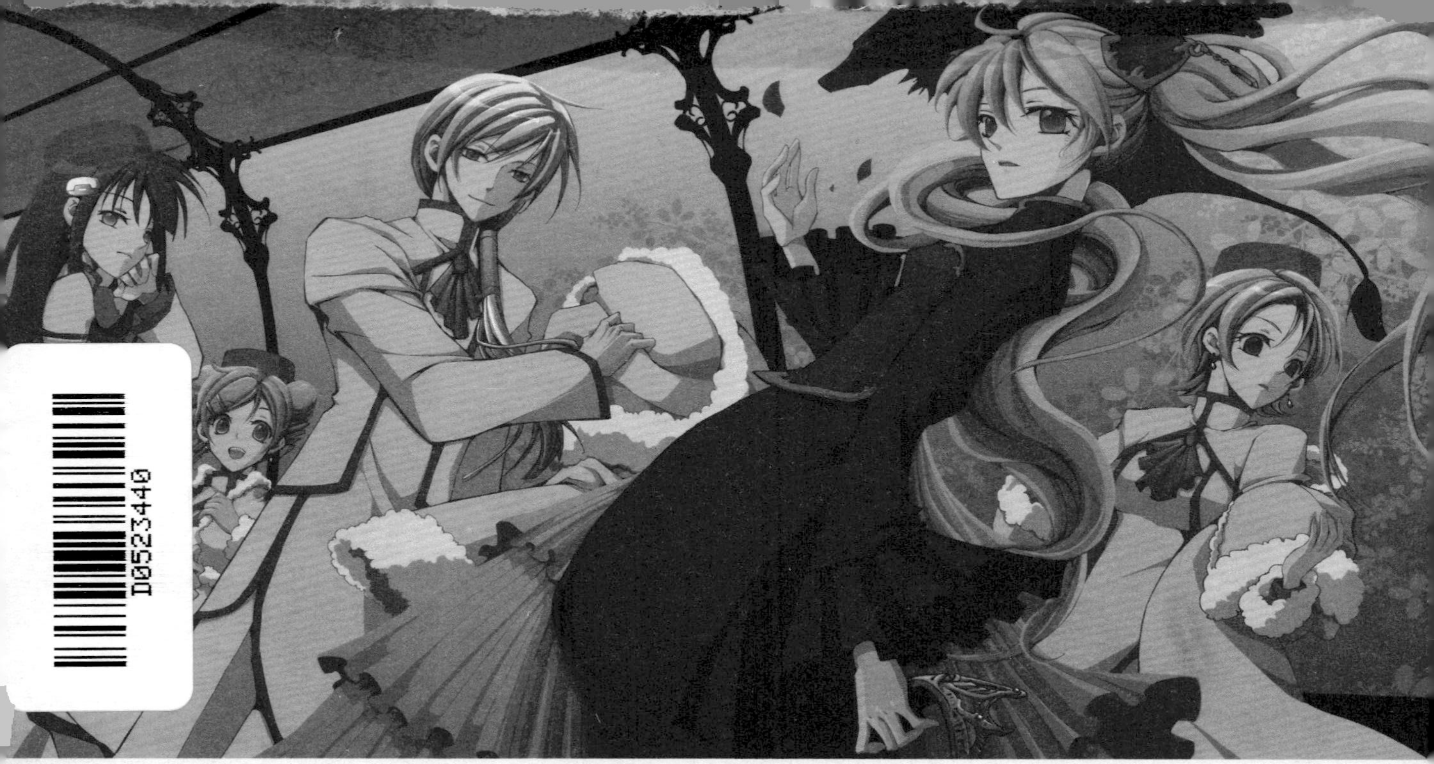

07 - G H O S T 11

Kapitel.61
"Out of Control"
5

Kapitel.62
"50/50"
25

Kapitel.63
"Cleaning House"
53

Kapitel.64
"Roseamanelle Ouka Barsburg"
87

Kapitel.65
"Tiashe: Part 1"
119

Kapitel.66
"Tiashe: Part 2"
151

Yukino Ichihara
Yuki Amemiya

07-GHOST
11

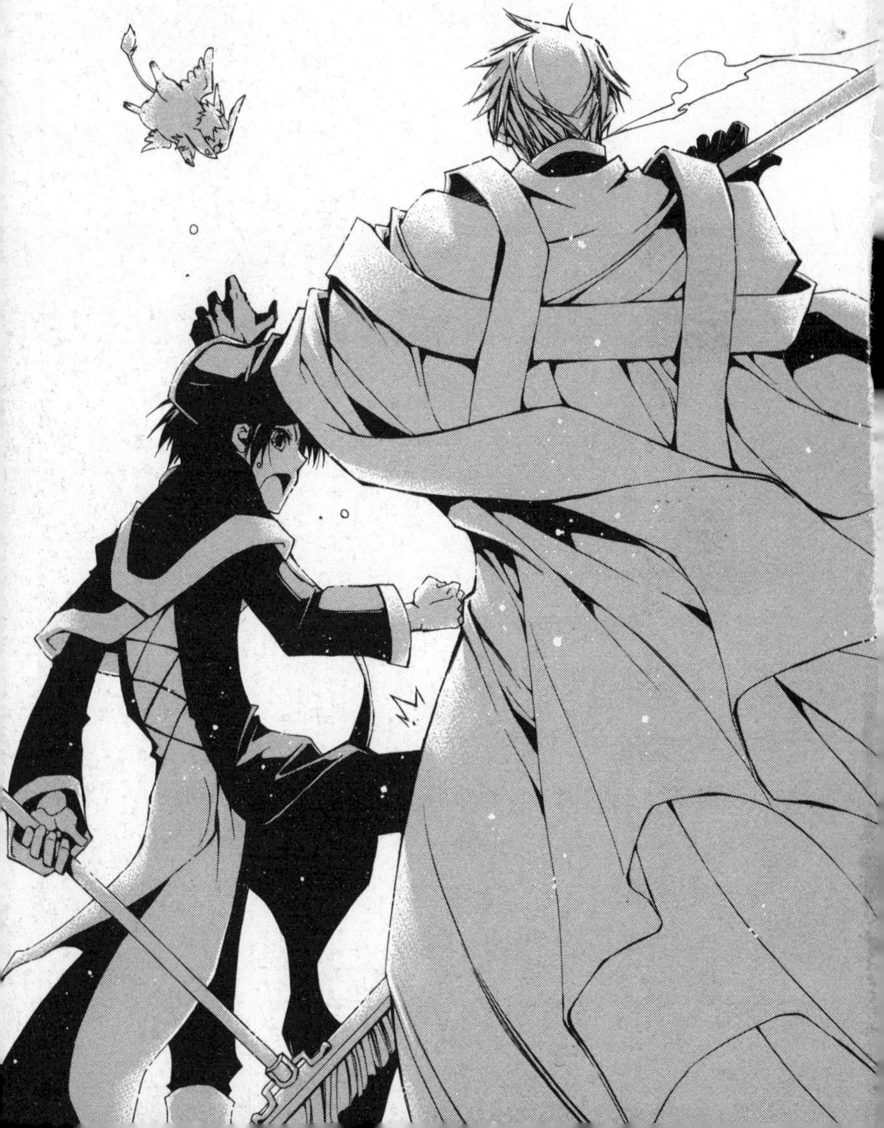

Characters

One thousand years ago, two equally powerful nations coexisted. One was the Barsburg Empire, protected by the Eye of Rafael. The other was the Raggs Kingdom, protected by the Eye of Mikael. Now that the Raggs Kingdom has been destroyed, things have changed...

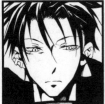

Frau

Bishop who saved Teito and now watches over him. He is Zehel of the Seven Ghosts. Currently disguised as tall, dark and handsome.

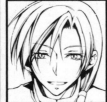

Hakuren

Teito's friend from the prestigious Oak family. Aimed to be a bishop, but is now the princess's tutor. Not fond of women.

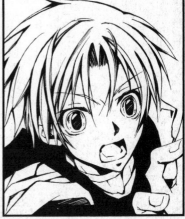

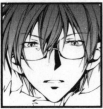

Castor

Bishop who can manipulate puppets. He watches over Teito and is Fest of the Seven Ghosts.

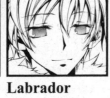

Labrador

Flower-loving bishop with the power of prophecy. He is Prophe of the Seven Ghosts.

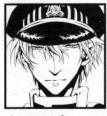

Ayanami

Imperial Army's Chief of Staff. Pursuing Teito, the vessel of the Eye of Mikael. He is the evil death god, Verloren.

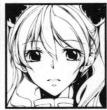

Ouka

First princess of the Barsburg Empire and vessel of the Eye of Rafael.

Teito Klein

Born a prince of Raggs, Teito was stripped of his memories and raised as a soldier by the military academy's chairman. He harbored the Eye of Mikael (an artifact said to bring either the world's salvation or destruction) in his right hand until the Black Hawks stole it. Currently Frau's apprentice...and blond.

Story

Teito is a student at the Barsburg Empire's military academy until the day he discovers that his father was the king of Raggs, the ruler of a kingdom the Barsburg Empire destroyed. He runs away, but loses his best friend to the diabolical Ayanami. As a first step in avenging Mikage's death, Teito becomes an apprentice bishop to obtain special privileges. He then embarks on a journey to the "Land of Seele," which holds the key to his past and the truth about the fall of Raggs. He obtains the Cursed Tickets in Districts 4, 5 and 6. In order to reach District 1, he and Frau enter the Hawkzile Race in disguise.

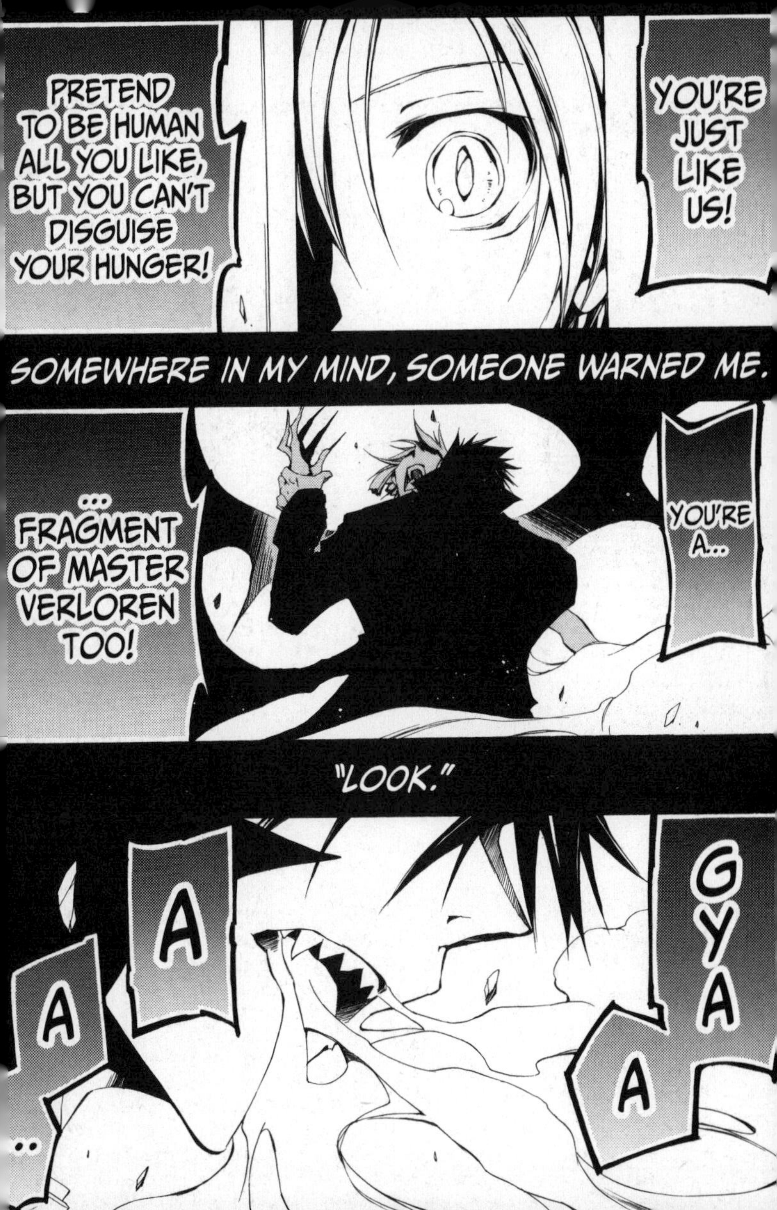
YOU'RE JUST LIKE US!
PRETEND TO BE HUMAN ALL YOU LIKE, BUT YOU CAN'T DISGUISE YOUR HUNGER!
SOMEWHERE IN MY MIND, SOMEONE WARNED ME.
YOU'RE A...
... FRAGMENT OF MASTER VERLOREN TOO!
"LOOK."
GYA
A
A
A
..

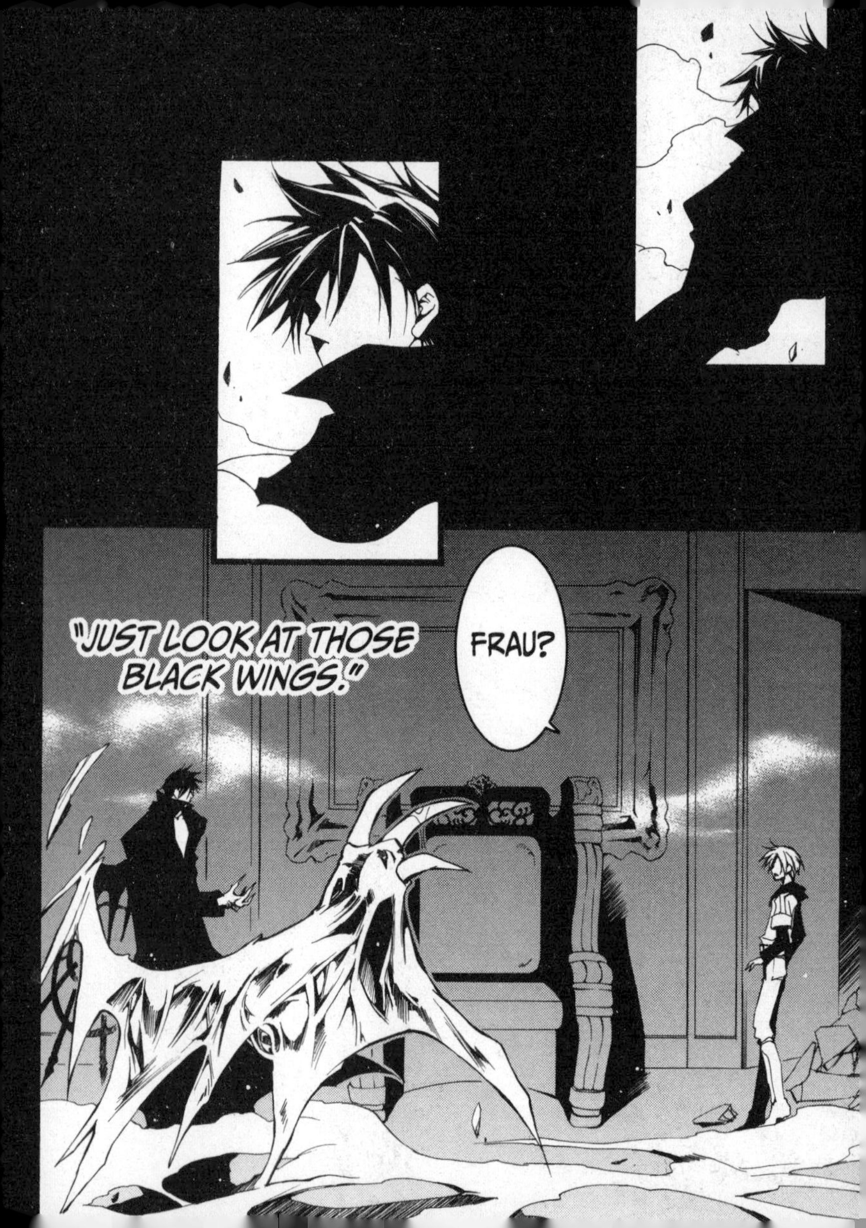
FRAU?
"JUST LOOK AT THOSE BLACK WINGS."

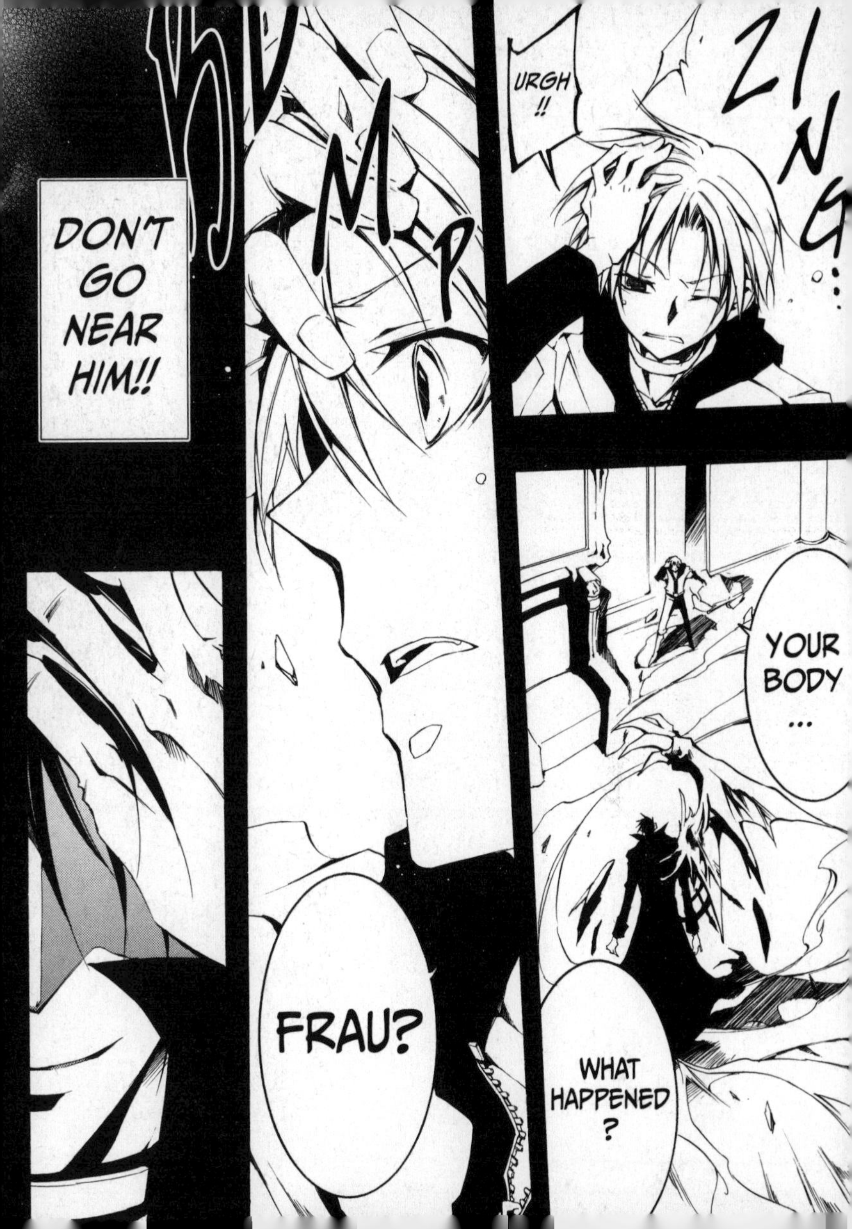
URGH !!
ZING..
YOUR BODY ...
WHAT HAPPENED ?
FRAU?
DON'T GO NEAR HIM!!

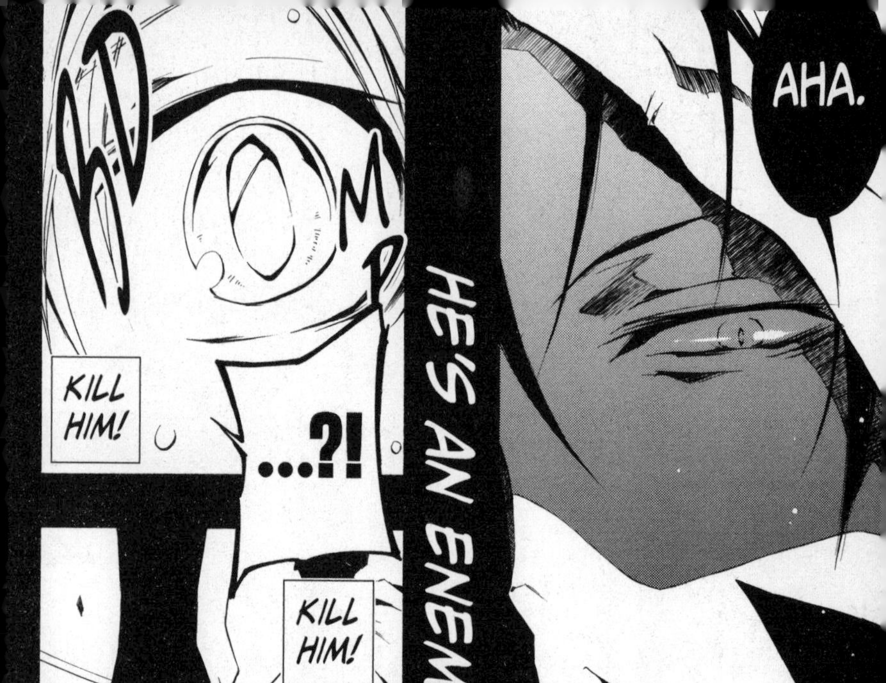
AHA.
CAUGHT YA.
HE'S AN ENEMY!!
BOOM
...?!
KILL HIM!
KILL HIM!
TAK...
FSH
KILL HIM!

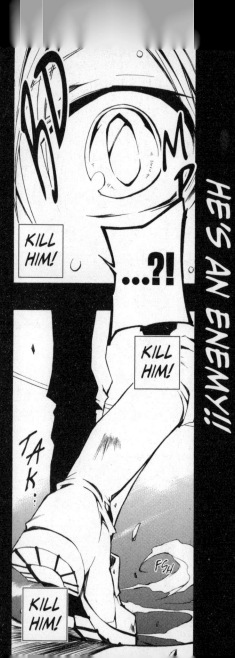

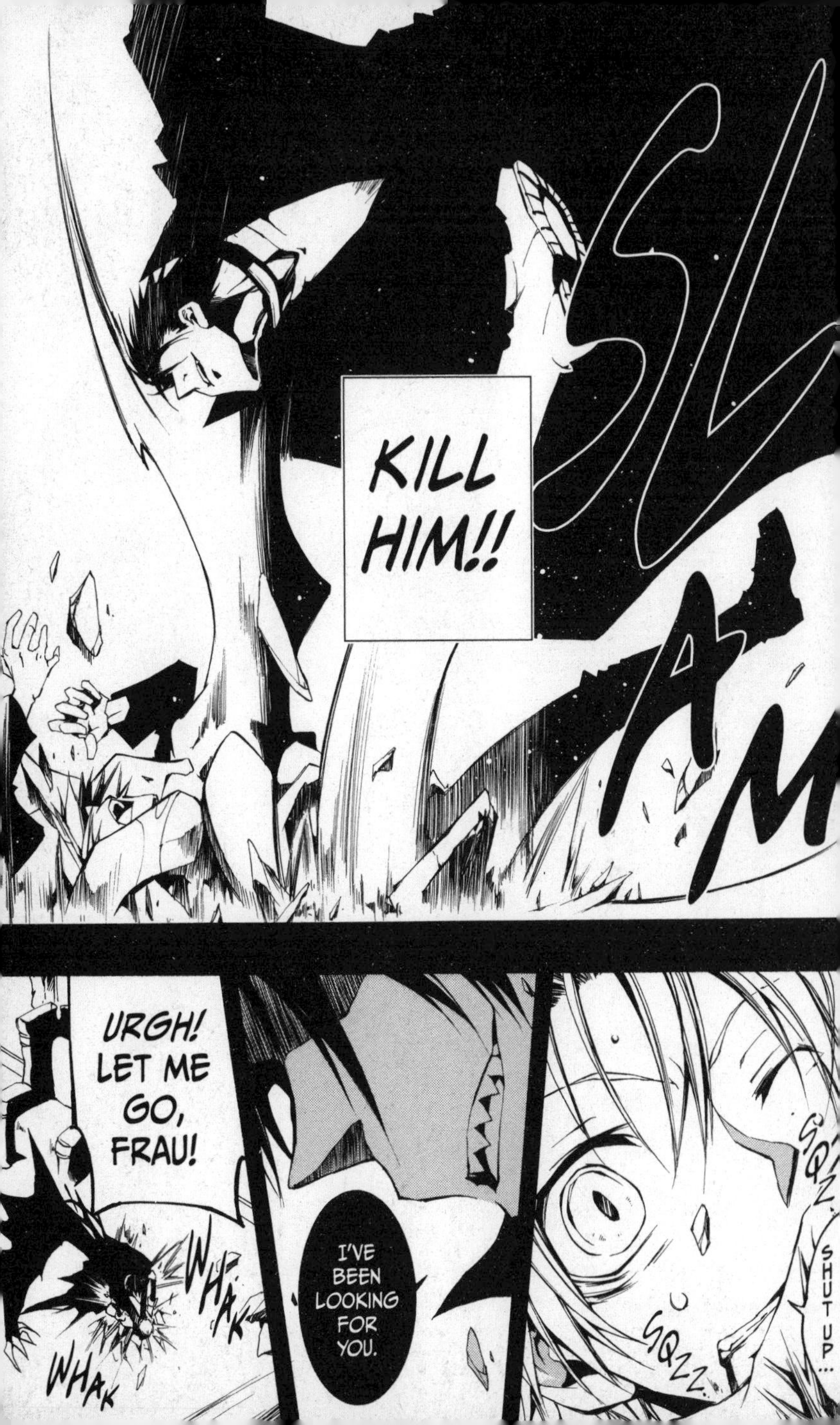
SLAM
KILL HIM!!
SQZZ...
SHUT UP...
SQZZ...
I'VE BEEN LOOKING FOR YOU.
URGH! LET ME GO, FRAU!
WHAK
WHAK

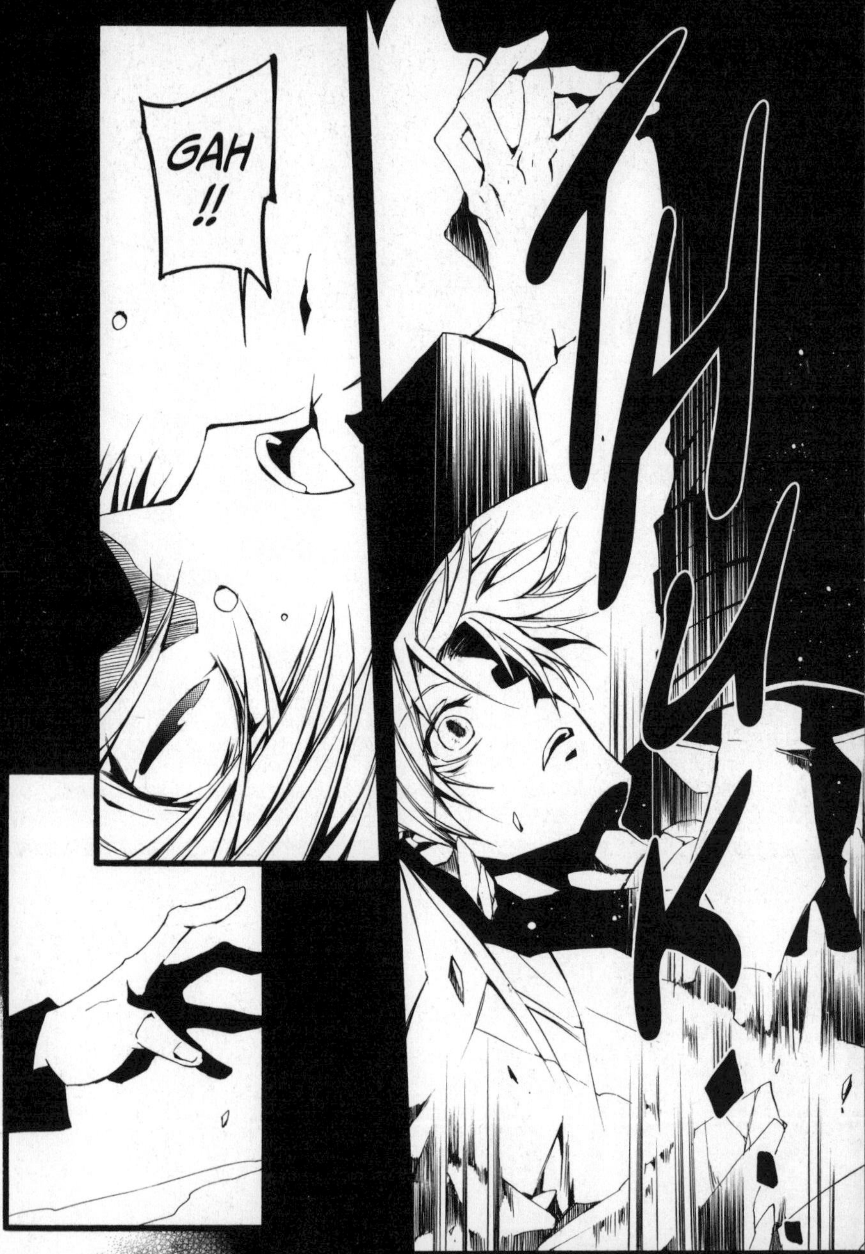
GAH !!

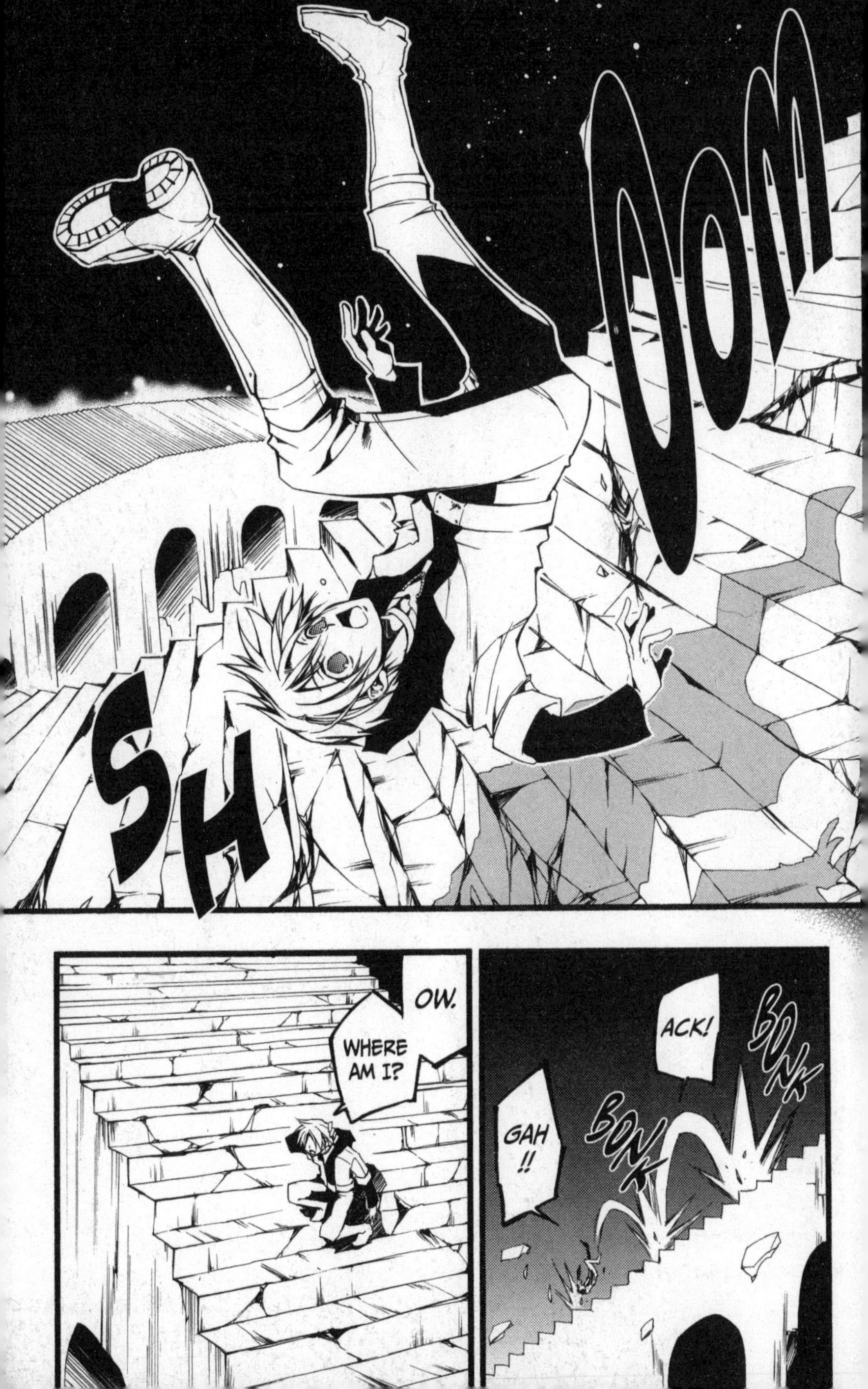
SHOOM
ACK!
BONK
BONK
GAH!!
OW.
WHERE AM I?

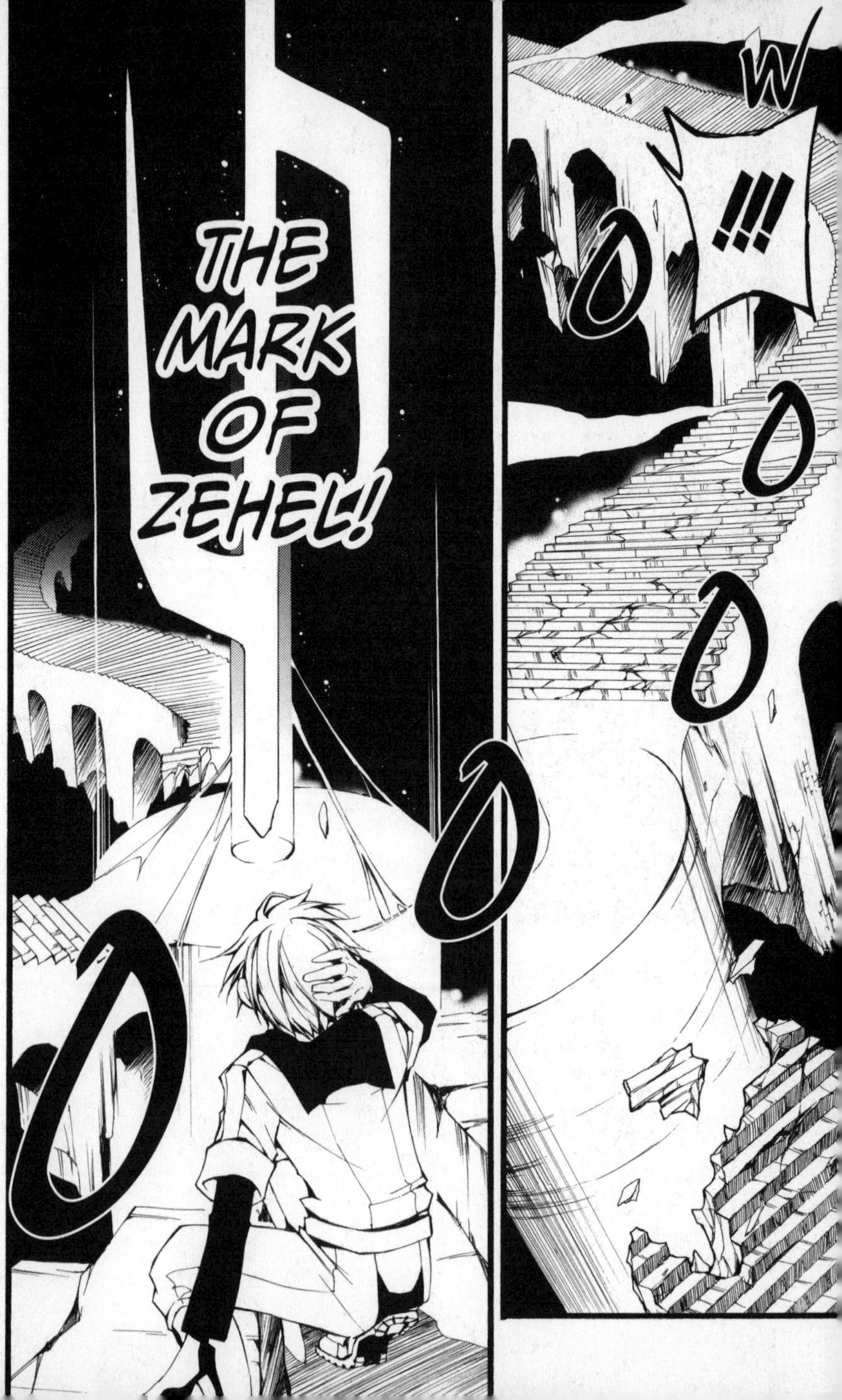
W
!!!
THE MARK OF ZEHEL!

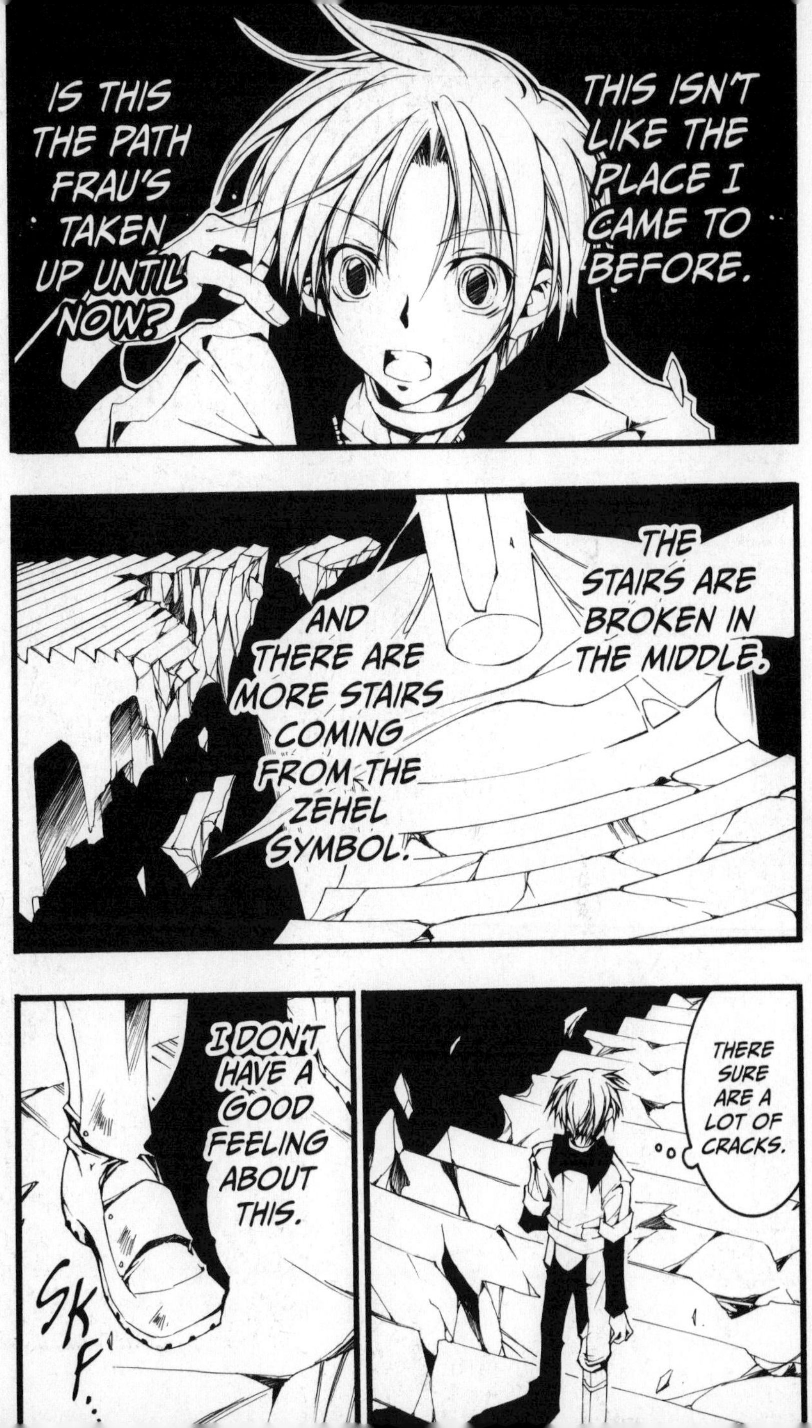

THIS ISN'T LIKE THE PLACE I CAME TO BEFORE.
IS THIS THE PATH FRAU'S TAKEN UP UNTIL NOW?
THE STAIRS ARE BROKEN IN THE MIDDLE.
AND THERE ARE MORE STAIRS COMING FROM THE ZEHEL SYMBOL.
THERE SURE ARE A LOT OF CRACKS.
I DON'T HAVE A GOOD FEELING ABOUT THIS.
SKF...

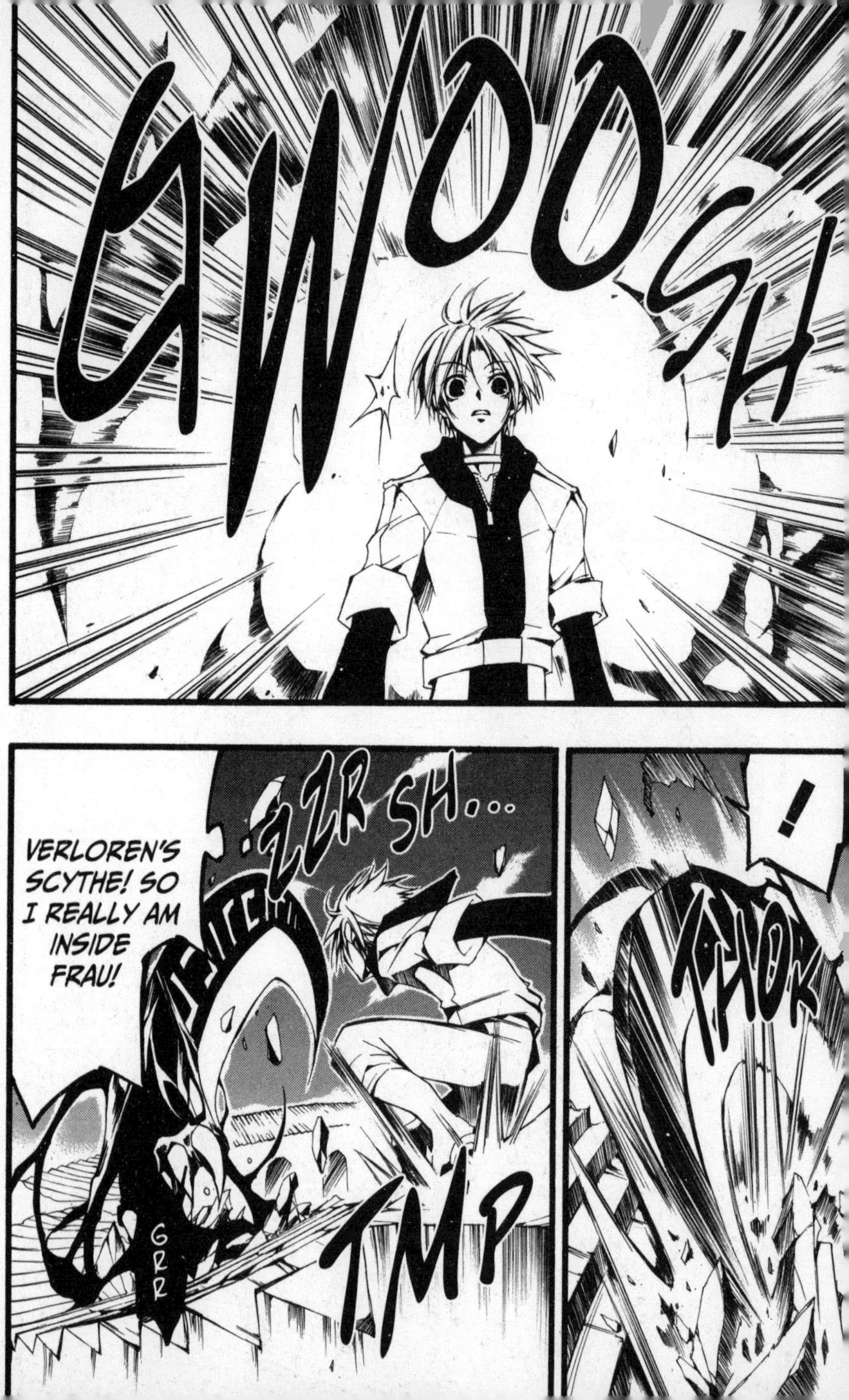
GWOOSH
!
TCHOK
ZZRSH...
VERLOREN'S SCYTHE! SO I REALLY AM INSIDE FRAU!
TMP
GRR

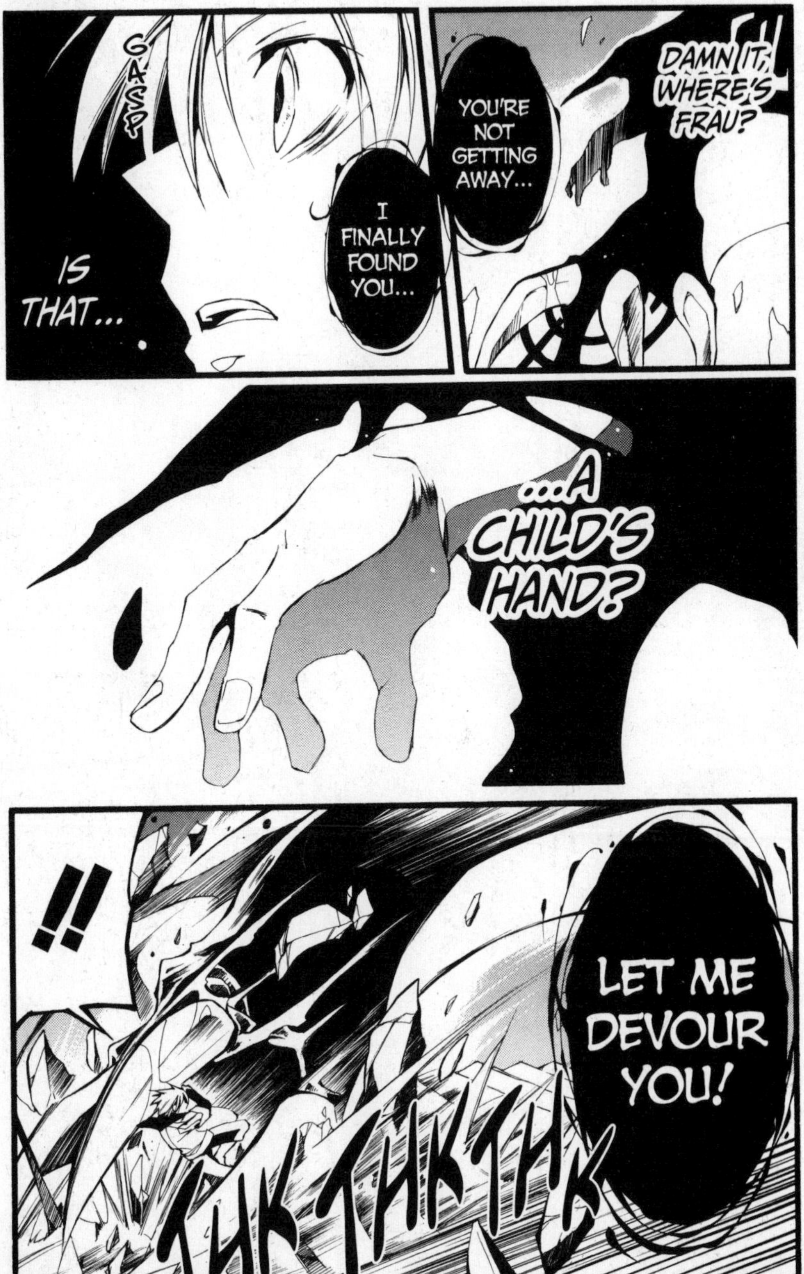
DAMN IT, WHERE'S FRAU?
YOU'RE NOT GETTING AWAY...
I FINALLY FOUND YOU...
GASP
IS THAT...
...A CHILD'S HAND?
LET ME DEVOUR YOU!
!!
THK THK THK THK

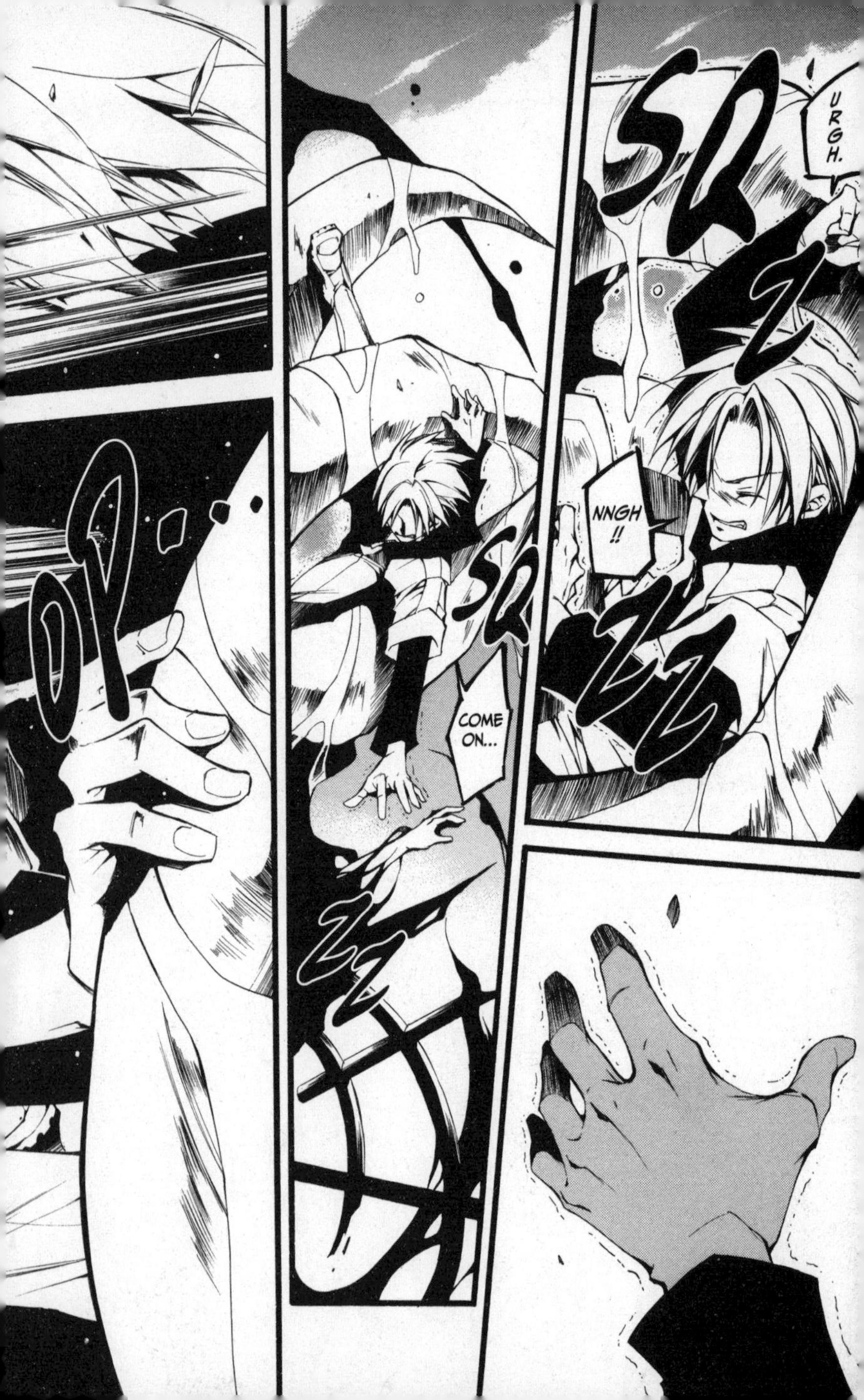
URGH.
NNGH!!
COME ON...

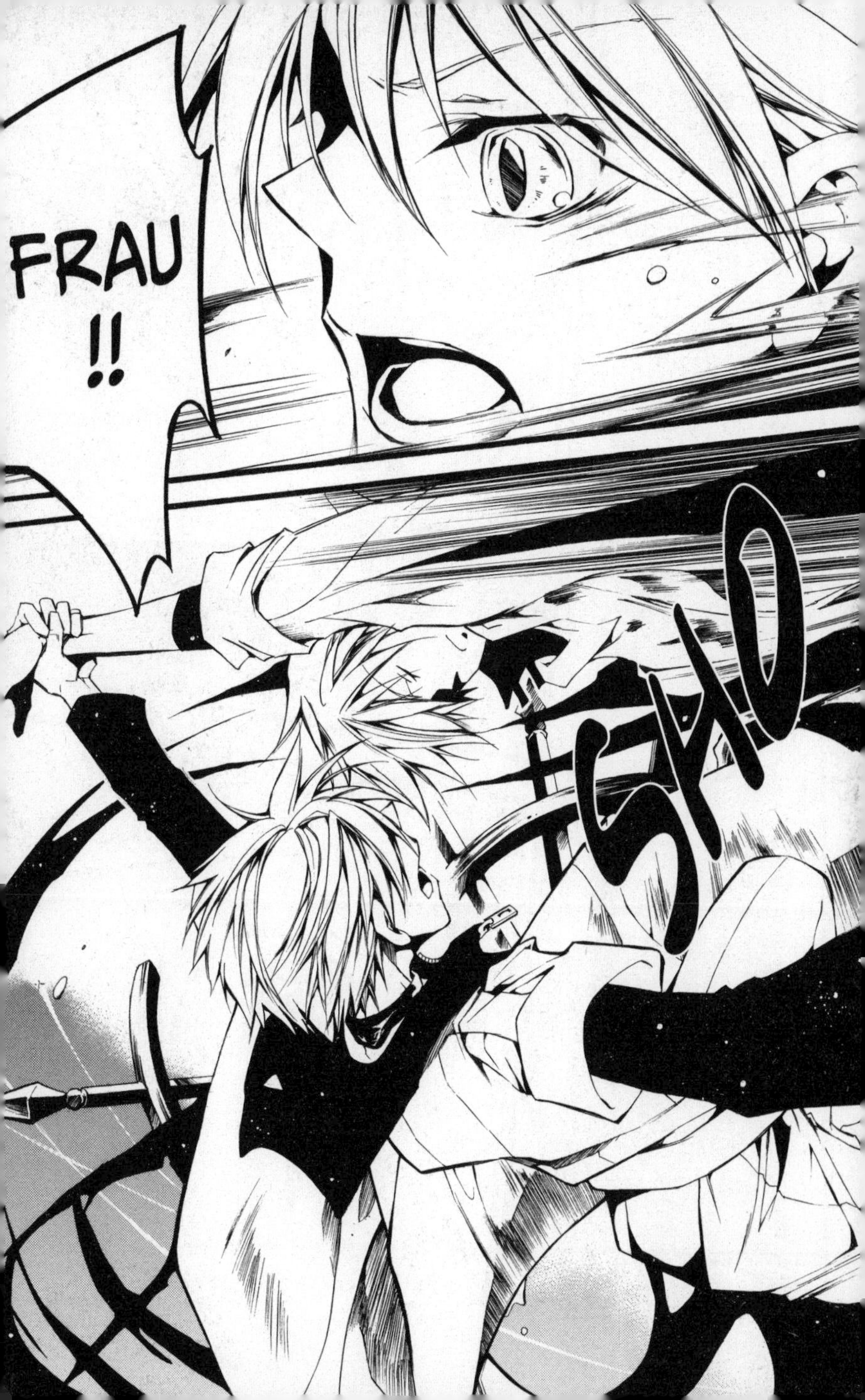
FRAU
!!
SHO

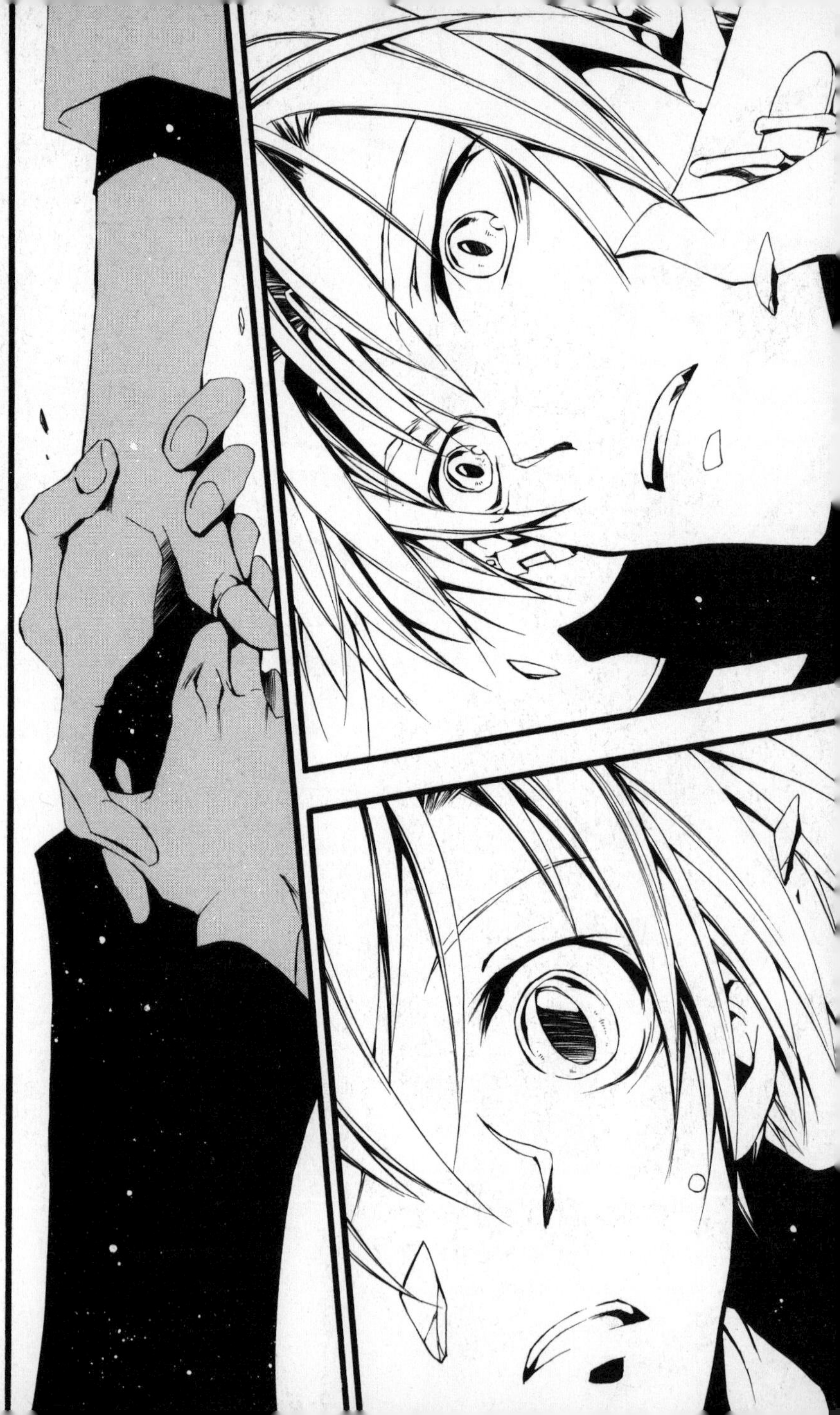

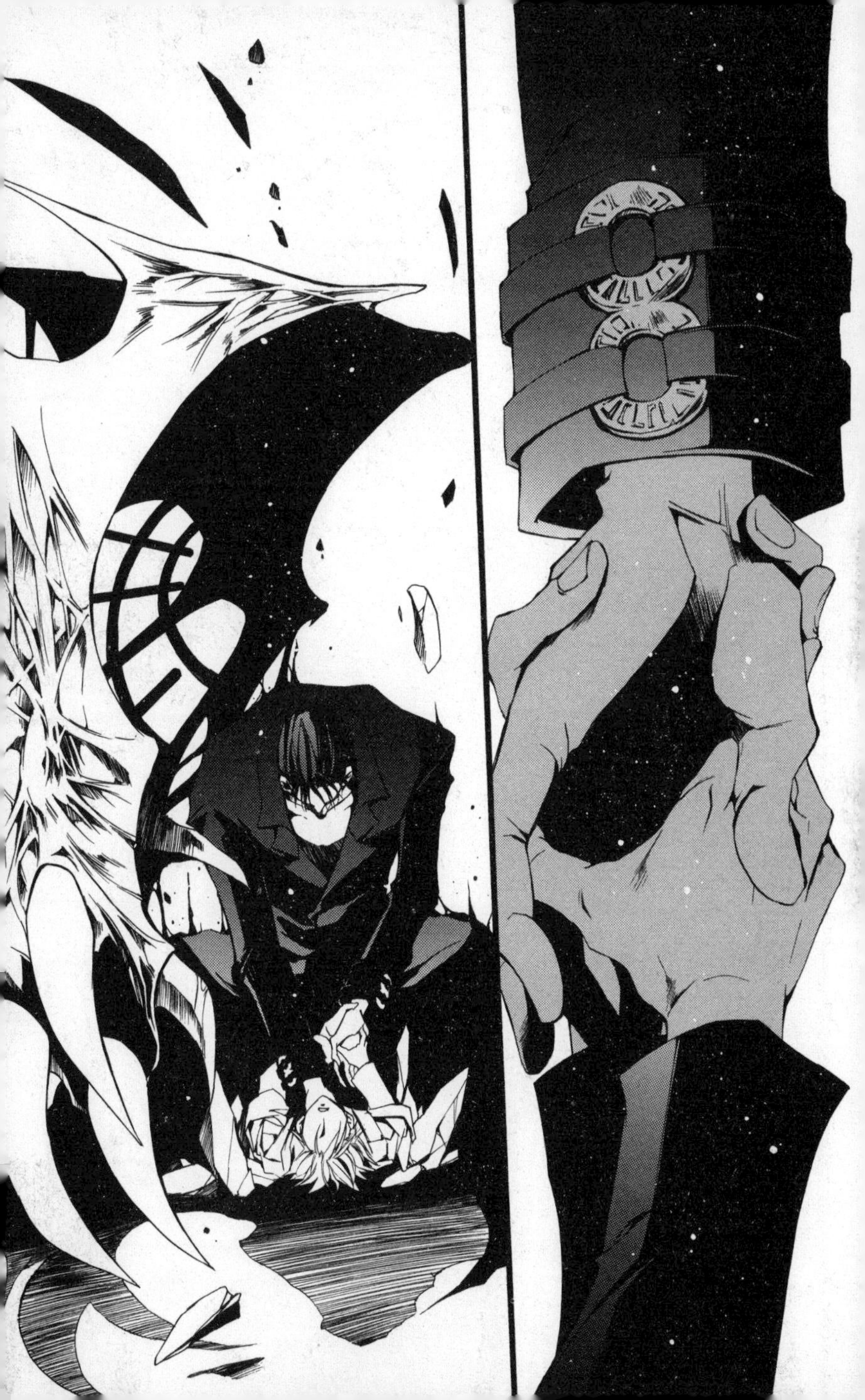

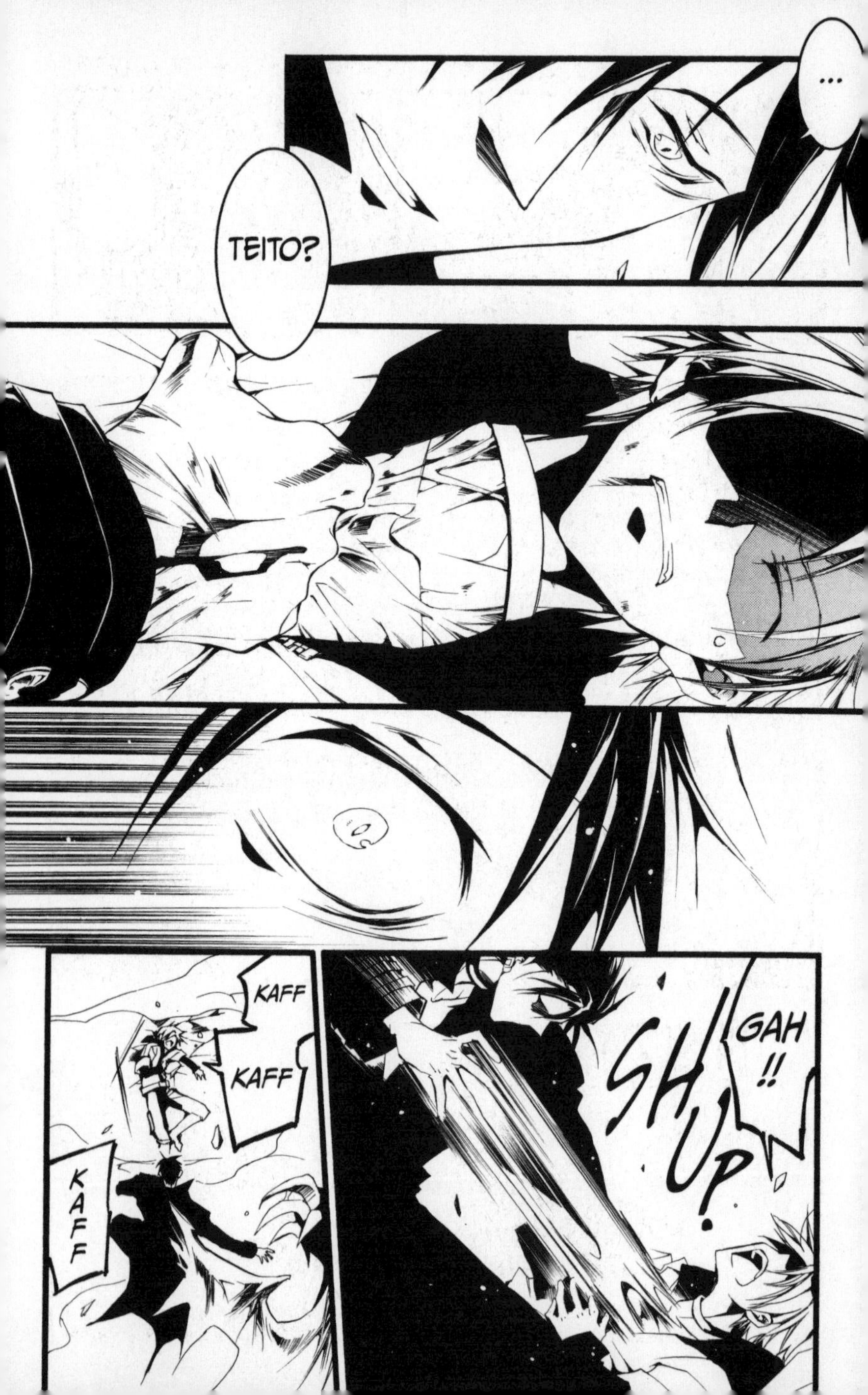
...
TEITO?
GAH !!
SHUP!
KAFF
KAFF
KAFF

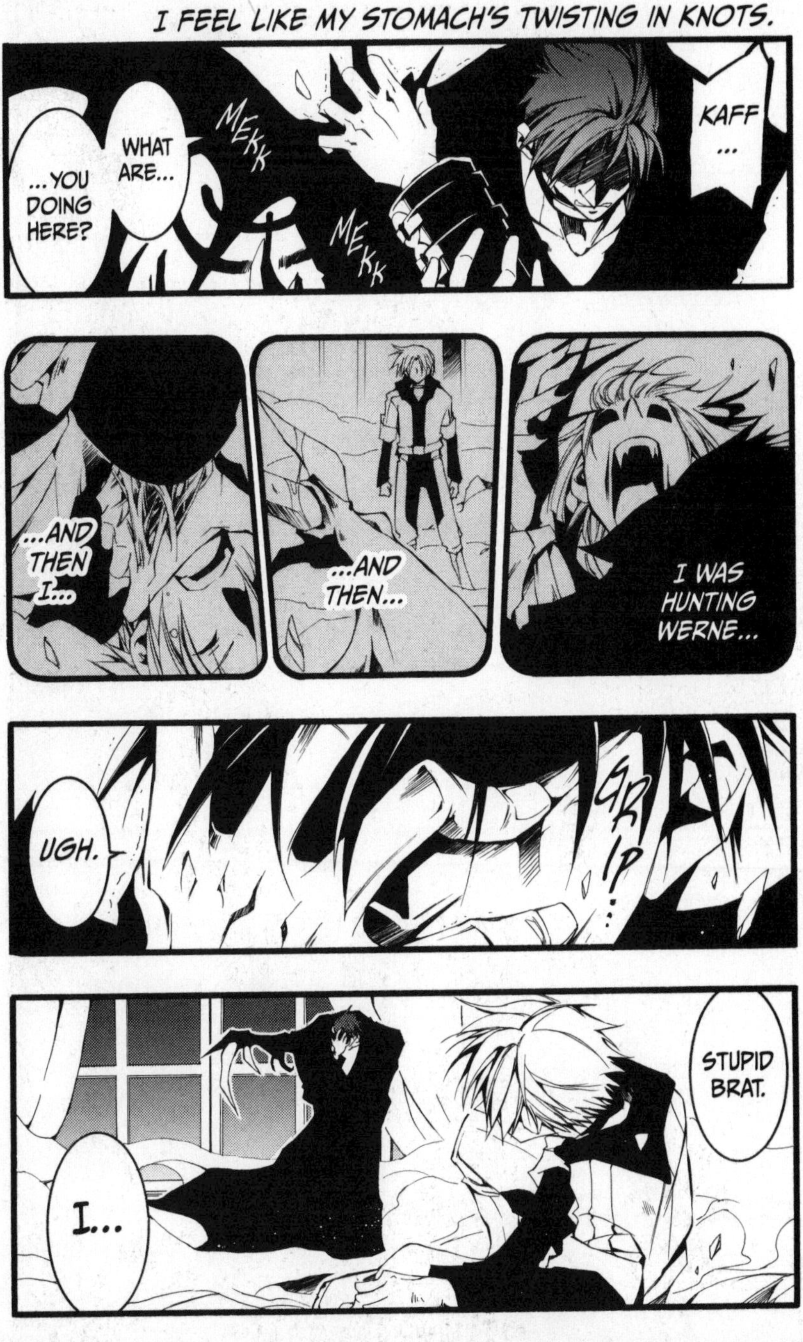
I FEEL LIKE MY STOMACH'S TWISTING IN KNOTS.
KAFF ...
MEKK
MEKK
WHAT ARE...
...YOU DOING HERE?
I WAS HUNTING WERNE...
...AND THEN...
...AND THEN I...
GRIP!...
UGH.
STUPID BRAT.
I...

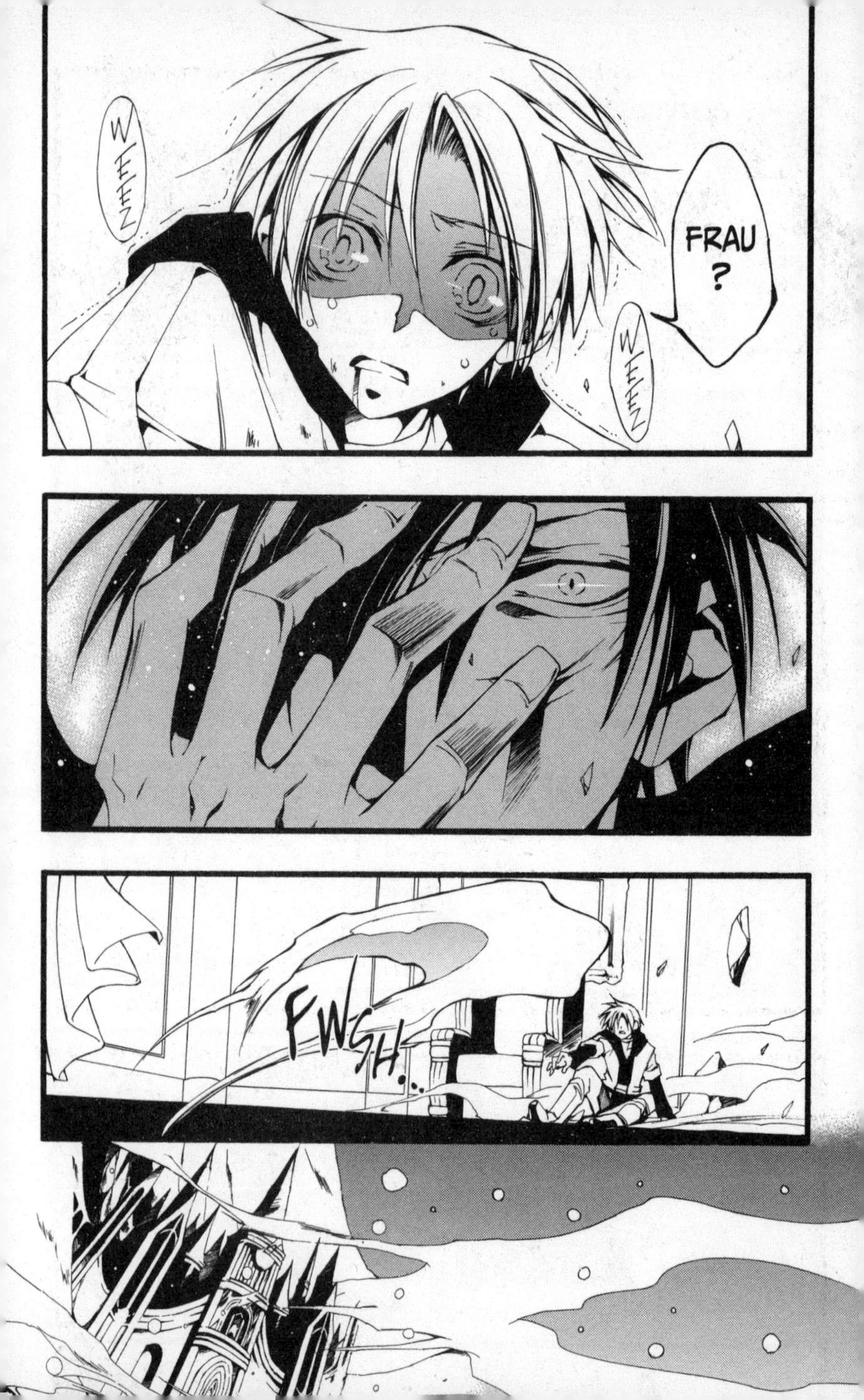
FRAU?
WEEZ
WEEZ
FWSH...

POOM

MIKAGE!!

BURUPYA

SORRY TO LEAVE YOU ALL ALONE.

BURUPYA?

YEAH. FRAU WENT SOME-WHERE.

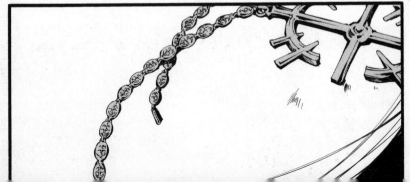

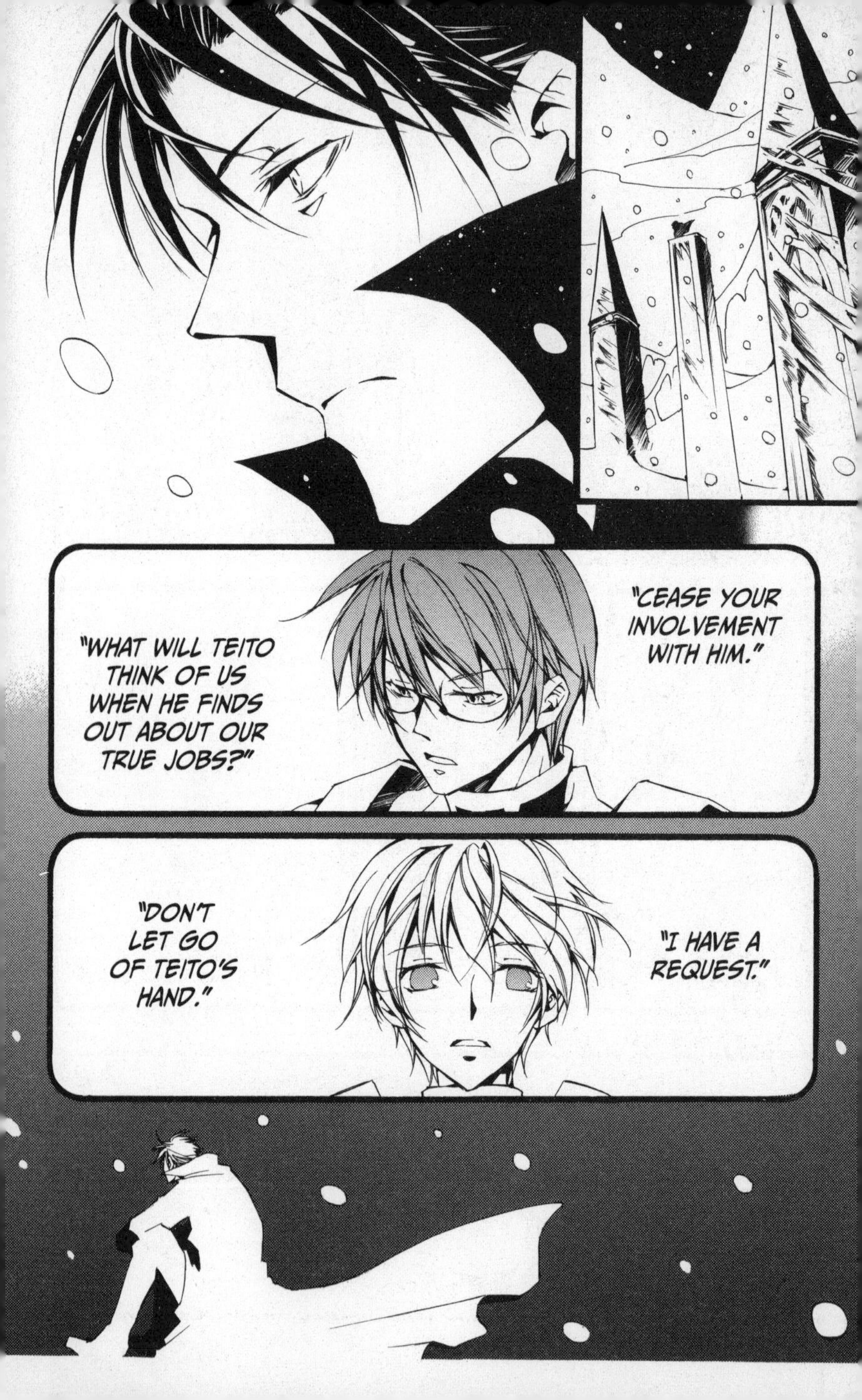
"CEASE YOUR INVOLVEMENT WITH HIM."
"WHAT WILL TEITO THINK OF US WHEN HE FINDS OUT ABOUT OUR TRUE JOBS?"
"I HAVE A REQUEST."
"DON'T LET GO OF TEITO'S HAND."

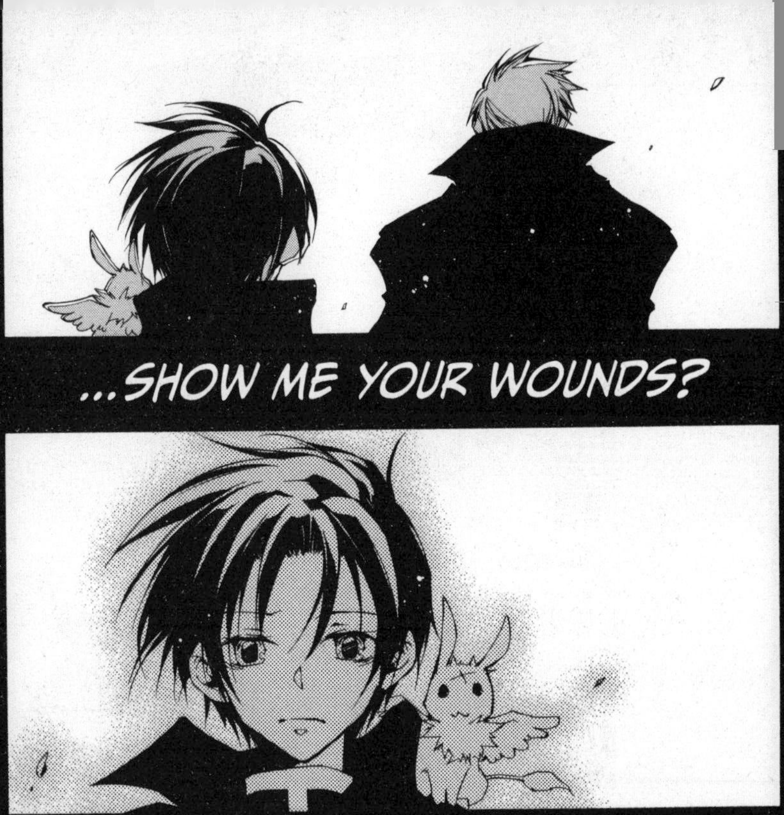
...SHOW ME YOUR WOUNDS?

Kapitel. 62 “50/50”

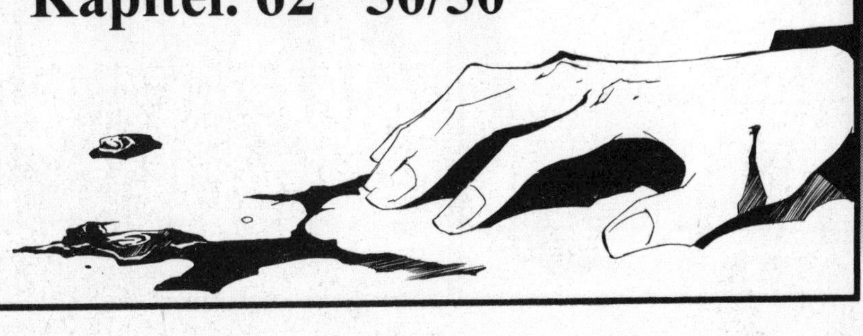

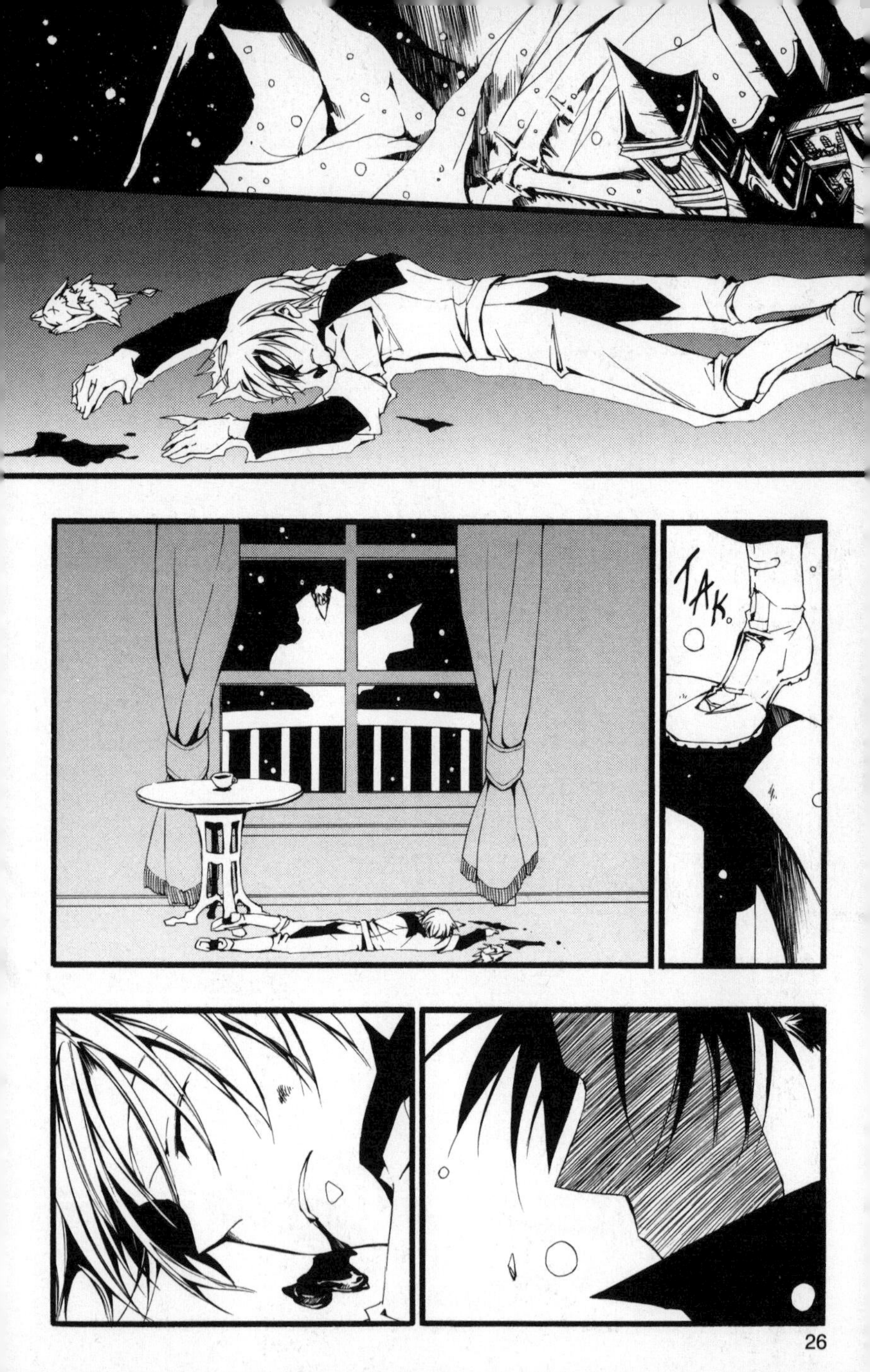
TAK.

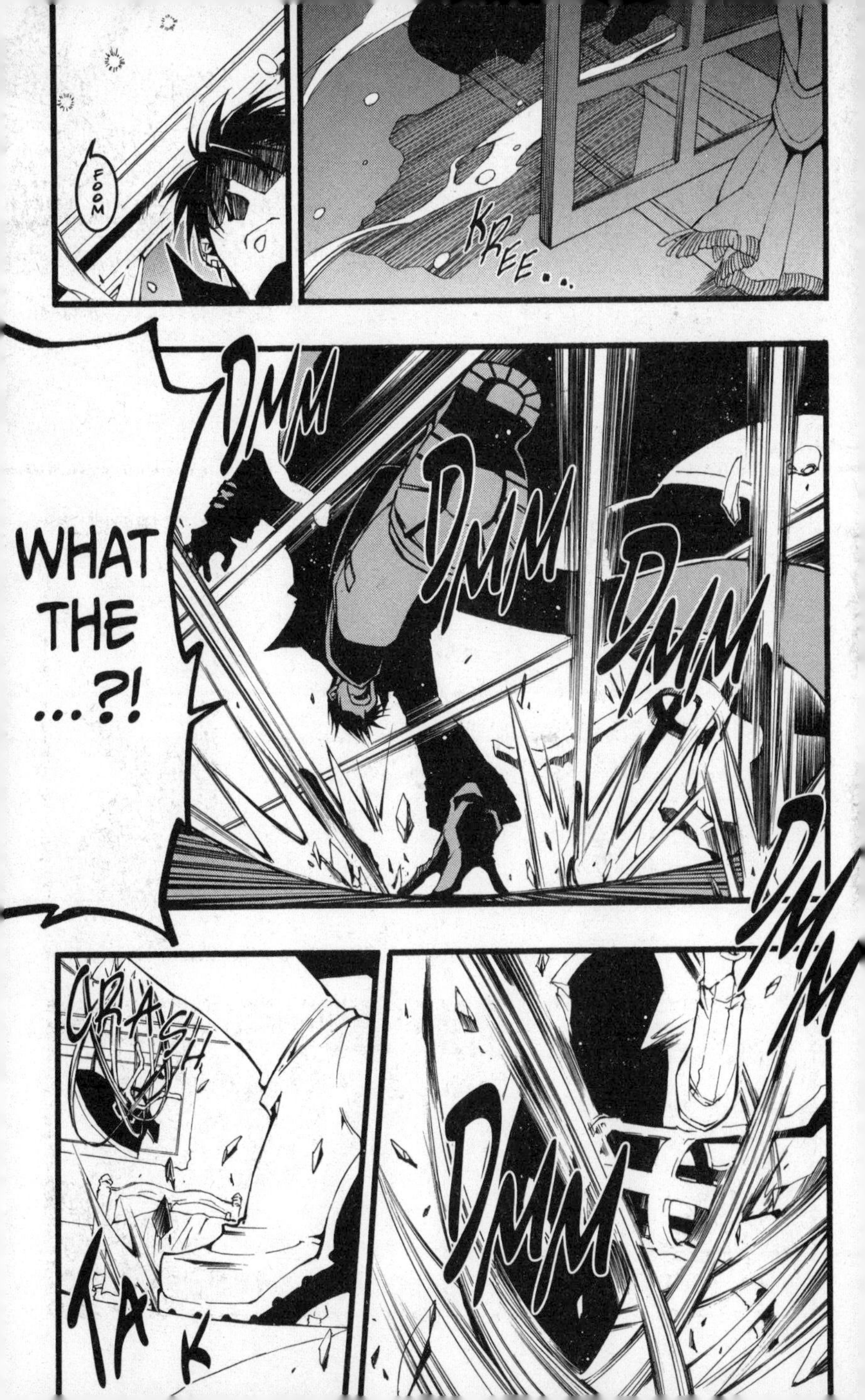
KREE...
FOOM
WHAT THE...?!
DMM
DMM
DMM
DMM
DMM
CRASH
TAK

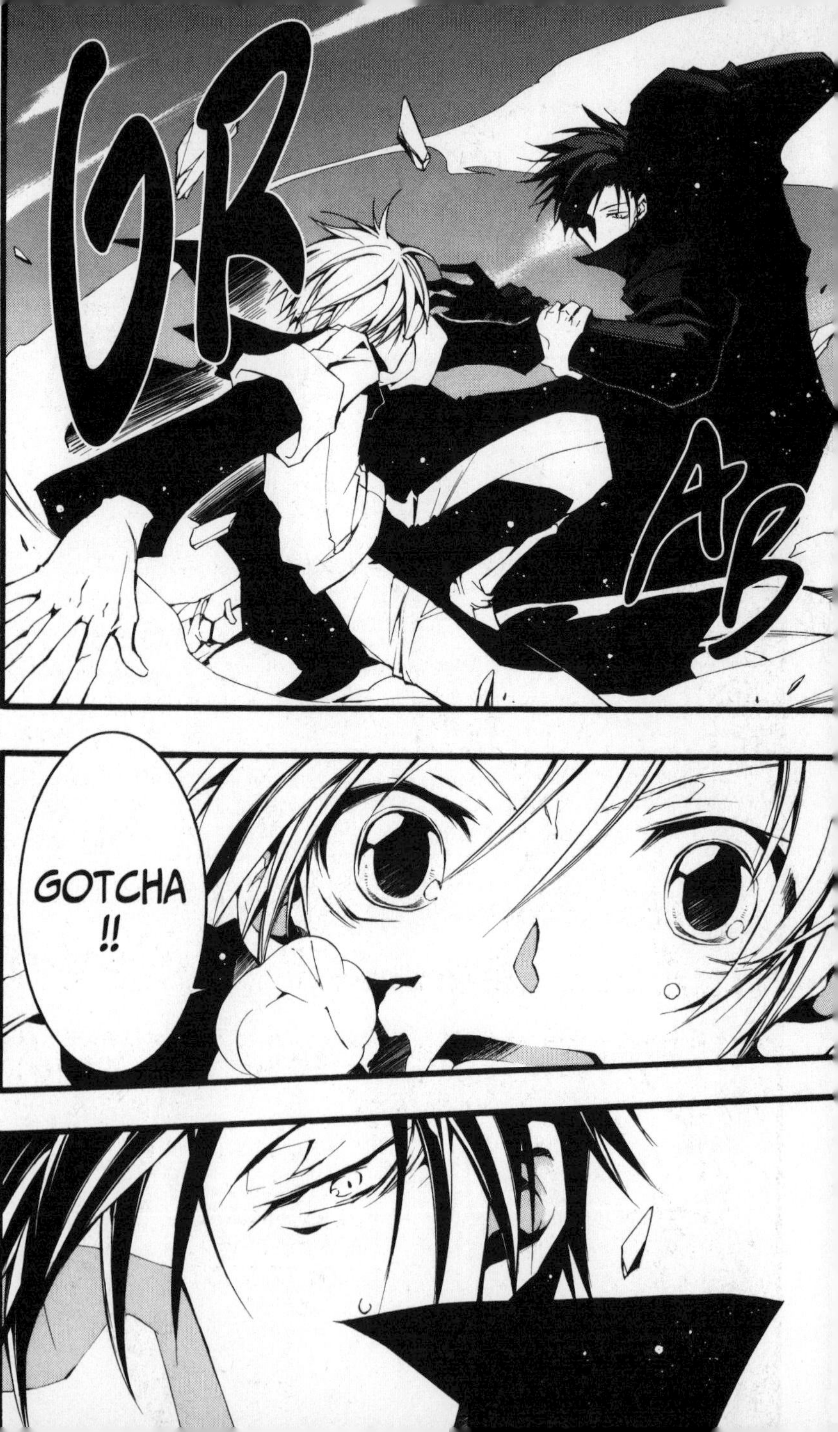
GRAB
GOTCHA !!

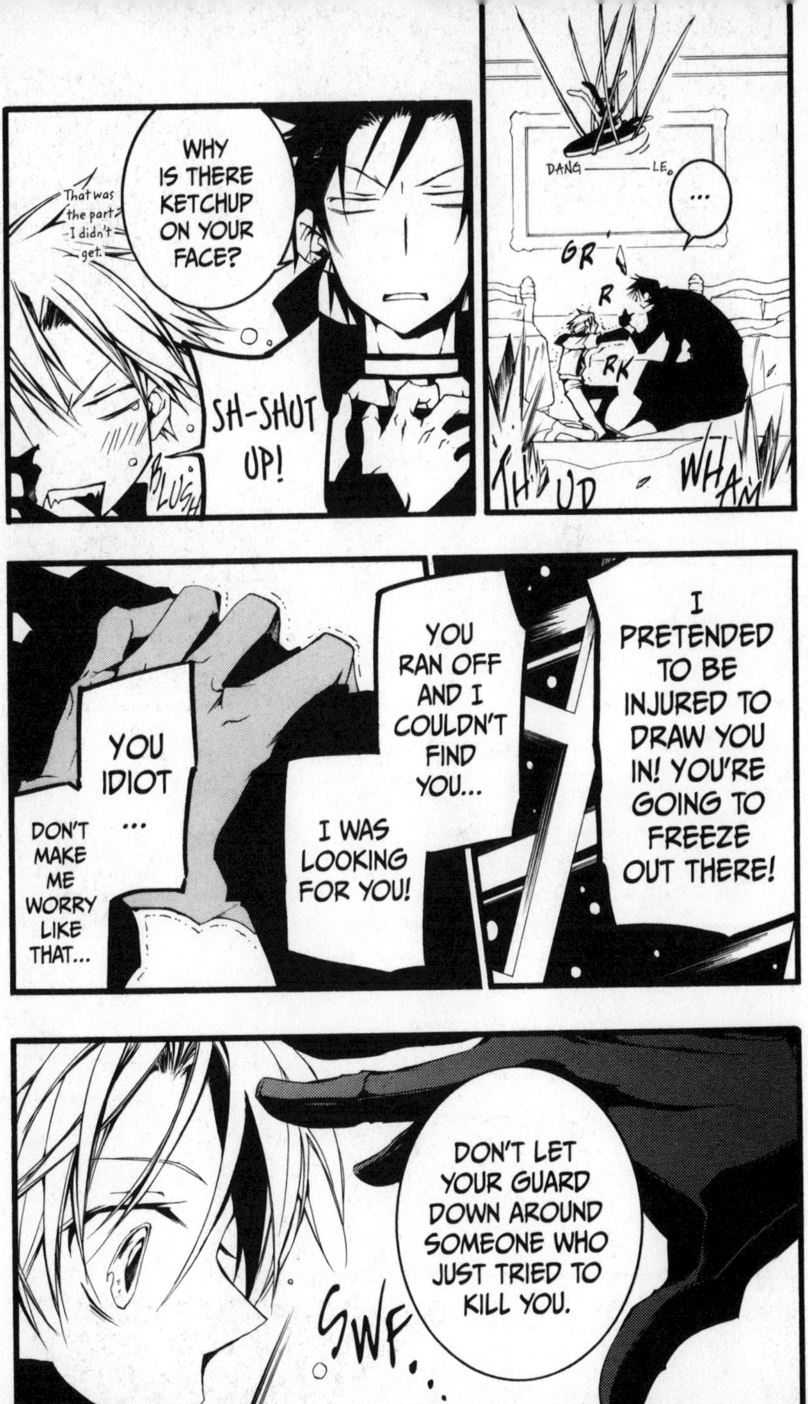
DANG———LE.
...
GRRRK
THUD
WHAM
WHY IS THERE KETCHUP ON YOUR FACE?
That was the part I didn't get.
SH-SHUT UP!
BLUSH
I PRETENDED TO BE INJURED TO DRAW YOU IN! YOU'RE GOING TO FREEZE OUT THERE!
YOU RAN OFF AND I COULDN'T FIND YOU...
I WAS LOOKING FOR YOU!
YOU IDIOT...
DON'T MAKE ME WORRY LIKE THAT...
DON'T LET YOUR GUARD DOWN AROUND SOMEONE WHO JUST TRIED TO KILL YOU.
SWF...

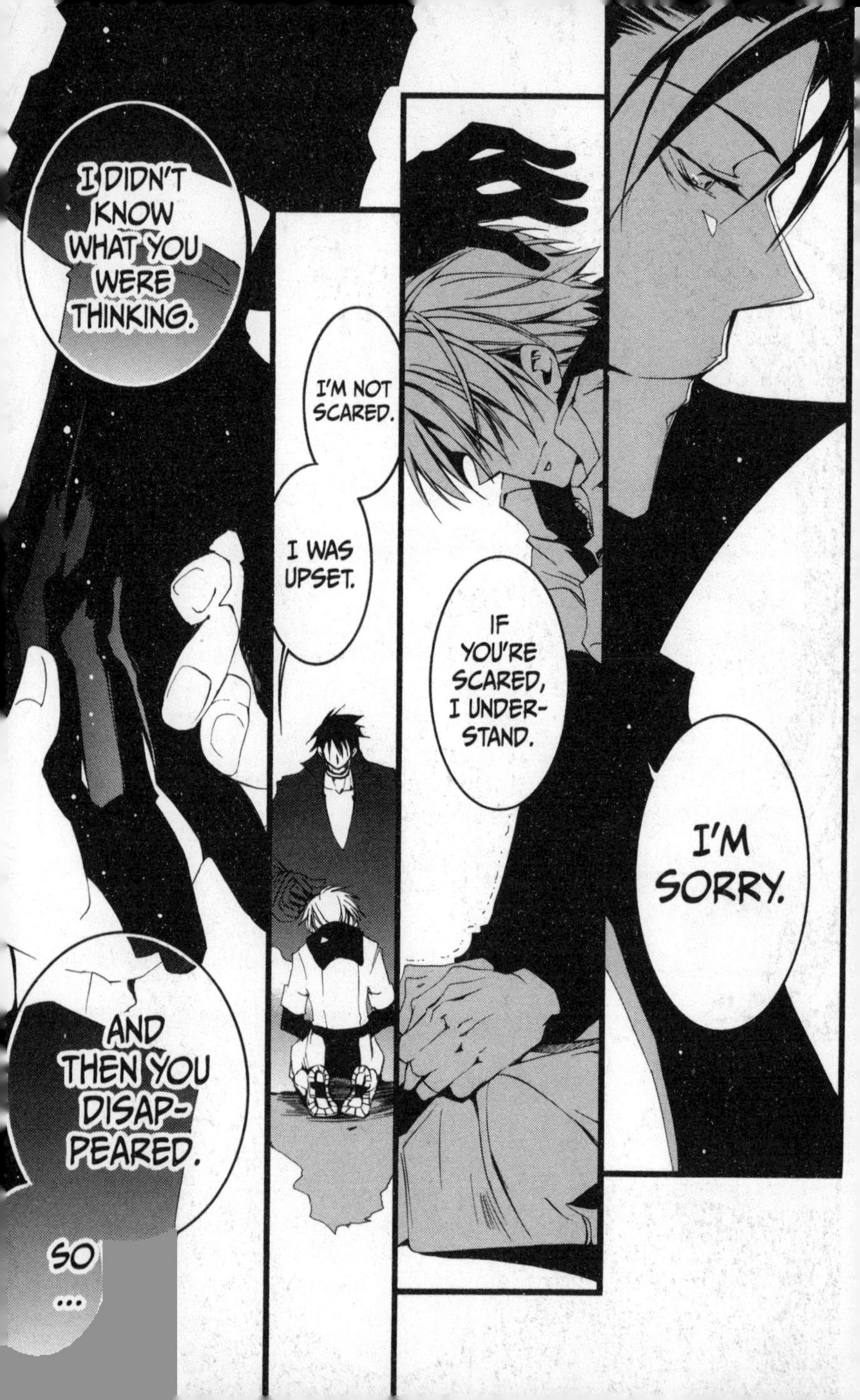
I'M SORRY.
IF YOU'RE SCARED, I UNDER-STAND.
I'M NOT SCARED.
I WAS UPSET.
I DIDN'T KNOW WHAT YOU WERE THINKING.
AND THEN YOU DISAP-PEARED.
SO ...

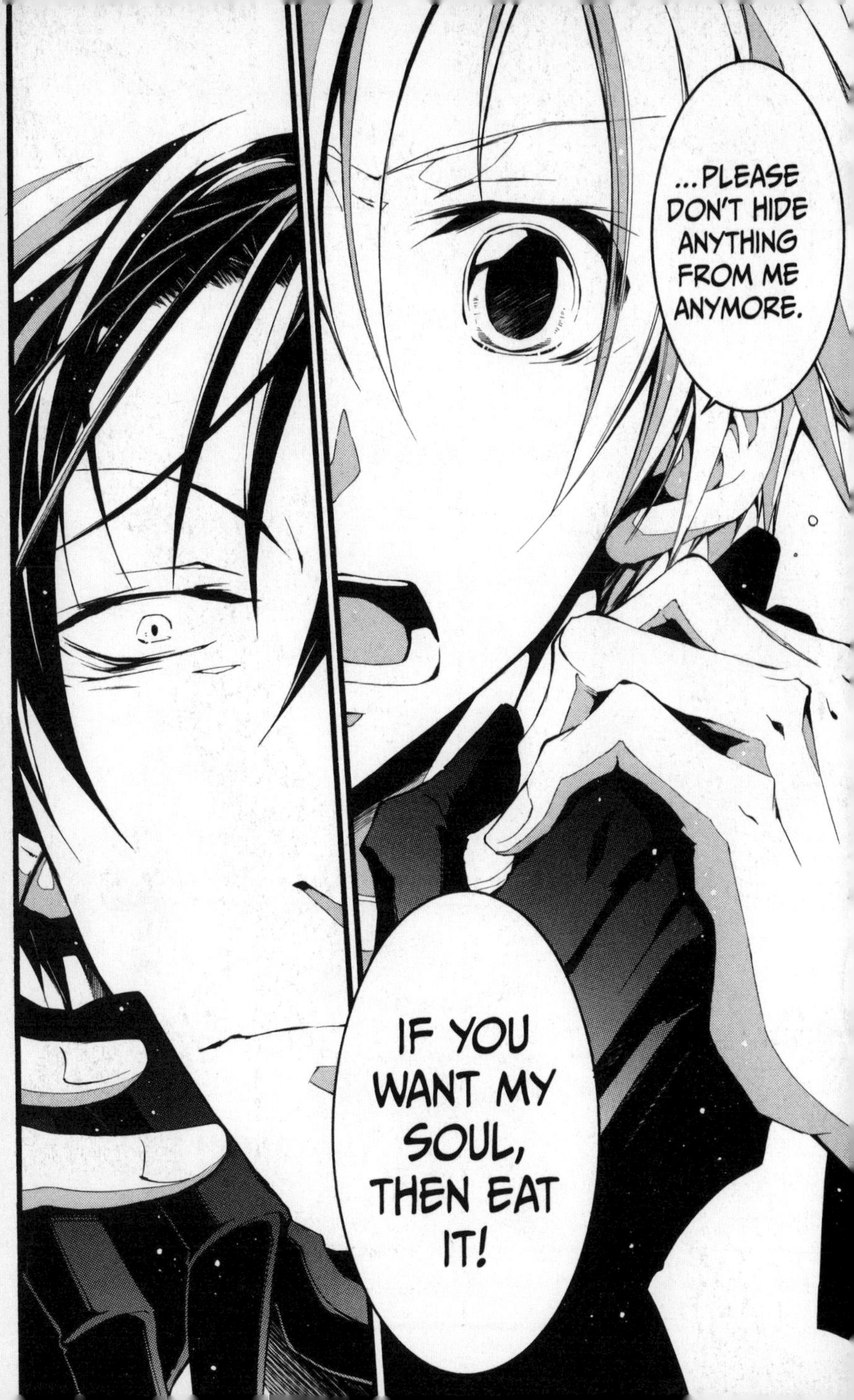
...PLEASE DON'T HIDE ANYTHING FROM ME ANYMORE.
IF YOU WANT MY SOUL, THEN EAT IT!

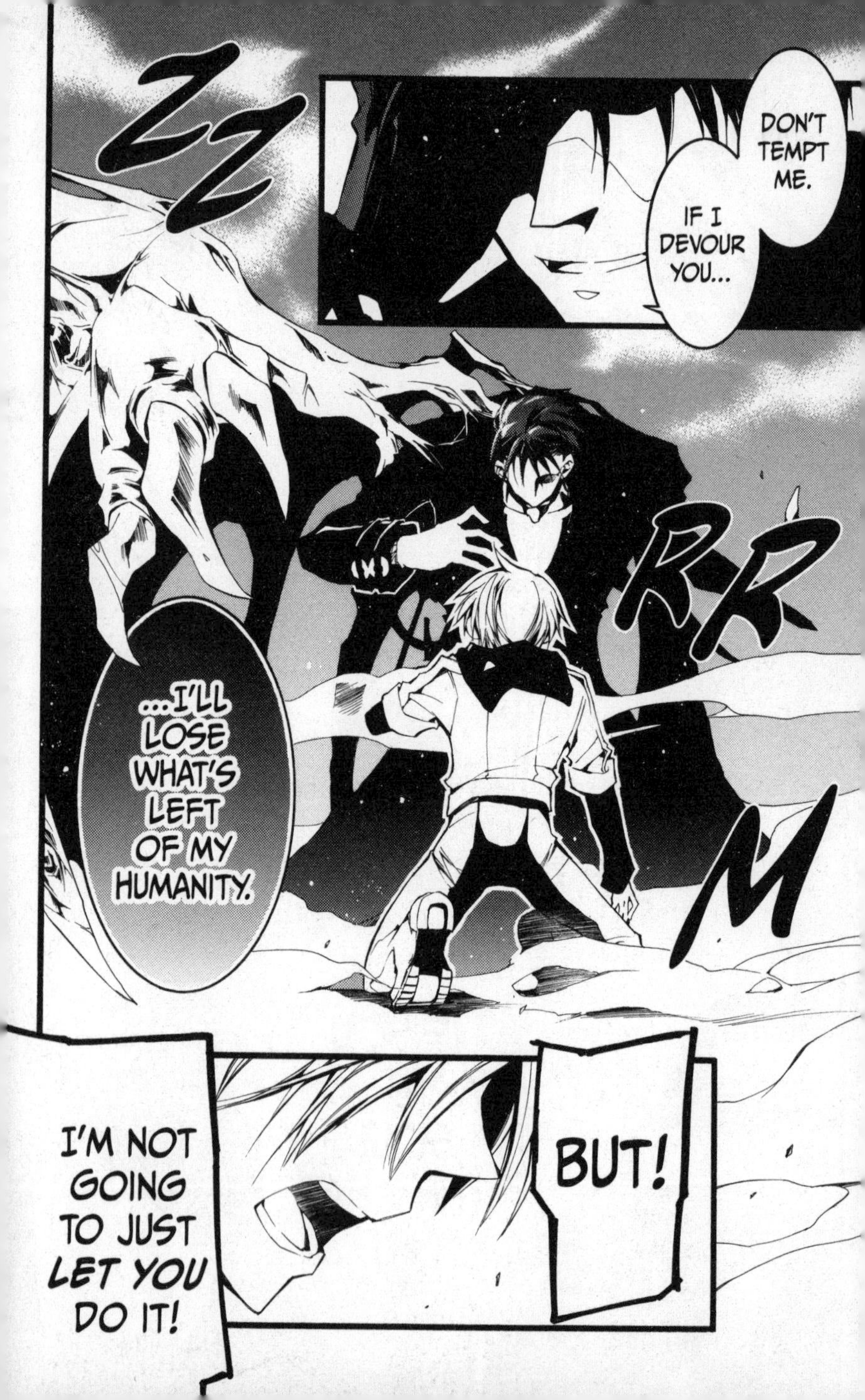
DON'T TEMPT ME.
IF I DEVOUR YOU...
ZZ
RRM
...I'LL LOSE WHAT'S LEFT OF MY HUMANITY.
BUT!
I'M NOT GOING TO JUST *LET YOU* DO IT!

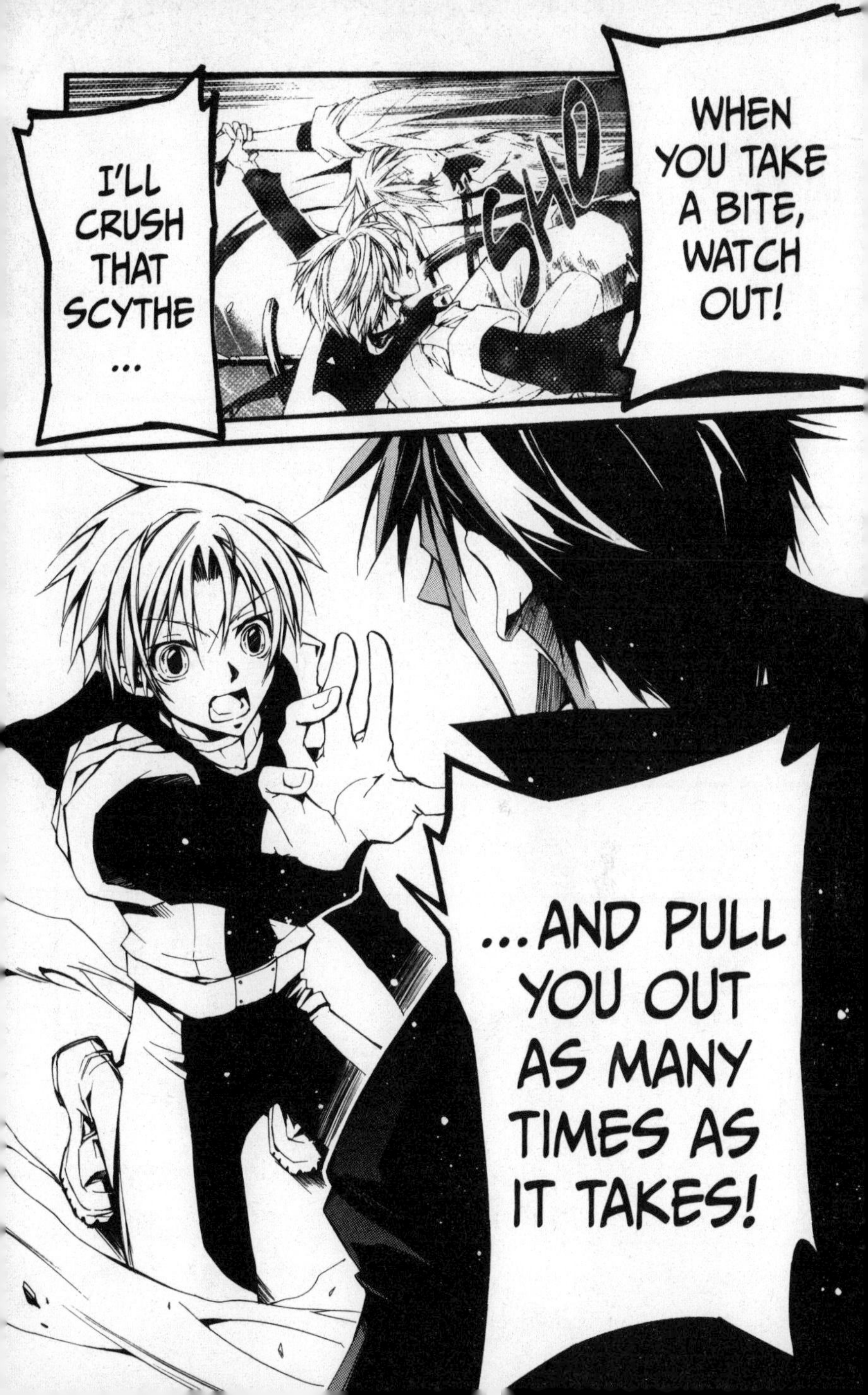
WHEN YOU TAKE A BITE, WATCH OUT!
SHO
I'LL CRUSH THAT SCYTHE ...
...AND PULL YOU OUT AS MANY TIMES AS IT TAKES!

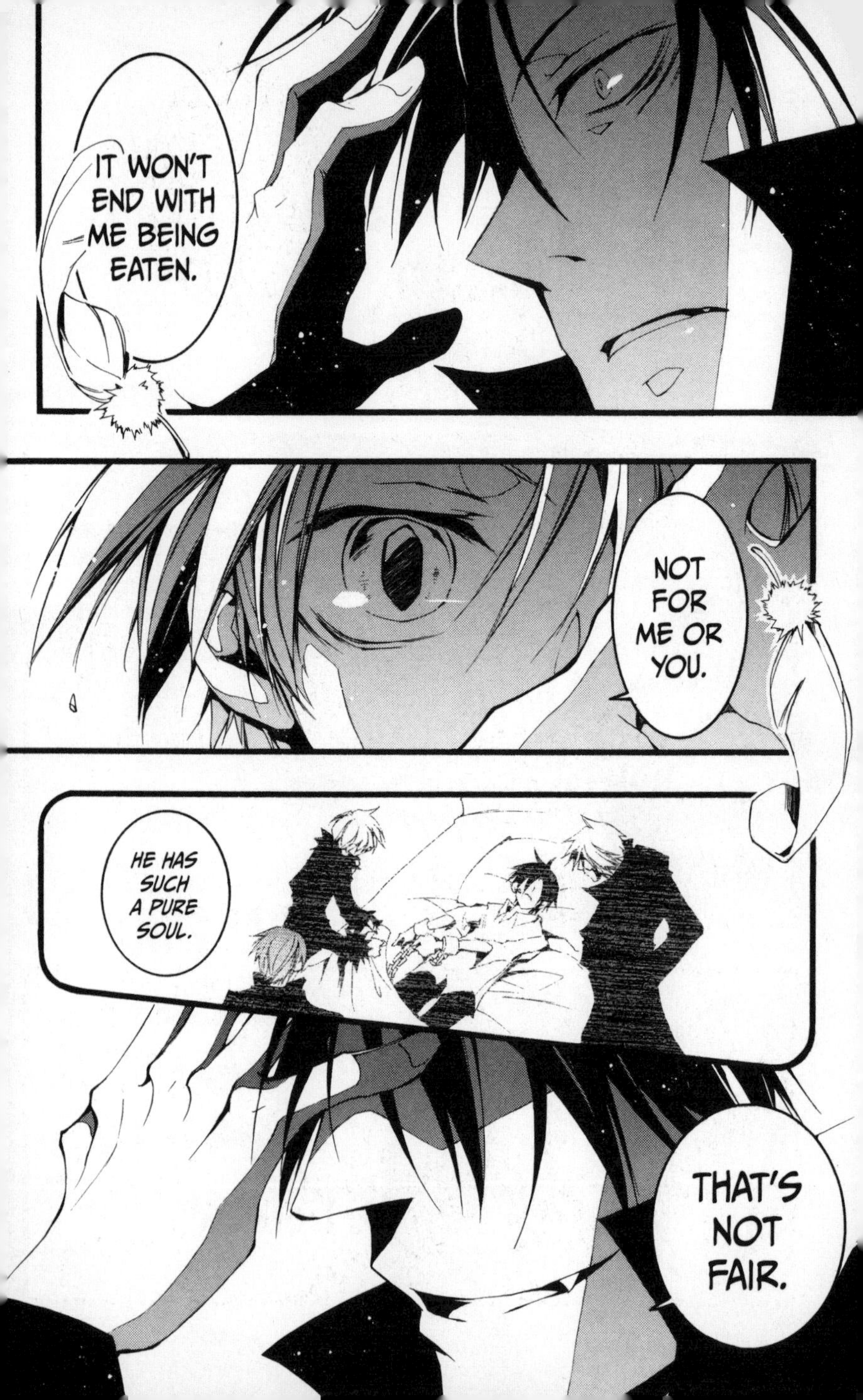
IT WON'T END WITH ME BEING EATEN.
NOT FOR ME OR YOU.
HE HAS SUCH A PURE SOUL.
THAT'S NOT FAIR.

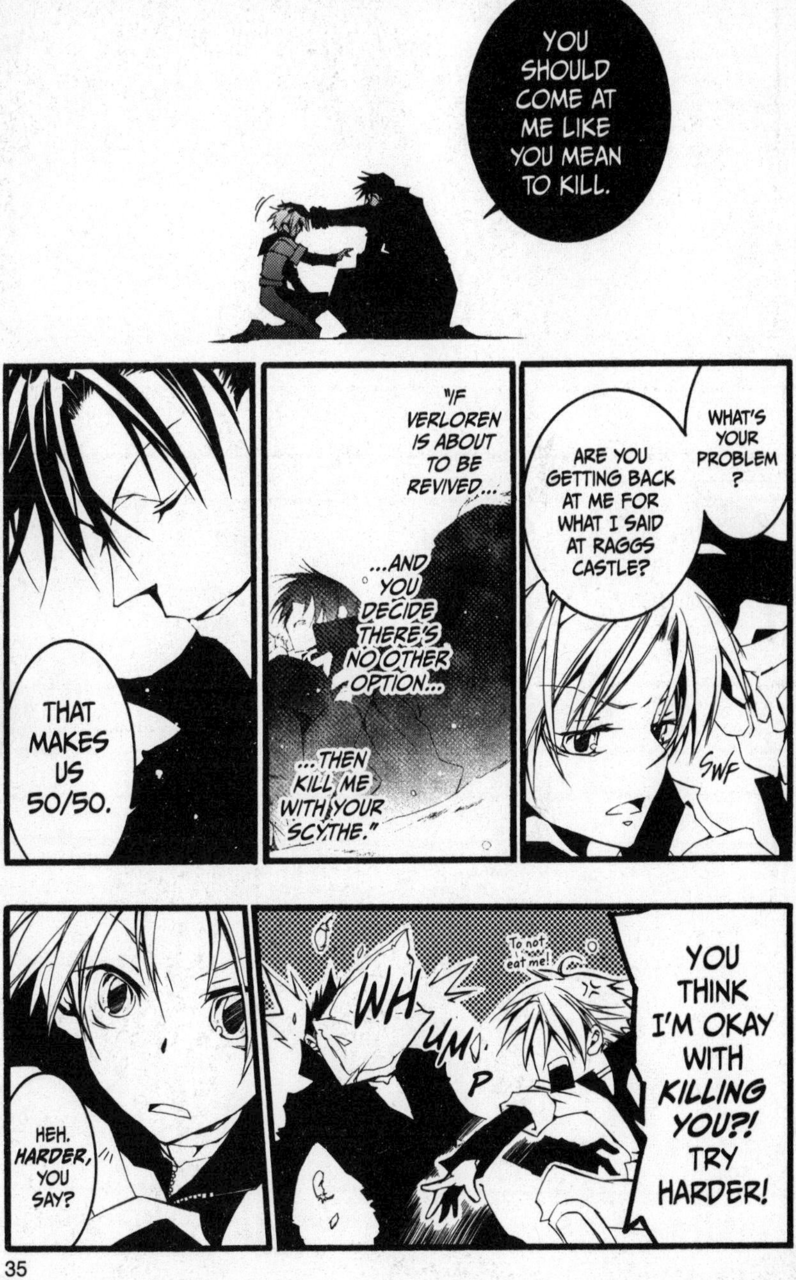
YOU SHOULD COME AT ME LIKE YOU MEAN TO KILL.
WHAT'S YOUR PROBLEM?
ARE YOU GETTING BACK AT ME FOR WHAT I SAID AT RAGGS CASTLE?
SWF
"IF VERLOREN IS ABOUT TO BE REVIVED...
...AND YOU DECIDE THERE'S NO OTHER OPTION...
...THEN KILL ME WITH YOUR SCYTHE."
THAT MAKES US 50/50.
YOU THINK I'M OKAY WITH *KILLING YOU?!* TRY HARDER!
To not eat me!
WHUMP
HEH. *HARDER,* YOU SAY?

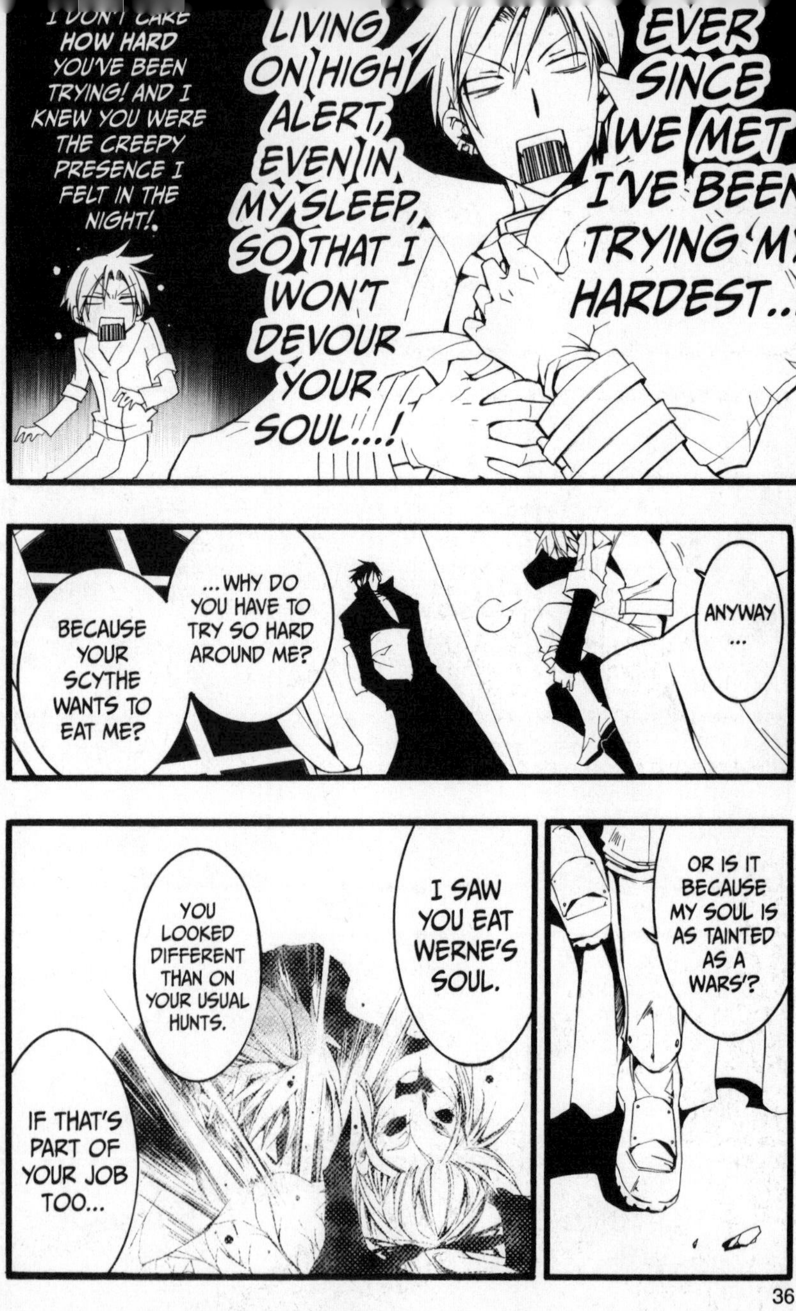
EVER SINCE WE MET I'VE BEEN TRYING MY HARDEST...!
LIVING ON HIGH ALERT, EVEN IN MY SLEEP, SO THAT I WON'T DEVOUR YOUR SOUL...!
I DON'T CARE HOW HARD YOU'VE BEEN TRYING! AND I KNEW YOU WERE THE CREEPY PRESENCE I FELT IN THE NIGHT!
ANYWAY...
...WHY DO YOU HAVE TO TRY SO HARD AROUND ME?
BECAUSE YOUR SCYTHE WANTS TO EAT ME?
OR IS IT BECAUSE MY SOUL IS AS TAINTED AS A WARS'?
I SAW YOU EAT WERNE'S SOUL.
YOU LOOKED DIFFERENT THAN ON YOUR USUAL HUNTS.
IF THAT'S PART OF YOUR JOB TOO...

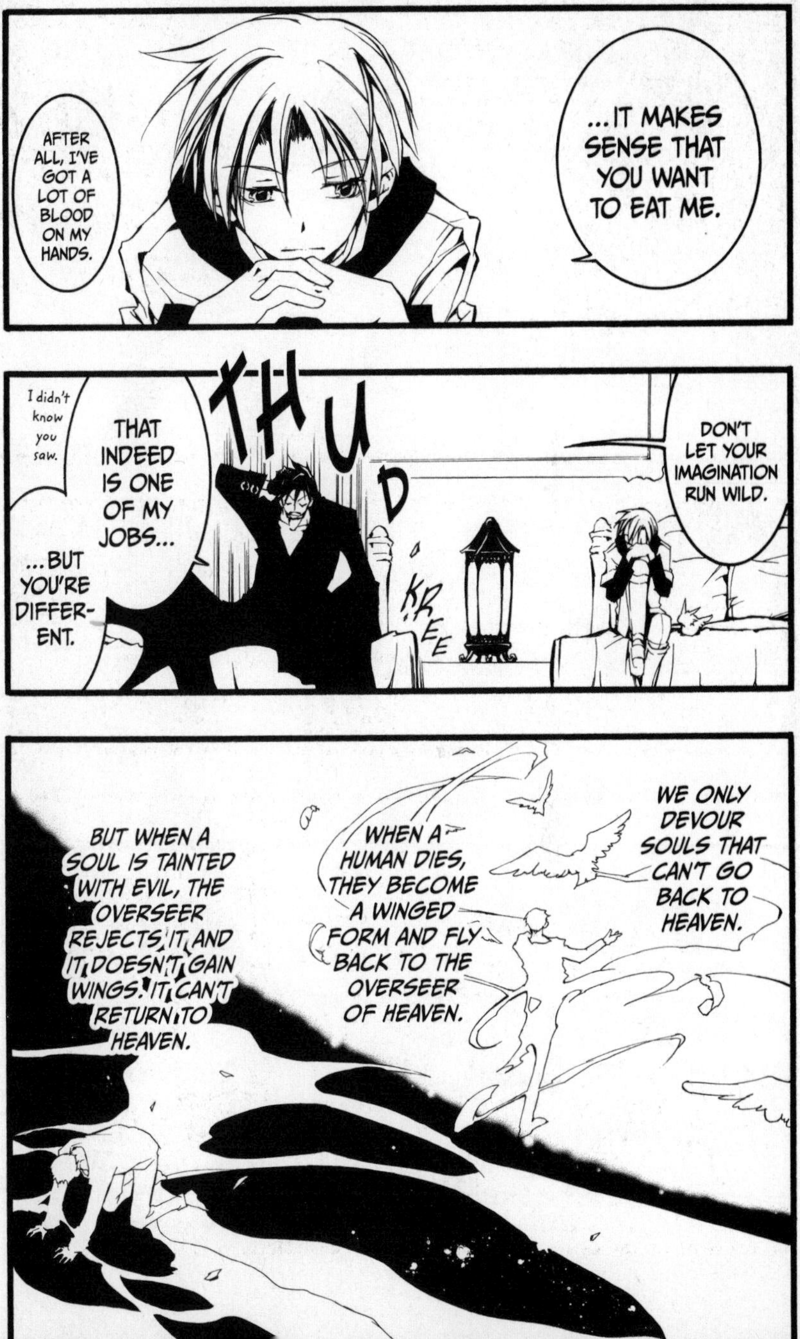
...IT MAKES SENSE THAT YOU WANT TO EAT ME.
AFTER ALL, I'VE GOT A LOT OF BLOOD ON MY HANDS.
DON'T LET YOUR IMAGINATION RUN WILD.
THUD
KREE
THAT INDEED IS ONE OF MY JOBS...
...BUT YOU'RE DIFFERENT.
I didn't know you saw.
WE ONLY DEVOUR SOULS THAT CAN'T GO BACK TO HEAVEN.
WHEN A HUMAN DIES, THEY BECOME A WINGED FORM AND FLY BACK TO THE OVERSEER OF HEAVEN.
BUT WHEN A SOUL IS TAINTED WITH EVIL, THE OVERSEER REJECTS IT AND IT DOESN'T GAIN WINGS. IT CAN'T RETURN TO HEAVEN.

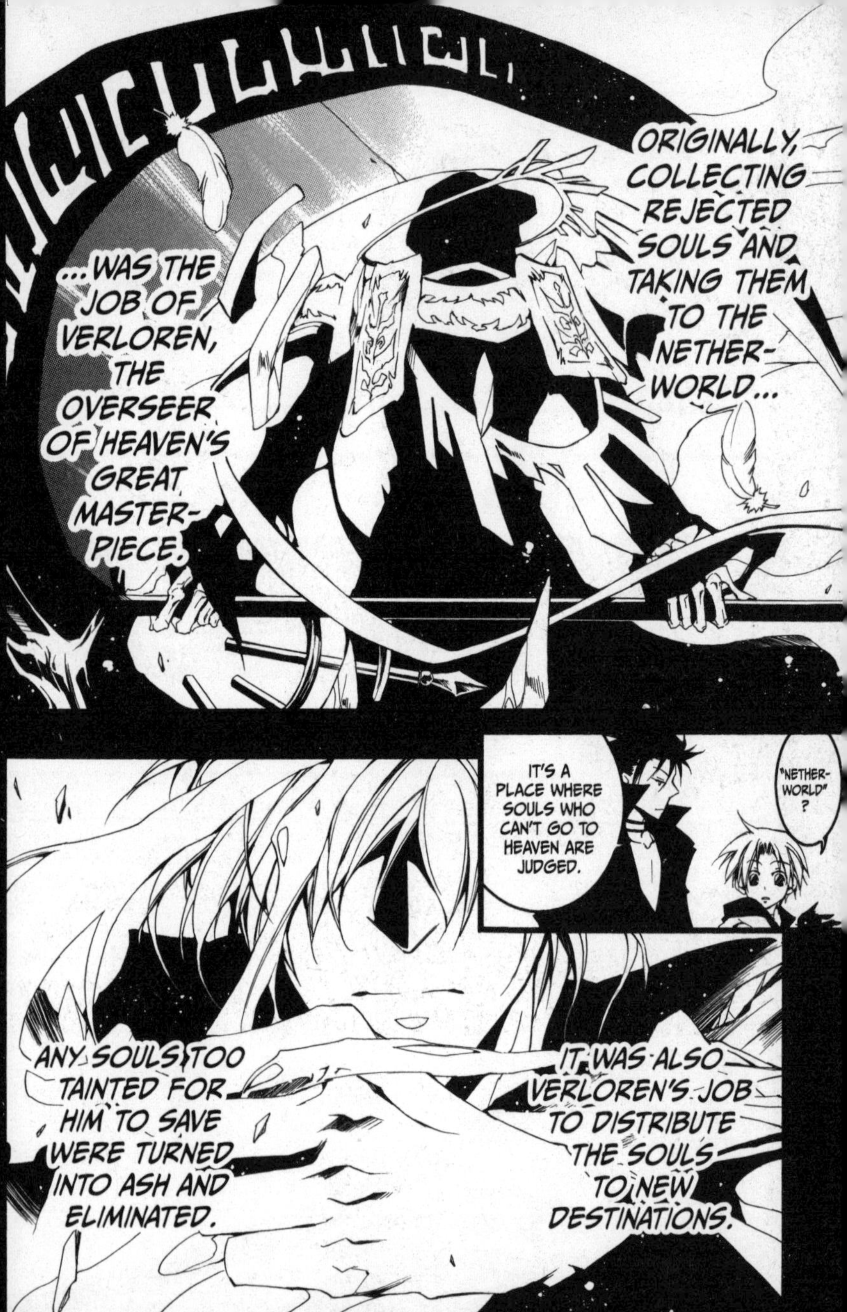
ORIGINALLY, COLLECTING REJECTED SOULS AND TAKING THEM TO THE NETHER-WORLD...
...WAS THE JOB OF VERLOREN, THE OVERSEER OF HEAVEN'S GREAT MASTER-PIECE.
"NETHER-WORLD"?
IT'S A PLACE WHERE SOULS WHO CAN'T GO TO HEAVEN ARE JUDGED.
IT WAS ALSO VERLOREN'S JOB TO DISTRIBUTE THE SOULS TO NEW DESTINATIONS.
ANY SOULS TOO TAINTED FOR HIM TO SAVE WERE TURNED INTO ASH AND ELIMINATED.

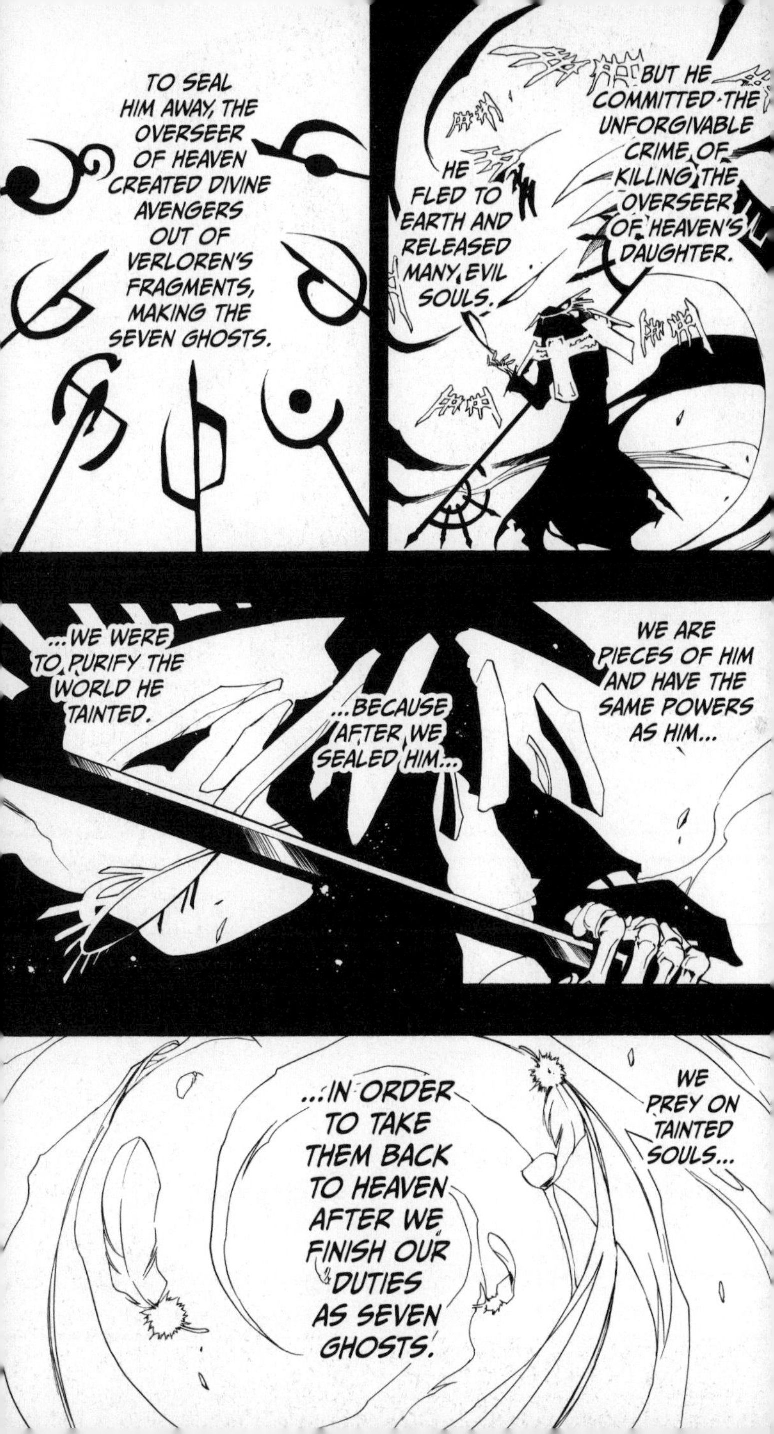
BUT HE COMMITTED THE UNFORGIVABLE CRIME OF KILLING THE OVERSEER OF HEAVEN'S DAUGHTER.
HE FLED TO EARTH AND RELEASED MANY EVIL SOULS.
TO SEAL HIM AWAY, THE OVERSEER OF HEAVEN CREATED DIVINE AVENGERS OUT OF VERLOREN'S FRAGMENTS, MAKING THE SEVEN GHOSTS.
WE ARE PIECES OF HIM AND HAVE THE SAME POWERS AS HIM...
...BECAUSE AFTER WE SEALED HIM...
...WE WERE TO PURIFY THE WORLD HE TAINTED.
WE PREY ON TAINTED SOULS...
...IN ORDER TO TAKE THEM BACK TO HEAVEN AFTER WE FINISH OUR DUTIES AS SEVEN GHOSTS.

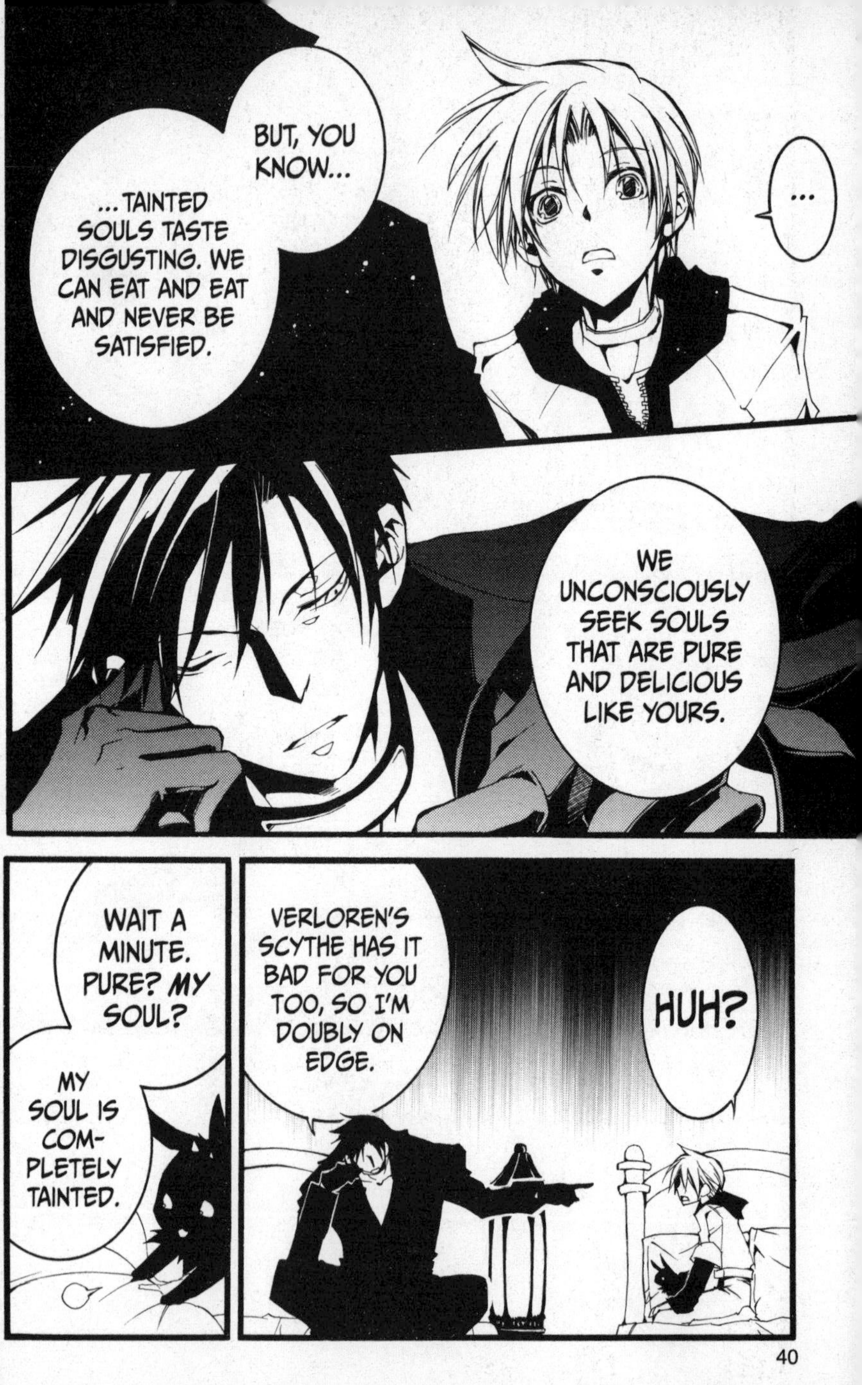
...
BUT, YOU KNOW...
...TAINTED SOULS TASTE DISGUSTING. WE CAN EAT AND EAT AND NEVER BE SATISFIED.
WE UNCONSCIOUSLY SEEK SOULS THAT ARE PURE AND DELICIOUS LIKE YOURS.
HUH?
VERLOREN'S SCYTHE HAS IT BAD FOR YOU TOO, SO I'M DOUBLY ON EDGE.
WAIT A MINUTE. PURE? *MY* SOUL?
MY SOUL IS COM-PLETELY TAINTED.

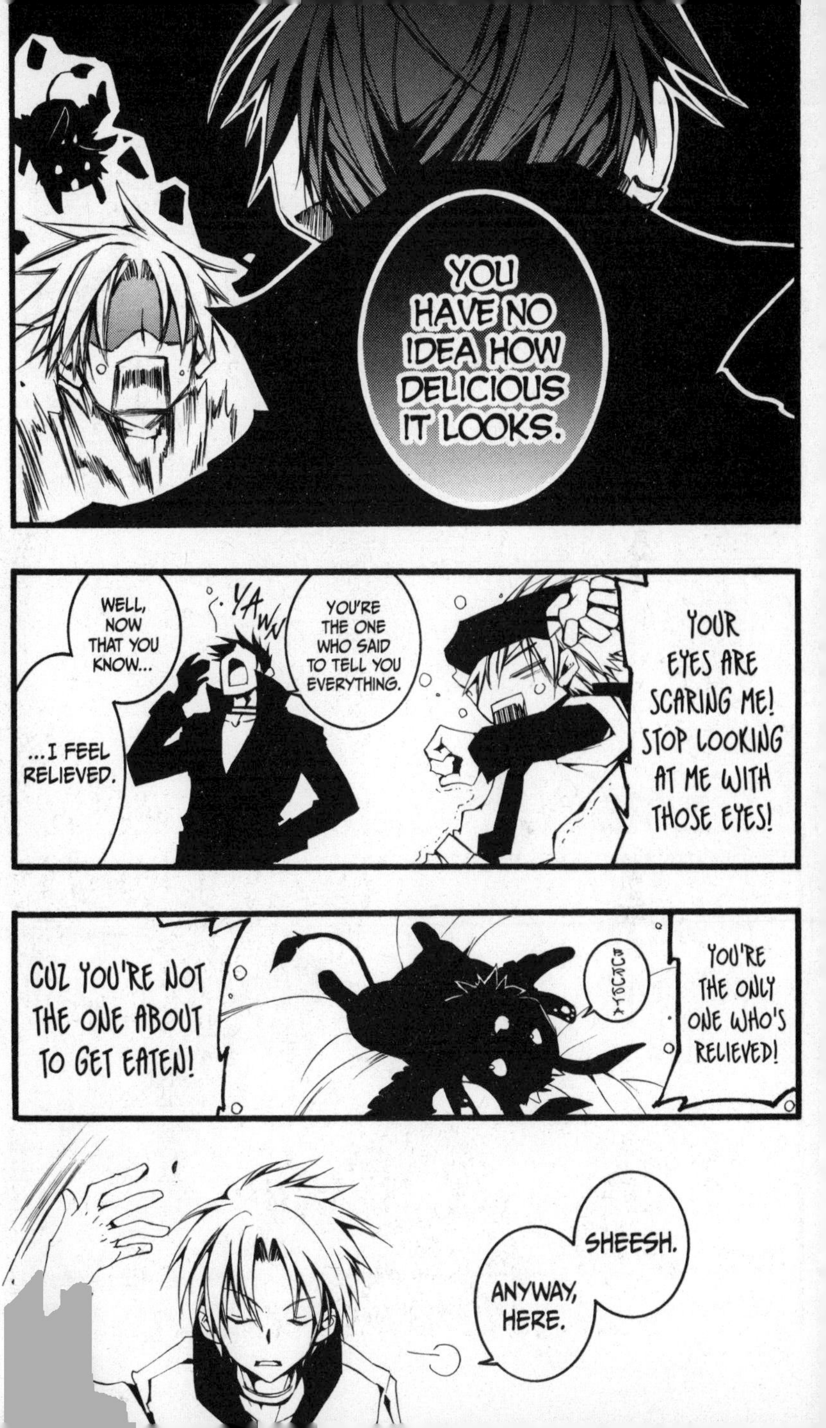
YOU HAVE NO IDEA HOW DELICIOUS IT LOOKS.
YOUR EYES ARE SCARING ME! STOP LOOKING AT ME WITH THOSE EYES!
YOU'RE THE ONE WHO SAID TO TELL YOU EVERYTHING.
YAWN
WELL, NOW THAT YOU KNOW...
...I FEEL RELIEVED.
YOU'RE THE ONLY ONE WHO'S RELIEVED!
CUZ YOU'RE NOT THE ONE ABOUT TO GET EATEN!
SHEESH.
ANYWAY, HERE.

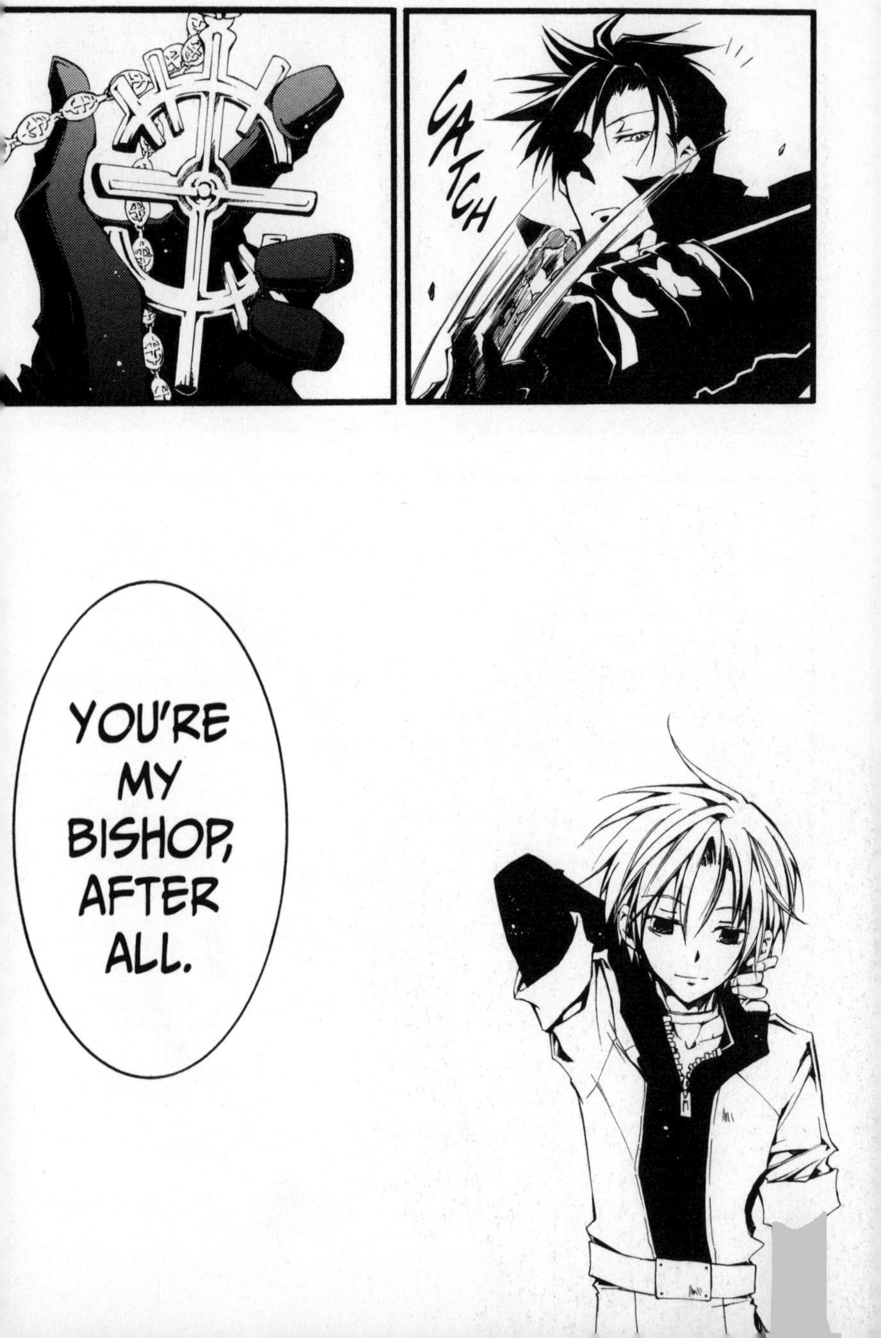
CATCH
YOU'RE MY BISHOP, AFTER ALL.

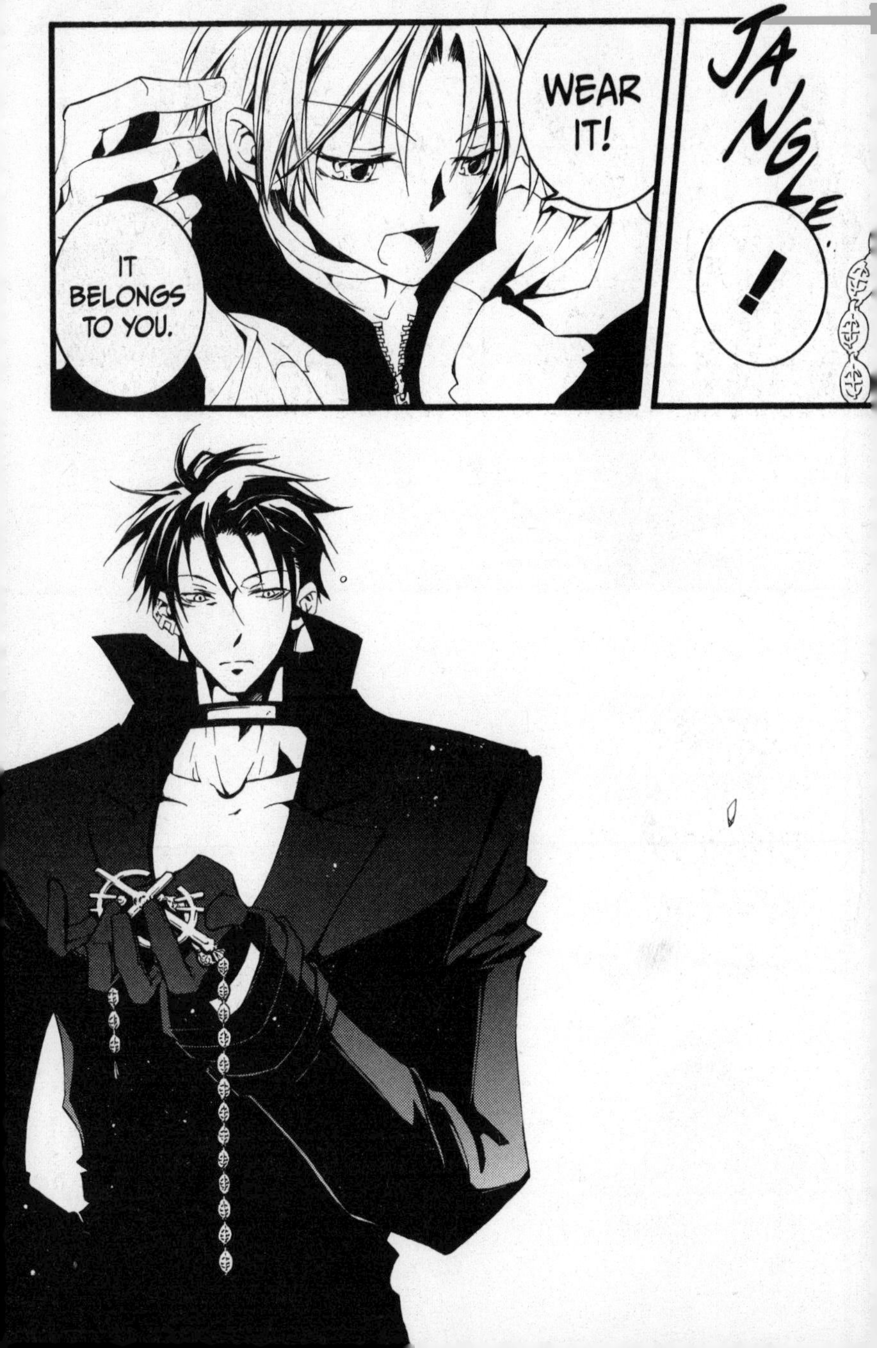
JANGLE...
!
WEAR IT!
IT BELONGS TO YOU.

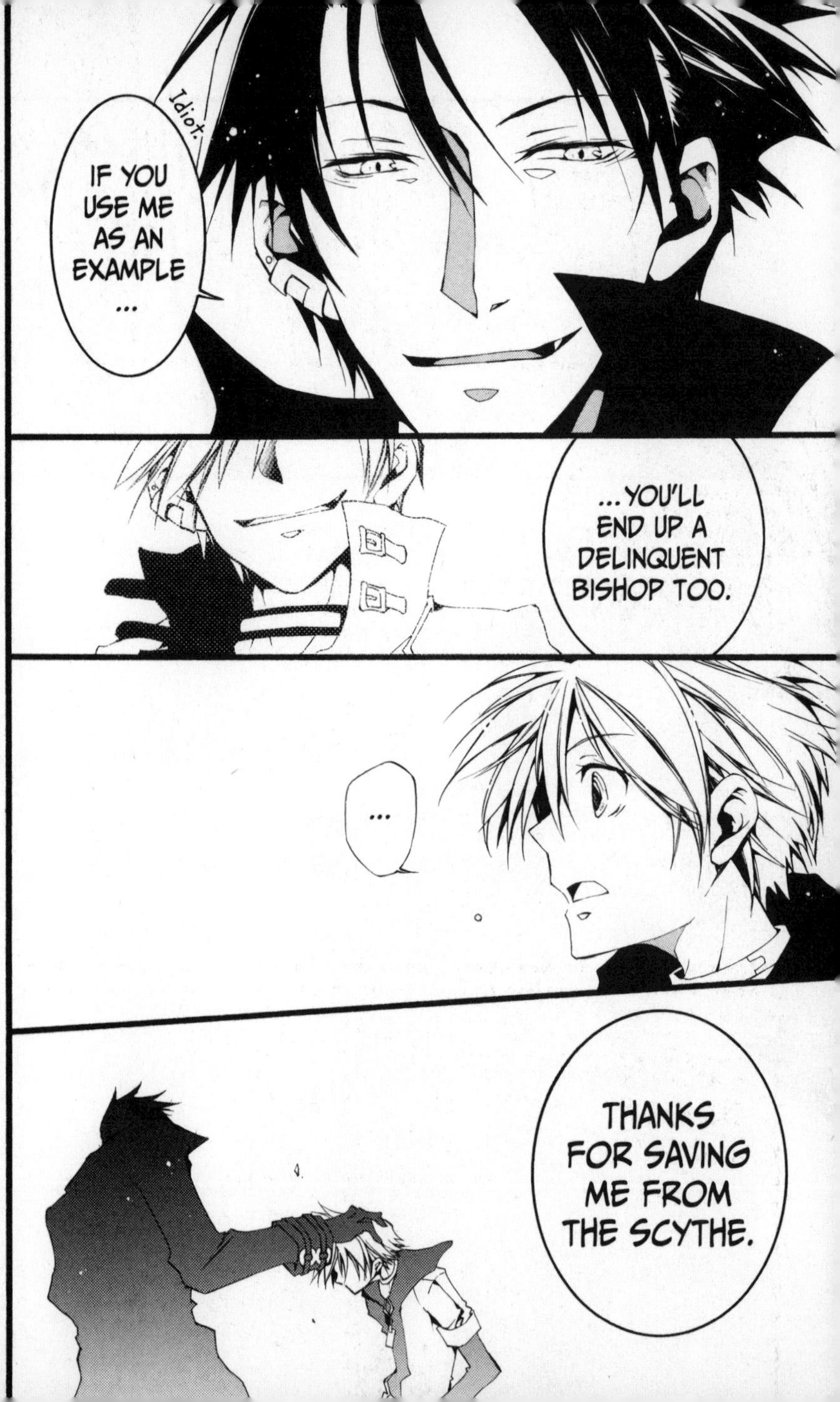
Idiot.
IF YOU USE ME AS AN EXAMPLE ...
...YOU'LL END UP A DELINQUENT BISHOP TOO.
...
THANKS FOR SAVING ME FROM THE SCYTHE.

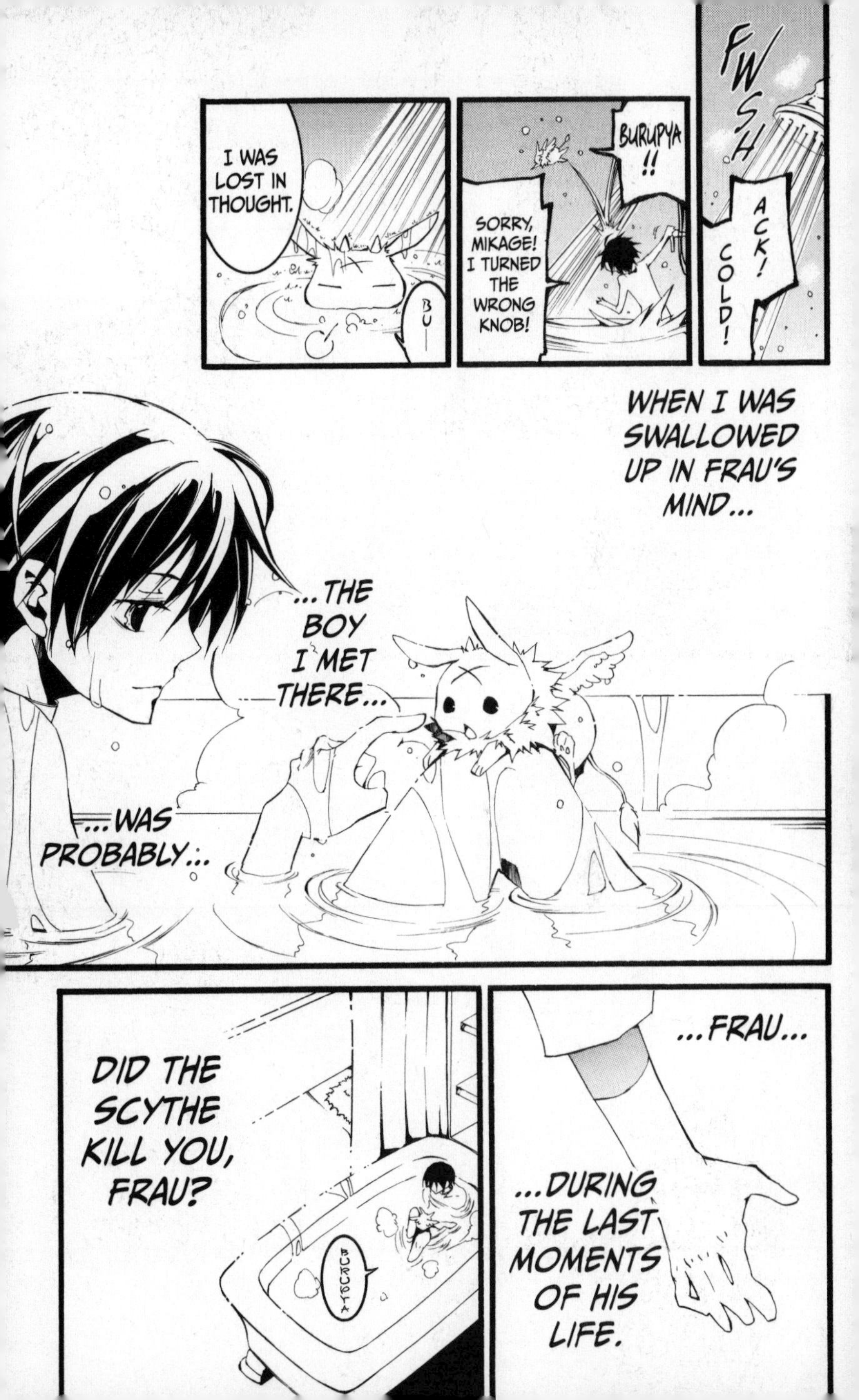
FWSH
ACK! COLD!
BURUPYA !!
SORRY, MIKAGE! I TURNED THE WRONG KNOB!
I WAS LOST IN THOUGHT.
BU
WHEN I WAS SWALLOWED UP IN FRAU'S MIND...
...THE BOY I MET THERE...
...WAS PROBABLY...
...FRAU...
...DURING THE LAST MOMENTS OF HIS LIFE.
DID THE SCYTHE KILL YOU, FRAU?
BURUPYA

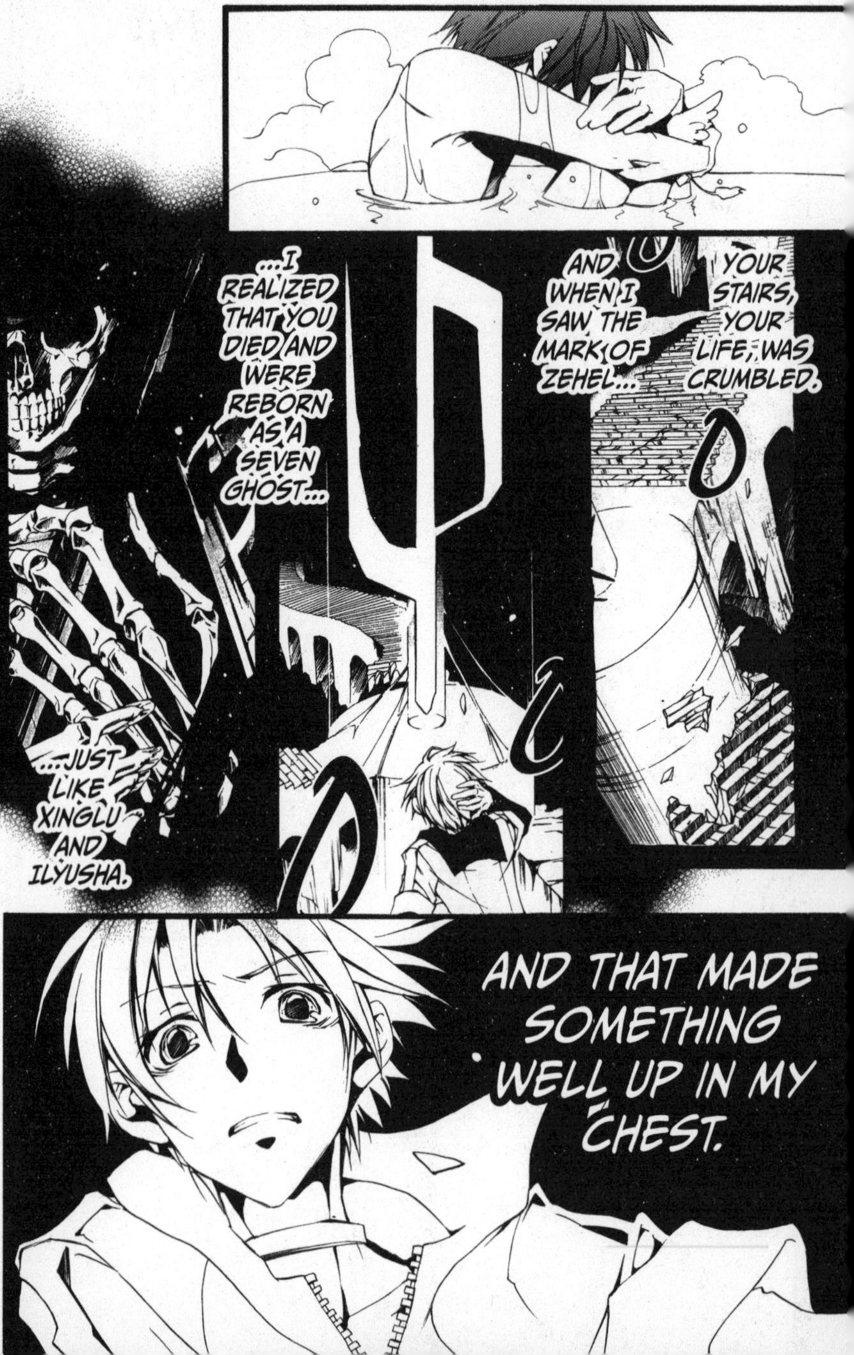
YOUR STAIRS, YOUR LIFE, WAS CRUMBLED.
AND WHEN I SAW THE MARK OF ZEHEL...
...I REALIZED THAT YOU DIED AND WERE REBORN AS A SEVEN GHOST...
...JUST LIKE XINGLU AND ILYUSHA.
AND THAT MADE SOMETHING WELL UP IN MY CHEST.

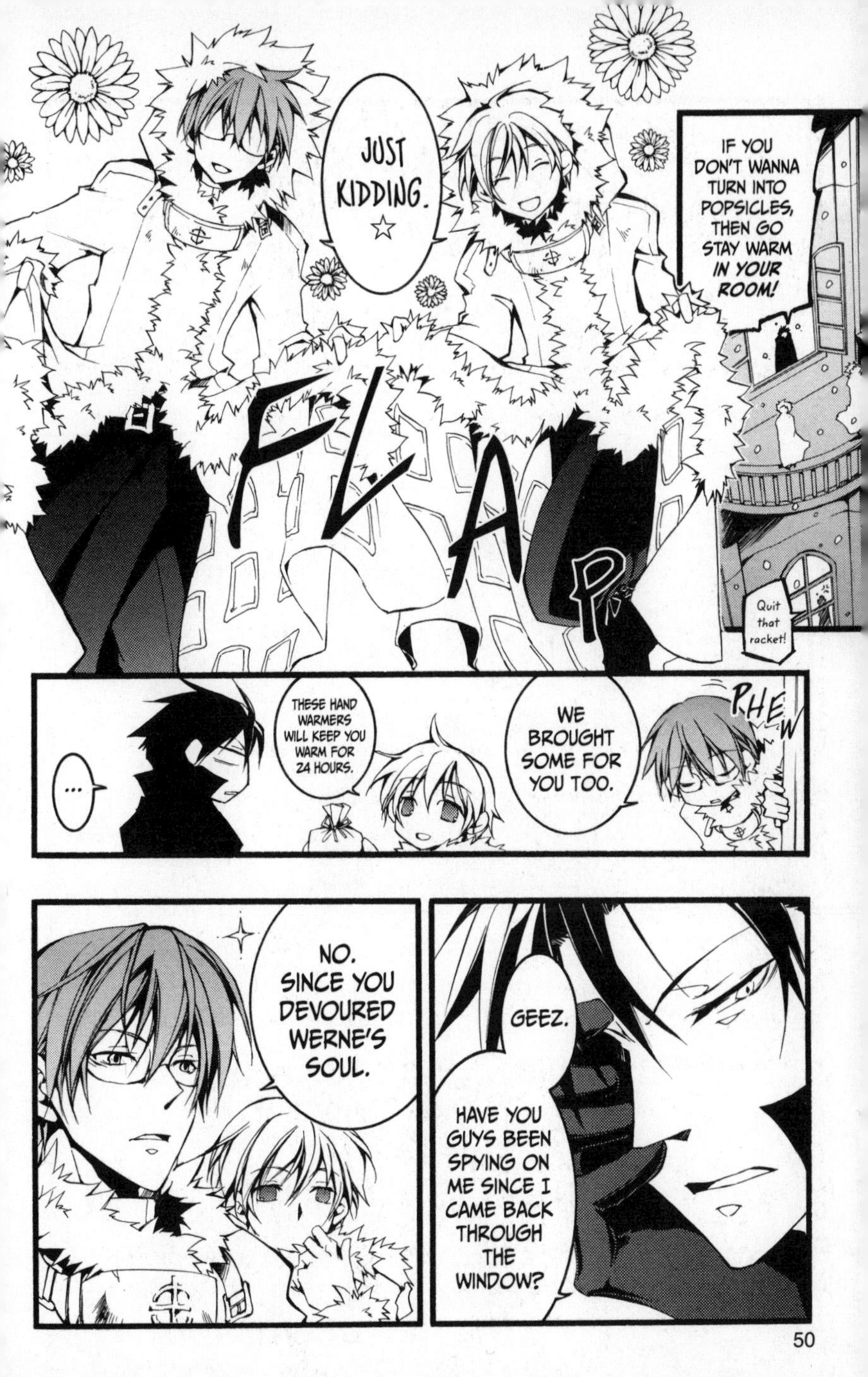
IF YOU DON'T WANNA TURN INTO POPSICLES, THEN GO STAY WARM IN YOUR ROOM!
Quit that racket!
JUST KIDDING. ☆
FLAP
PHEW
WE BROUGHT SOME FOR YOU TOO.
THESE HAND WARMERS WILL KEEP YOU WARM FOR 24 HOURS.
...
GEEZ.
HAVE YOU GUYS BEEN SPYING ON ME SINCE I CAME BACK THROUGH THE WINDOW?
NO. SINCE YOU DEVOURED WERNE'S SOUL.

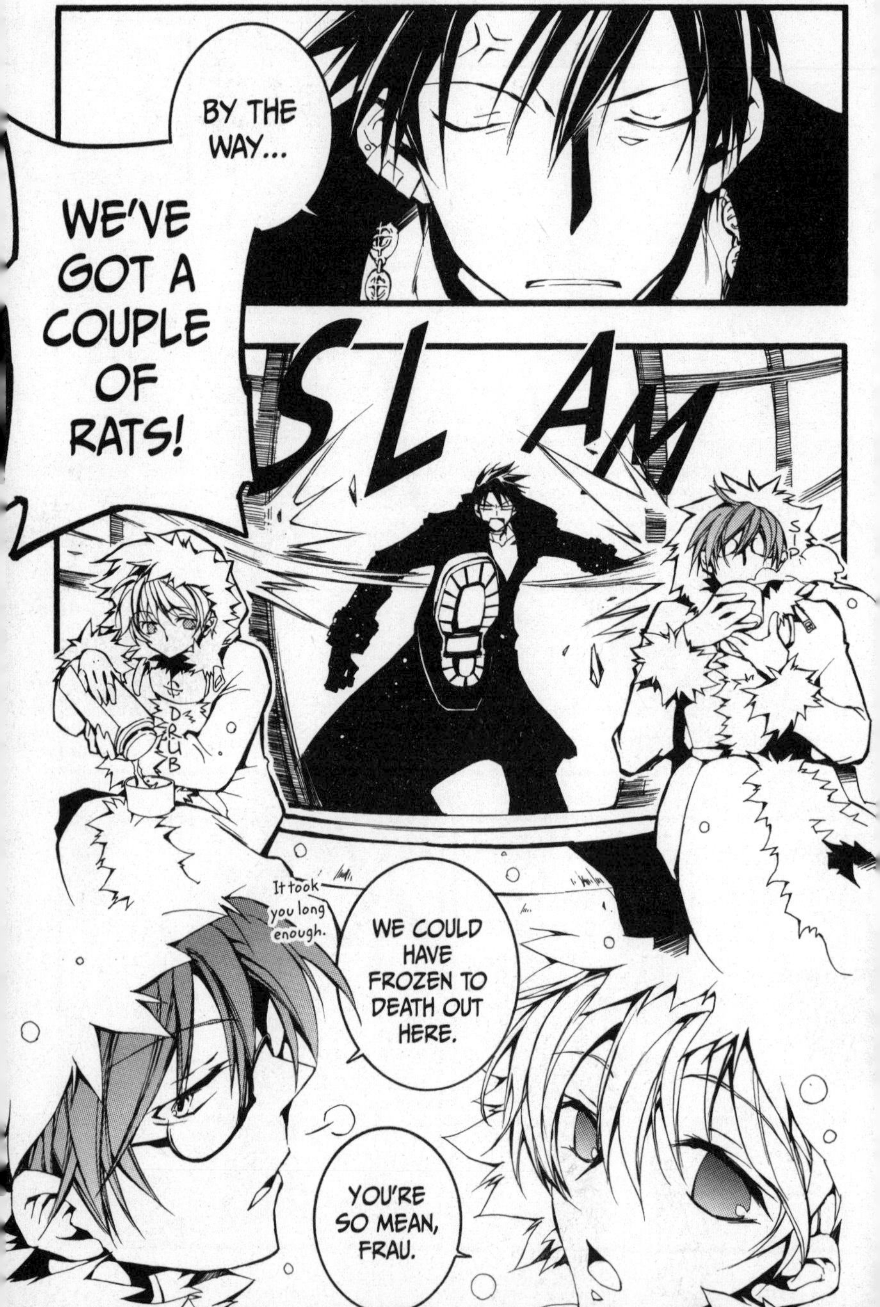
BY THE WAY...
WE'VE GOT A COUPLE OF RATS!
SLAM
SIP
DRUB
It took you long enough.
WE COULD HAVE FROZEN TO DEATH OUT HERE.
YOU'RE SO MEAN, FRAU.

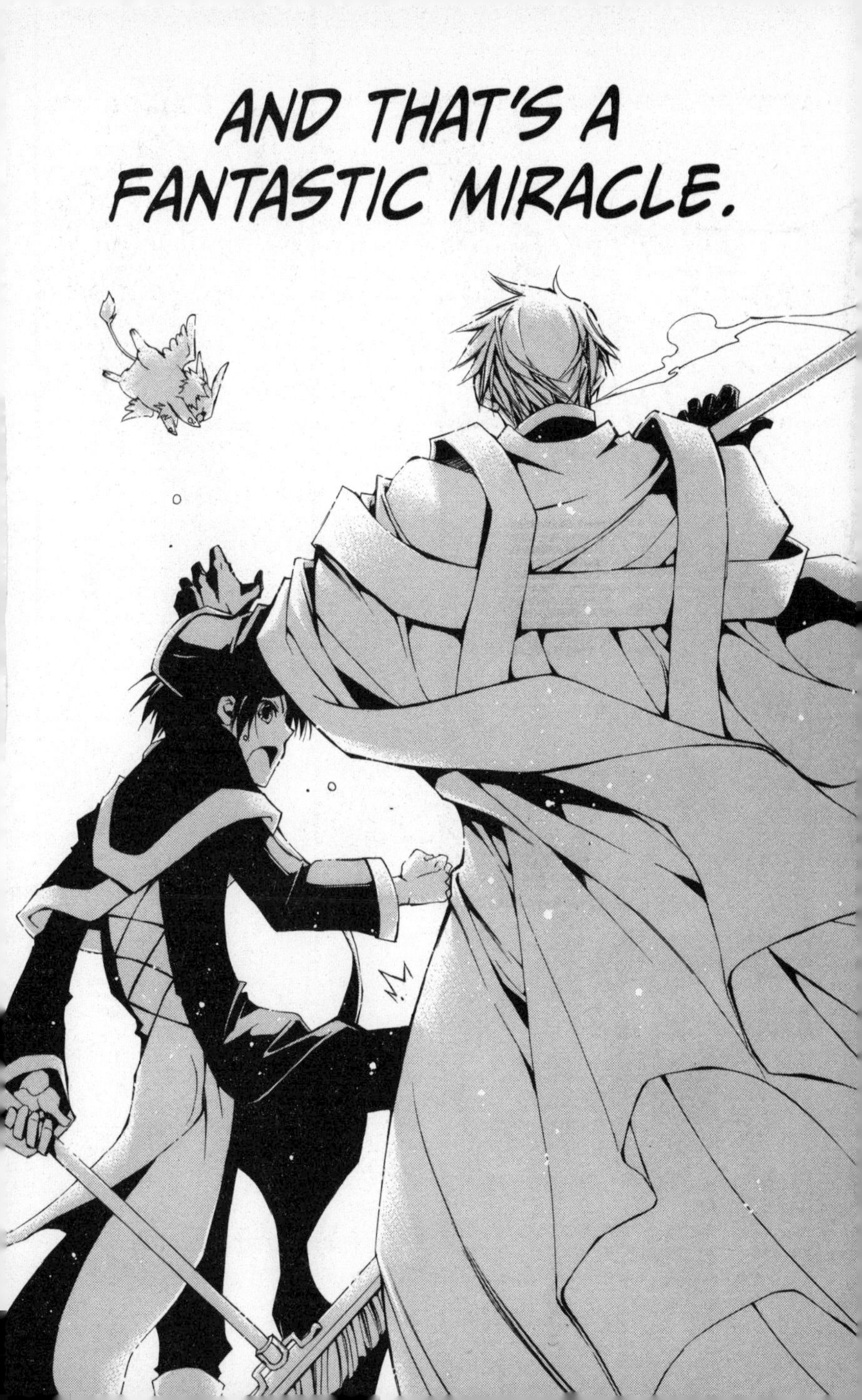
AND THAT'S A FANTASTIC MIRACLE.

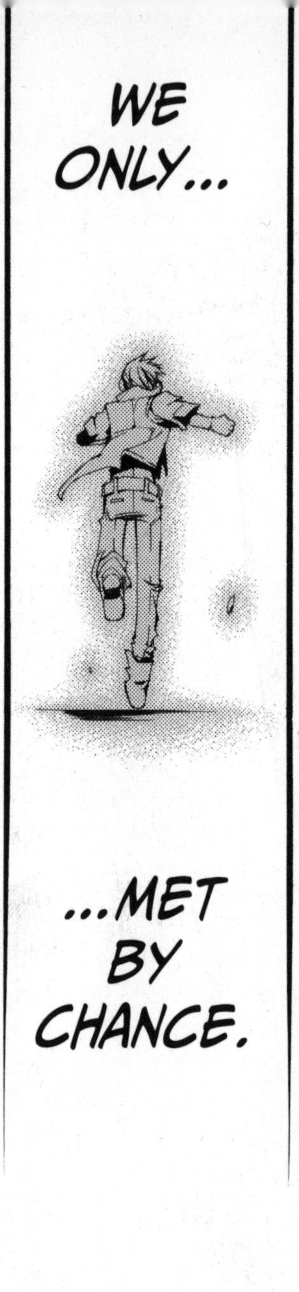
WE ONLY...
...MET BY CHANCE.
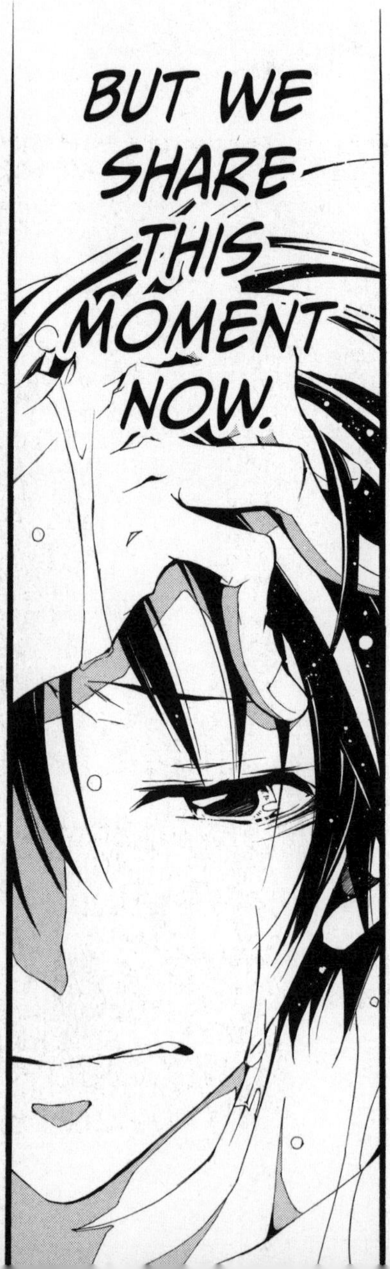
BUT WE SHARE THIS MOMENT NOW.

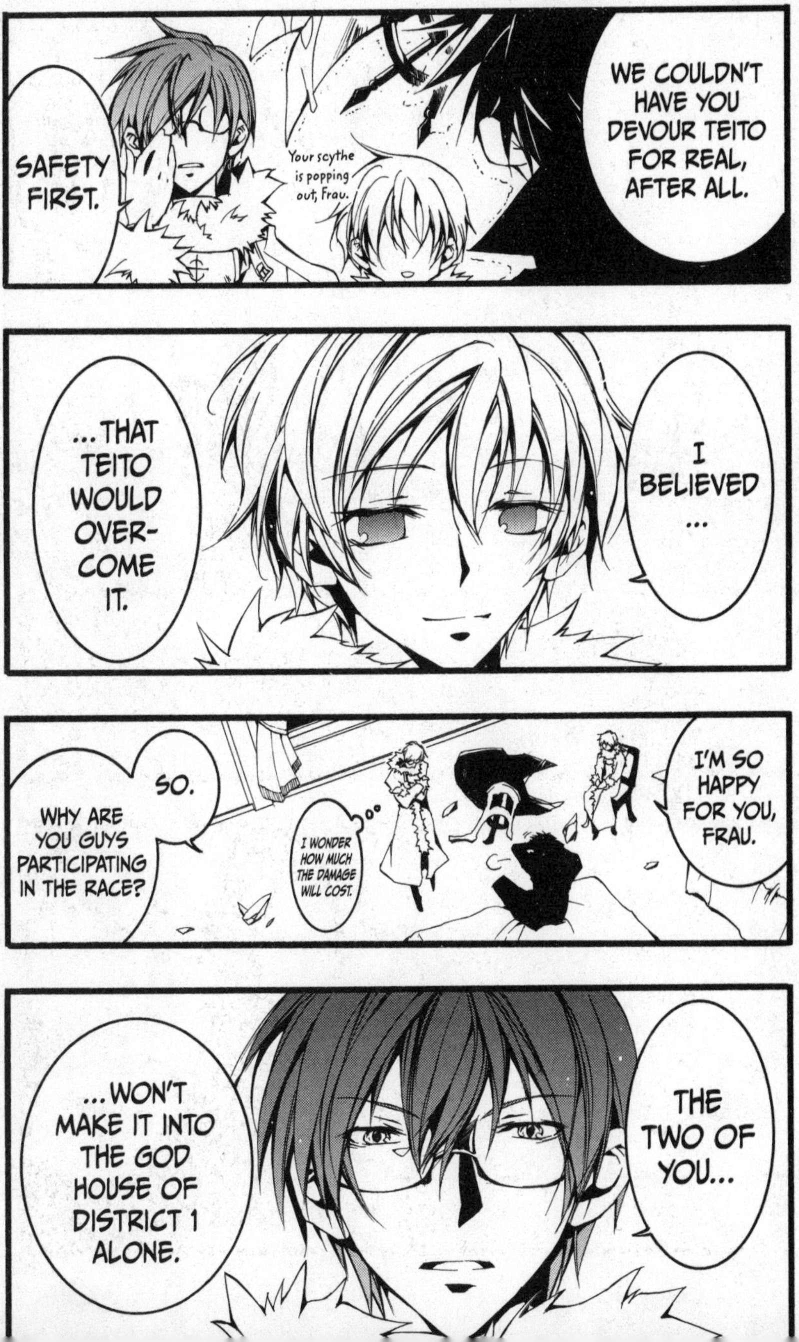
WE COULDN'T HAVE YOU DEVOUR TEITO FOR REAL, AFTER ALL.
Your scythe is popping out, Frau.
SAFETY FIRST.
I BELIEVED...
...THAT TEITO WOULD OVER-COME IT.
I'M SO HAPPY FOR YOU, FRAU.
I WONDER HOW MUCH THE DAMAGE WILL COST.
SO.
WHY ARE YOU GUYS PARTICIPATING IN THE RACE?
THE TWO OF YOU...
...WON'T MAKE IT INTO THE GOD HOUSE OF DISTRICT 1 ALONE.

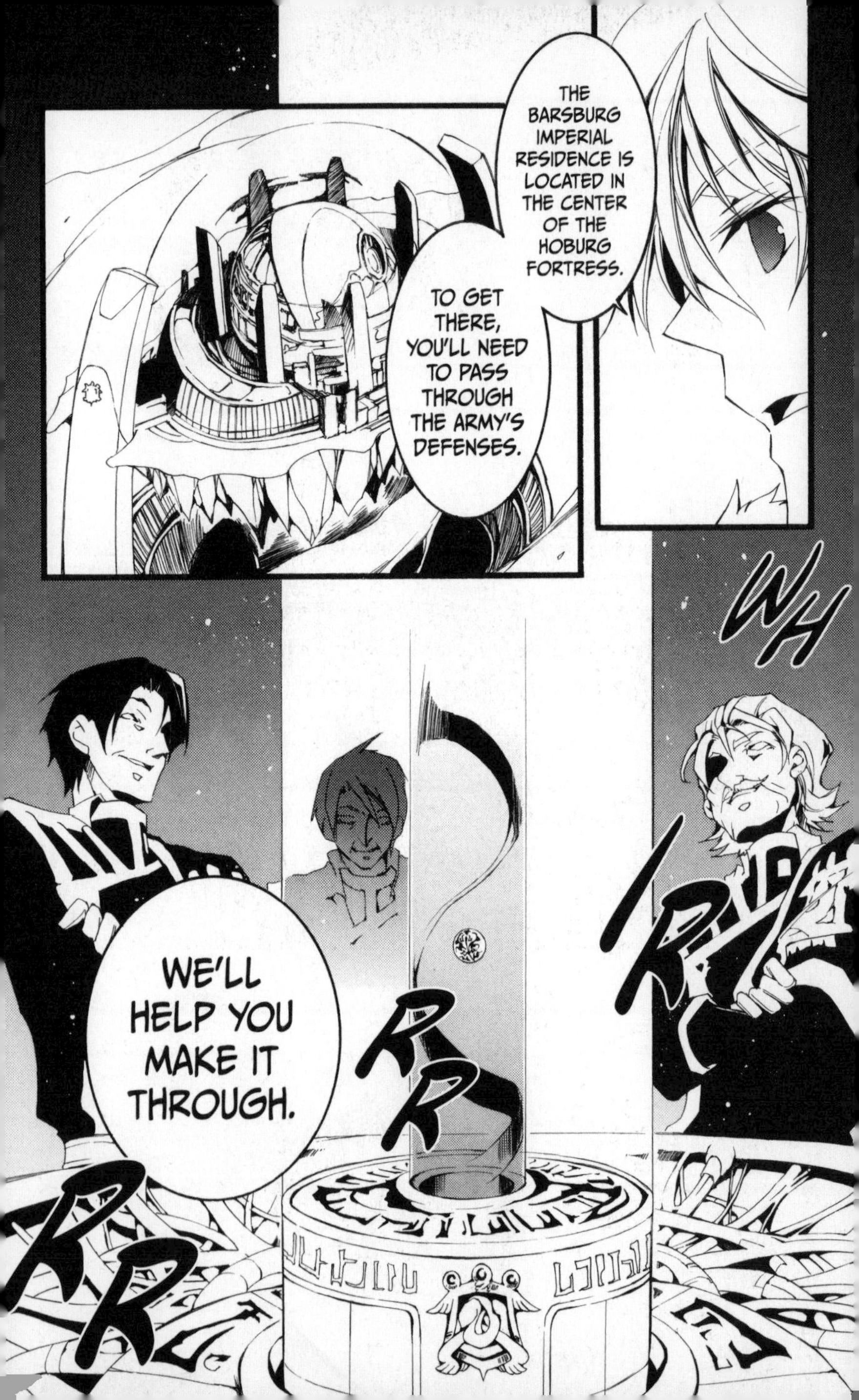

THE BARSBURG IMPERIAL RESIDENCE IS LOCATED IN THE CENTER OF THE HOBURG FORTRESS.
TO GET THERE, YOU'LL NEED TO PASS THROUGH THE ARMY'S DEFENSES.
WHIRR
WE'LL HELP YOU MAKE IT THROUGH.
RR
RR

Kapitel. 63 "Cleaning House"

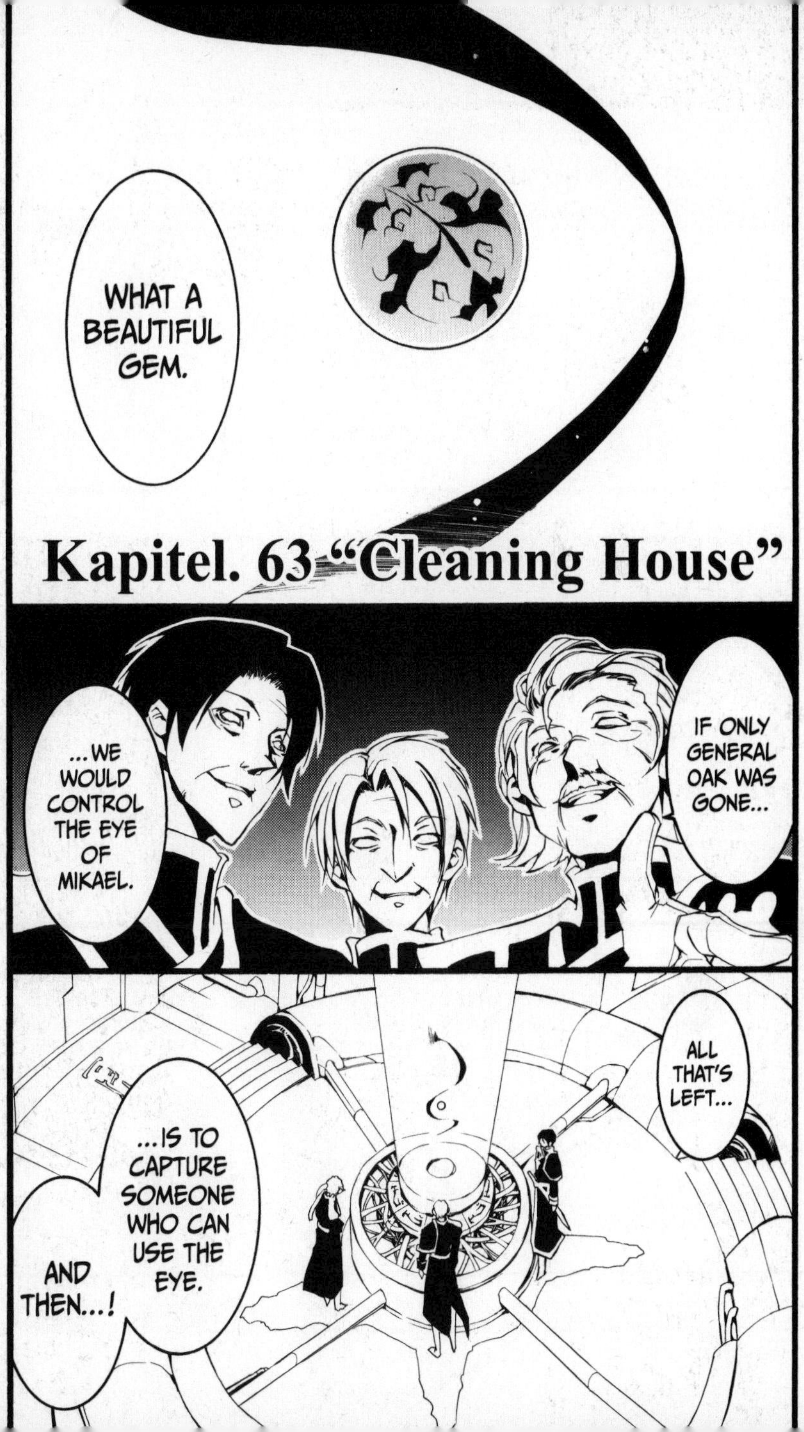
WHAT A BEAUTIFUL GEM.
IF ONLY GENERAL OAK WAS GONE...
...WE WOULD CONTROL THE EYE OF MIKAEL.
ALL THAT'S LEFT...
...IS TO CAPTURE SOMEONE WHO CAN USE THE EYE.
AND THEN...!

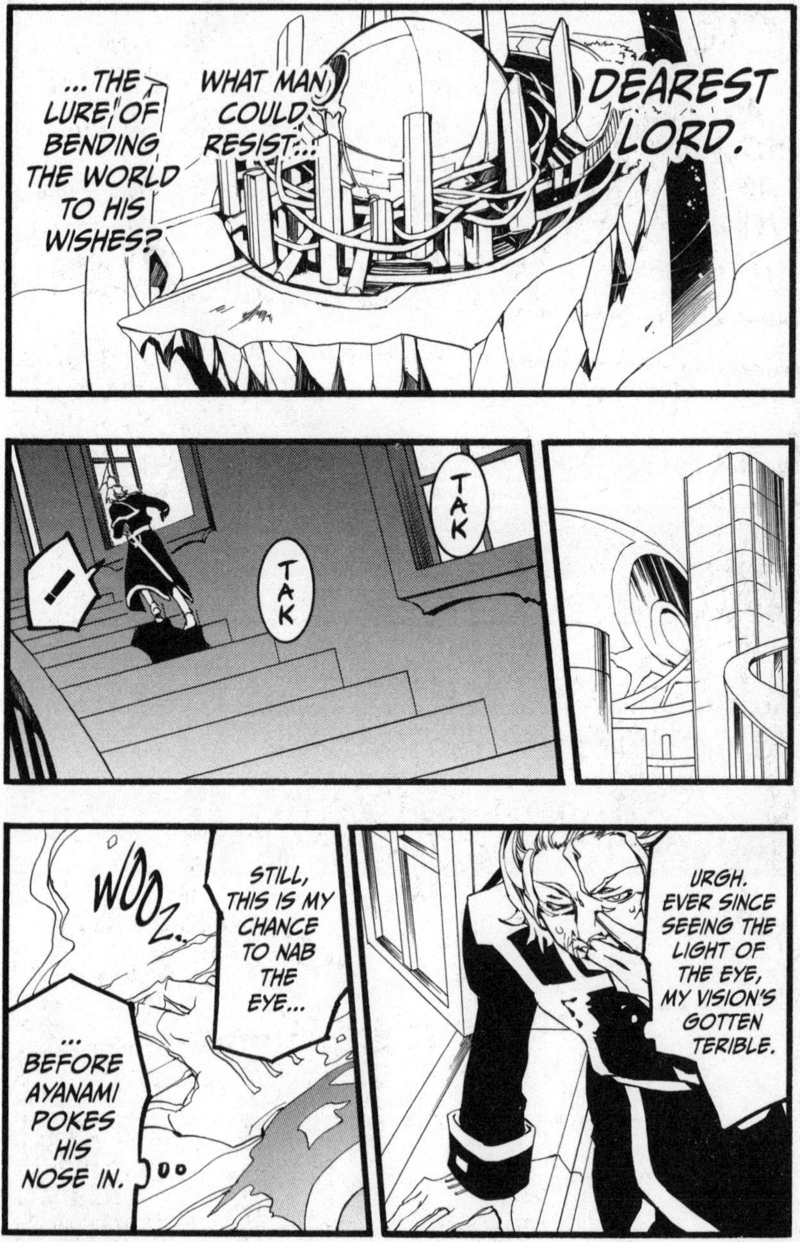
DEAREST LORD.
WHAT MAN COULD RESIST...
...THE LURE OF BENDING THE WORLD TO HIS WISHES?
TAK
TAK
!
URGH. EVER SINCE SEEING THE LIGHT OF THE EYE, MY VISION'S GOTTEN TERIBLE.
WOOZ..
STILL, THIS IS MY CHANCE TO NAB THE EYE...
...BEFORE AYANAMI POKES HIS NOSE IN.

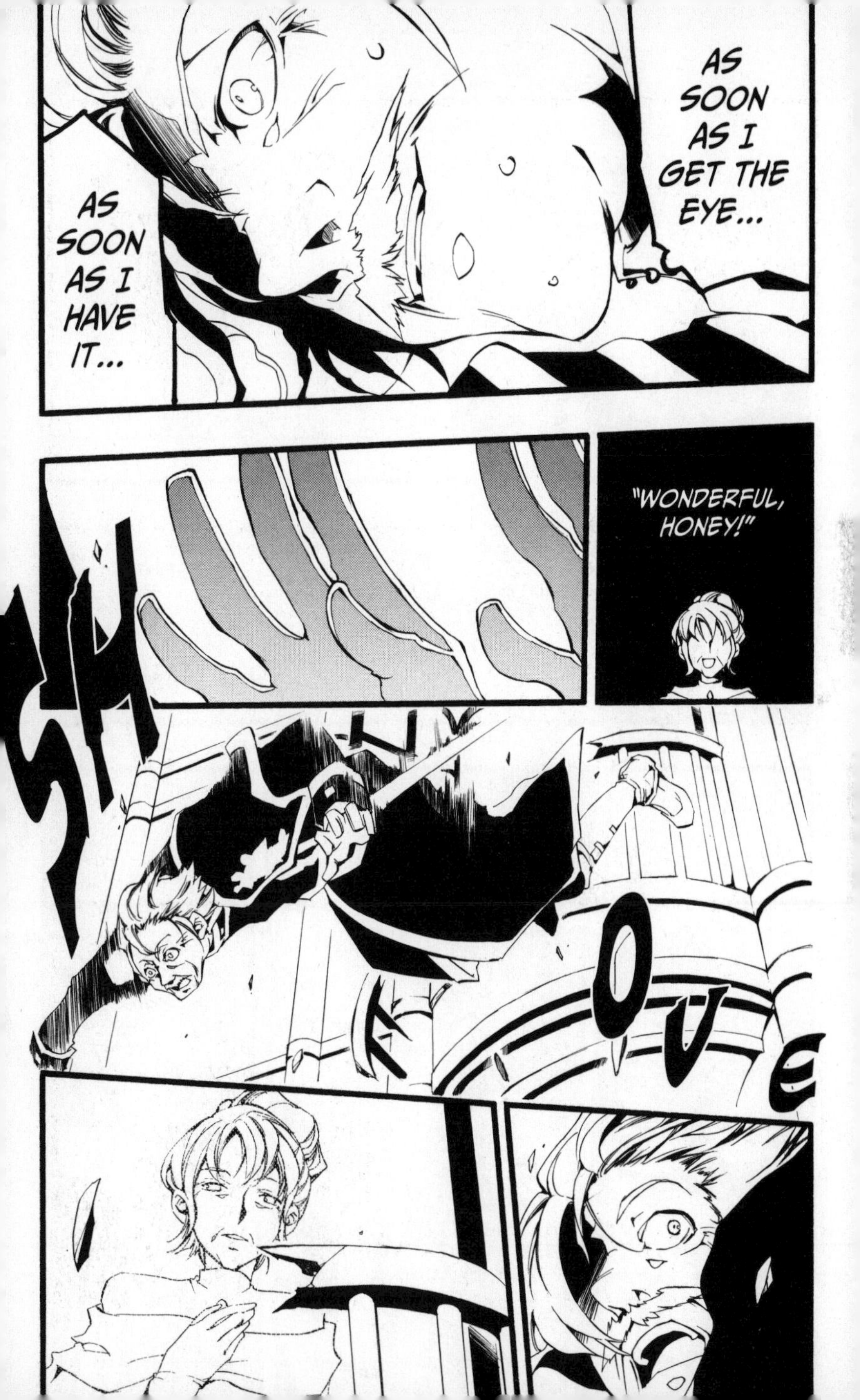
AS SOON AS I GET THE EYE...
AS SOON AS I HAVE IT...
"WONDERFUL, HONEY!"
SHOVE

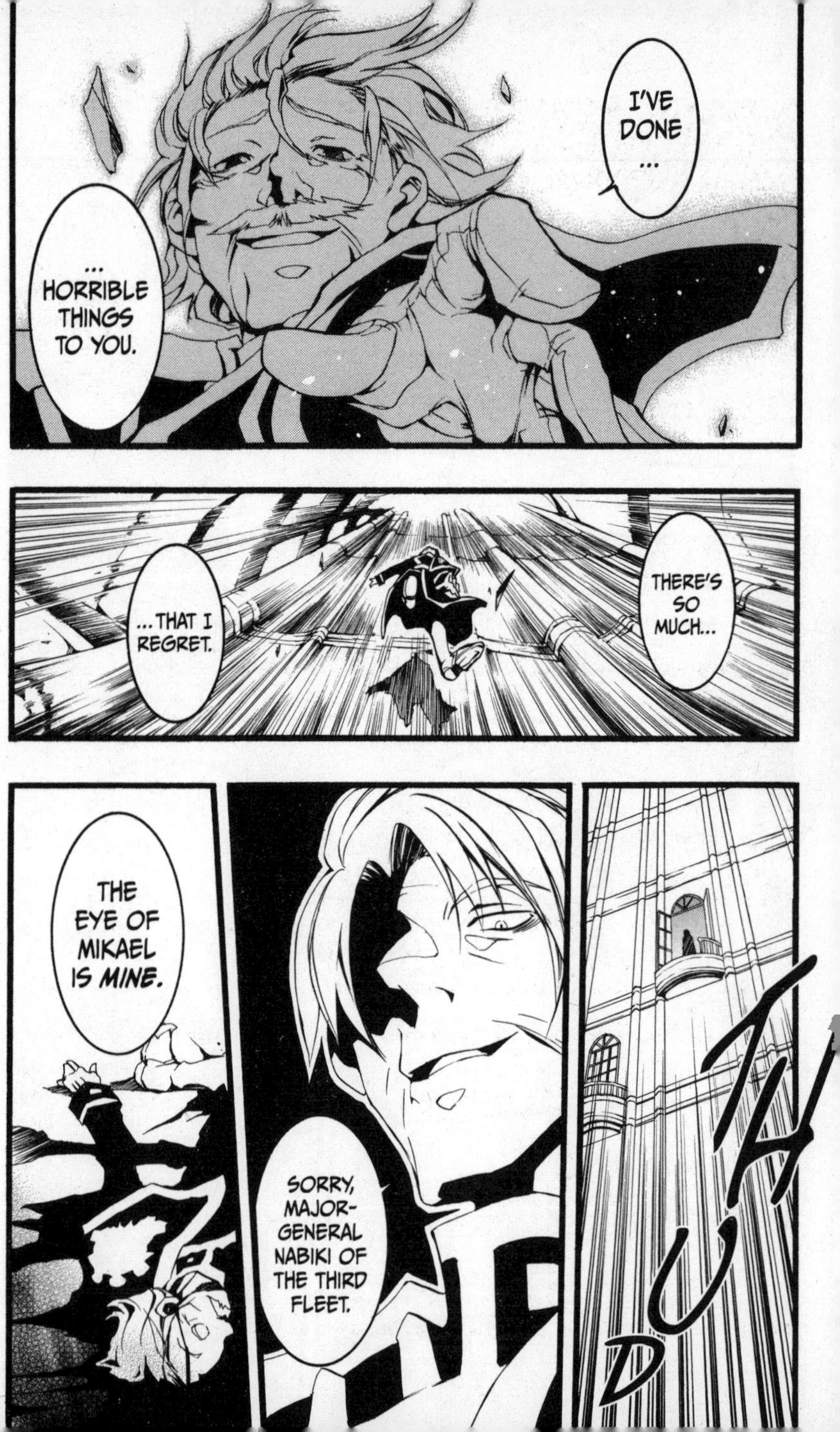
I'VE DONE ...
... HORRIBLE THINGS TO YOU.
THERE'S SO MUCH...
...THAT I REGRET.
SORRY, MAJOR-GENERAL NABIKI OF THE THIRD FLEET.
THE EYE OF MIKAEL IS *MINE*.

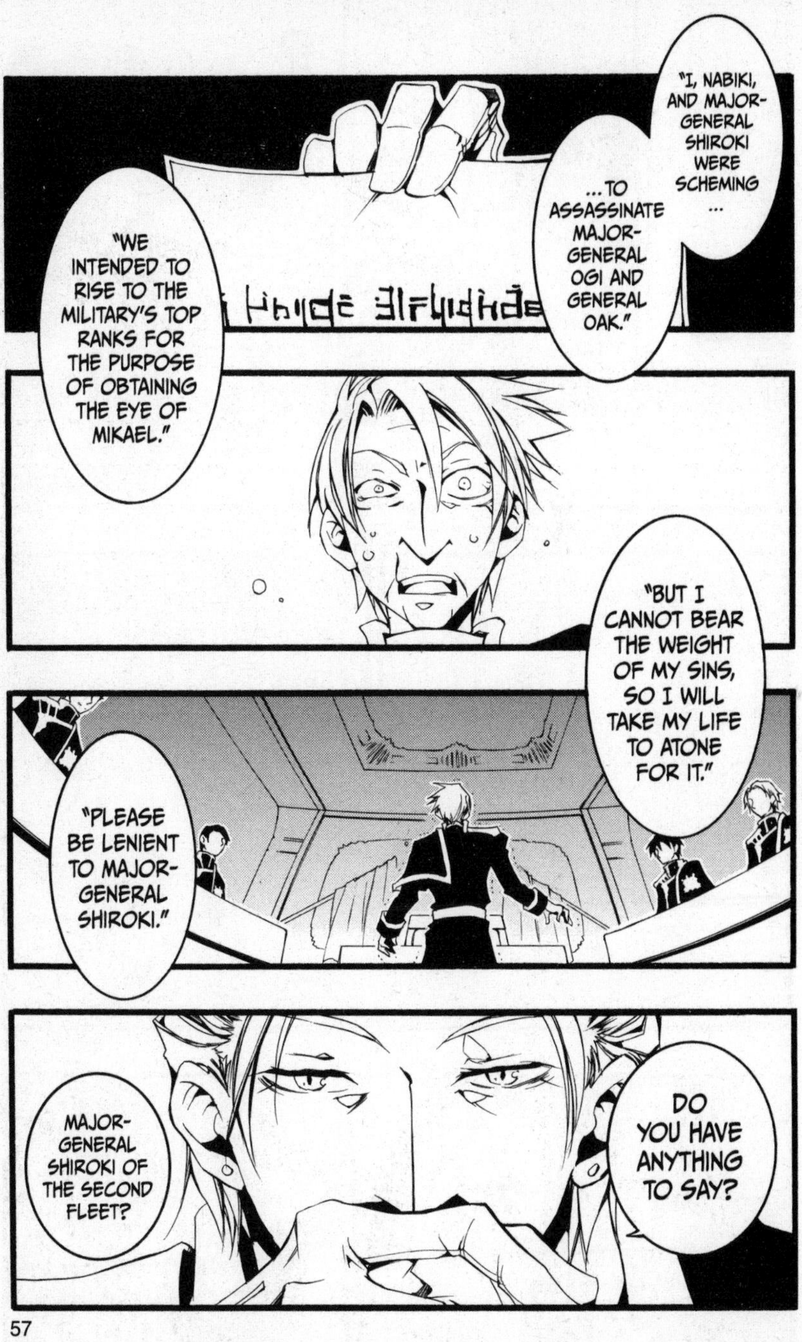
"I, NABIKI, AND MAJOR-GENERAL SHIROKI WERE SCHEMING ...
...TO ASSASSINATE MAJOR-GENERAL OGI AND GENERAL OAK."
"WE INTENDED TO RISE TO THE MILITARY'S TOP RANKS FOR THE PURPOSE OF OBTAINING THE EYE OF MIKAEL."
"BUT I CANNOT BEAR THE WEIGHT OF MY SINS, SO I WILL TAKE MY LIFE TO ATONE FOR IT."
"PLEASE BE LENIENT TO MAJOR-GENERAL SHIROKI."
DO YOU HAVE ANYTHING TO SAY?
MAJOR-GENERAL SHIROKI OF THE SECOND FLEET?

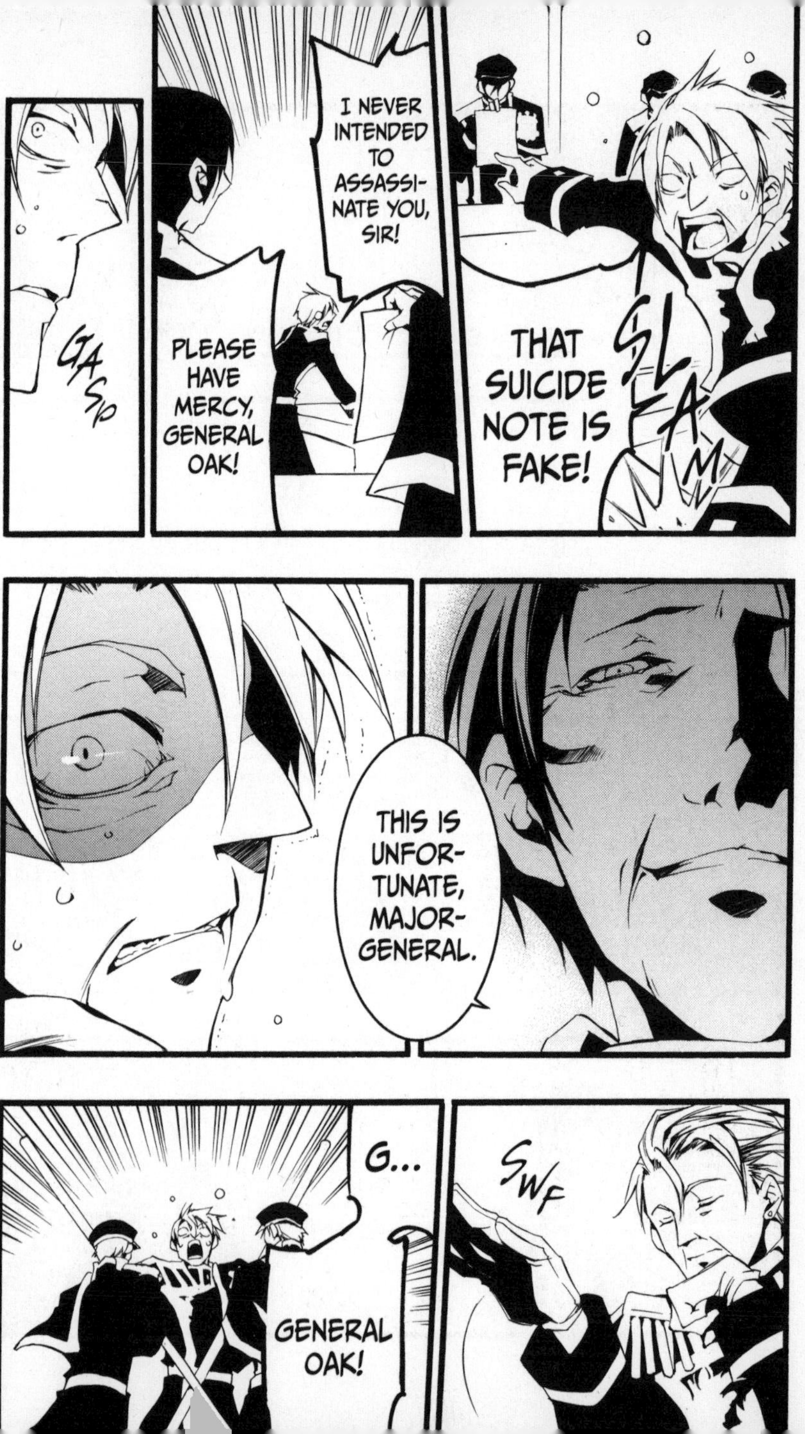
THAT SUICIDE NOTE IS FAKE!
SLAM
I NEVER INTENDED TO ASSASSI-NATE YOU, SIR!
PLEASE HAVE MERCY, GENERAL OAK!
GASP
THIS IS UNFOR-TUNATE, MAJOR-GENERAL.
SWF
G...
GENERAL OAK!

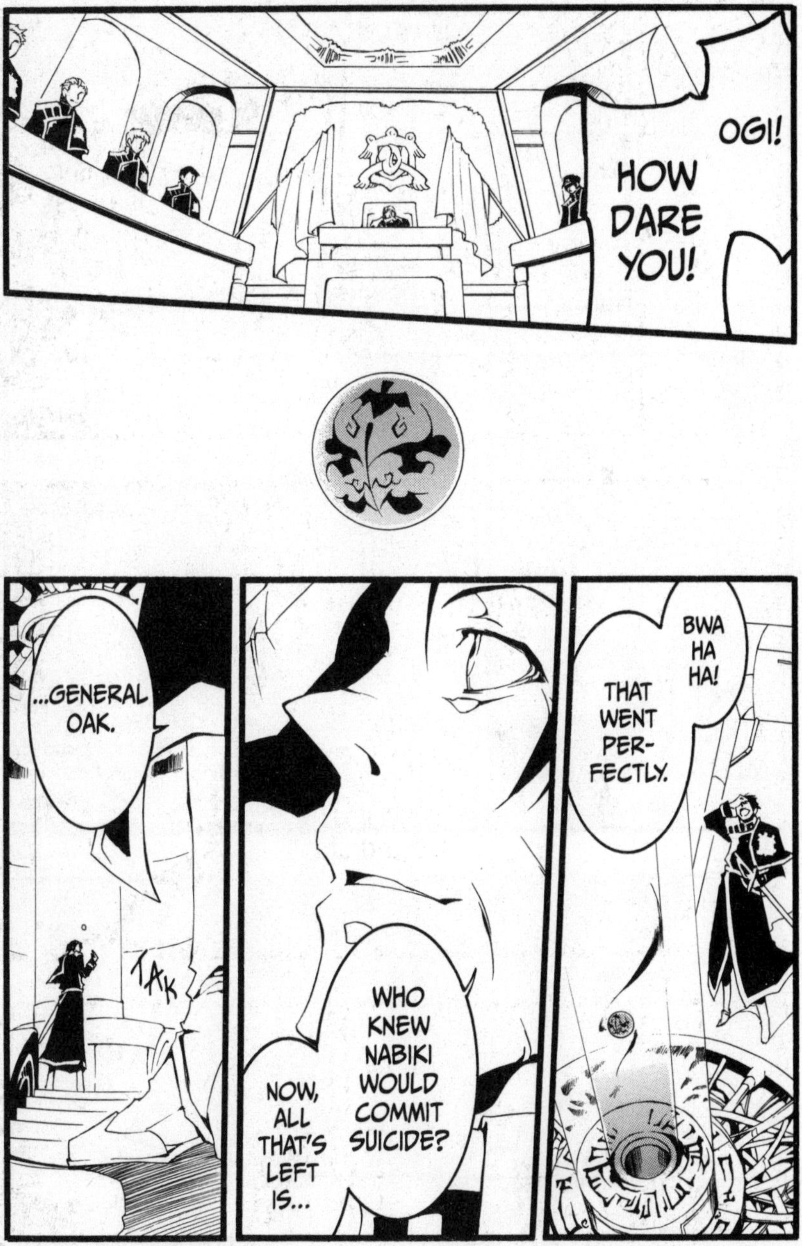
OGI! HOW DARE YOU!
BWA HA HA!
THAT WENT PERFECTLY.
WHO KNEW NABIKI WOULD COMMIT SUICIDE?
NOW, ALL THAT'S LEFT IS...
TAK
...GENERAL OAK.

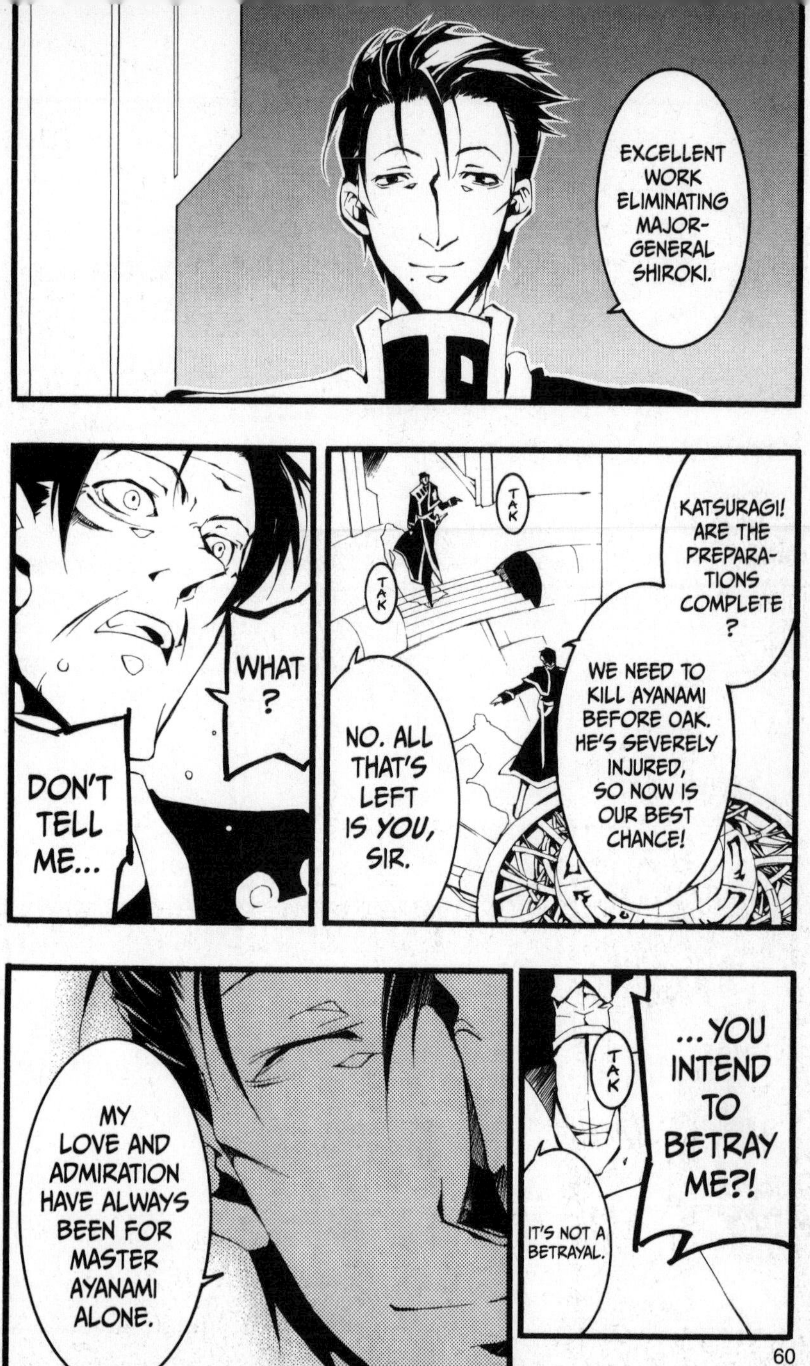
EXCELLENT WORK ELIMINATING MAJOR-GENERAL SHIROKI.
TAK
TAK
KATSURAGI! ARE THE PREPARATIONS COMPLETE?
WE NEED TO KILL AYANAMI BEFORE OAK. HE'S SEVERELY INJURED, SO NOW IS OUR BEST CHANCE!
NO. ALL THAT'S LEFT IS *YOU*, SIR.
WHAT?
DON'T TELL ME...
...YOU INTEND TO BETRAY ME?!
TAK
IT'S NOT A BETRAYAL.
MY LOVE AND ADMIRATION HAVE ALWAYS BEEN FOR MASTER AYANAMI ALONE.

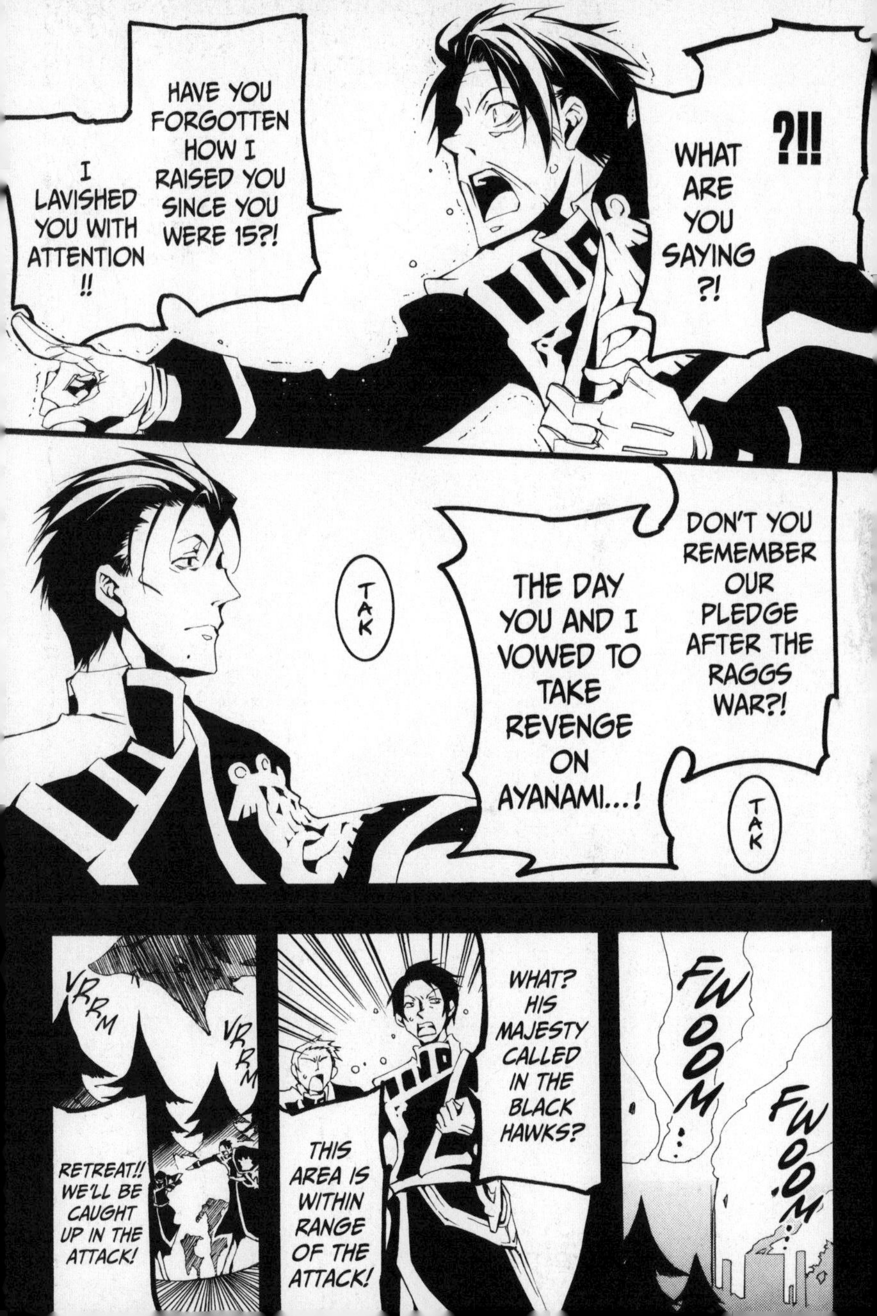
?!!
WHAT ARE YOU SAYING?!
HAVE YOU FORGOTTEN HOW I RAISED YOU SINCE YOU WERE 15?!
I LAVISHED YOU WITH ATTENTION!!
TAK
DON'T YOU REMEMBER OUR PLEDGE AFTER THE RAGGS WAR?!
THE DAY YOU AND I VOWED TO TAKE REVENGE ON AYANAMI...!
TAK
FWOOM...
FWOOM...
WHAT? HIS MAJESTY CALLED IN THE BLACK HAWKS?
THIS AREA IS WITHIN RANGE OF THE ATTACK!
VRRM
VRRM
RETREAT!! WE'LL BE CAUGHT UP IN THE ATTACK!

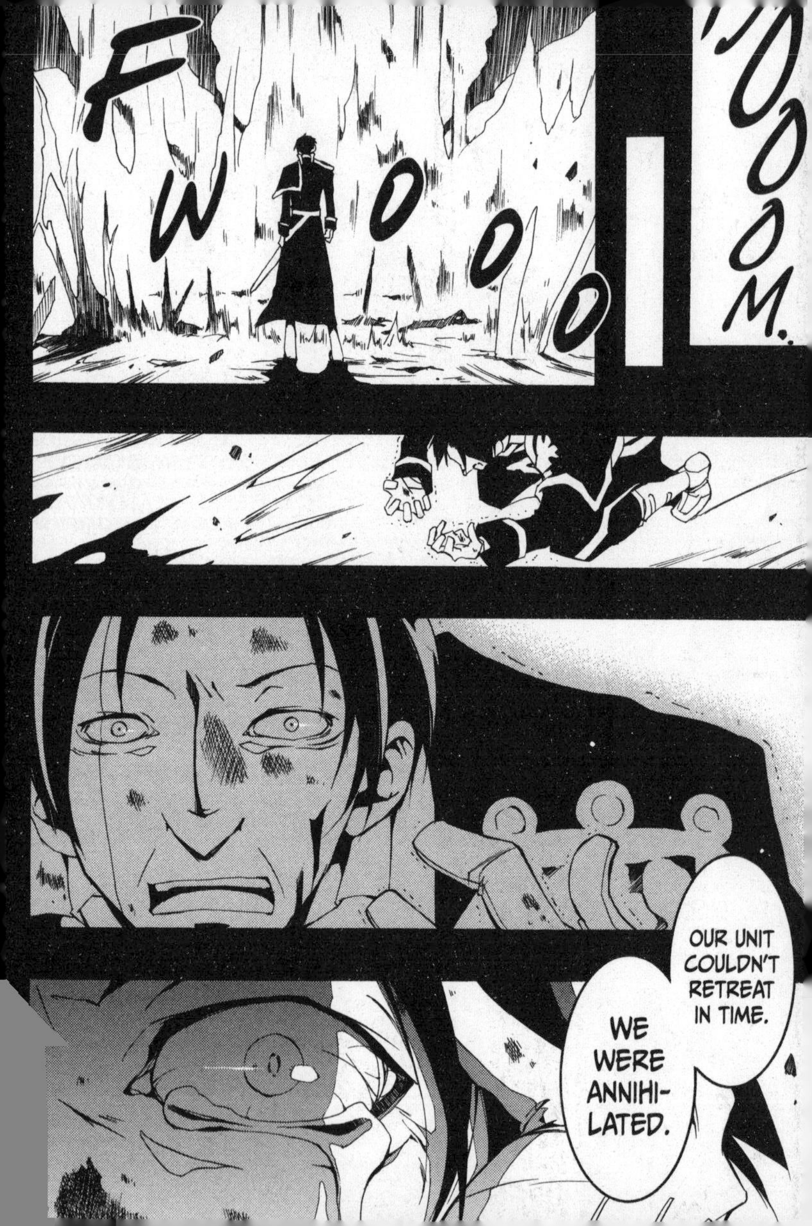
FWOOOO
OOOOM..
OUR UNIT COULDN'T RETREAT IN TIME.
WE WERE ANNIHI-LATED.

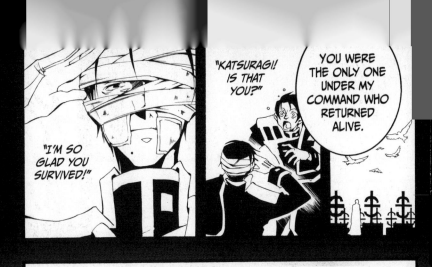

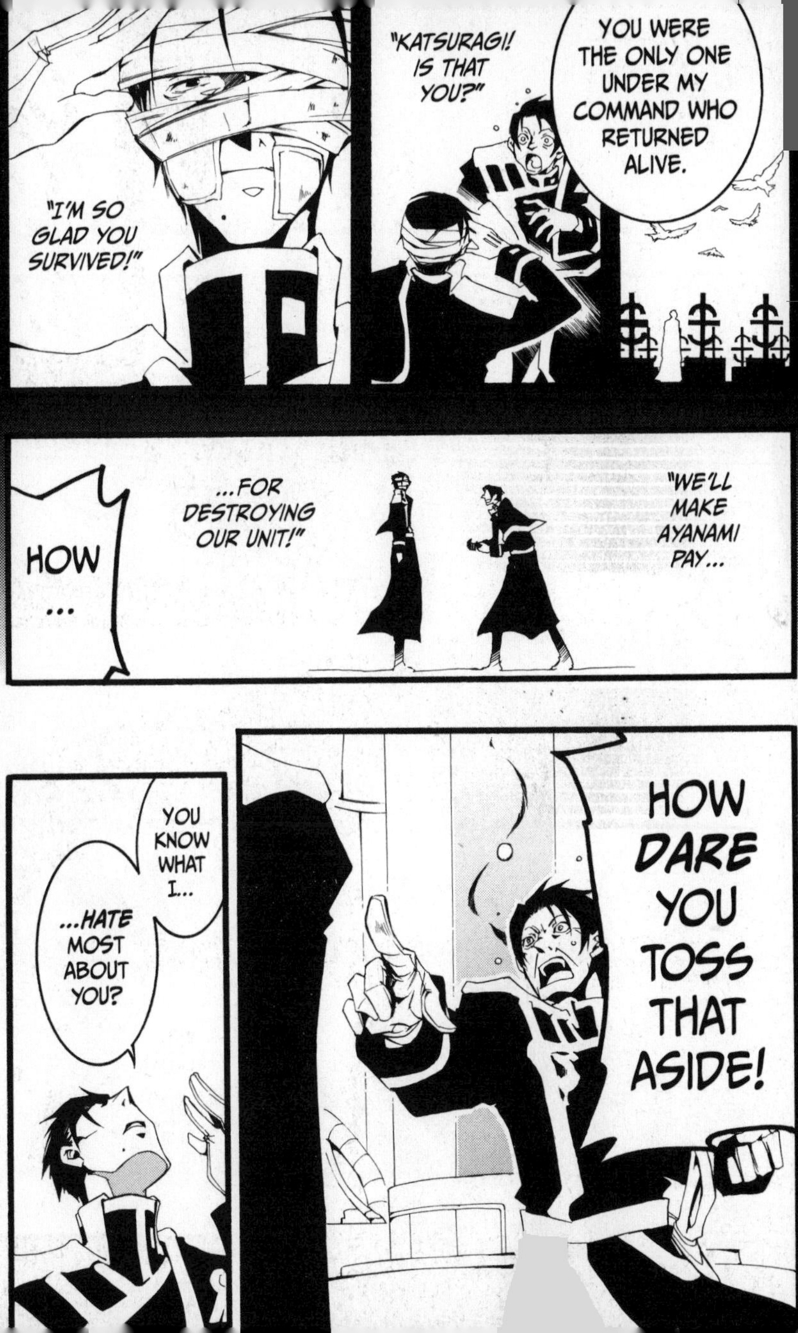
YOU WERE THE ONLY ONE UNDER MY COMMAND WHO RETURNED ALIVE.
"KATSURAGI! IS THAT YOU?"
"I'M SO GLAD YOU SURVIVED!"
"WE'LL MAKE AYANAMI PAY...
...FOR DESTROYING OUR UNIT!"
HOW ...
HOW DARE YOU TOSS THAT ASIDE!
YOU KNOW WHAT I...
...HATE MOST ABOUT YOU?

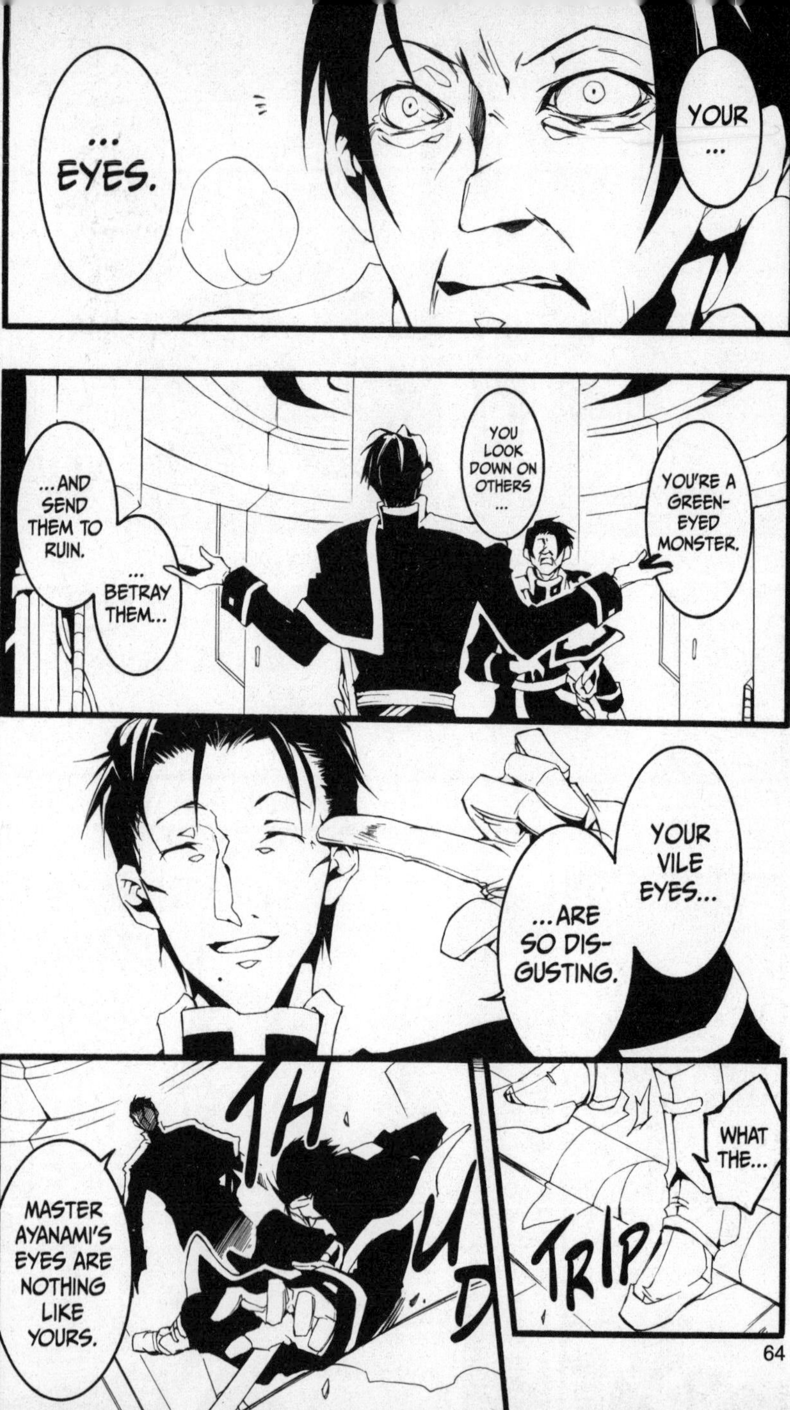
YOUR ...
... EYES.
YOU'RE A GREEN-EYED MONSTER.
YOU LOOK DOWN ON OTHERS ...
... BETRAY THEM...
...AND SEND THEM TO RUIN.
YOUR VILE EYES...
...ARE SO DIS-GUSTING.
WHAT THE...
TRIP
THUD
MASTER AYANAMI'S EYES ARE NOTHING LIKE YOURS.

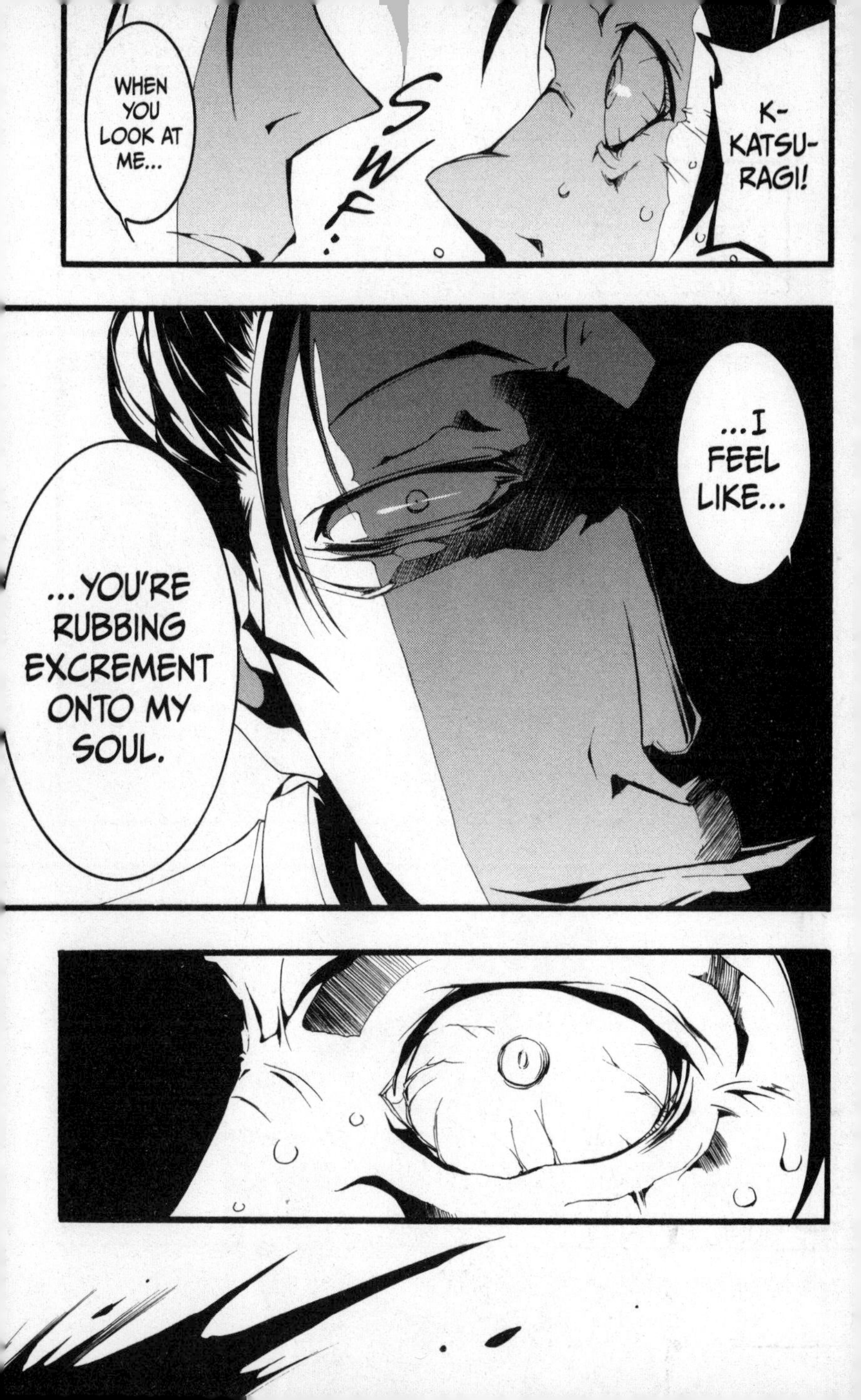
K-KATSURAGI!
SWF...
WHEN YOU LOOK AT ME...
...I FEEL LIKE...
...YOU'RE RUBBING EXCREMENT ONTO MY SOUL.

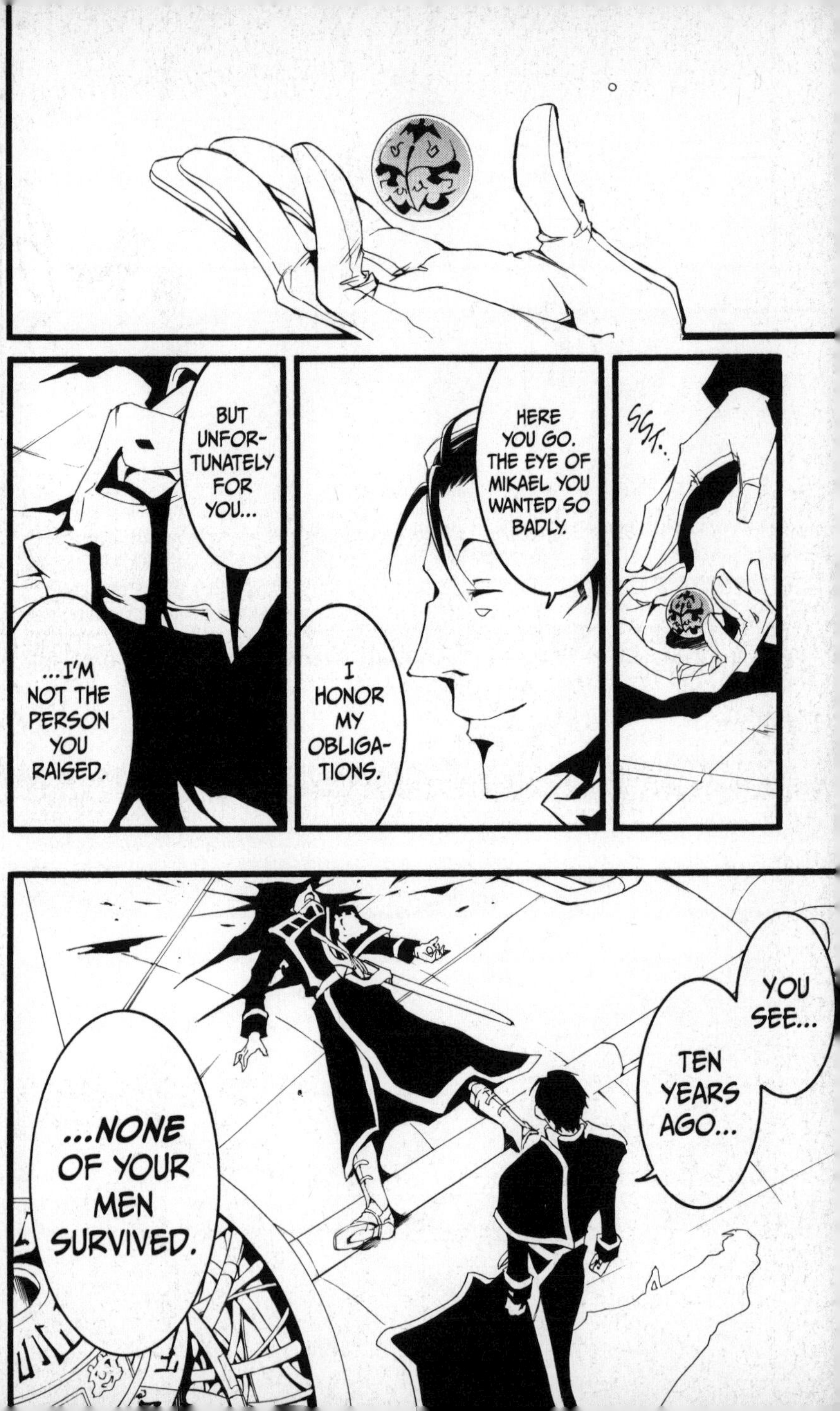
SSST...
HERE YOU GO. THE EYE OF MIKAEL YOU WANTED SO BADLY.
I HONOR MY OBLIGATIONS.
BUT UNFORTUNATELY FOR YOU...
...I'M NOT THE PERSON YOU RAISED.
YOU SEE...
TEN YEARS AGO...
...NONE OF YOUR MEN SURVIVED.

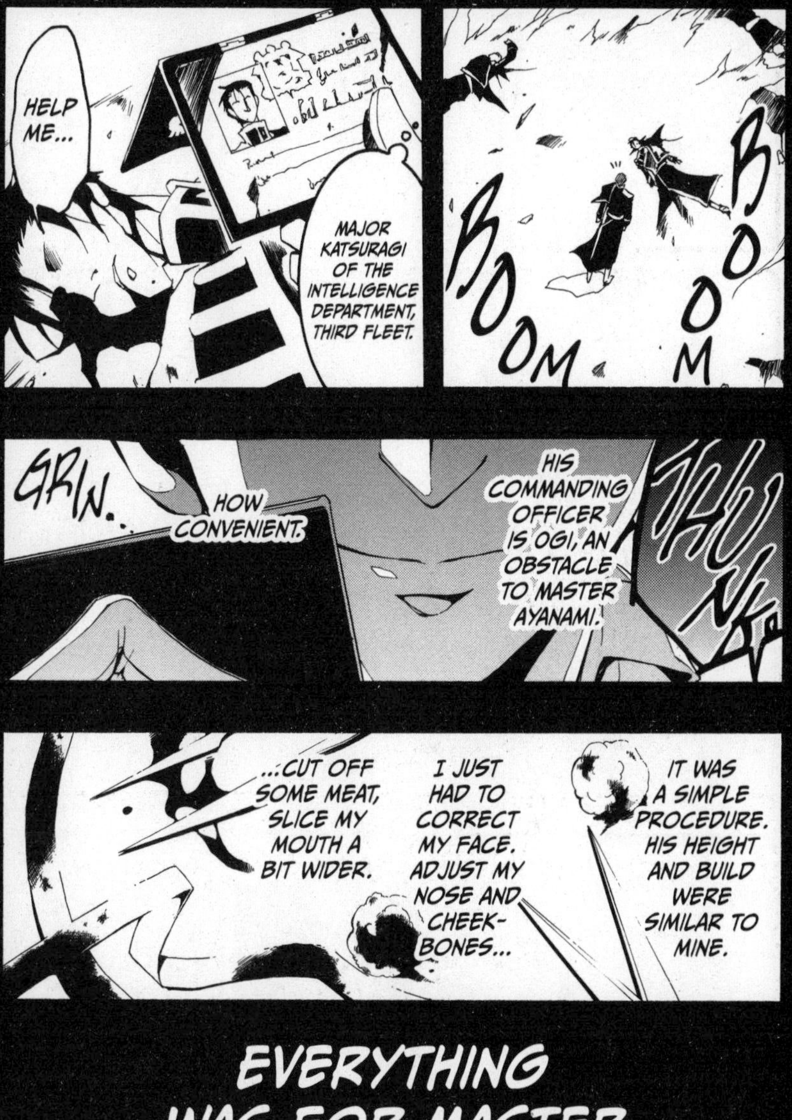
BOOM
BOOM
MAJOR KATSURAGI OF THE INTELLIGENCE DEPARTMENT, THIRD FLEET.
HELP ME...
THUNK
HIS COMMANDING OFFICER IS OGI, AN OBSTACLE TO MASTER AYANAMI.
HOW CONVENIENT.
GRIN...
IT WAS A SIMPLE PROCEDURE. HIS HEIGHT AND BUILD WERE SIMILAR TO MINE.
I JUST HAD TO CORRECT MY FACE. ADJUST MY NOSE AND CHEEK-BONES...
...CUT OFF SOME MEAT, SLICE MY MOUTH A BIT WIDER.
EVERYTHING WAS FOR MASTER AYANAMI.

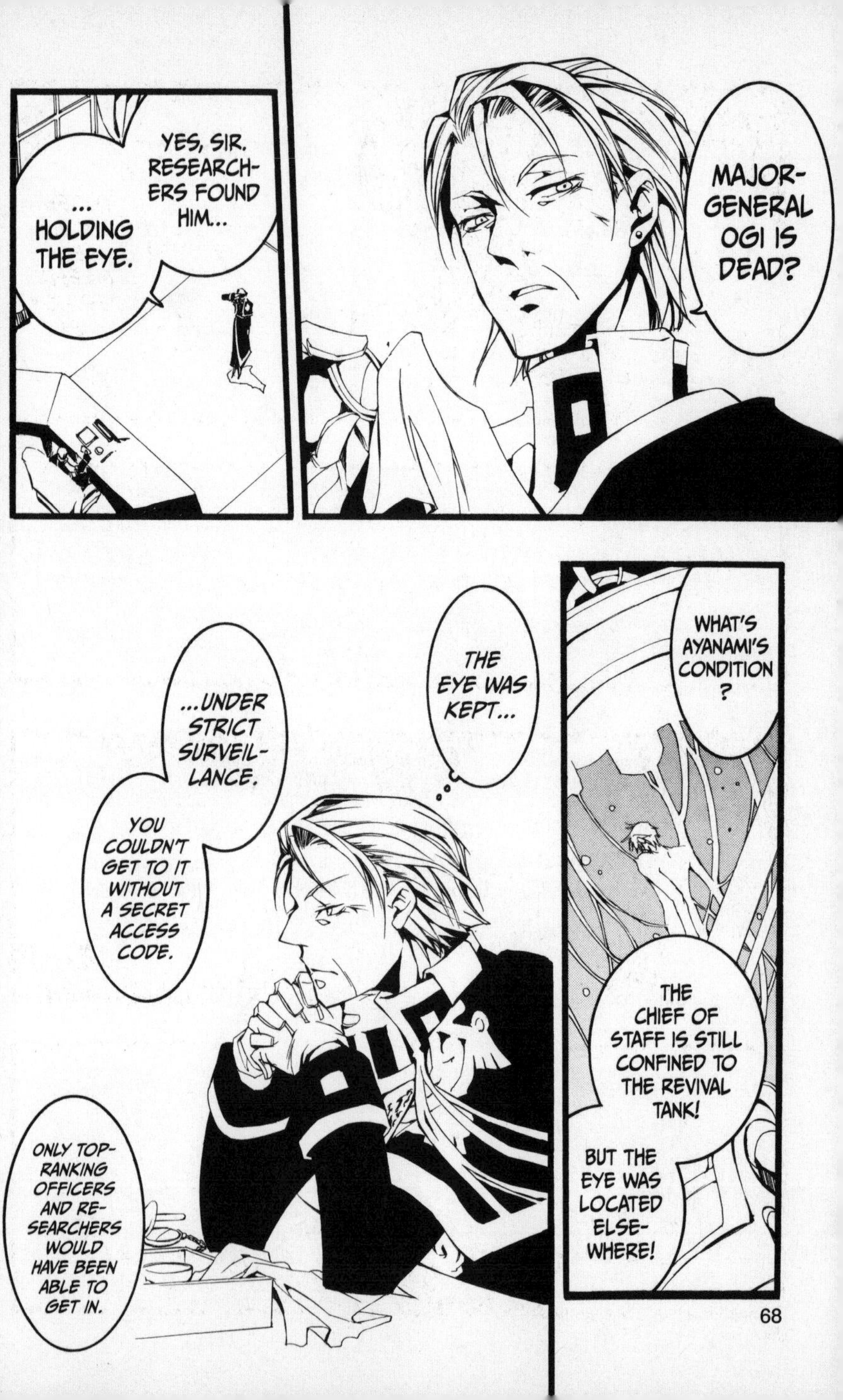
MAJOR-GENERAL OGI IS DEAD?
YES, SIR. RESEARCHERS FOUND HIM...
... HOLDING THE EYE.
WHAT'S AYANAMI'S CONDITION?
THE CHIEF OF STAFF IS STILL CONFINED TO THE REVIVAL TANK!
BUT THE EYE WAS LOCATED ELSEWHERE!
THE EYE WAS KEPT...
...UNDER STRICT SURVEILLANCE.
YOU COULDN'T GET TO IT WITHOUT A SECRET ACCESS CODE.
ONLY TOP-RANKING OFFICERS AND RESEARCHERS WOULD HAVE BEEN ABLE TO GET IN.

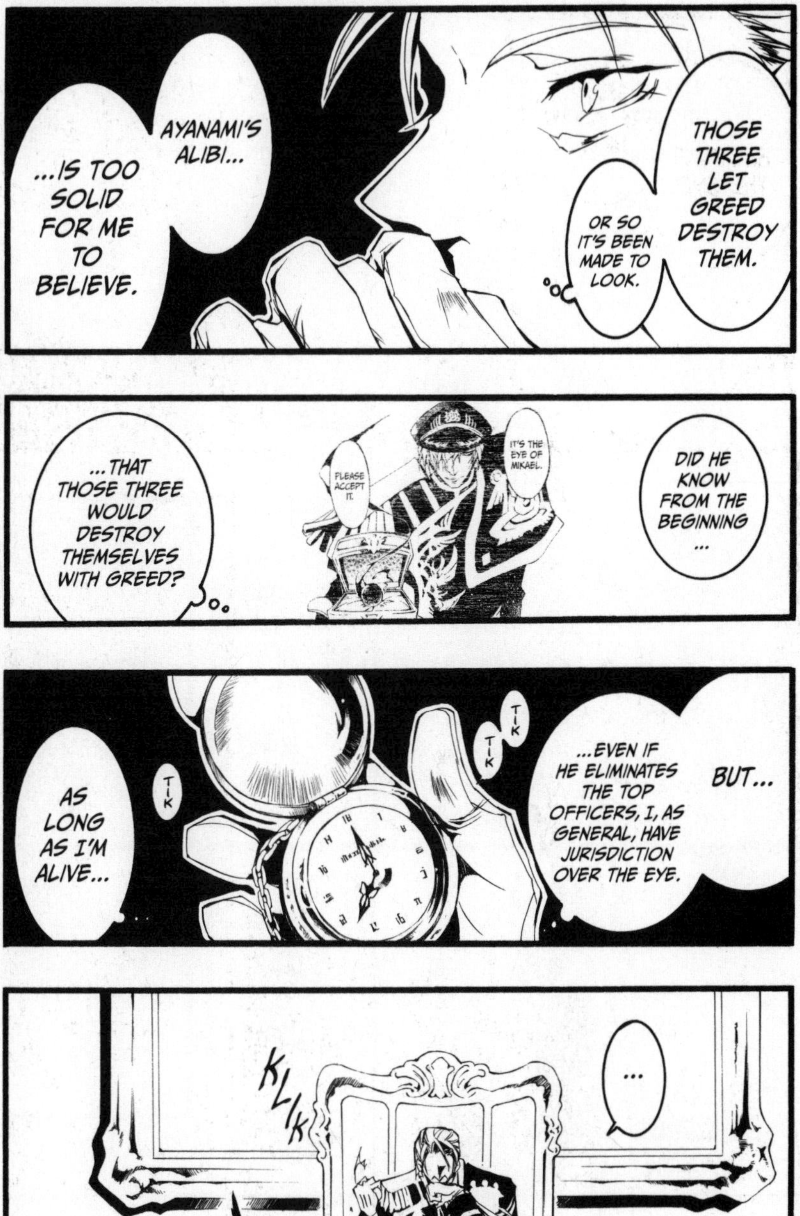
THOSE THREE LET GREED DESTROY THEM.
OR SO IT'S BEEN MADE TO LOOK.
AYANAMI'S ALIBI...
...IS TOO SOLID FOR ME TO BELIEVE.
DID HE KNOW FROM THE BEGINNING ...
IT'S THE EYE OF MIKAEL.
PLEASE ACCEPT IT.
...THAT THOSE THREE WOULD DESTROY THEMSELVES WITH GREED?
BUT...
...EVEN IF HE ELIMINATES THE TOP OFFICERS, I, AS GENERAL, HAVE JURISDICTION OVER THE EYE.
TIK
TIK
TIK
AS LONG AS I'M ALIVE...
...
KLIK

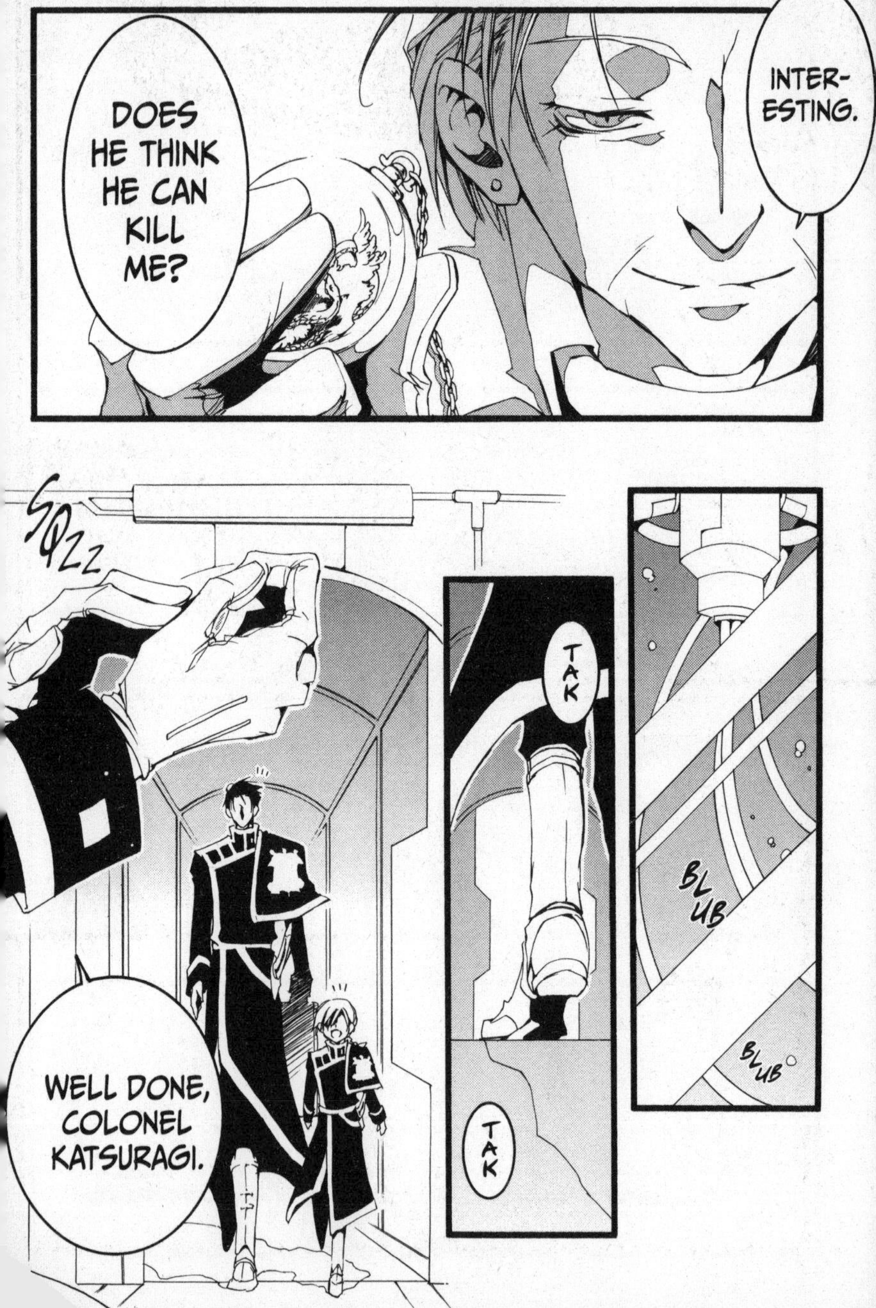
INTER-ESTING.
DOES HE THINK HE CAN KILL ME?
BLUB
BLUB
TAK
TAK
SQZZ
WELL DONE, COLONEL KATSURAGI.

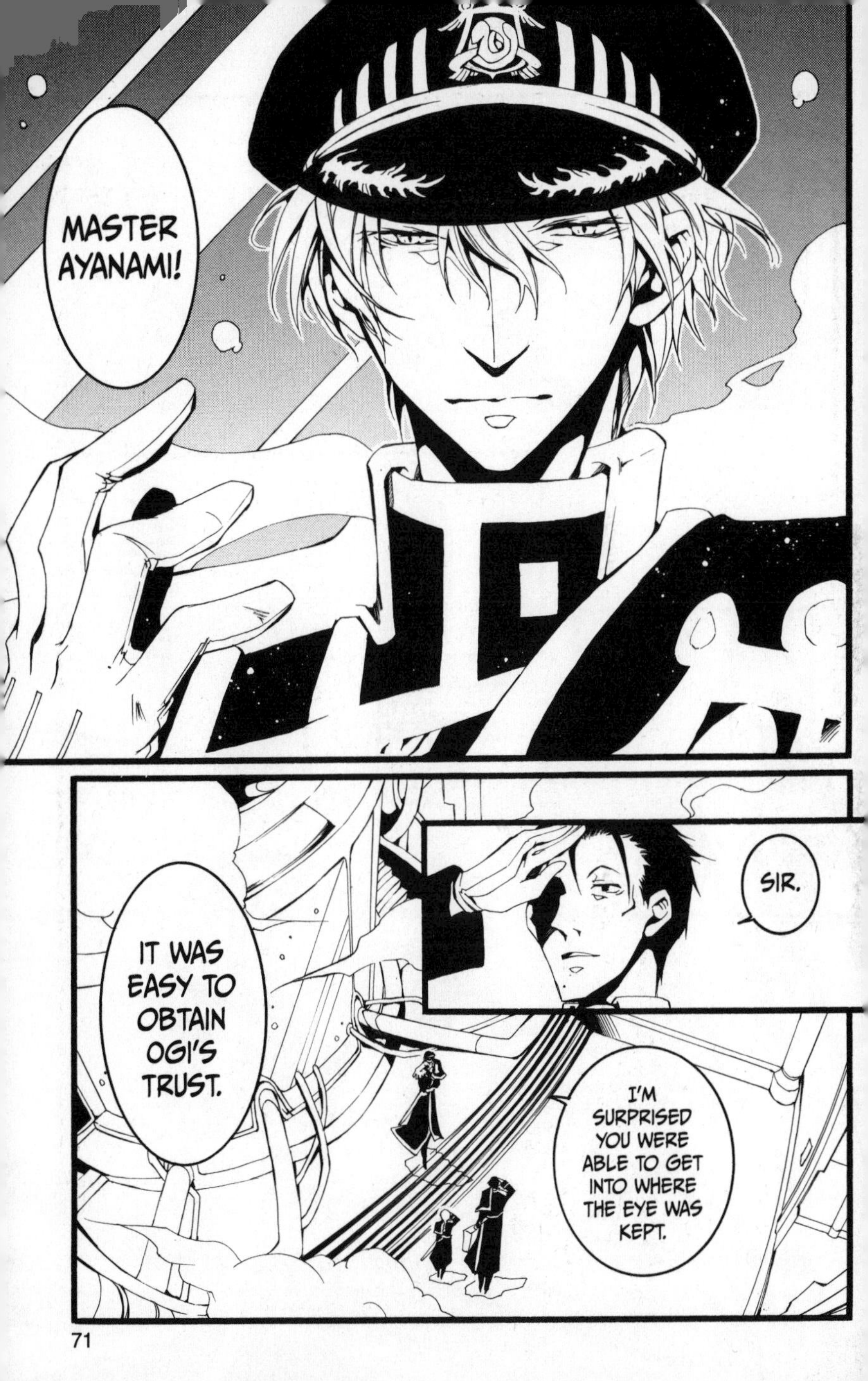
MASTER AYANAMI!
SIR.
IT WAS EASY TO OBTAIN OGI'S TRUST.
I'M SURPRISED YOU WERE ABLE TO GET INTO WHERE THE EYE WAS KEPT.

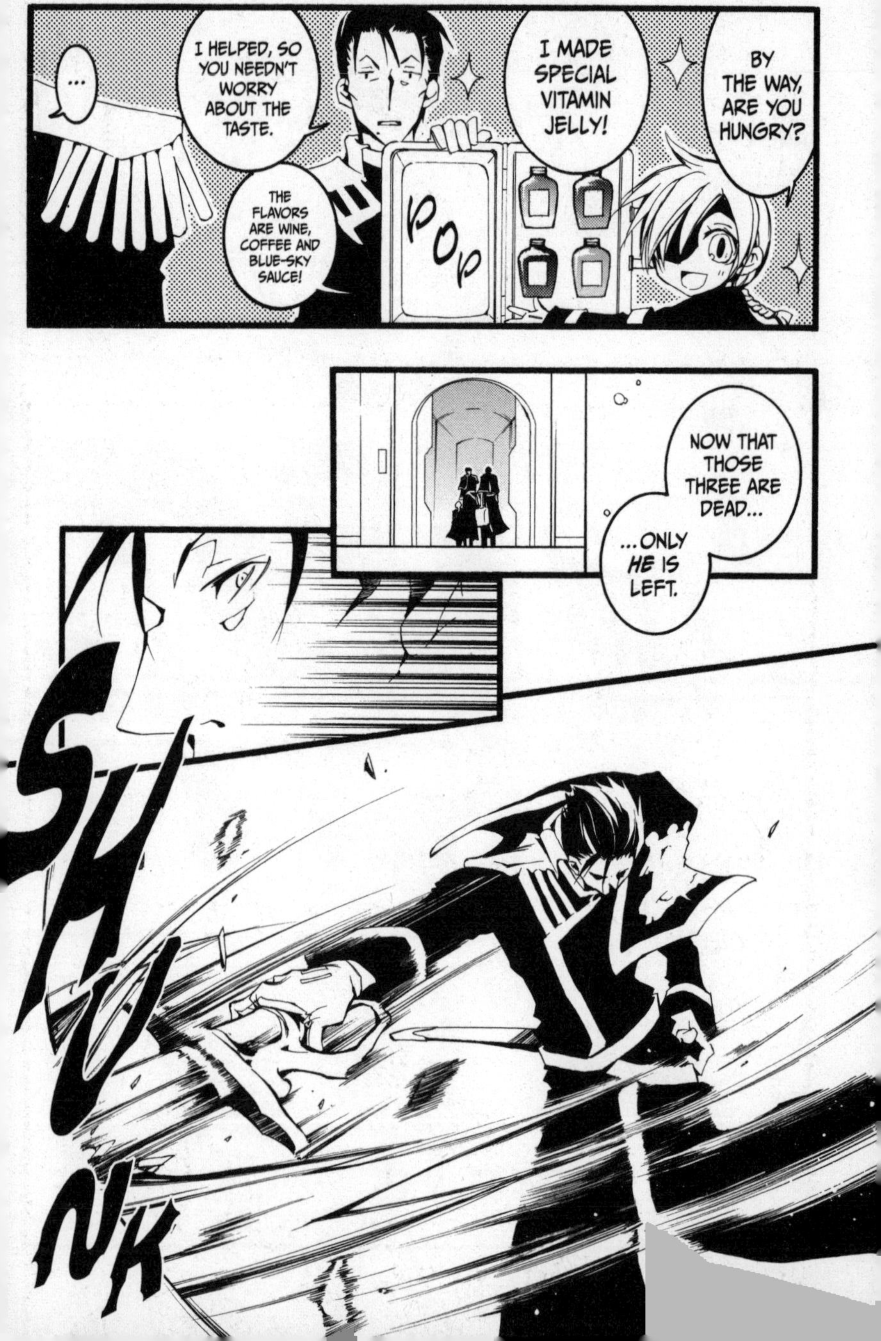
BY THE WAY, ARE YOU HUNGRY?
I MADE SPECIAL VITAMIN JELLY!
POP
THE FLAVORS ARE WINE, COFFEE AND BLUE-SKY SAUCE!
I HELPED, SO YOU NEEDN'T WORRY ABOUT THE TASTE.
...
NOW THAT THOSE THREE ARE DEAD...
...ONLY *HE* IS LEFT.
SHUNK

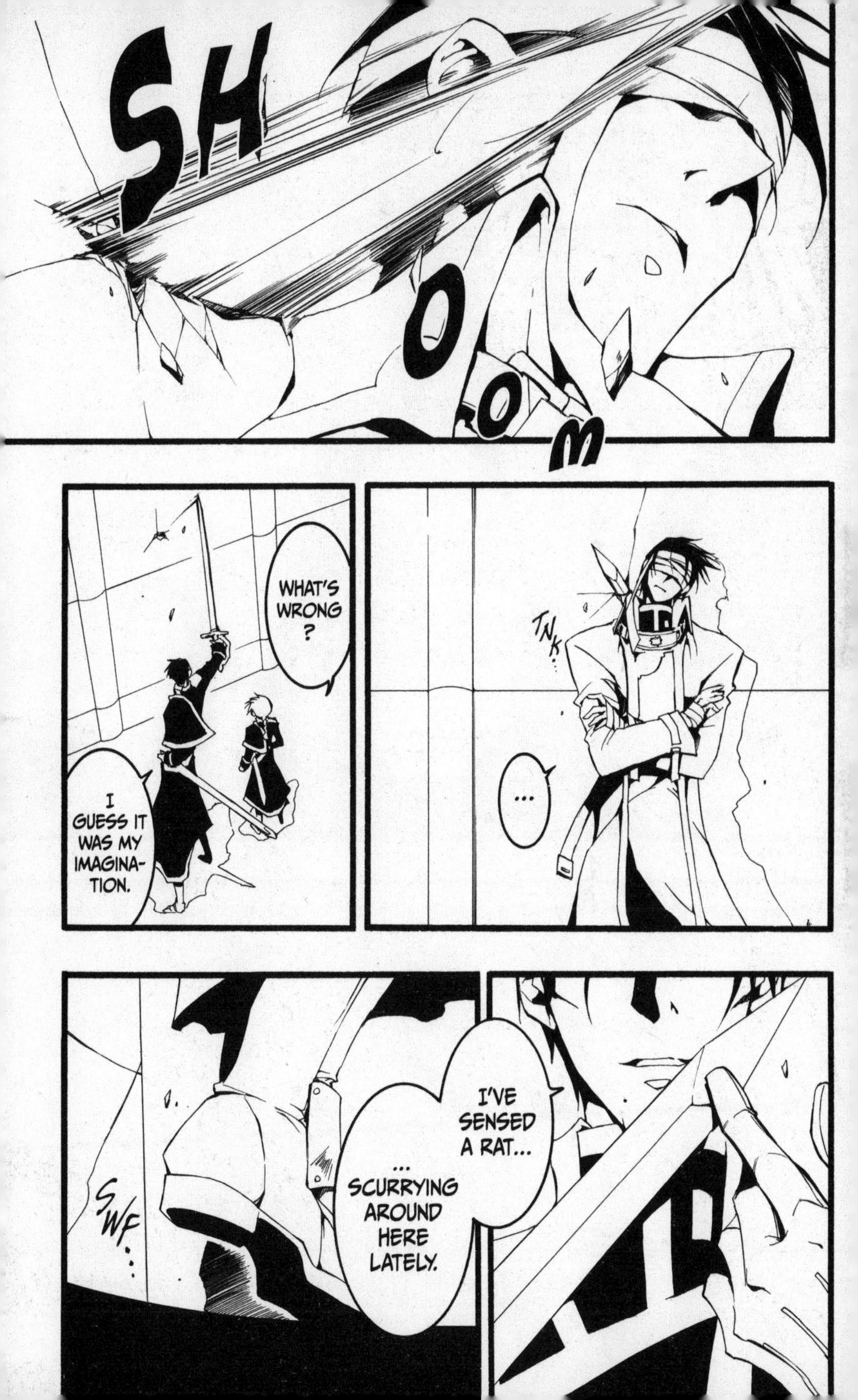
SHOOOM
TNK...
...
WHAT'S WRONG?
I GUESS IT WAS MY IMAGINATION.
I'VE SENSED A RAT...
... SCURRYING AROUND HERE LATELY.
SWF...

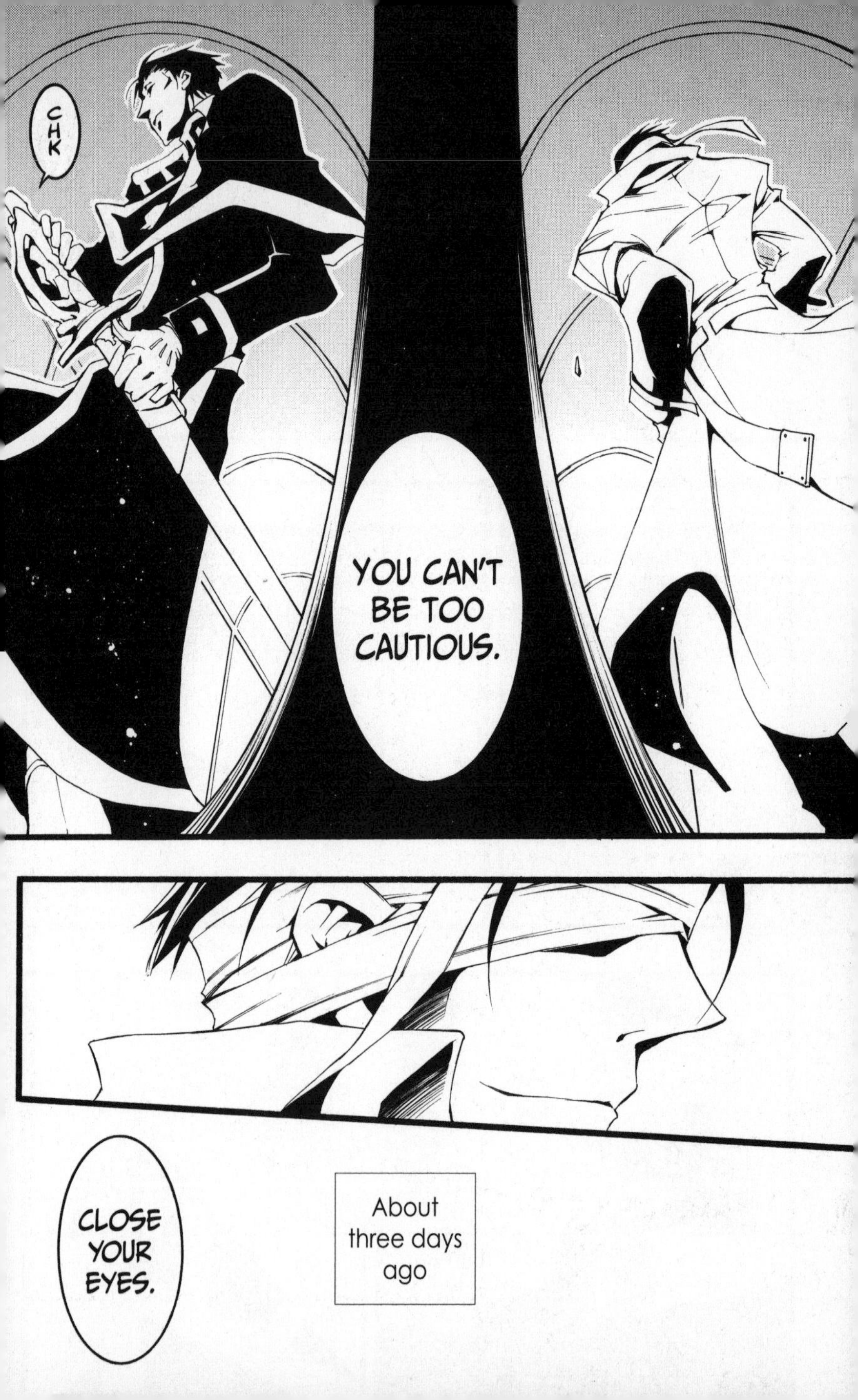
CHK
YOU CAN'T BE TOO CAUTIOUS.
About three days ago
CLOSE YOUR EYES.

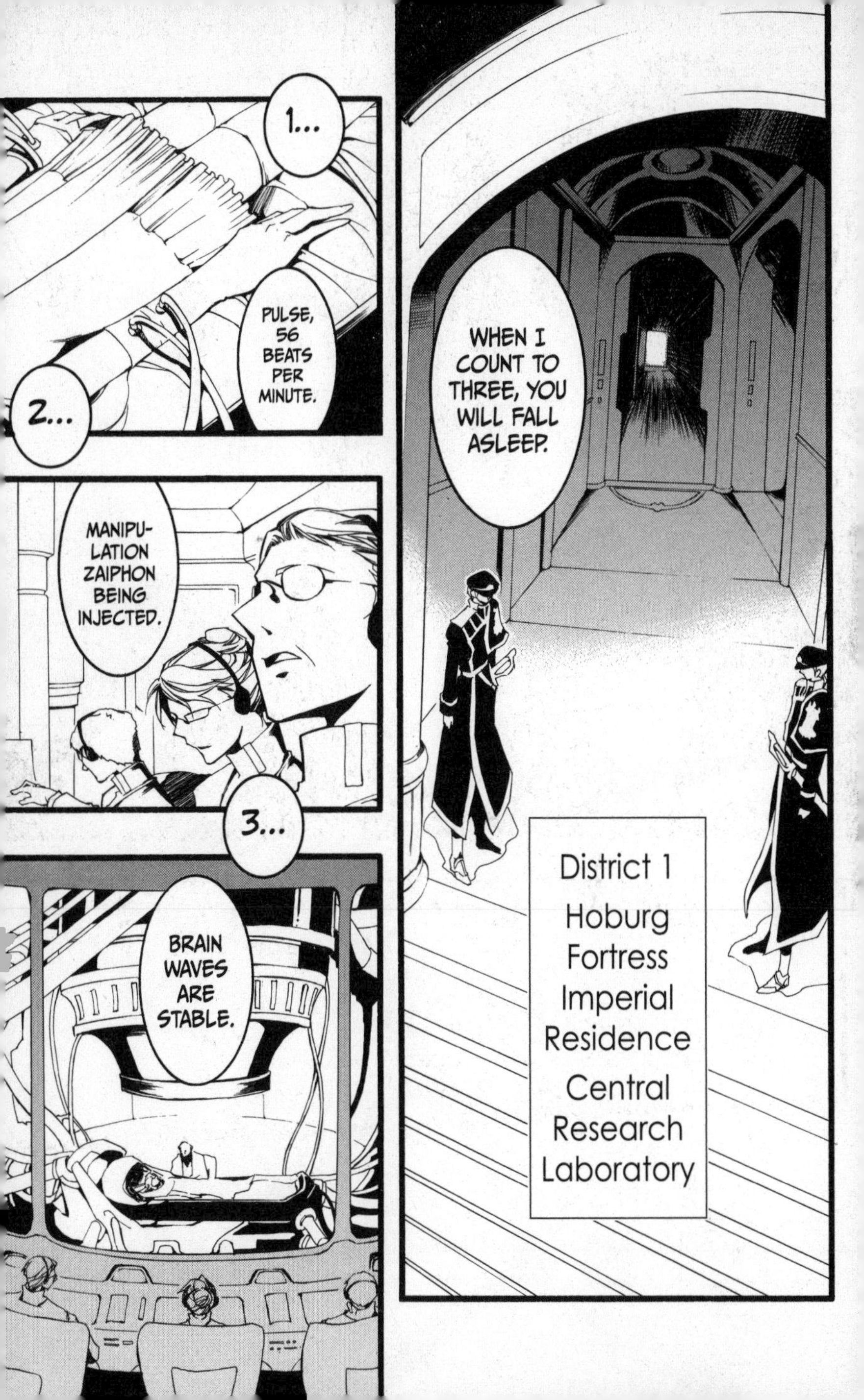
WHEN I COUNT TO THREE, YOU WILL FALL ASLEEP.
District 1 Hoburg Fortress Imperial Residence Central Research Laboratory
1...
PULSE, 56 BEATS PER MINUTE.
2...
MANIPULATION ZAIPHON BEING INJECTED.
3...
BRAIN WAVES ARE STABLE.

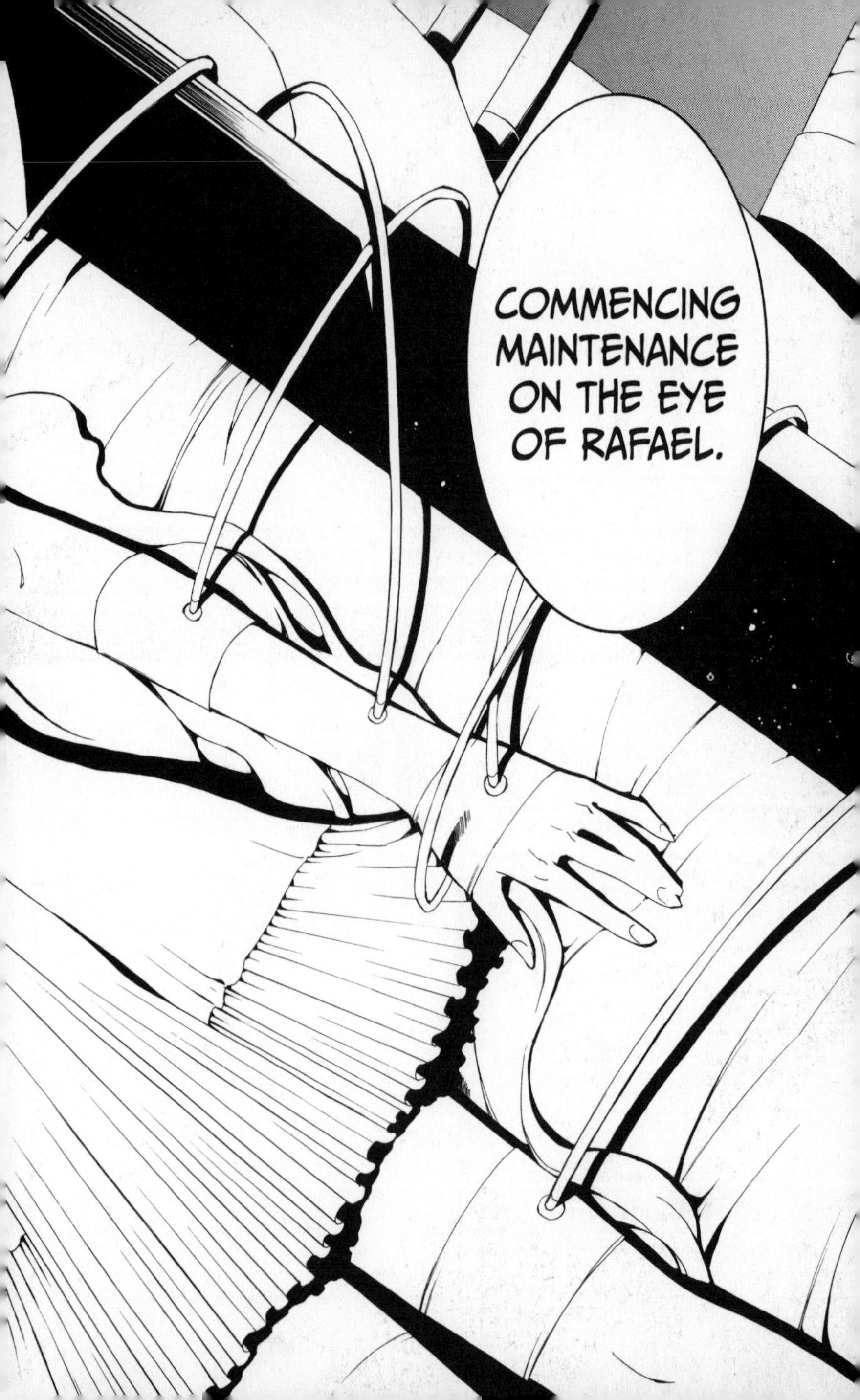
COMMENCING MAINTENANCE ON THE EYE OF RAFAEL.

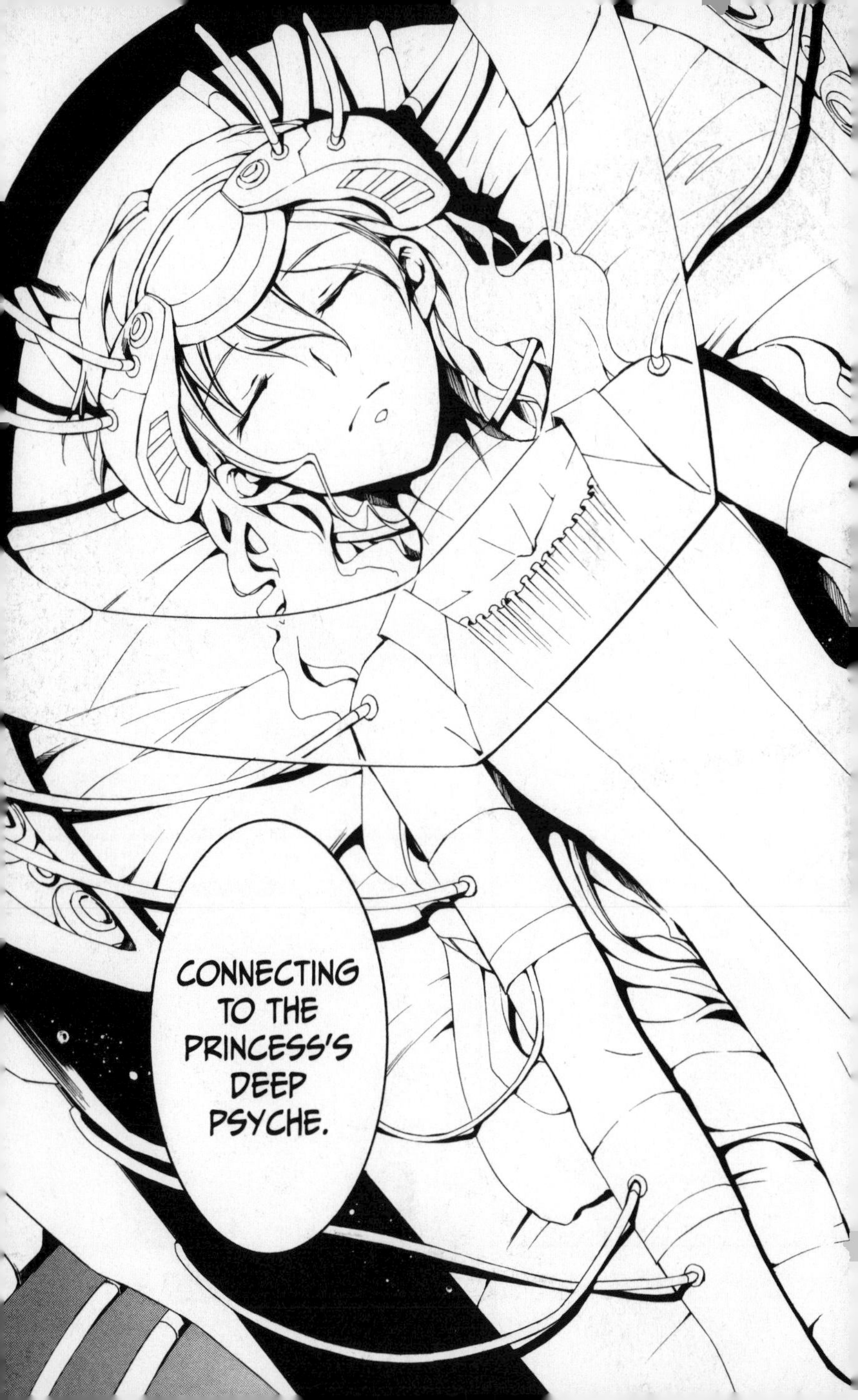
CONNECTING TO THE PRINCESS'S DEEP PSYCHE.

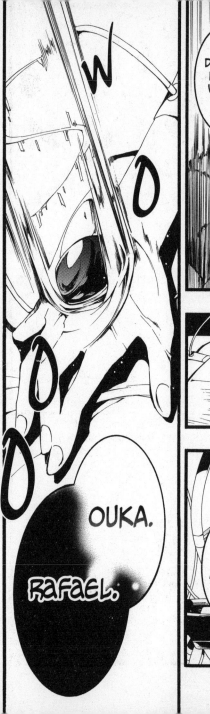

OUKA.

RAFAEL.

DO YOU KNOW WHO I AM?

VWEE...E

DR. NANASE...

YES. GOOD GIRL.

WHICH ONE ARE YOU TODAY?

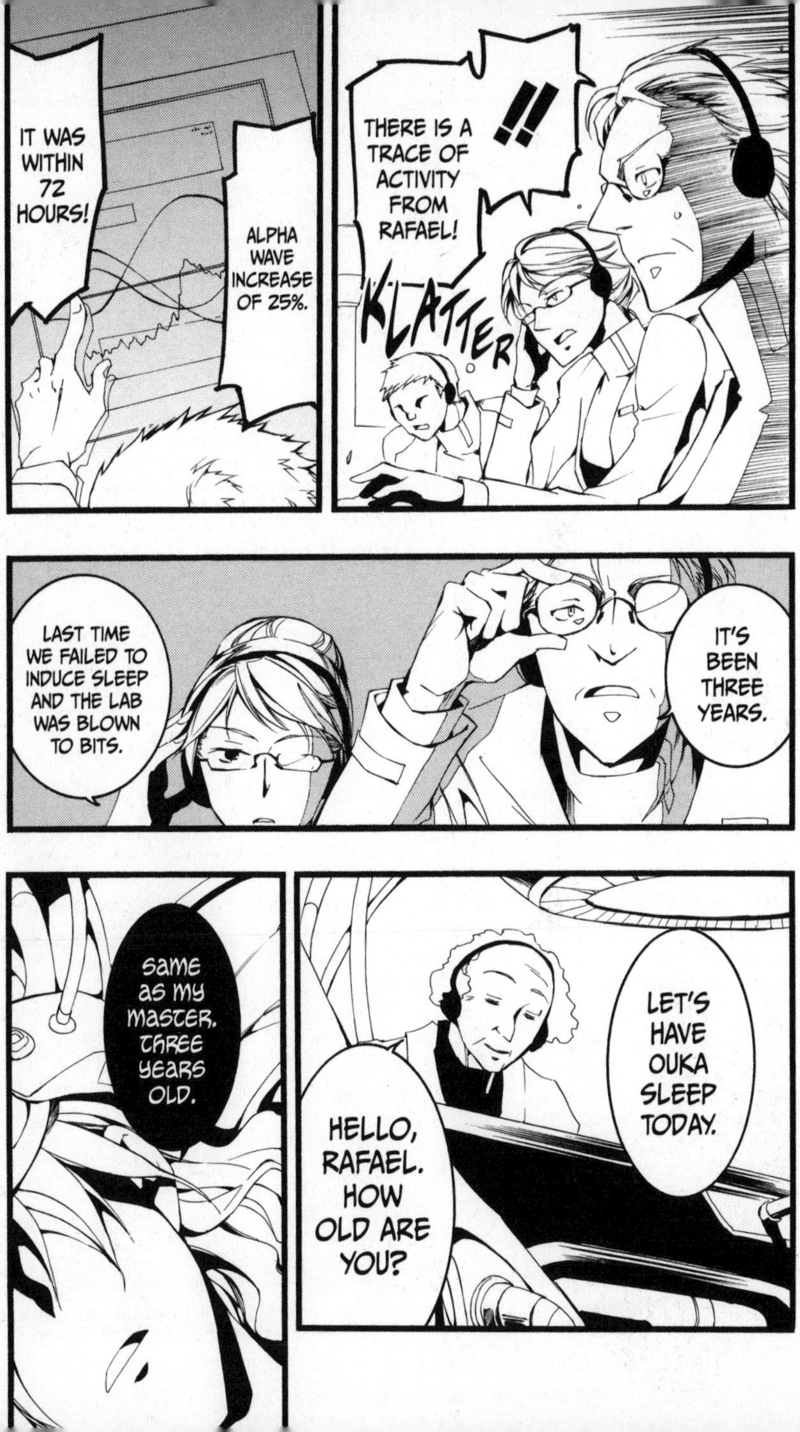
!!
THERE IS A TRACE OF ACTIVITY FROM RAFAEL!
KLATTER
ALPHA WAVE INCREASE OF 25%.
IT WAS WITHIN 72 HOURS!
IT'S BEEN THREE YEARS.
LAST TIME WE FAILED TO INDUCE SLEEP AND THE LAB WAS BLOWN TO BITS.
LET'S HAVE OUKA SLEEP TODAY.
HELLO, RAFAEL. HOW OLD ARE YOU?
Same as my master. Three years old.

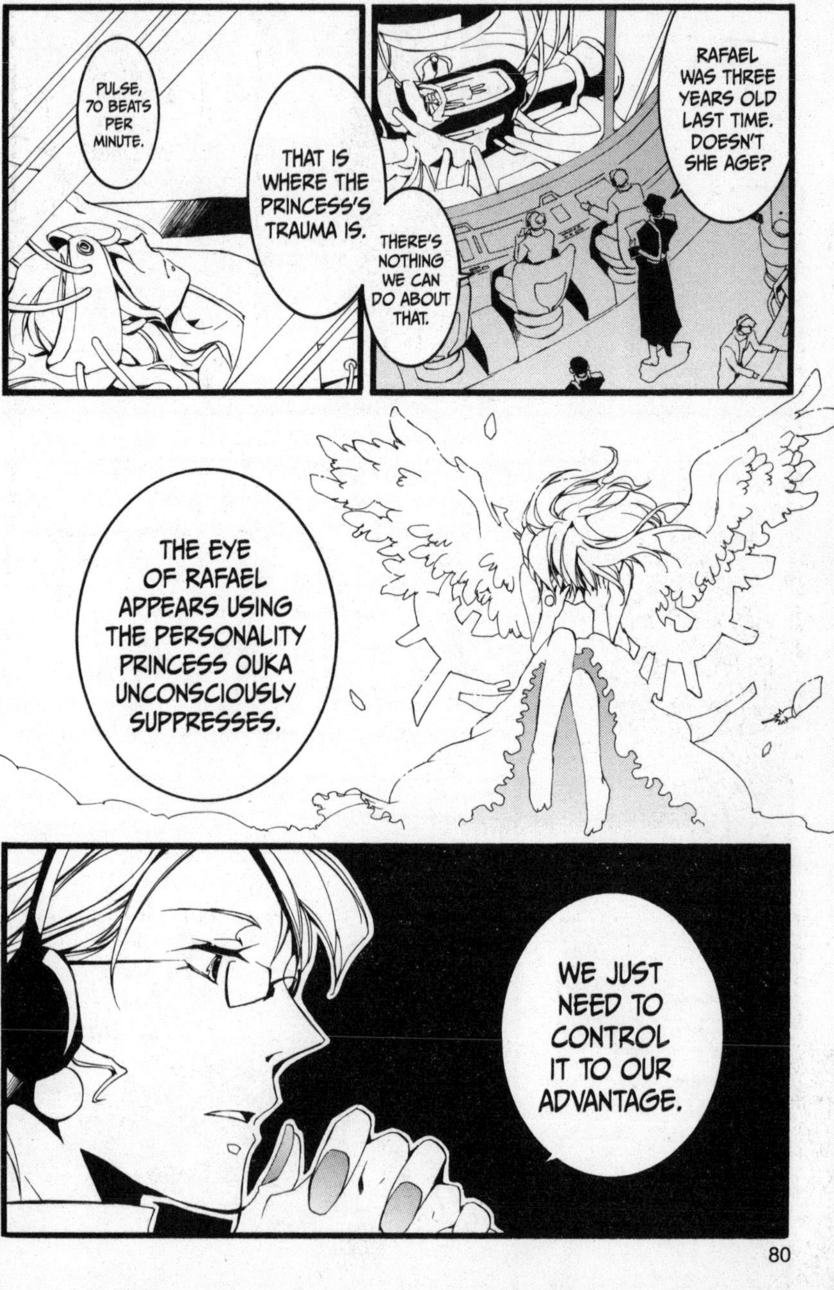
RAFAEL WAS THREE YEARS OLD LAST TIME. DOESN'T SHE AGE?
THAT IS WHERE THE PRINCESS'S TRAUMA IS.
THERE'S NOTHING WE CAN DO ABOUT THAT.
PULSE, 70 BEATS PER MINUTE.
THE EYE OF RAFAEL APPEARS USING THE PERSONALITY PRINCESS OUKA UNCONSCIOUSLY SUPPRESSES.
WE JUST NEED TO CONTROL IT TO OUR ADVANTAGE.

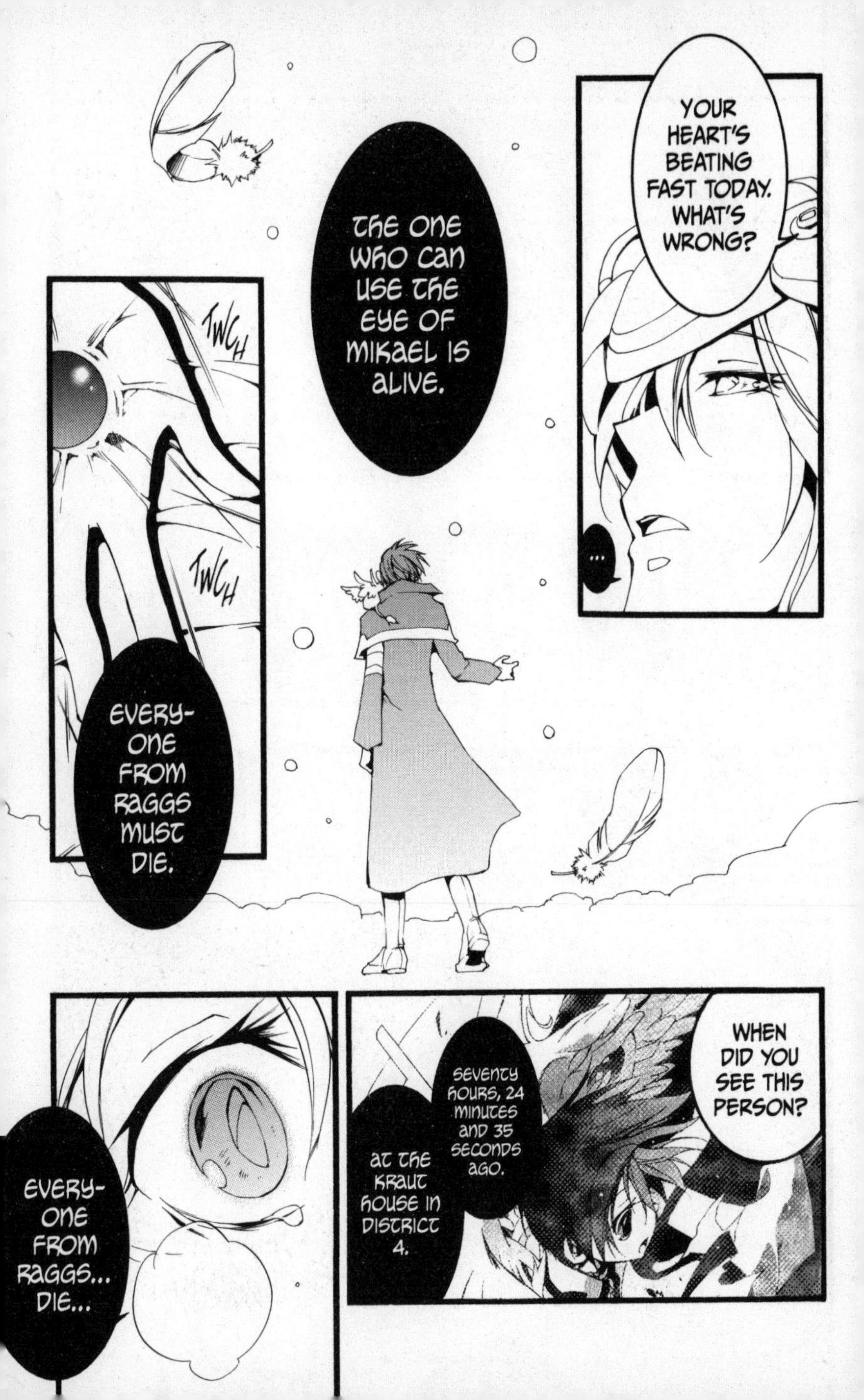
YOUR HEART'S BEATING FAST TODAY. WHAT'S WRONG?
...
THE ONE WHO CAN USE THE EYE OF MIKAEL IS ALIVE.
TWCH
TWCH
EVERY-ONE FROM RAGGS MUST DIE.
WHEN DID YOU SEE THIS PERSON?
SEVENTY HOURS, 24 MINUTES AND 35 SECONDS AGO.
AT THE KRAUT HOUSE IN DISTRICT 4.
EVERY-ONE FROM RAGGS... DIE...

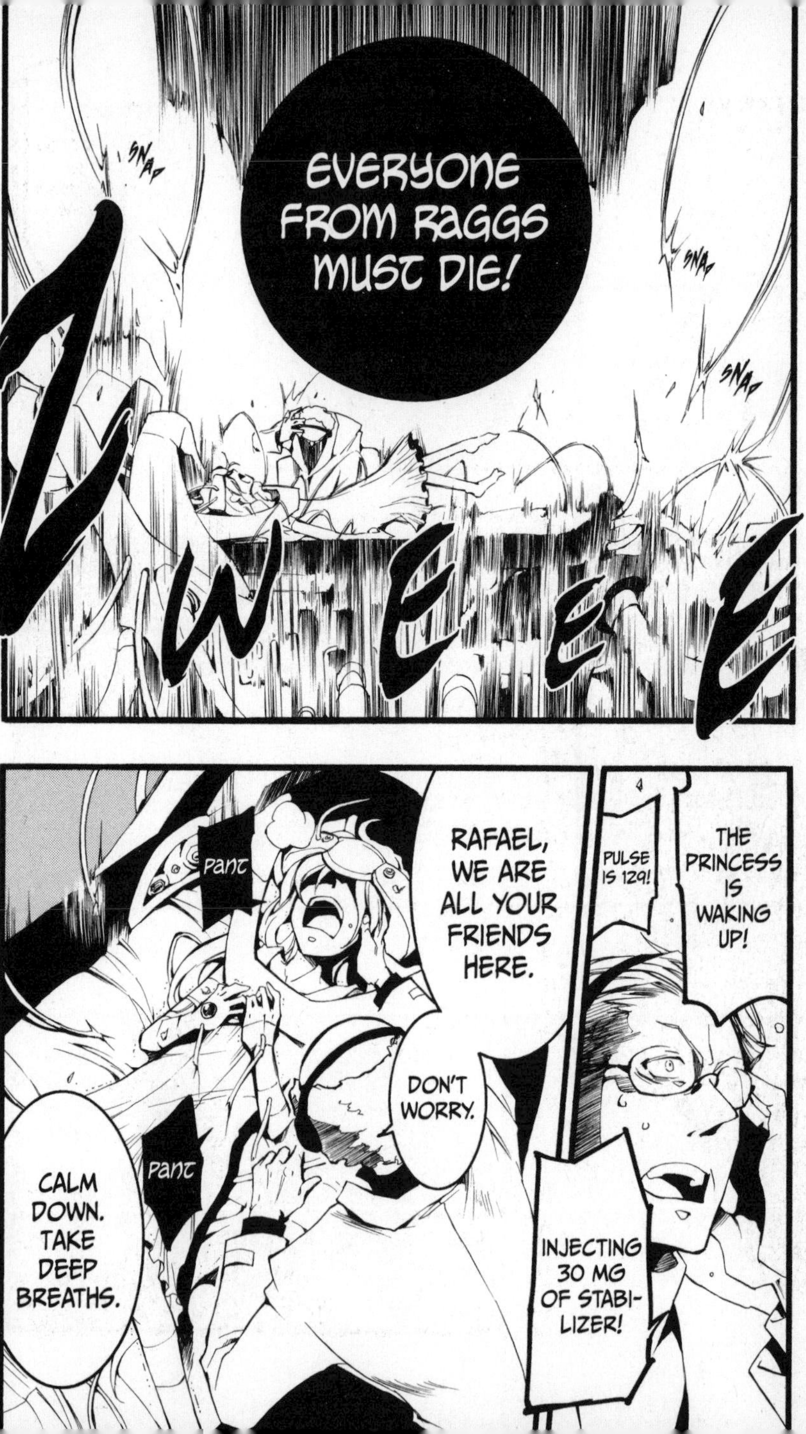
SNAP
SNAP
SNAP
EVERYONE FROM RAGGS MUST DIE!
THE PRINCESS IS WAKING UP!
PULSE IS 129!
RAFAEL, WE ARE ALL YOUR FRIENDS HERE.
pant
DON'T WORRY.
INJECTING 30 MG OF STABI-LIZER!
pant
CALM DOWN. TAKE DEEP BREATHS.

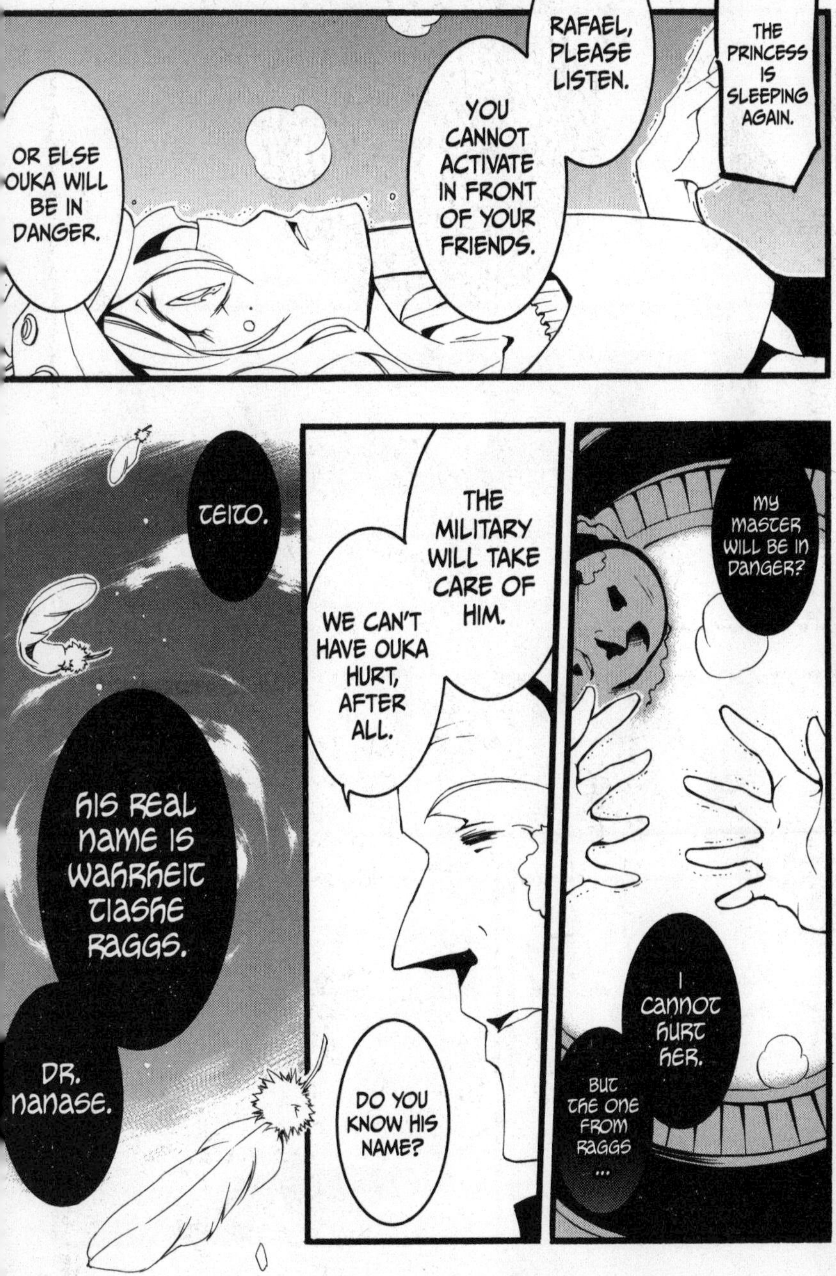
THE PRINCESS IS SLEEPING AGAIN.
RAFAEL, PLEASE LISTEN.
YOU CANNOT ACTIVATE IN FRONT OF YOUR FRIENDS.
OR ELSE OUKA WILL BE IN DANGER.
MY MASTER WILL BE IN DANGER?
I CANNOT HURT HER.
BUT THE ONE FROM RAGGS...
THE MILITARY WILL TAKE CARE OF HIM.
WE CAN'T HAVE OUKA HURT, AFTER ALL.
DO YOU KNOW HIS NAME?
TEITO.
HIS REAL NAME IS WAHRHEIT TIASHE RAGGS.
DR. NANASE.

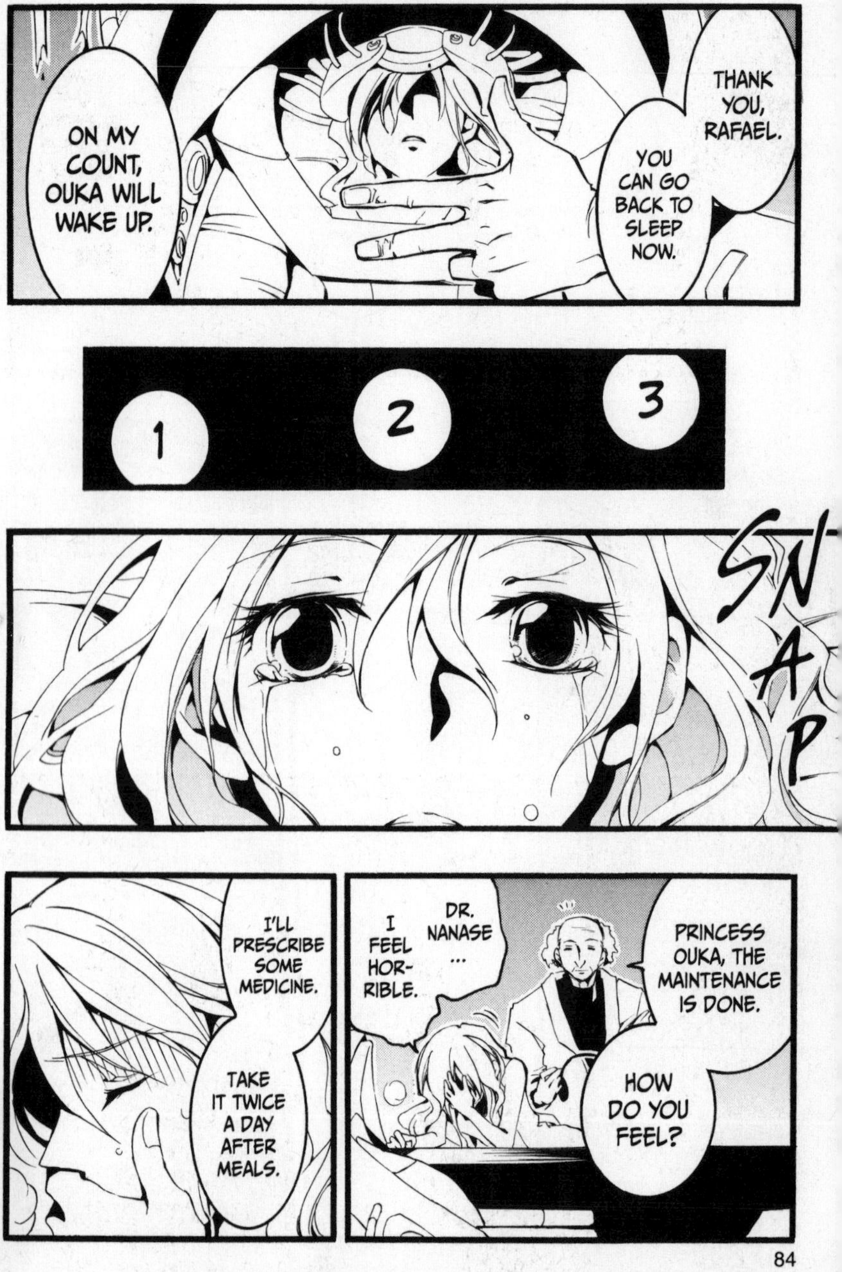
THANK YOU, RAFAEL.
YOU CAN GO BACK TO SLEEP NOW.
ON MY COUNT, OUKA WILL WAKE UP.
1
2
3
SNAP
PRINCESS OUKA, THE MAINTENANCE IS DONE.
HOW DO YOU FEEL?
DR. NANASE...
I FEEL HOR-RIBLE.
I'LL PRESCRIBE SOME MEDICINE.
TAKE IT TWICE A DAY AFTER MEALS.

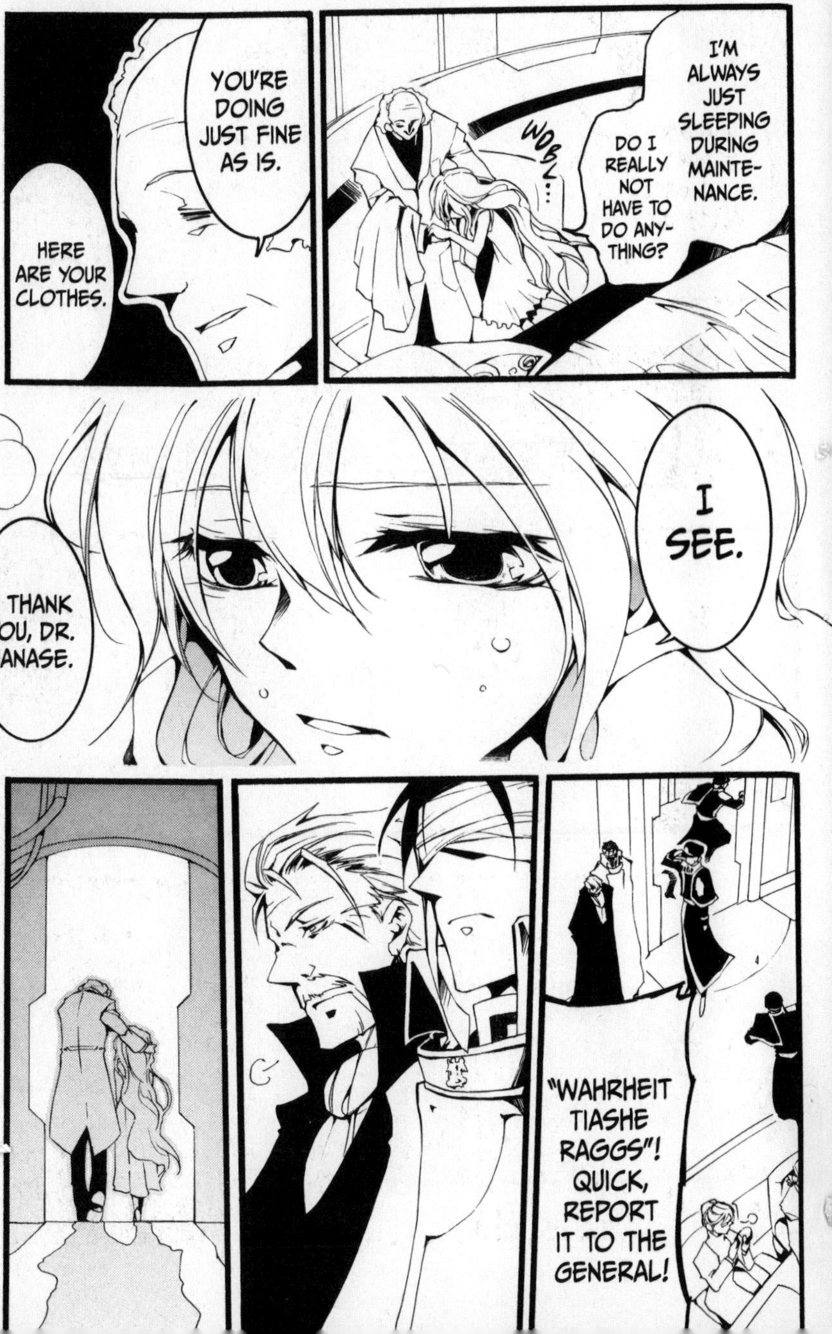
I'M ALWAYS JUST SLEEPING DURING MAINTE-NANCE.
DO I REALLY NOT HAVE TO DO ANY-THING?
WOBL...
YOU'RE DOING JUST FINE AS IS.
HERE ARE YOUR CLOTHES.
I SEE.
I THANK YOU, DR. NANASE.
"WAHRHEIT TIASHE RAGGS"! QUICK, REPORT IT TO THE GENERAL!

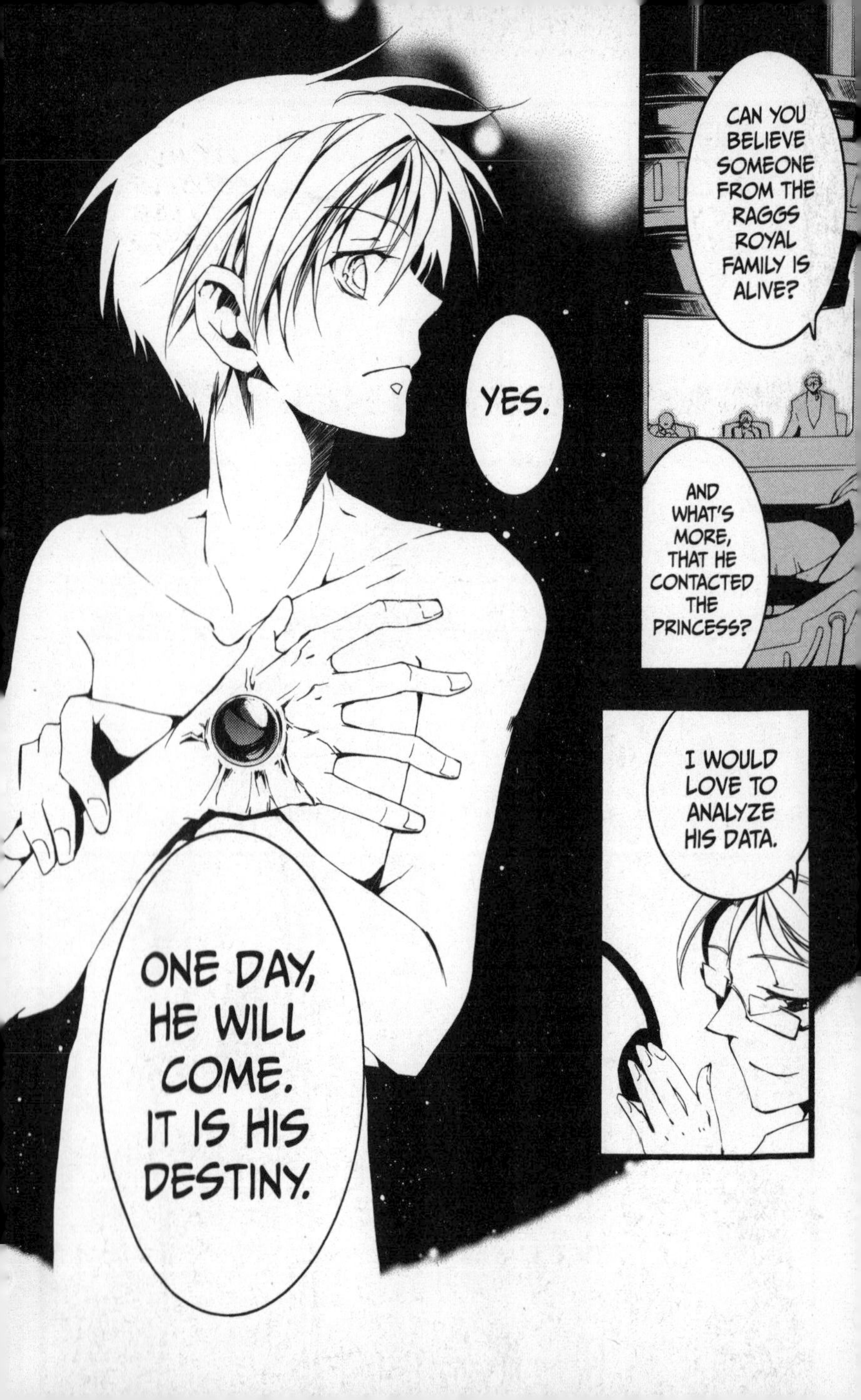
CAN YOU BELIEVE SOMEONE FROM THE RAGGS ROYAL FAMILY IS ALIVE?
AND WHAT'S MORE, THAT HE CONTACTED THE PRINCESS?
I WOULD LOVE TO ANALYZE HIS DATA.
YES.
ONE DAY, HE WILL COME. IT IS HIS DESTINY.

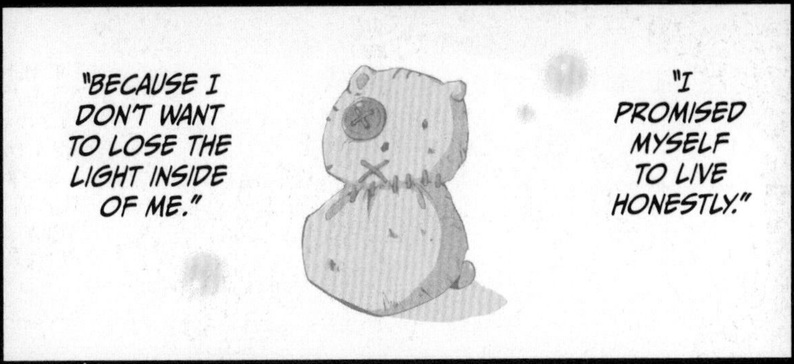
"I PROMISED MYSELF TO LIVE HONESTLY."
"BECAUSE I DON'T WANT TO LOSE THE LIGHT INSIDE OF ME."

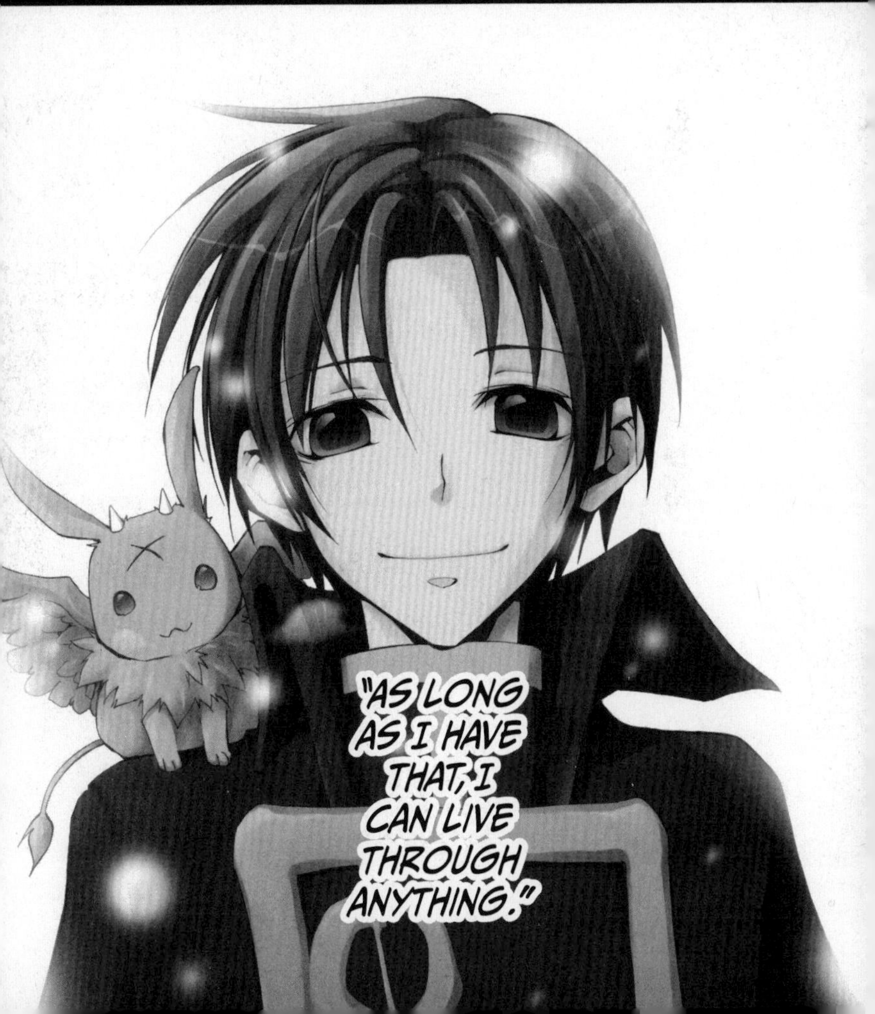
"AS LONG AS I HAVE THAT, I CAN LIVE THROUGH ANYTHING."

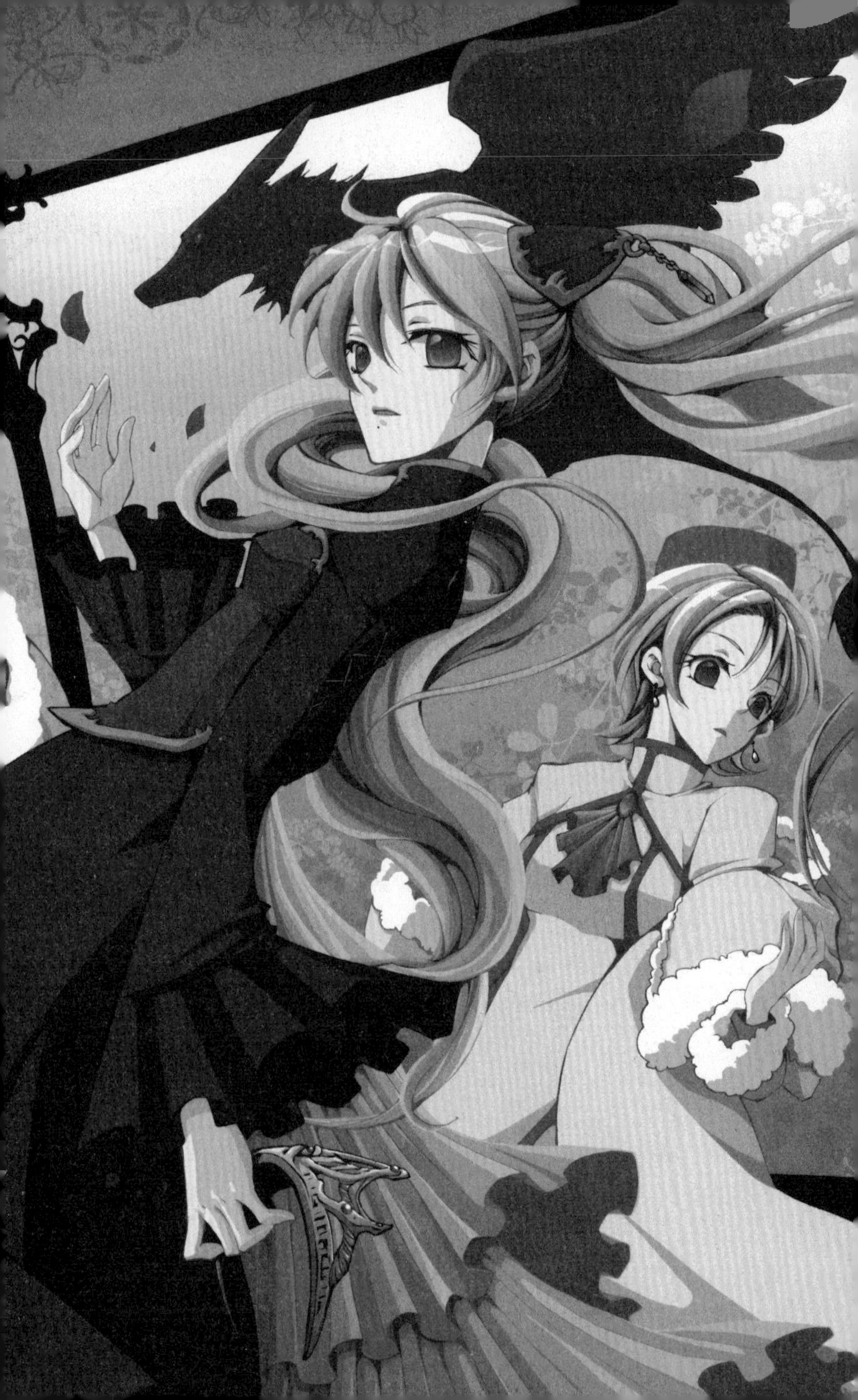

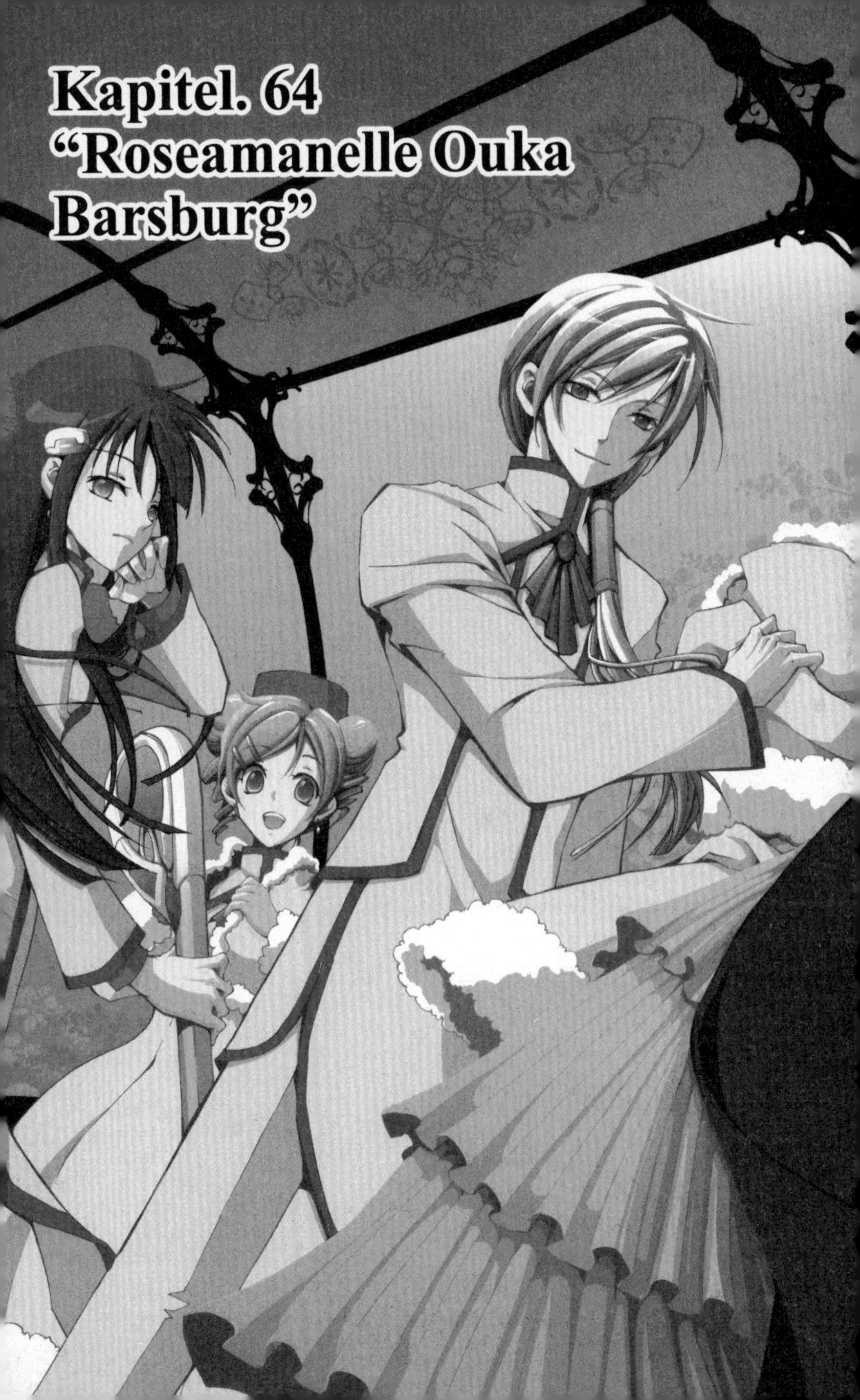
Kapitel. 64
“Roseamanelle Ouka Barsburg”

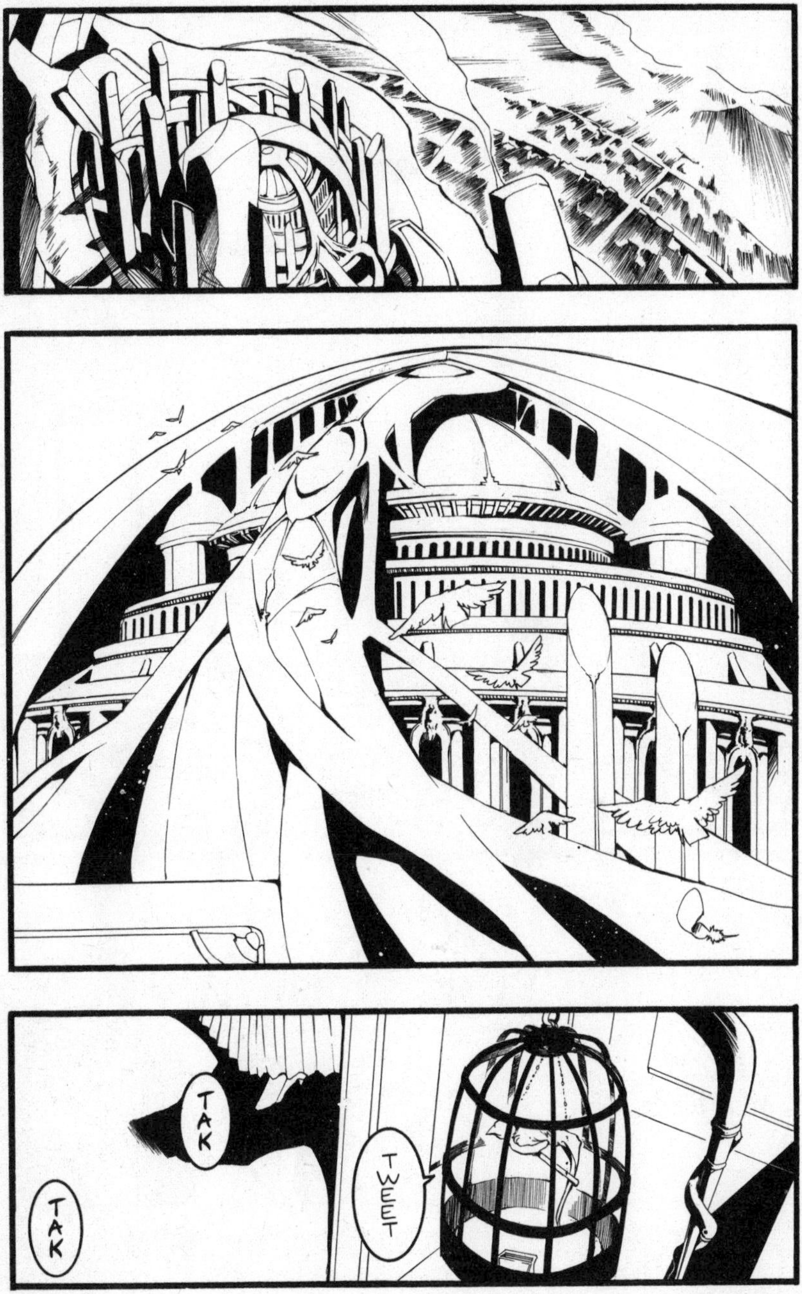
TWEET
TAK
TAK

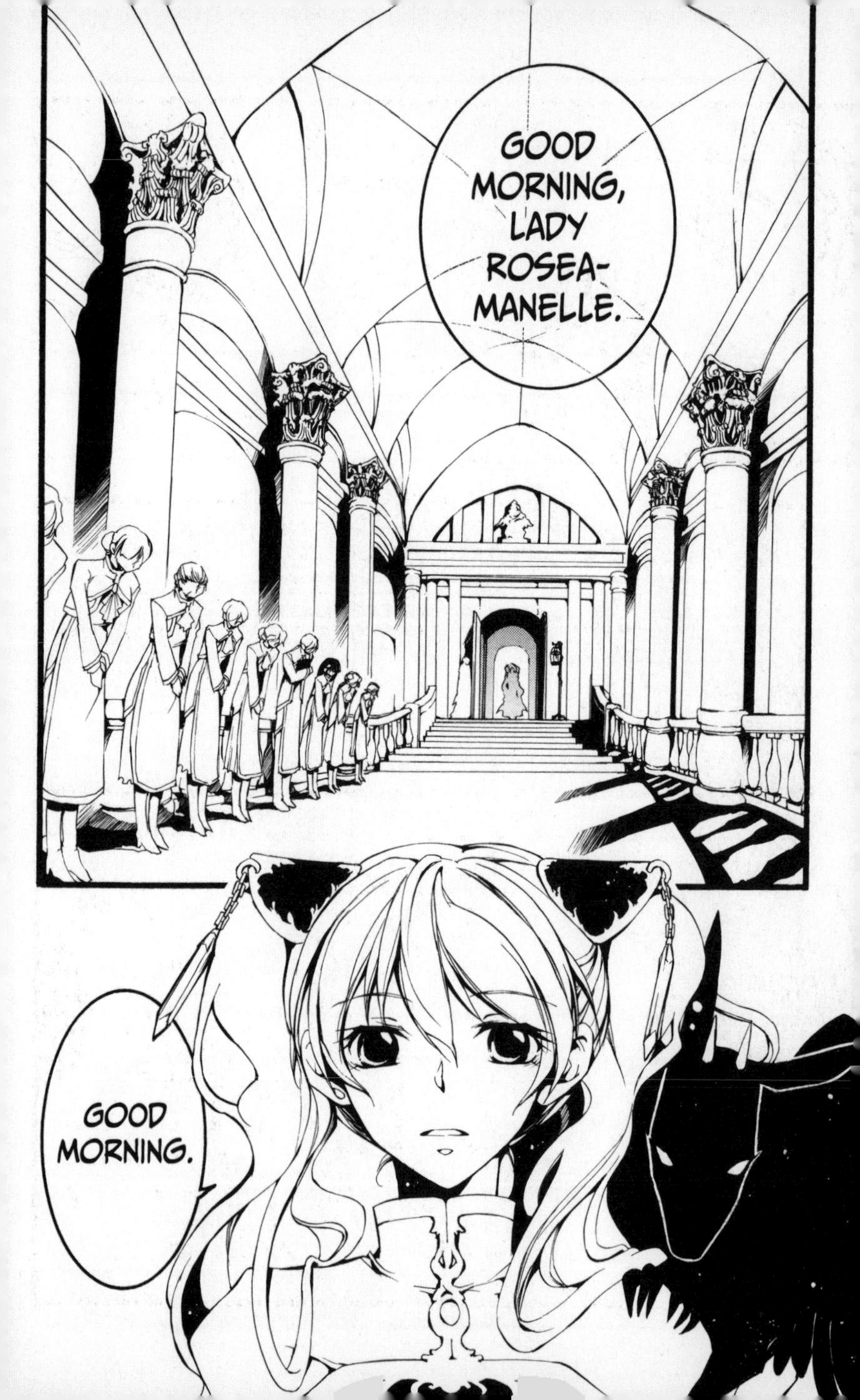
GOOD MORNING, LADY ROSEA-MANELLE.
GOOD MORNING.

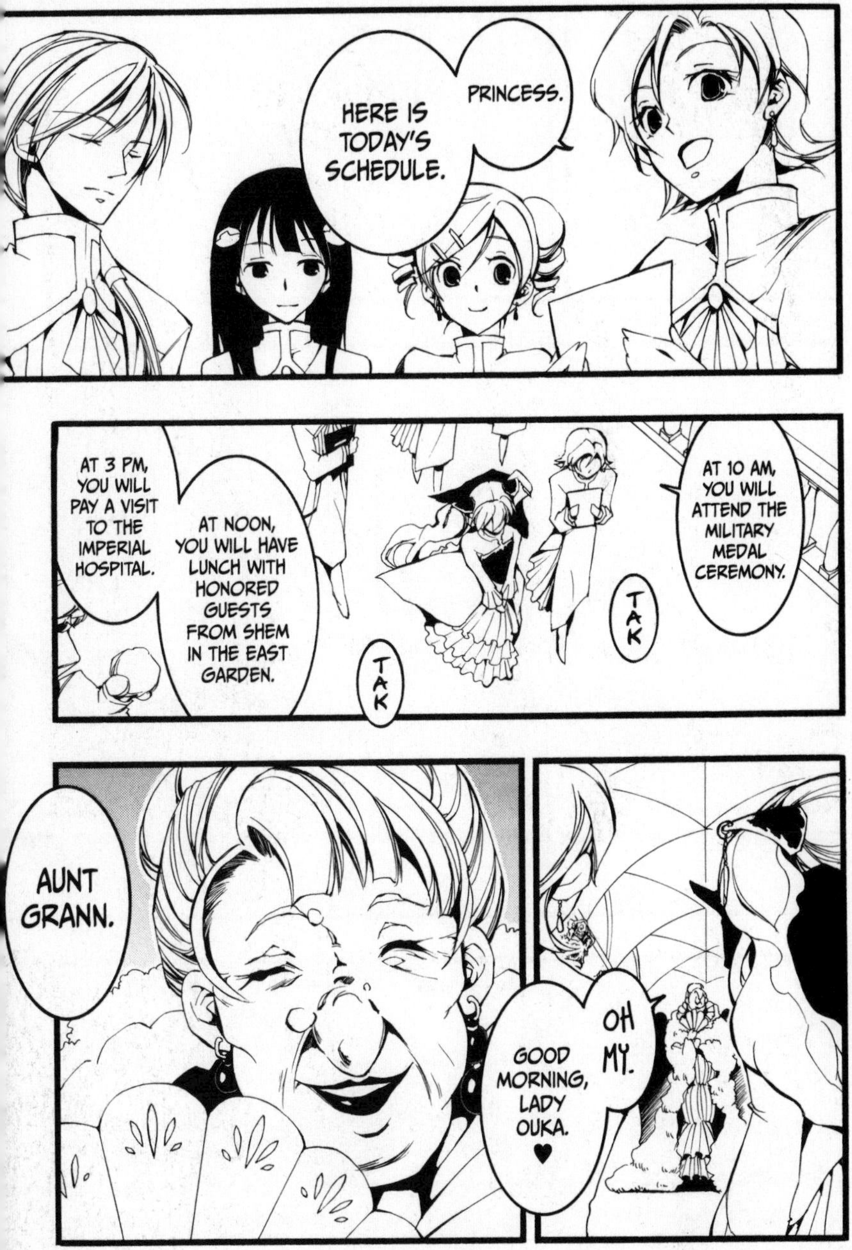
PRINCESS.
HERE IS TODAY'S SCHEDULE.
AT 10 AM, YOU WILL ATTEND THE MILITARY MEDAL CEREMONY.
TAK
TAK
AT NOON, YOU WILL HAVE LUNCH WITH HONORED GUESTS FROM SHEM IN THE EAST GARDEN.
AT 3 PM, YOU WILL PAY A VISIT TO THE IMPERIAL HOSPITAL.
OH MY.
GOOD MORNING, LADY OUKA. ♥
AUNT GRANN.

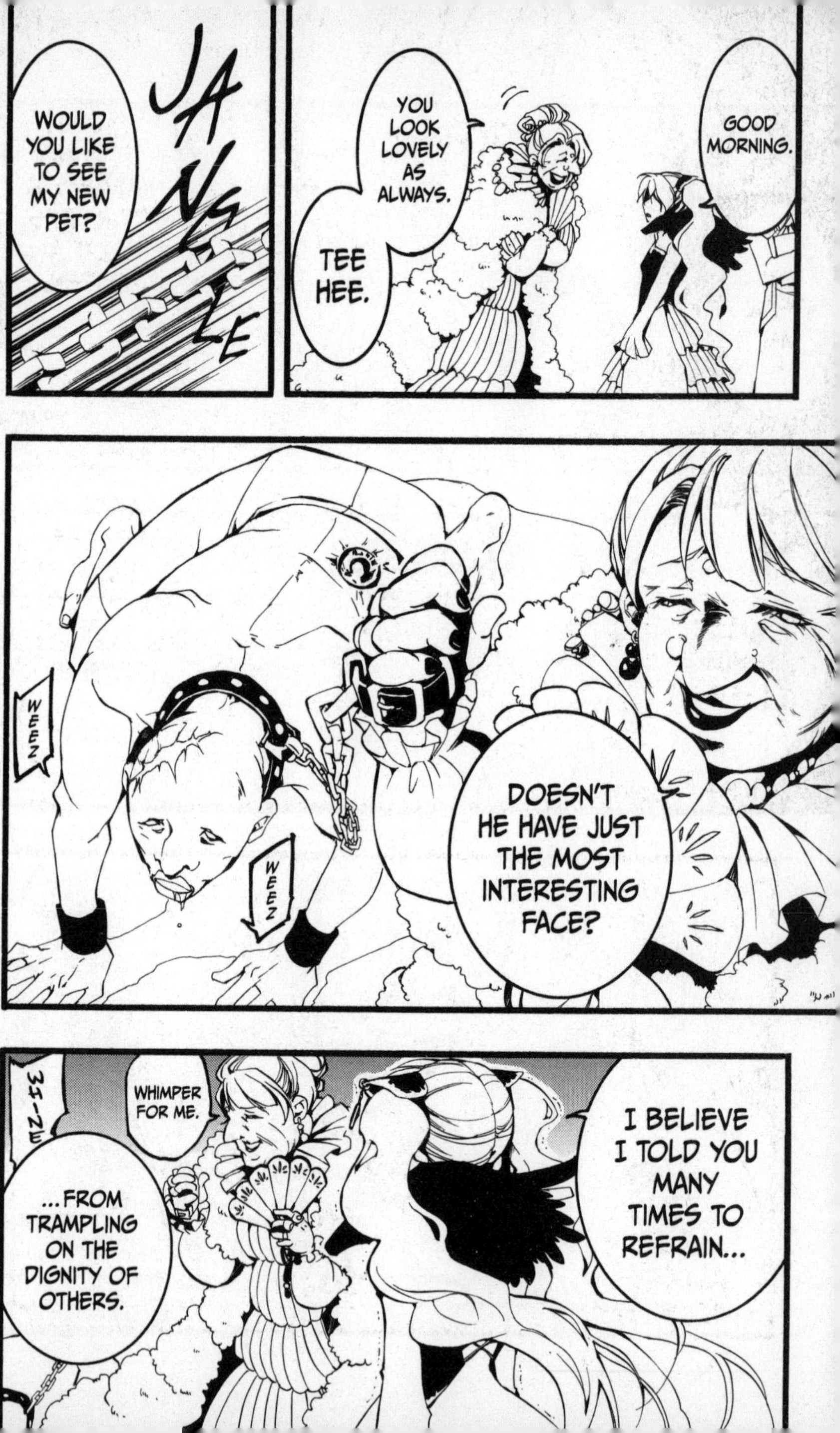
GOOD MORNING.
YOU LOOK LOVELY AS ALWAYS.
TEE HEE.
JANGLE
WOULD YOU LIKE TO SEE MY NEW PET?
DOESN'T HE HAVE JUST THE MOST INTERESTING FACE?
WEEZ
WEEZ
I BELIEVE I TOLD YOU MANY TIMES TO REFRAIN...
WHIMPER FOR ME.
WHINE
...FROM TRAMPLING ON THE DIGNITY OF OTHERS.

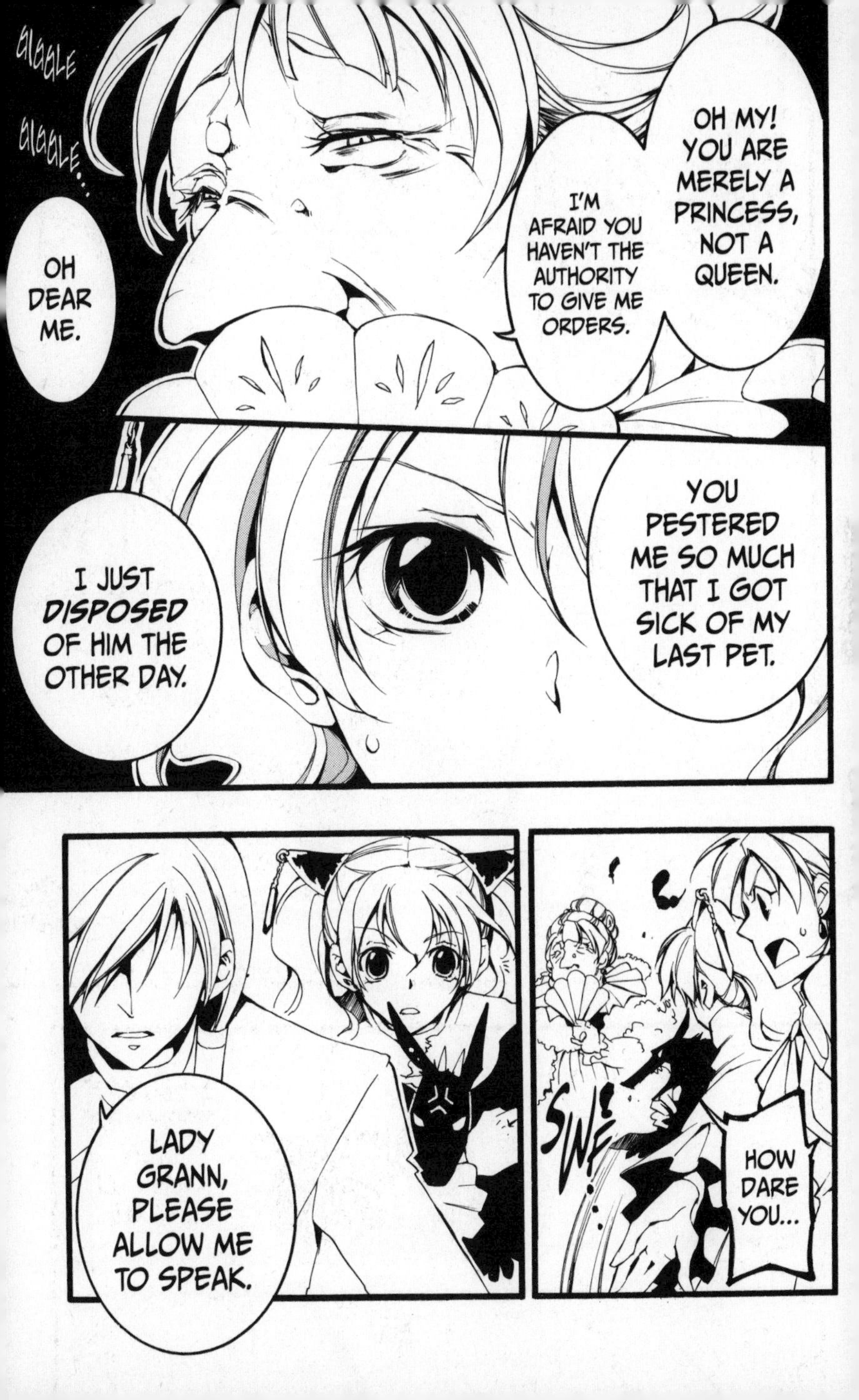
OH MY! YOU ARE MERELY A PRINCESS, NOT A QUEEN.
I'M AFRAID YOU HAVEN'T THE AUTHORITY TO GIVE ME ORDERS.
GIGGLE
GIGGLE...
OH DEAR ME.
YOU PESTERED ME SO MUCH THAT I GOT SICK OF MY LAST PET.
I JUST *DISPOSED* OF HIM THE OTHER DAY.
HOW DARE YOU...
LADY GRANN, PLEASE ALLOW ME TO SPEAK.

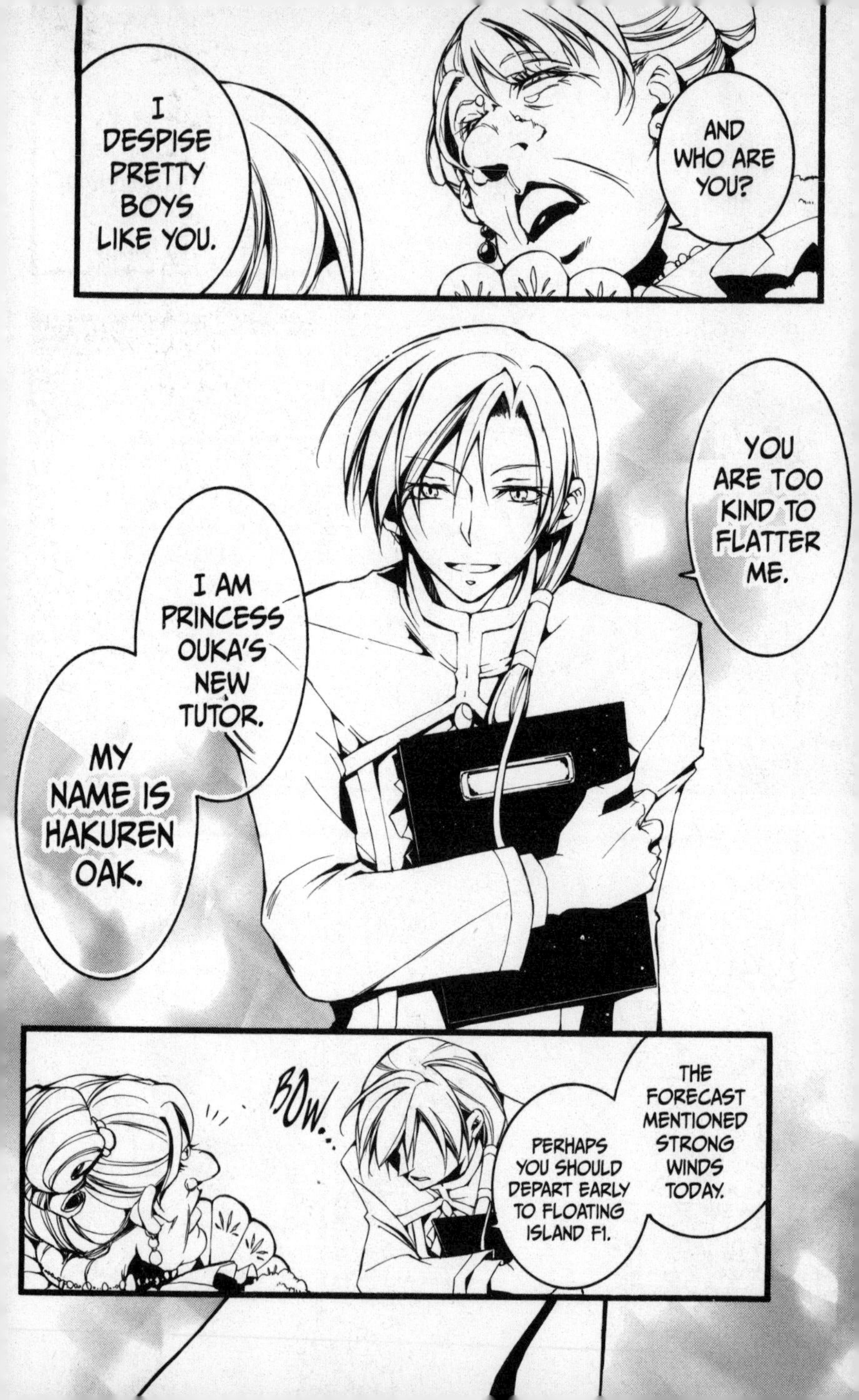
AND WHO ARE YOU?
I DESPISE PRETTY BOYS LIKE YOU.
YOU ARE TOO KIND TO FLATTER ME.
I AM PRINCESS OUKA'S NEW TUTOR.
MY NAME IS HAKUREN OAK.
THE FORECAST MENTIONED STRONG WINDS TODAY.
PERHAPS YOU SHOULD DEPART EARLY TO FLOATING ISLAND F1.
BOW...

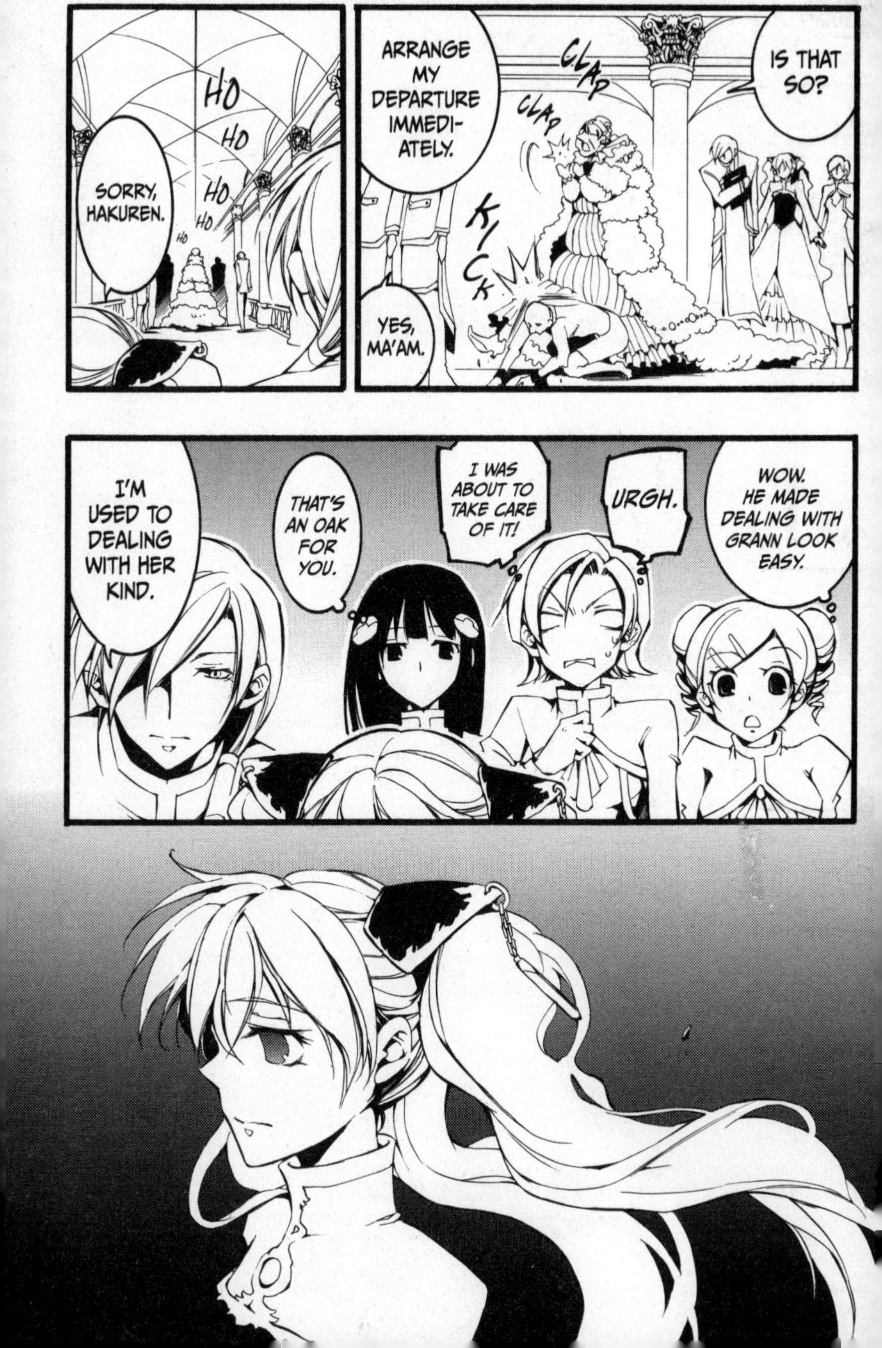
IS THAT SO?
CLAP
CLAP
ARRANGE MY DEPARTURE IMMEDIATELY.
KICK
YES, MA'AM.
HO HO HO HO HO
SORRY, HAKUREN.
WOW. HE MADE DEALING WITH GRANN LOOK EASY.
URGH.
I WAS ABOUT TO TAKE CARE OF IT!
THAT'S AN OAK FOR YOU.
I'M USED TO DEALING WITH HER KIND.

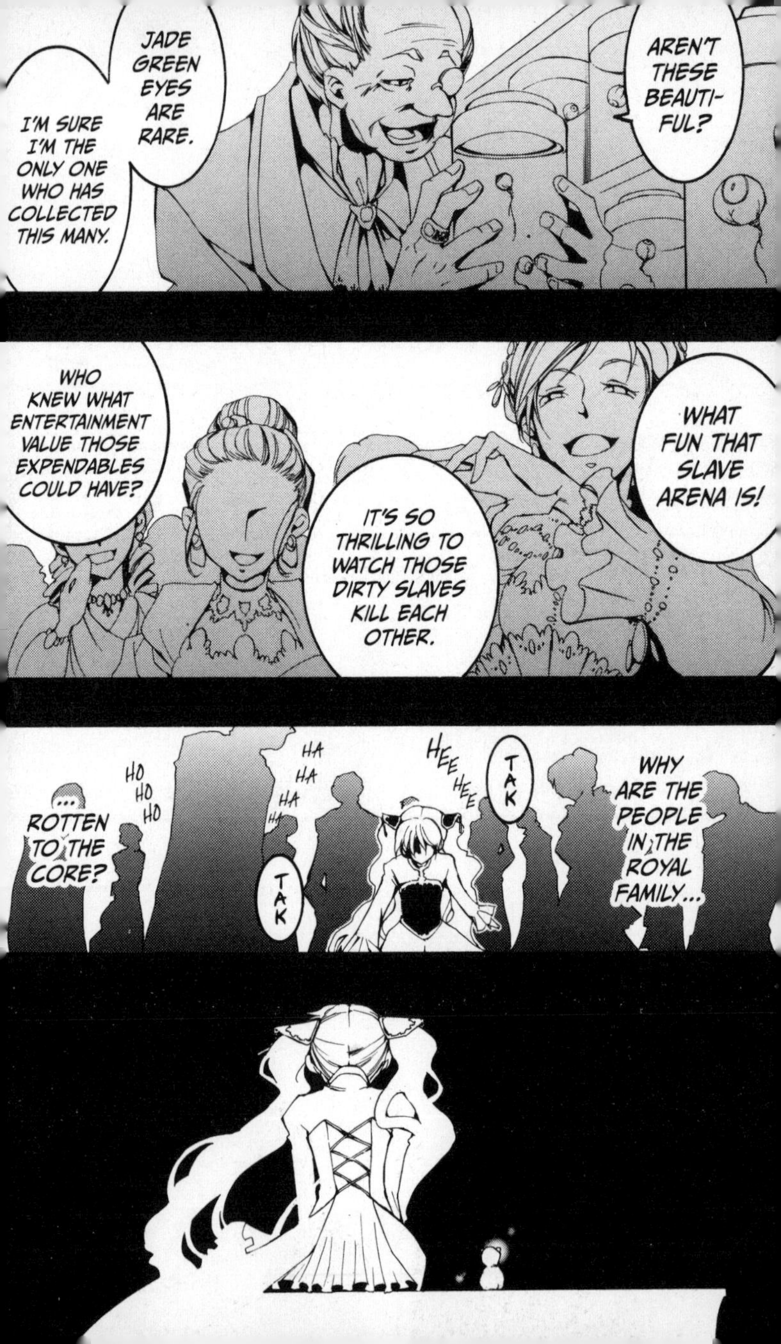
AREN'T THESE BEAUTIFUL?
JADE GREEN EYES ARE RARE.
I'M SURE I'M THE ONLY ONE WHO HAS COLLECTED THIS MANY.
WHAT FUN THAT SLAVE ARENA IS!
IT'S SO THRILLING TO WATCH THOSE DIRTY SLAVES KILL EACH OTHER.
WHO KNEW WHAT ENTERTAINMENT VALUE THOSE EXPENDABLES COULD HAVE?
WHY ARE THE PEOPLE IN THE ROYAL FAMILY...
TAK
HEE HEE
HA HA HA HA
TAK
HO HO HO
...
ROTTEN TO THE CORE?

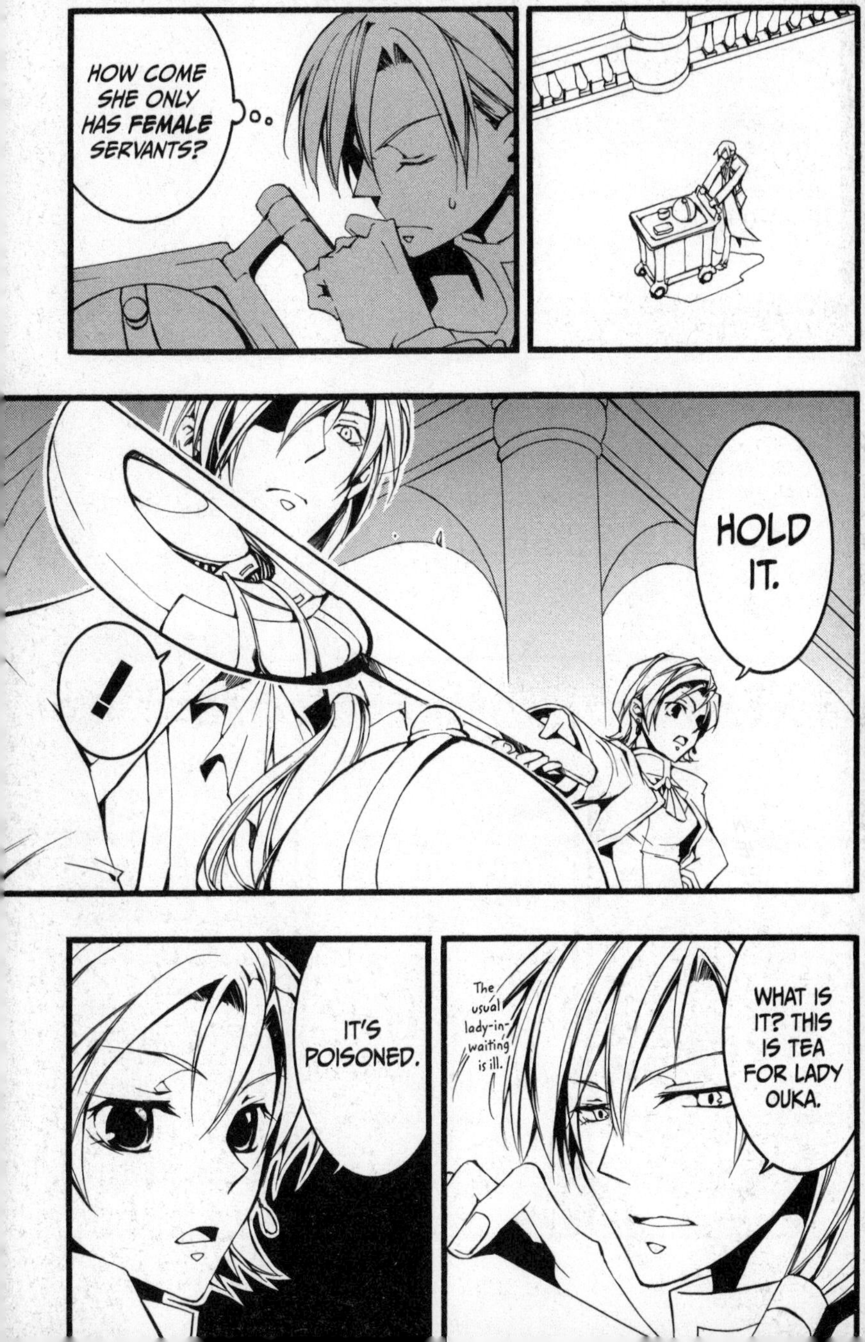
HOW COME SHE ONLY HAS FEMALE SERVANTS?
HOLD IT.
!
WHAT IS IT? THIS IS TEA FOR LADY OUKA.
The usual lady-in-waiting is ill.
IT'S POISONED.

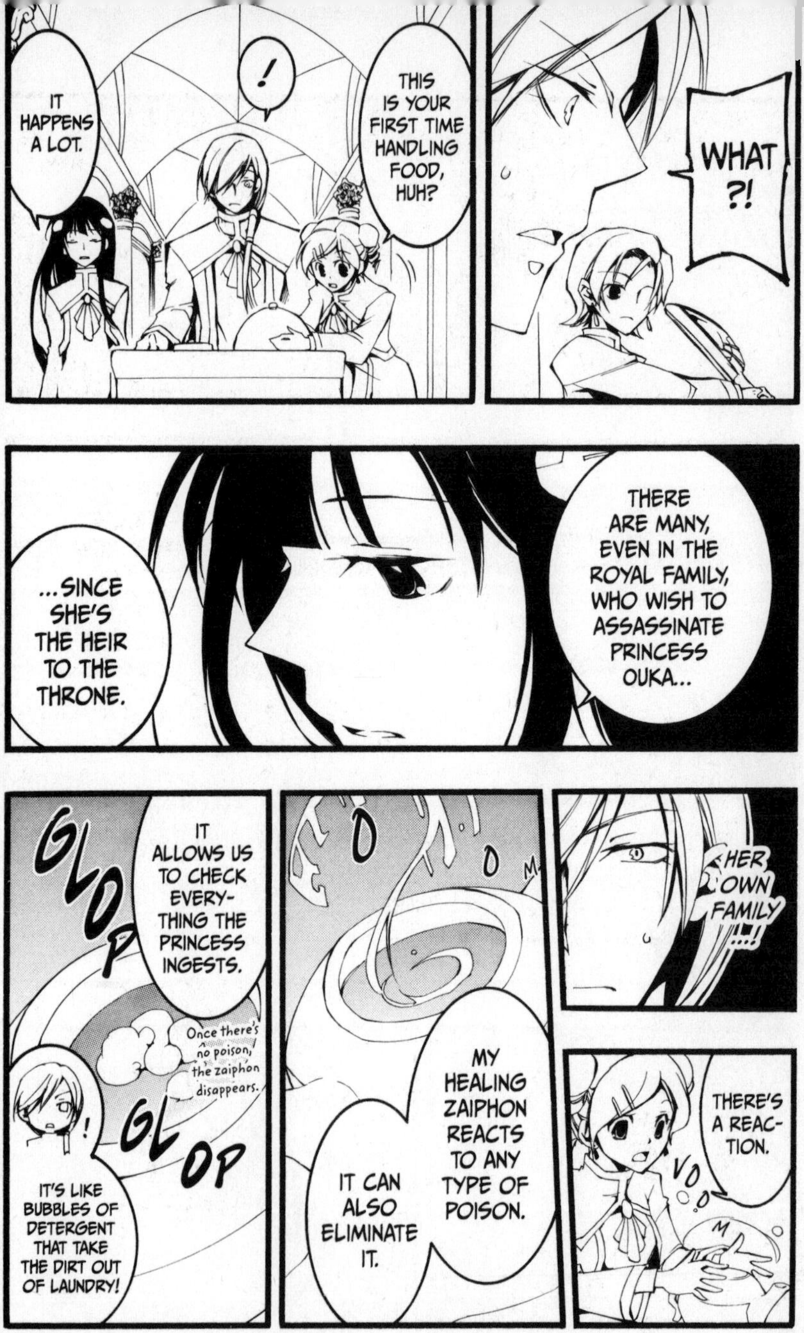
WHAT?!
THIS IS YOUR FIRST TIME HANDLING FOOD, HUH?
!
IT HAPPENS A LOT.
THERE ARE MANY, EVEN IN THE ROYAL FAMILY, WHO WISH TO ASSASSINATE PRINCESS OUKA...
...SINCE SHE'S THE HEIR TO THE THRONE.
HER OWN FAMILY...!
THERE'S A REACTION.
VOOM
MY HEALING ZAIPHON REACTS TO ANY TYPE OF POISON.
IT CAN ALSO ELIMINATE IT.
IT ALLOWS US TO CHECK EVERYTHING THE PRINCESS INGESTS.
GLOP
GLOP
Once there's no poison, the zaiphon disappears.
!
IT'S LIKE BUBBLES OF DETERGENT THAT TAKE THE DIRT OUT OF LAUNDRY!

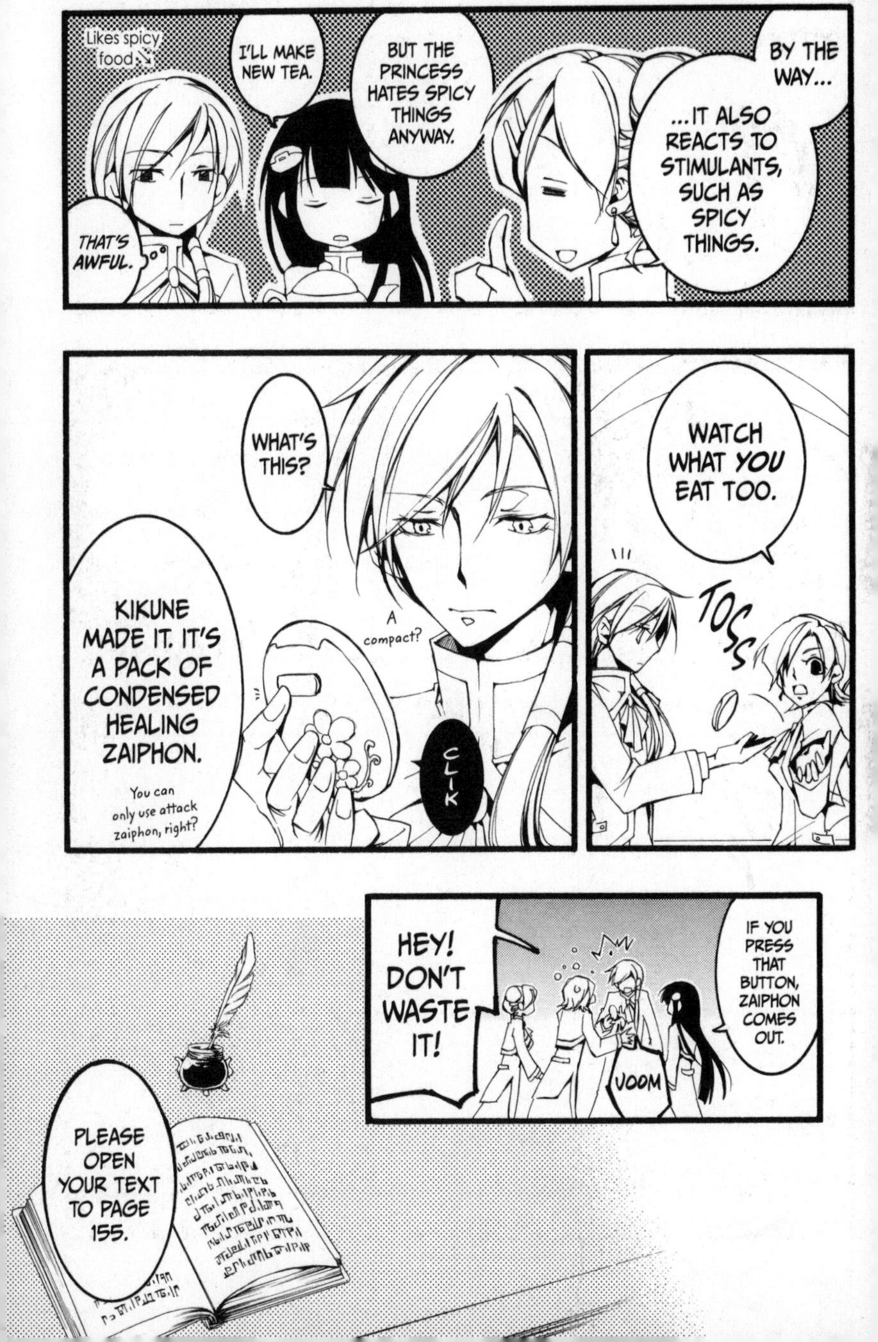
BY THE WAY...
...IT ALSO REACTS TO STIMULANTS, SUCH AS SPICY THINGS.
BUT THE PRINCESS HATES SPICY THINGS ANYWAY.
I'LL MAKE NEW TEA.
Likes spicy food
THAT'S AWFUL.
WATCH WHAT *YOU* EAT TOO.
TOSS
WHAT'S THIS?
A compact?
CLIK
KIKUNE MADE IT. IT'S A PACK OF CONDENSED HEALING ZAIPHON.
You can only use attack zaiphon, right?
IF YOU PRESS THAT BUTTON, ZAIPHON COMES OUT.
HEY! DON'T WASTE IT!
VOOM
PLEASE OPEN YOUR TEXT TO PAGE 155.

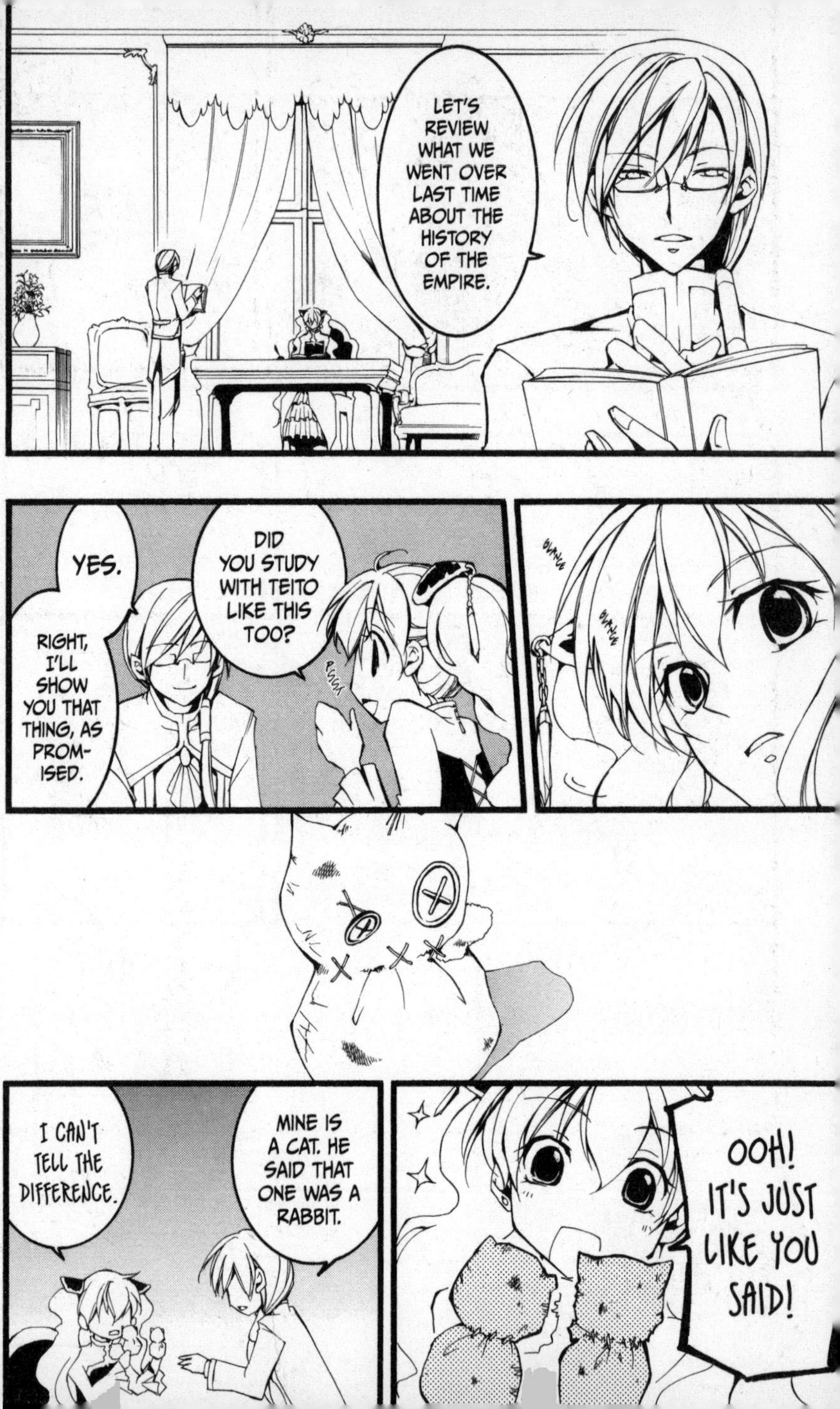
LET'S REVIEW WHAT WE WENT OVER LAST TIME ABOUT THE HISTORY OF THE EMPIRE.
GLANCE
GLANCE
DID YOU STUDY WITH TEITO LIKE THIS TOO?
YES.
RIGHT, I'LL SHOW YOU THAT THING, AS PROMISED.
OOH! IT'S JUST LIKE YOU SAID!
MINE IS A CAT. HE SAID THAT ONE WAS A RABBIT.
I CAN'T TELL THE DIFFERENCE.

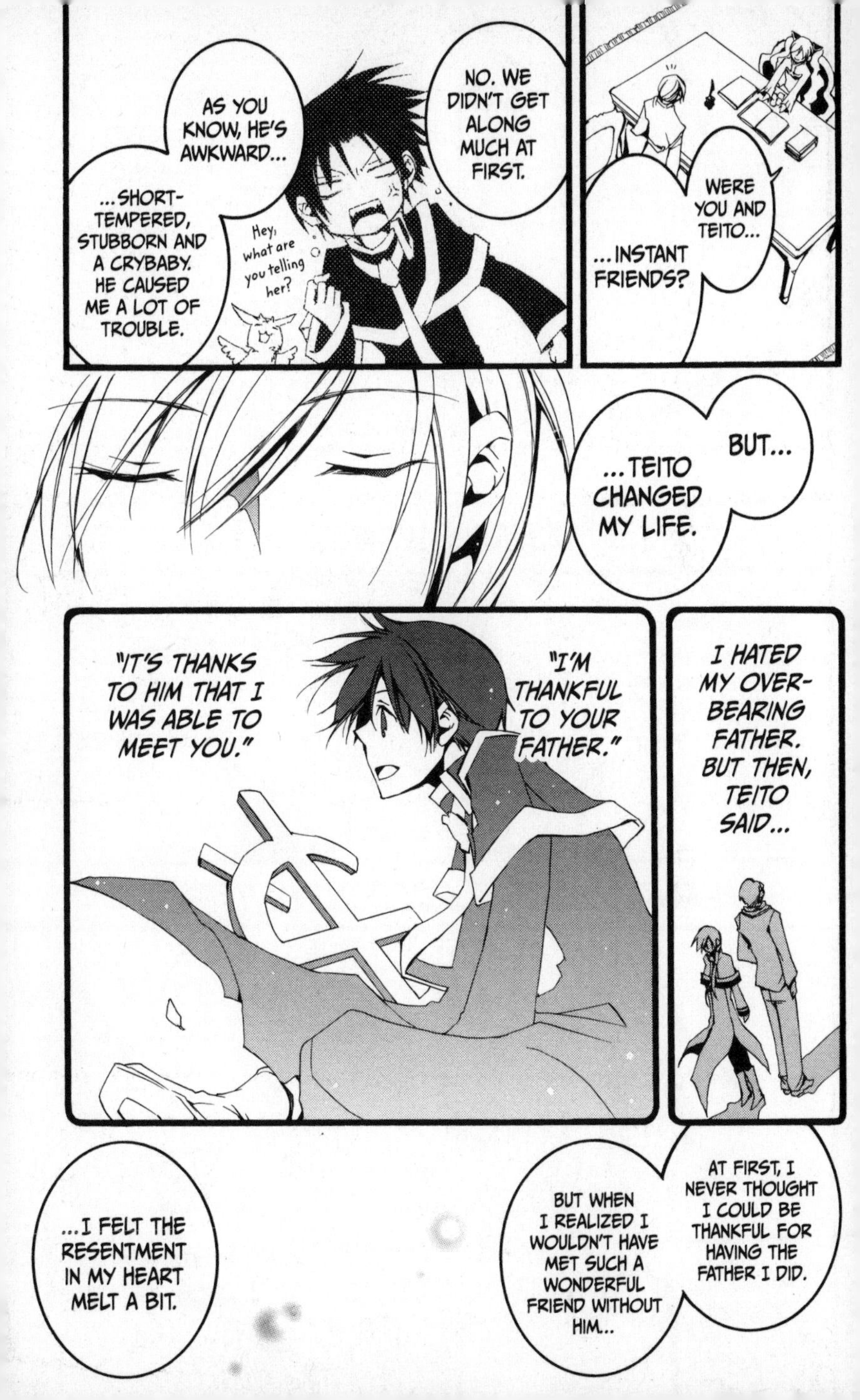
WERE YOU AND TEITO...
...INSTANT FRIENDS?
NO. WE DIDN'T GET ALONG MUCH AT FIRST.
AS YOU KNOW, HE'S AWKWARD...
...SHORT-TEMPERED, STUBBORN AND A CRYBABY. HE CAUSED ME A LOT OF TROUBLE.
Hey, what are you telling her?
BUT...
...TEITO CHANGED MY LIFE.
I HATED MY OVER-BEARING FATHER. BUT THEN, TEITO SAID...
"I'M THANKFUL TO YOUR FATHER."
"IT'S THANKS TO HIM THAT I WAS ABLE TO MEET YOU."
AT FIRST, I NEVER THOUGHT I COULD BE THANKFUL FOR HAVING THE FATHER I DID.
BUT WHEN I REALIZED I WOULDN'T HAVE MET SUCH A WONDERFUL FRIEND WITHOUT HIM...
...I FELT THE RESENTMENT IN MY HEART MELT A BIT.

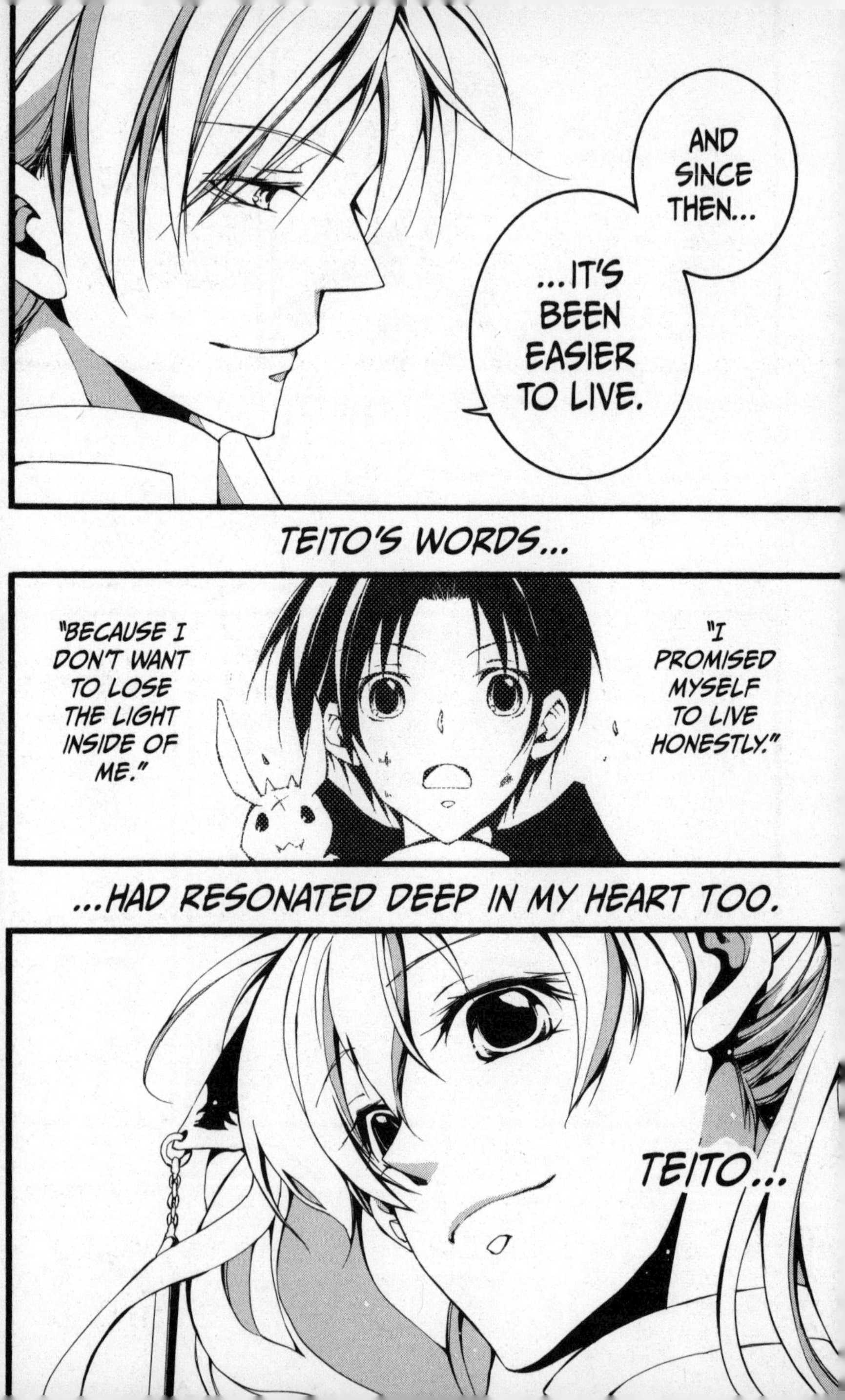
AND SINCE THEN...
...IT'S BEEN EASIER TO LIVE.
TEITO'S WORDS...
"I PROMISED MYSELF TO LIVE HONESTLY."
"BECAUSE I DON'T WANT TO LOSE THE LIGHT INSIDE OF ME."
...HAD RESONATED DEEP IN MY HEART TOO.
TEITO...

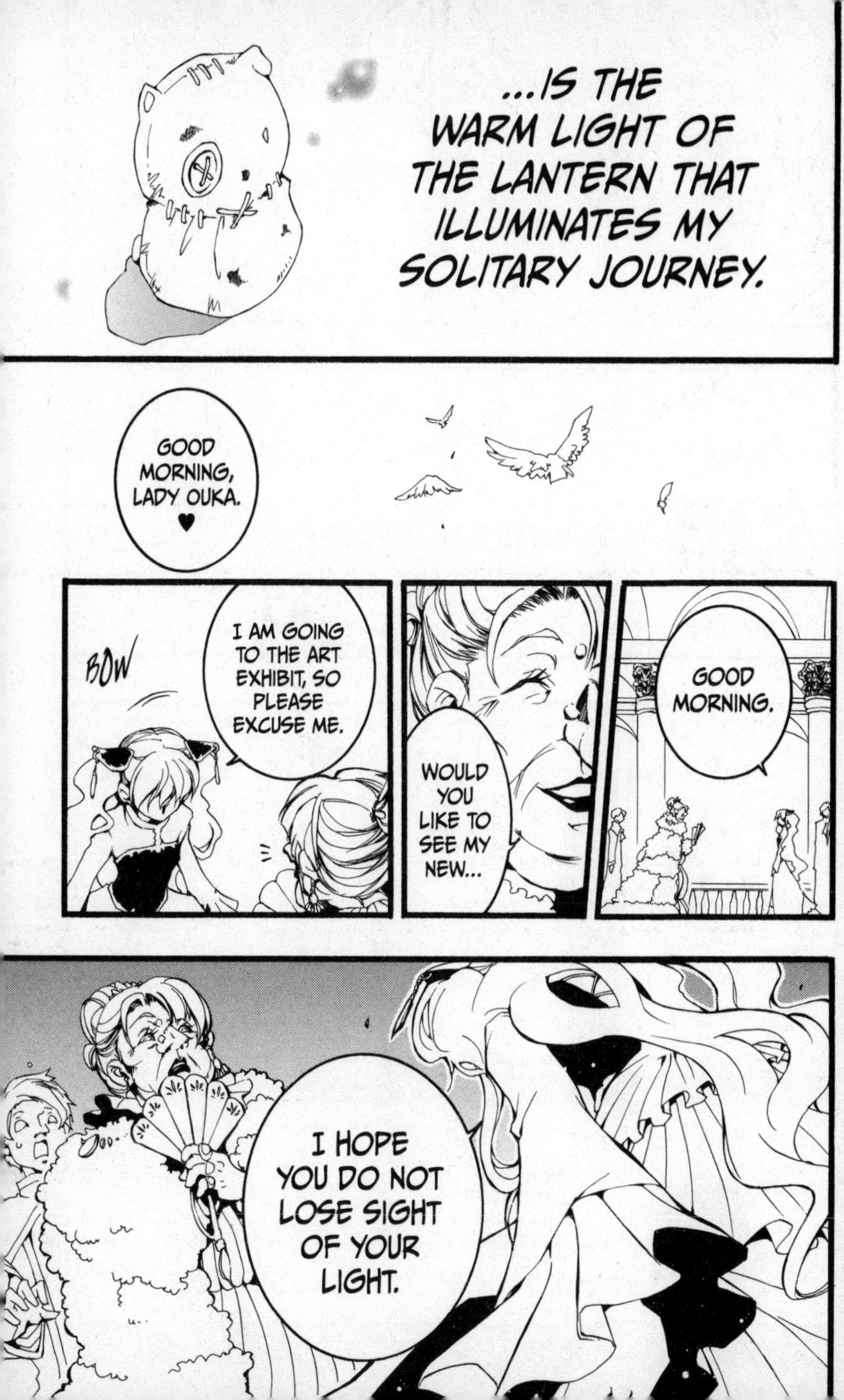
...IS THE WARM LIGHT OF THE LANTERN THAT ILLUMINATES MY SOLITARY JOURNEY.
GOOD MORNING, LADY OUKA. ♥
GOOD MORNING.
WOULD YOU LIKE TO SEE MY NEW...
I AM GOING TO THE ART EXHIBIT, SO PLEASE EXCUSE ME.
BOW
I HOPE YOU DO NOT LOSE SIGHT OF YOUR LIGHT.

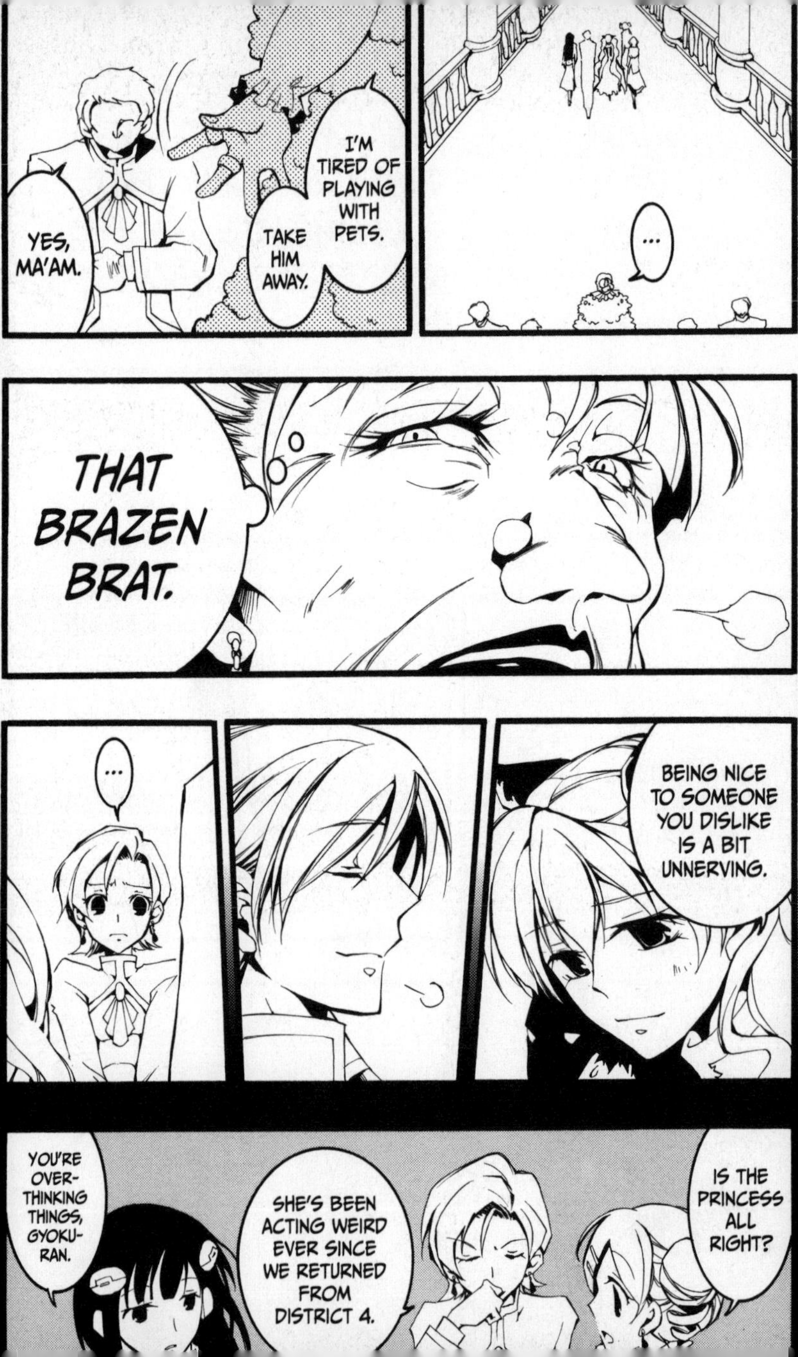
...
I'M TIRED OF PLAYING WITH PETS.
TAKE HIM AWAY.
YES, MA'AM.
THAT BRAZEN BRAT.
BEING NICE TO SOMEONE YOU DISLIKE IS A BIT UNNERVING.
...
IS THE PRINCESS ALL RIGHT?
SHE'S BEEN ACTING WEIRD EVER SINCE WE RETURNED FROM DISTRICT 4.
YOU'RE OVER-THINKING THINGS, GYOKU-RAN.

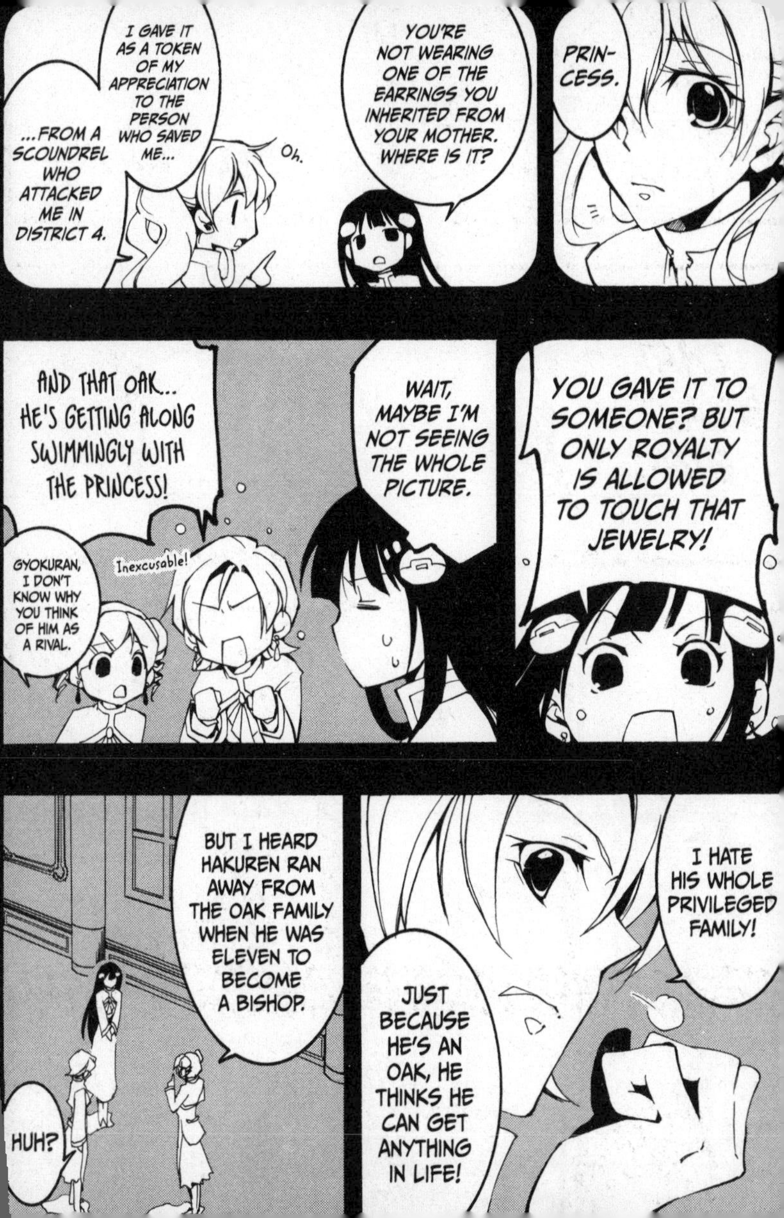
PRIN-CESS.
YOU'RE NOT WEARING ONE OF THE EARRINGS YOU INHERITED FROM YOUR MOTHER. WHERE IS IT?
Oh.
I GAVE IT AS A TOKEN OF MY APPRECIATION TO THE PERSON WHO SAVED ME...
...FROM A SCOUNDREL WHO ATTACKED ME IN DISTRICT 4.
YOU GAVE IT TO SOMEONE? BUT ONLY ROYALTY IS ALLOWED TO TOUCH THAT JEWELRY!
WAIT, MAYBE I'M NOT SEEING THE WHOLE PICTURE.
AND THAT OAK... HE'S GETTING ALONG SWIMMINGLY WITH THE PRINCESS!
Inexcusable!
GYOKURAN, I DON'T KNOW WHY YOU THINK OF HIM AS A RIVAL.
I HATE HIS WHOLE PRIVILEGED FAMILY!
JUST BECAUSE HE'S AN OAK, HE THINKS HE CAN GET ANYTHING IN LIFE!
BUT I HEARD HAKUREN RAN AWAY FROM THE OAK FAMILY WHEN HE WAS ELEVEN TO BECOME A BISHOP.
HUH?

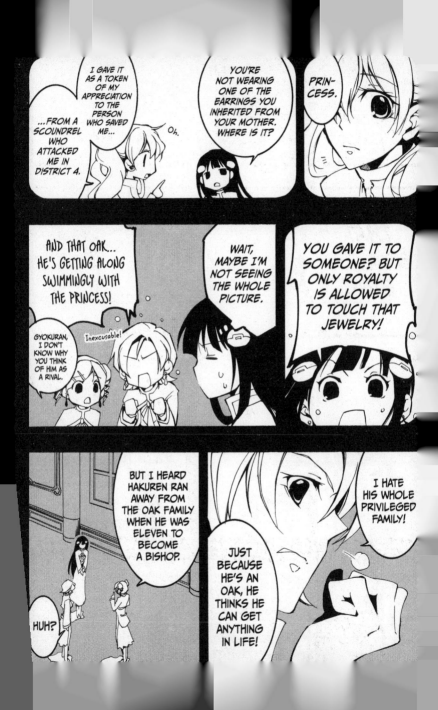

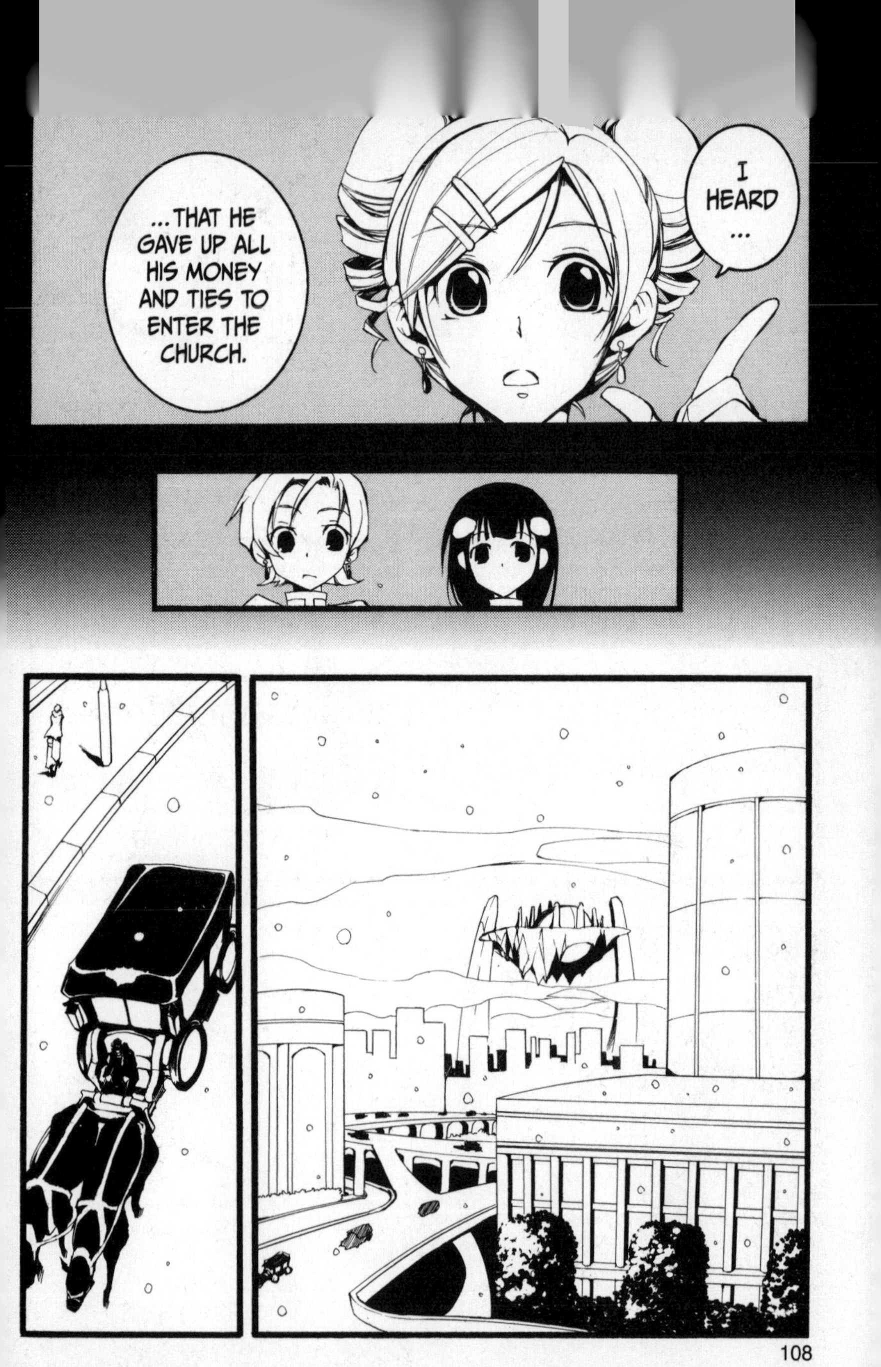
I HEARD ...
...THAT HE GAVE UP ALL HIS MONEY AND TIES TO ENTER THE CHURCH.

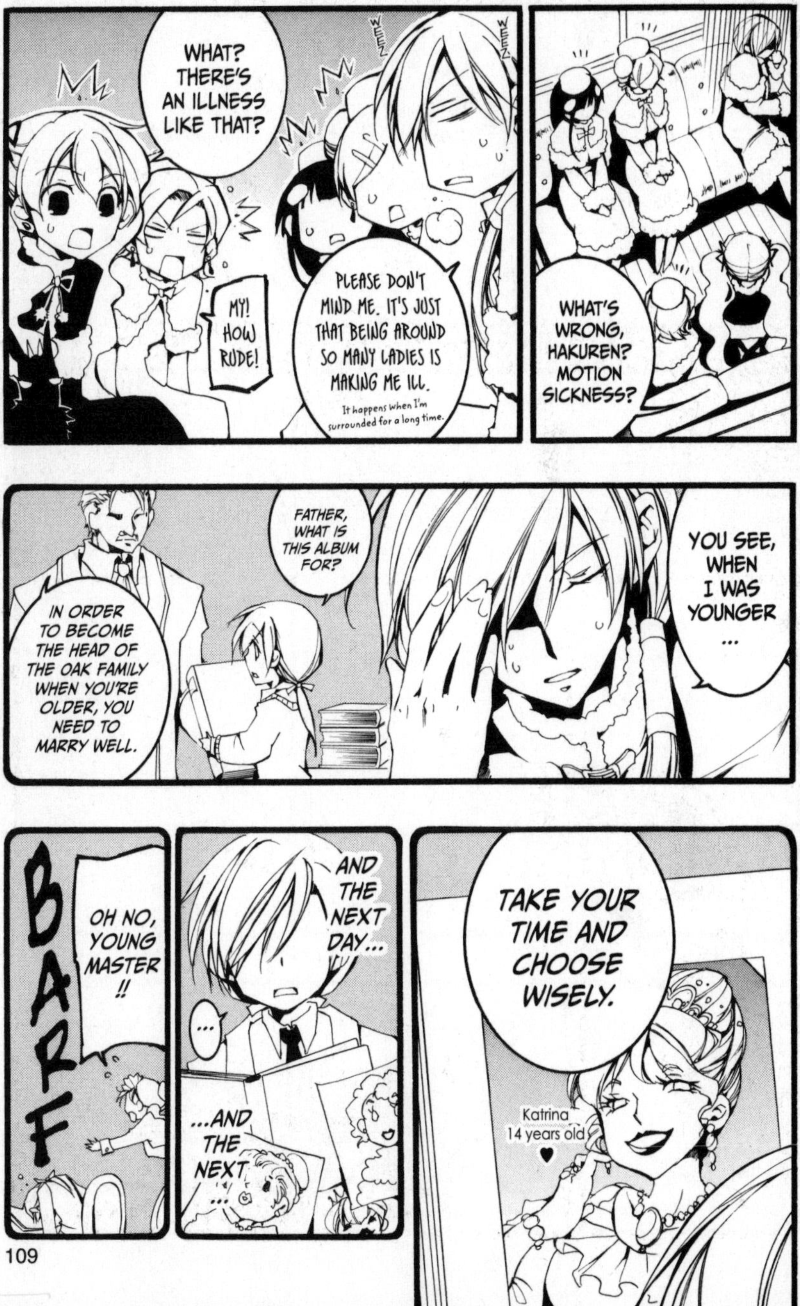
WHAT'S WRONG, HAKUREN? MOTION SICKNESS?
WEEZ
WEEZ
PLEASE DON'T MIND ME. IT'S JUST THAT BEING AROUND SO MANY LADIES IS MAKING ME ILL.
It happens when I'm surrounded for a long time.
WHAT? THERE'S AN ILLNESS LIKE THAT?
MY! HOW RUDE!
YOU SEE, WHEN I WAS YOUNGER...
FATHER, WHAT IS THIS ALBUM FOR?
IN ORDER TO BECOME THE HEAD OF THE OAK FAMILY WHEN YOU'RE OLDER, YOU NEED TO MARRY WELL.
TAKE YOUR TIME AND CHOOSE WISELY.
Katrina 14 years old ♥
AND THE NEXT DAY...
...
...AND THE NEXT...
BARF
OH NO, YOUNG MASTER!!

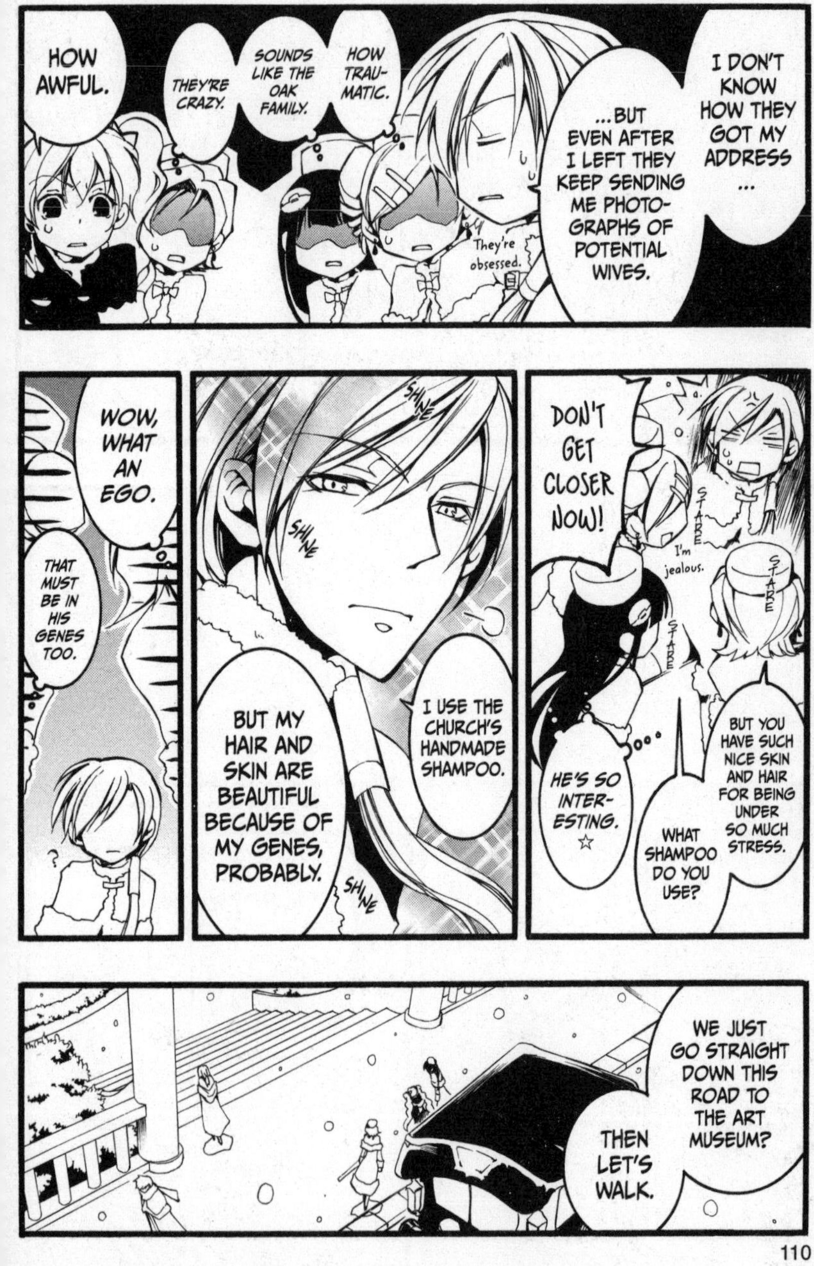
I DON'T KNOW HOW THEY GOT MY ADDRESS ...
...BUT EVEN AFTER I LEFT THEY KEEP SENDING ME PHOTOGRAPHS OF POTENTIAL WIVES.
They're obsessed.
HOW TRAUMATIC.
SOUNDS LIKE THE OAK FAMILY.
THEY'RE CRAZY.
HOW AWFUL.
STARE
STARE
DON'T GET CLOSER NOW!
I'm jealous.
STARE
BUT YOU HAVE SUCH NICE SKIN AND HAIR FOR BEING UNDER SO MUCH STRESS.
WHAT SHAMPOO DO YOU USE?
HE'S SO INTERESTING. ☆
SHINE
SHINE
I USE THE CHURCH'S HANDMADE SHAMPOO.
BUT MY HAIR AND SKIN ARE BEAUTIFUL BECAUSE OF MY GENES, PROBABLY.
SHINE
WOW, WHAT AN EGO.
THAT MUST BE IN HIS GENES TOO.
WE JUST GO STRAIGHT DOWN THIS ROAD TO THE ART MUSEUM?
THEN LET'S WALK.

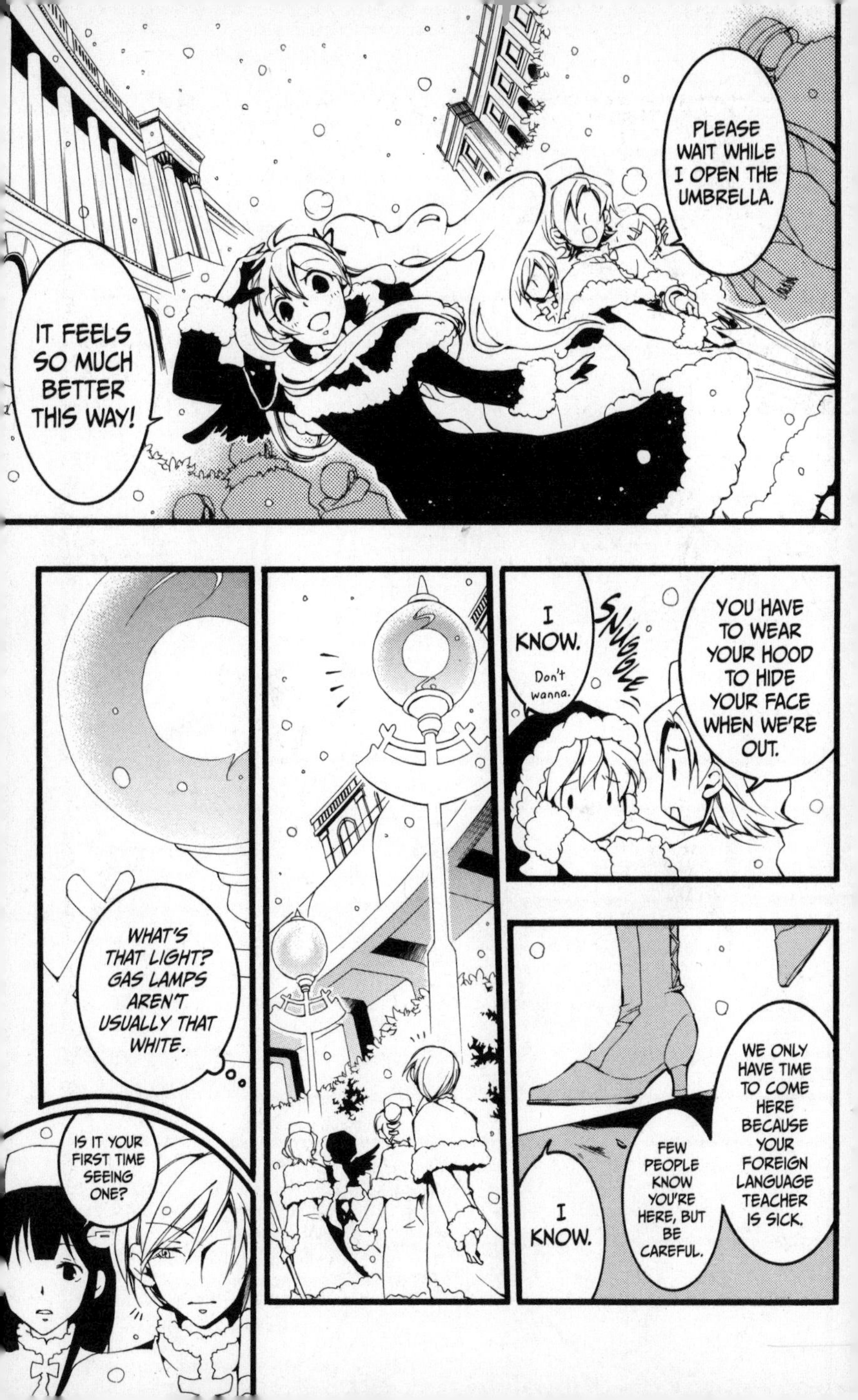
PLEASE WAIT WHILE I OPEN THE UMBRELLA.
IT FEELS SO MUCH BETTER THIS WAY!
YOU HAVE TO WEAR YOUR HOOD TO HIDE YOUR FACE WHEN WE'RE OUT.
SNUGGLE
I KNOW.
Don't wanna.
WE ONLY HAVE TIME TO COME HERE BECAUSE YOUR FOREIGN LANGUAGE TEACHER IS SICK.
FEW PEOPLE KNOW YOU'RE HERE, BUT BE CAREFUL.
I KNOW.
WHAT'S THAT LIGHT? GAS LAMPS AREN'T USUALLY THAT WHITE.
IS IT YOUR FIRST TIME SEEING ONE?

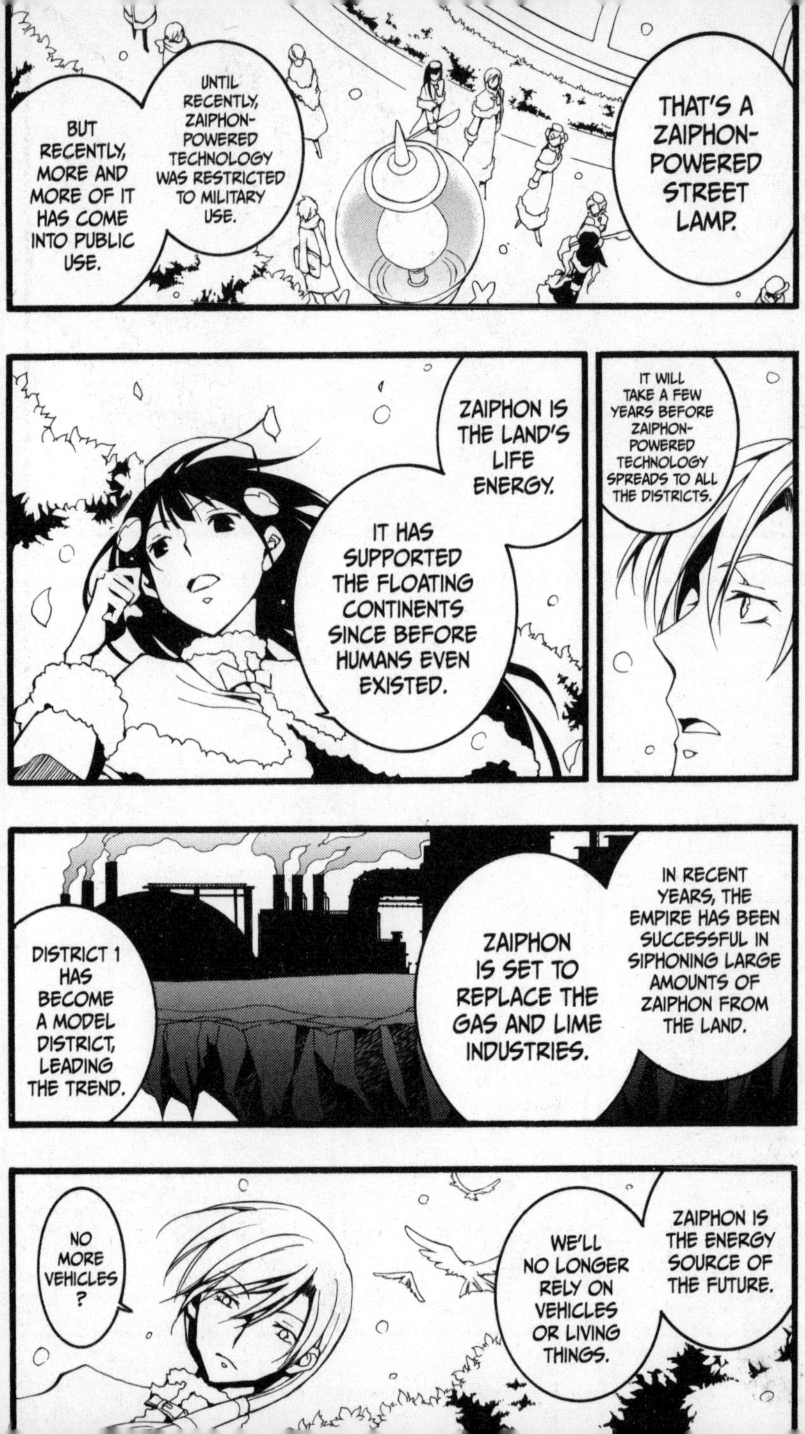
THAT'S A ZAIPHON-POWERED STREET LAMP.
UNTIL RECENTLY, ZAIPHON-POWERED TECHNOLOGY WAS RESTRICTED TO MILITARY USE.
BUT RECENTLY, MORE AND MORE OF IT HAS COME INTO PUBLIC USE.
IT WILL TAKE A FEW YEARS BEFORE ZAIPHON-POWERED TECHNOLOGY SPREADS TO ALL THE DISTRICTS.
ZAIPHON IS THE LAND'S LIFE ENERGY.
IT HAS SUPPORTED THE FLOATING CONTINENTS SINCE BEFORE HUMANS EVEN EXISTED.
IN RECENT YEARS, THE EMPIRE HAS BEEN SUCCESSFUL IN SIPHONING LARGE AMOUNTS OF ZAIPHON FROM THE LAND.
ZAIPHON IS SET TO REPLACE THE GAS AND LIME INDUSTRIES.
DISTRICT 1 HAS BECOME A MODEL DISTRICT, LEADING THE TREND.
ZAIPHON IS THE ENERGY SOURCE OF THE FUTURE.
WE'LL NO LONGER RELY ON VEHICLES OR LIVING THINGS.
NO MORE VEHICLES?

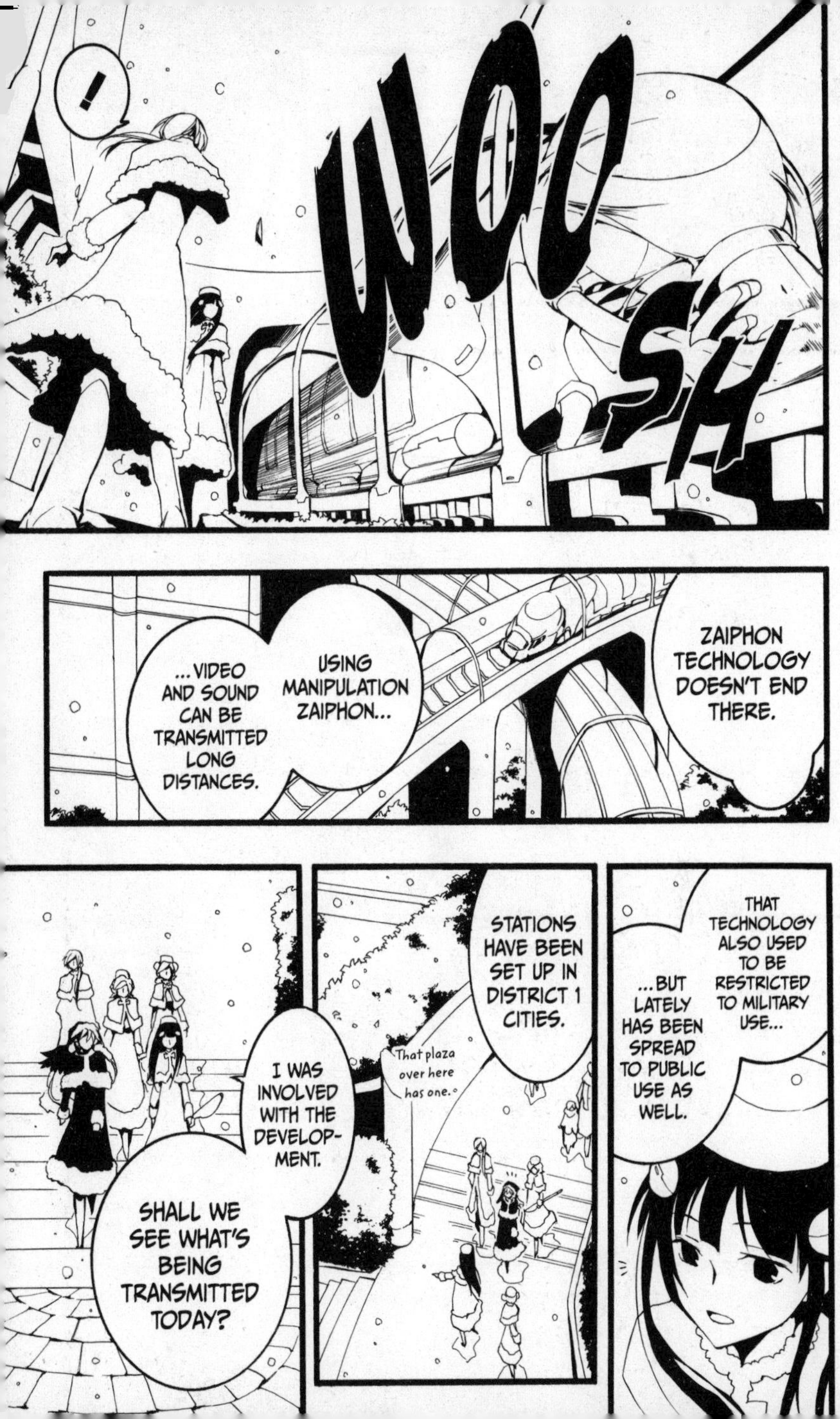
WOOSH
!
ZAIPHON TECHNOLOGY DOESN'T END THERE.
USING MANIPULATION ZAIPHON...
...VIDEO AND SOUND CAN BE TRANSMITTED LONG DISTANCES.
THAT TECHNOLOGY ALSO USED TO BE RESTRICTED TO MILITARY USE...
...BUT LATELY HAS BEEN SPREAD TO PUBLIC USE AS WELL.
STATIONS HAVE BEEN SET UP IN DISTRICT 1 CITIES.
That plaza over here has one.
I WAS INVOLVED WITH THE DEVELOPMENT.
SHALL WE SEE WHAT'S BEING TRANSMITTED TODAY?

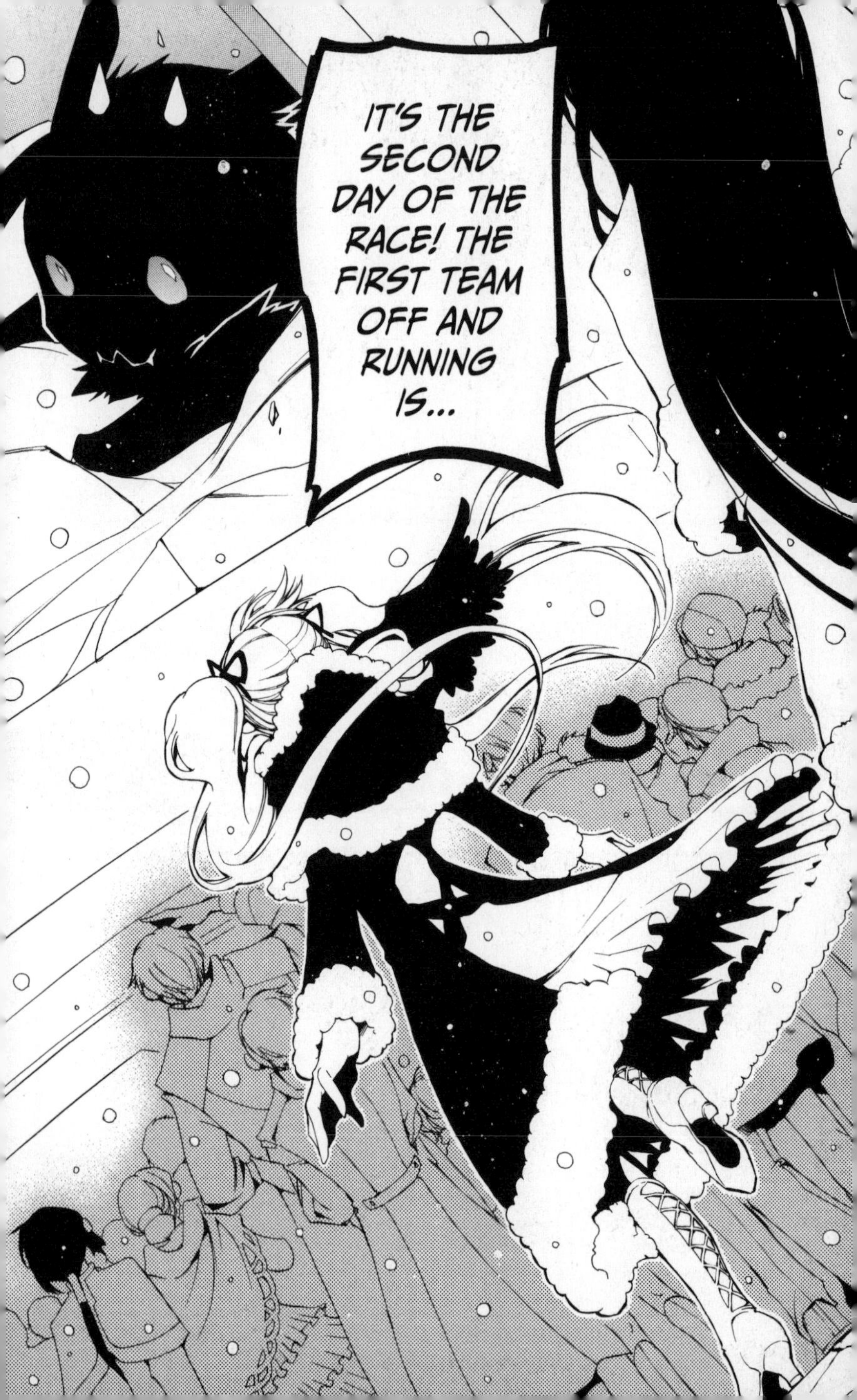
IT'S THE SECOND DAY OF THE RACE! THE FIRST TEAM OFF AND RUNNING IS...

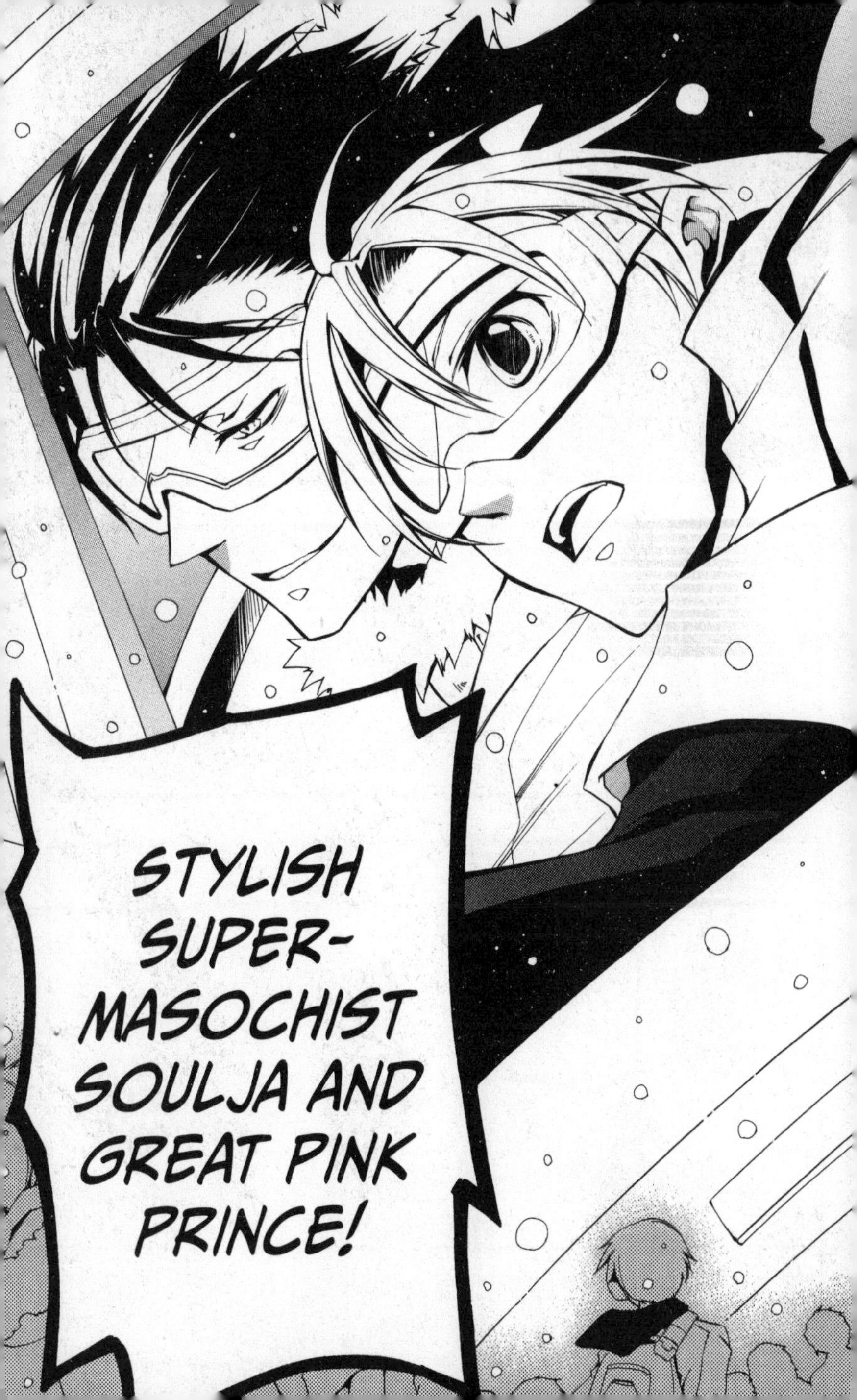
STYLISH SUPER-MASOCHIST SOULJA AND GREAT PINK PRINCE!

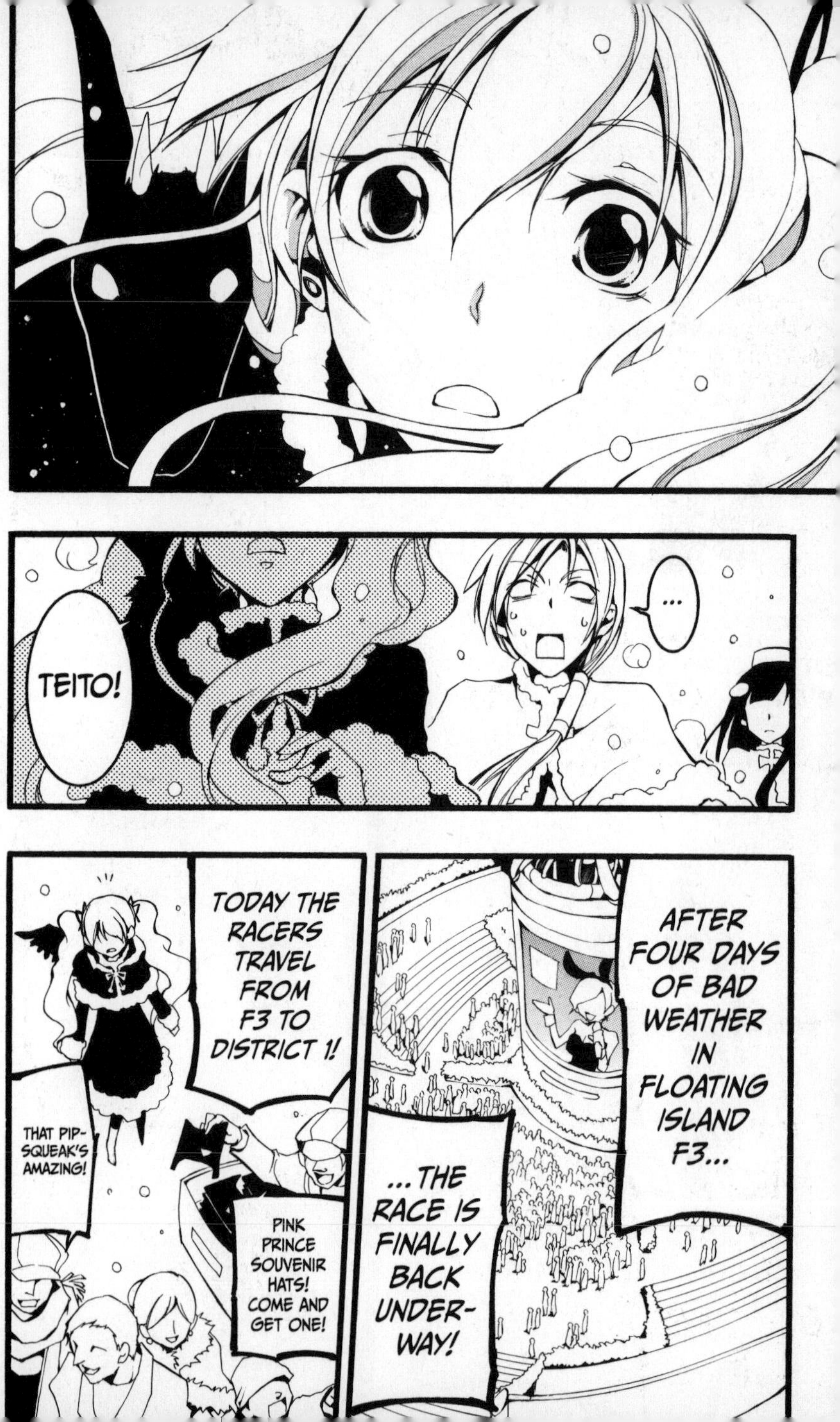
...
TEITO!
AFTER FOUR DAYS OF BAD WEATHER IN FLOATING ISLAND F3...
...THE RACE IS FINALLY BACK UNDER-WAY!
TODAY THE RACERS TRAVEL FROM F3 TO DISTRICT 1!
THAT PIP-SQUEAK'S AMAZING!
PINK PRINCE SOUVENIR HATS! COME AND GET ONE!

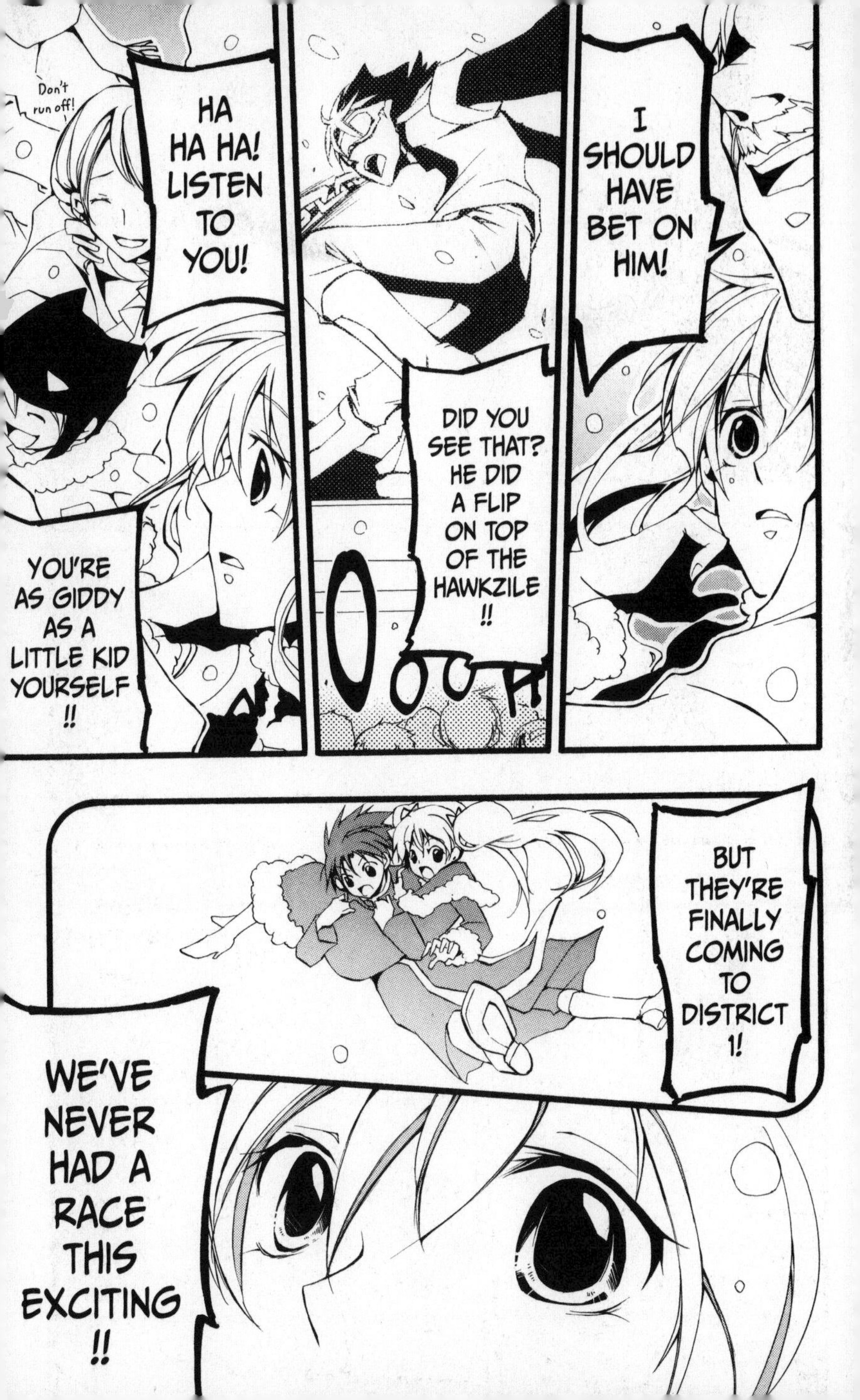
I SHOULD HAVE BET ON HIM!
DID YOU SEE THAT? HE DID A FLIP ON TOP OF THE HAWKZILE!!
OOOH!
HA HA HA! LISTEN TO YOU!
Don't run off!
YOU'RE AS GIDDY AS A LITTLE KID YOURSELF!!
BUT THEY'RE FINALLY COMING TO DISTRICT 1!
WE'VE NEVER HAD A RACE THIS EXCITING!!

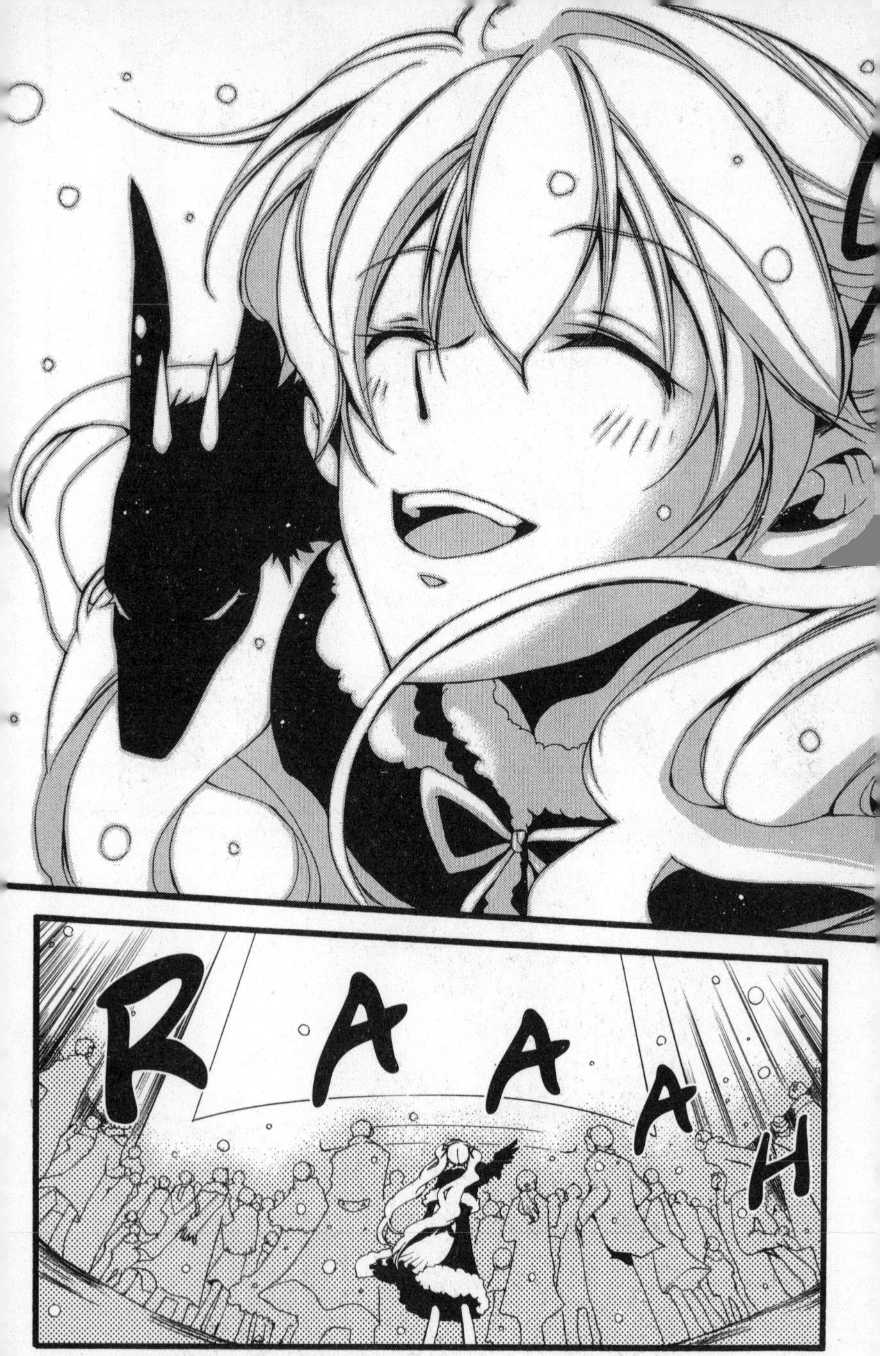
RAAAH

Kapitel. 65 "Tiashe: Part 1"

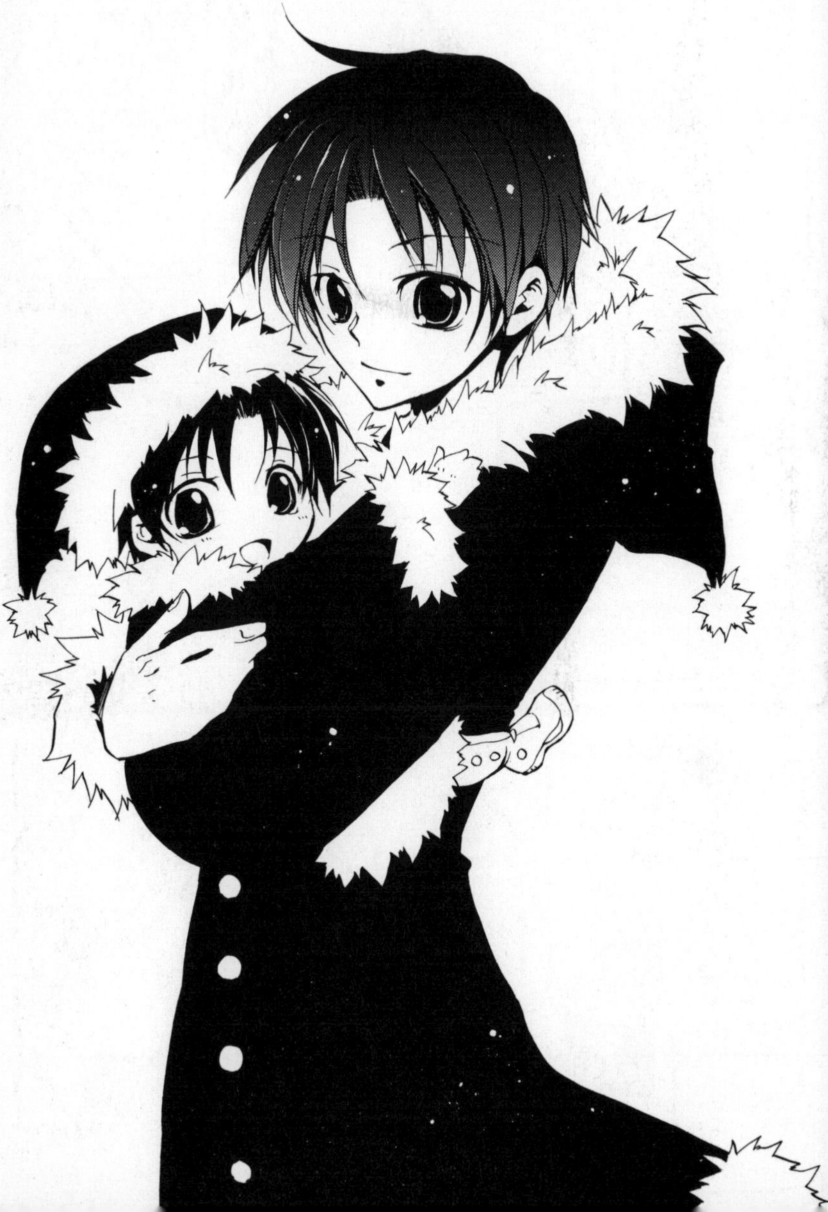

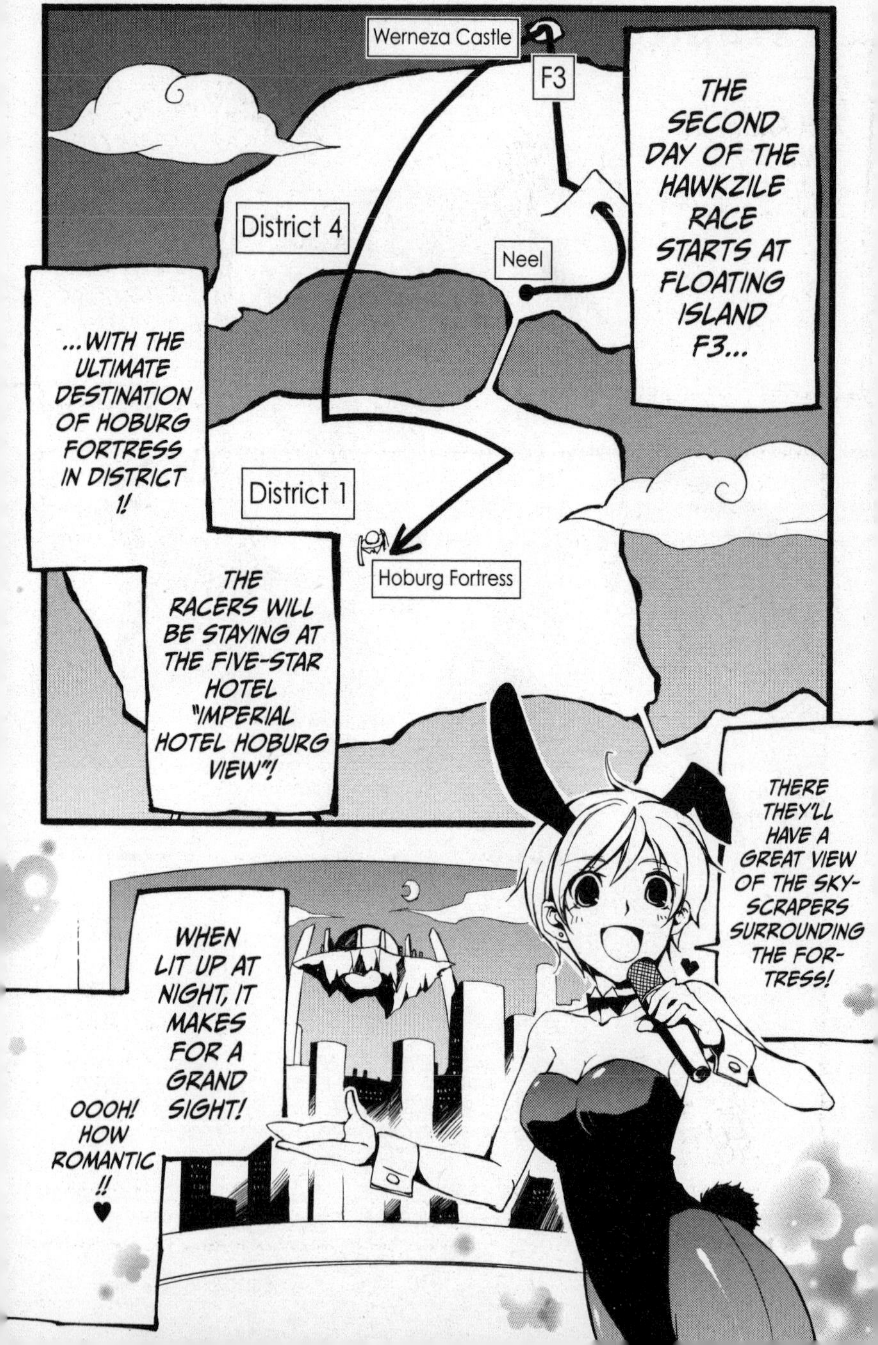
THE SECOND DAY OF THE HAWKZILE RACE STARTS AT FLOATING ISLAND F3...
Werneza Castle
F3
Neel
District 4
District 1
Hoburg Fortress
...WITH THE ULTIMATE DESTINATION OF HOBURG FORTRESS IN DISTRICT 1!
THE RACERS WILL BE STAYING AT THE FIVE-STAR HOTEL "IMPERIAL HOTEL HOBURG VIEW"!
THERE THEY'LL HAVE A GREAT VIEW OF THE SKY-SCRAPERS SURROUNDING THE FOR-TRESS! ♥
WHEN LIT UP AT NIGHT, IT MAKES FOR A GRAND SIGHT!
OOOH! HOW ROMANTIC!! ♥

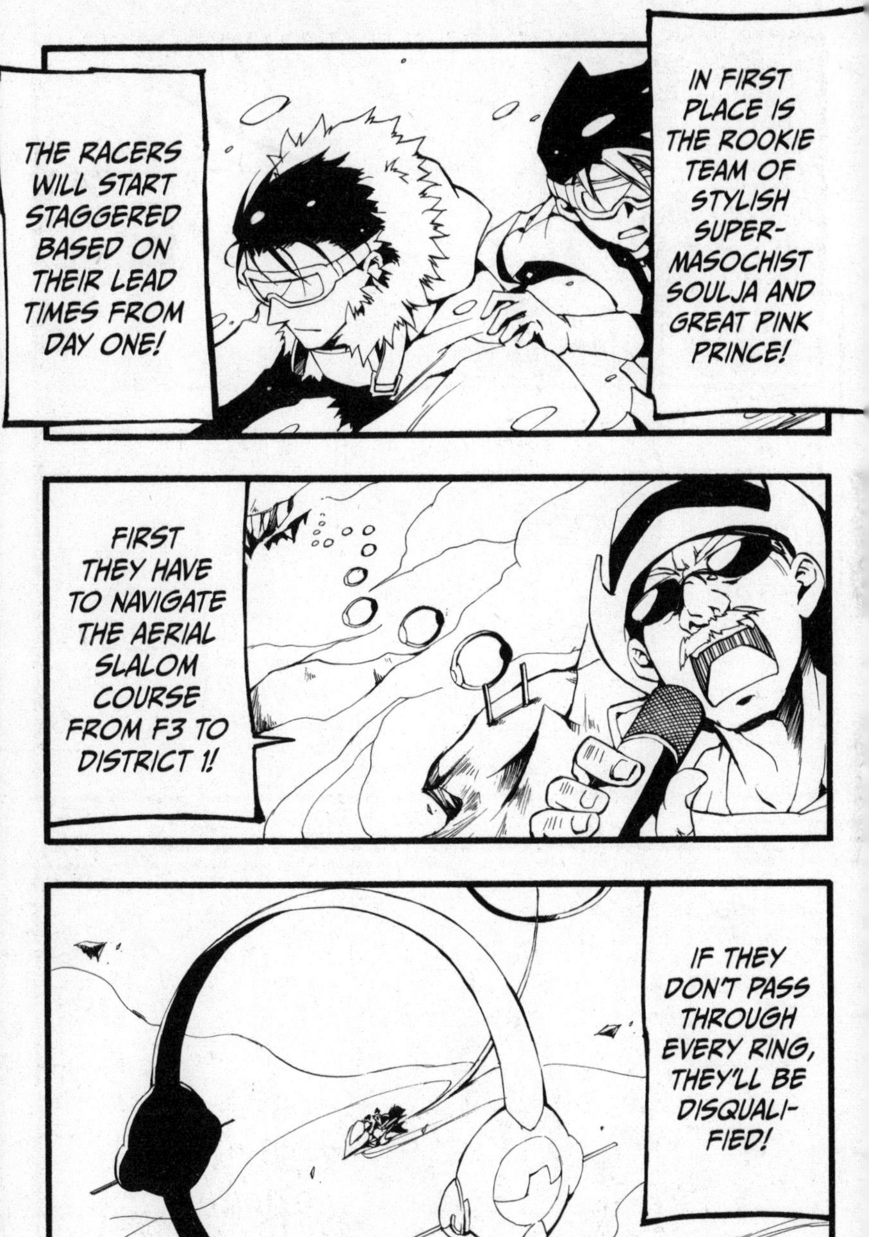
IN FIRST PLACE IS THE ROOKIE TEAM OF STYLISH SUPER-MASOCHIST SOULJA AND GREAT PINK PRINCE!
THE RACERS WILL START STAGGERED BASED ON THEIR LEAD TIMES FROM DAY ONE!
FIRST THEY HAVE TO NAVIGATE THE AERIAL SLALOM COURSE FROM F3 TO DISTRICT 1!
IF THEY DON'T PASS THROUGH EVERY RING, THEY'LL BE DISQUALIFIED!

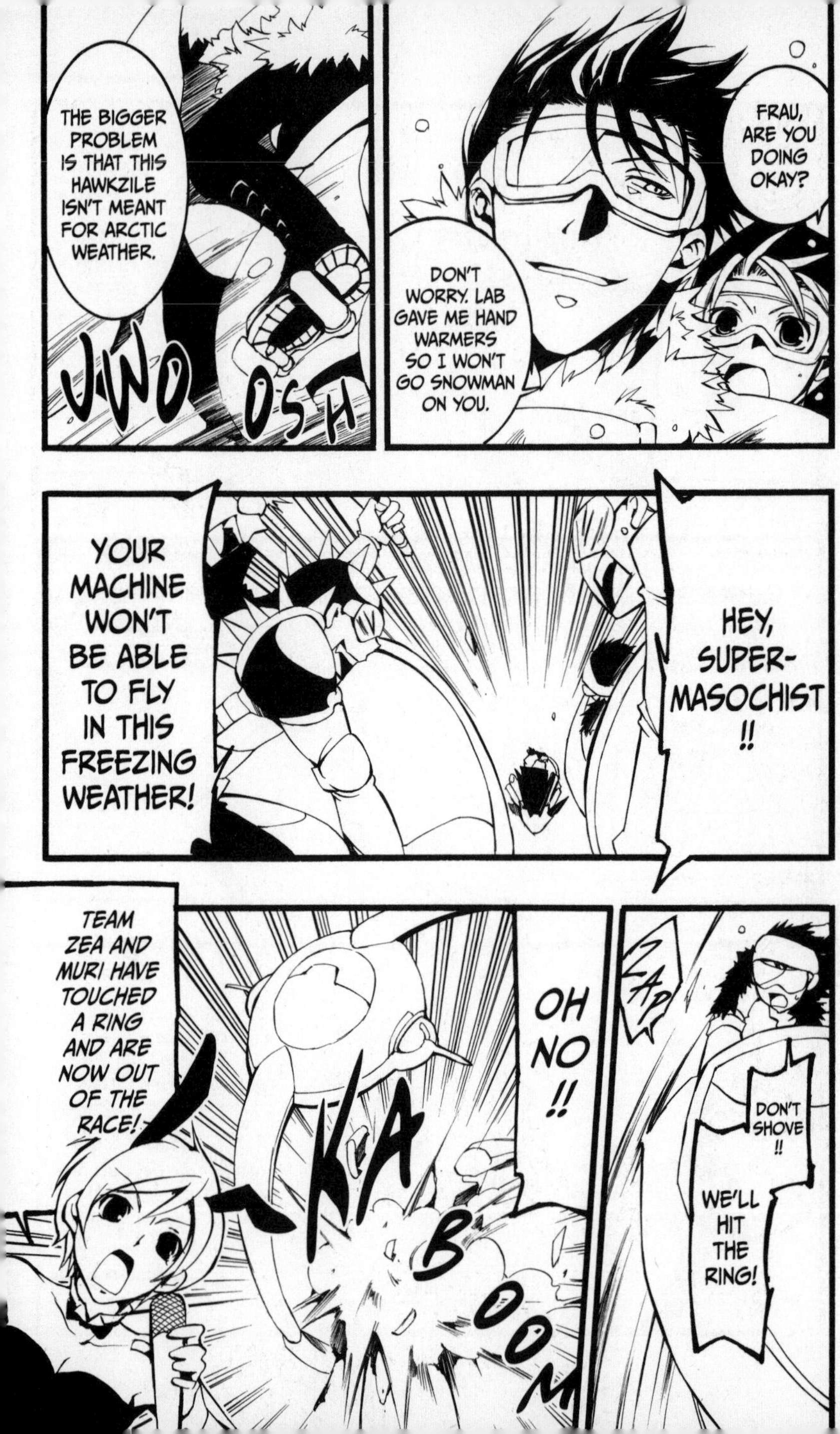
FRAU, ARE YOU DOING OKAY?
DON'T WORRY. LAB GAVE ME HAND WARMERS SO I WON'T GO SNOWMAN ON YOU.
THE BIGGER PROBLEM IS THAT THIS HAWKZILE ISN'T MEANT FOR ARCTIC WEATHER.
VWOOSH
HEY, SUPER-MASOCHIST!!
YOUR MACHINE WON'T BE ABLE TO FLY IN THIS FREEZING WEATHER!
ZAP
DON'T SHOVE!!
WE'LL HIT THE RING!
OH NO!!
TEAM ZEA AND MURI HAVE TOUCHED A RING AND ARE NOW OUT OF THE RACE!
KABOOOOM

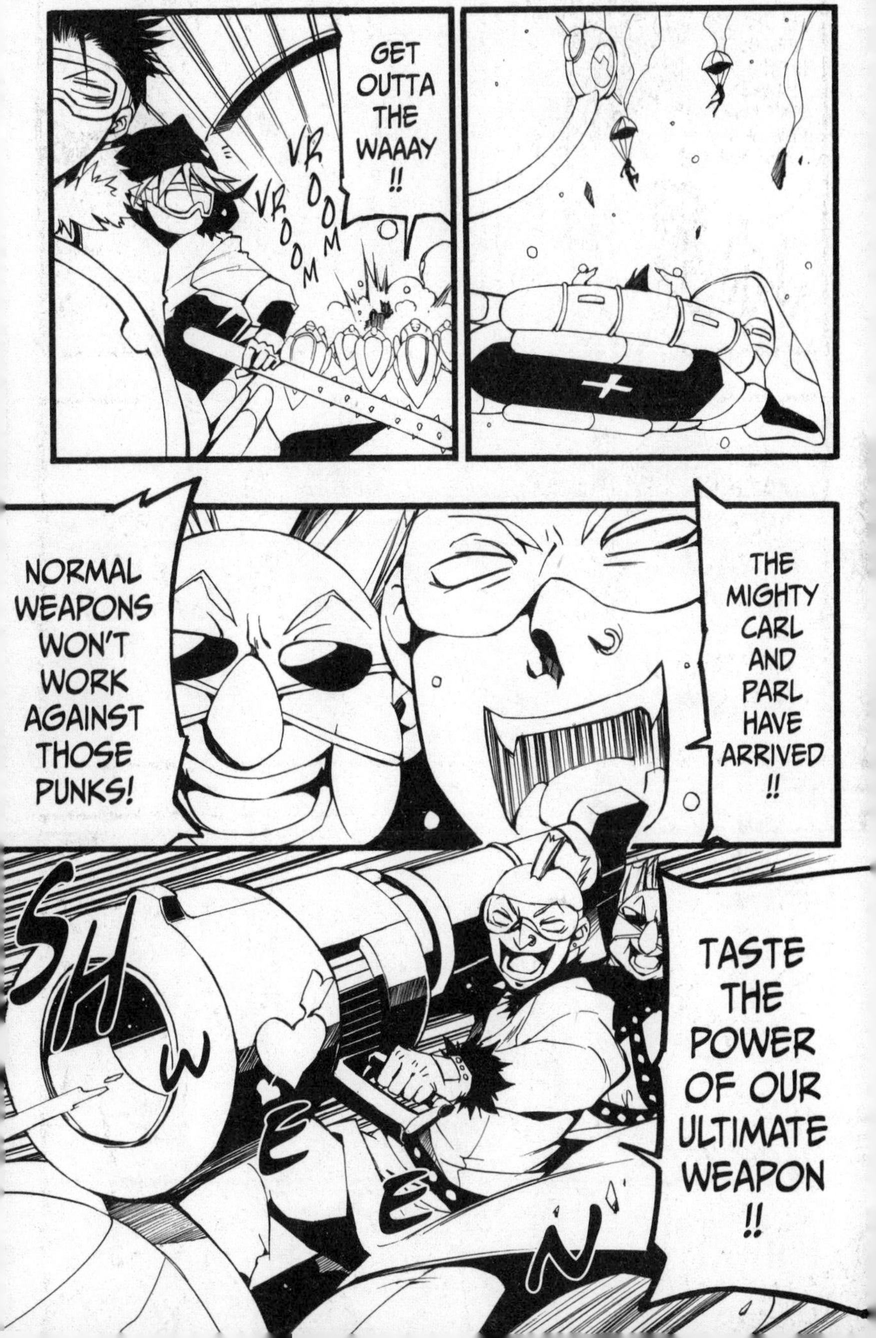
GET OUTTA THE WAAAY!!
VROOOM
VROOOM
THE MIGHTY CARL AND PARL HAVE ARRIVED!!
NORMAL WEAPONS WON'T WORK AGAINST THOSE PUNKS!
TASTE THE POWER OF OUR ULTIMATE WEAPON!!
SHWEEN

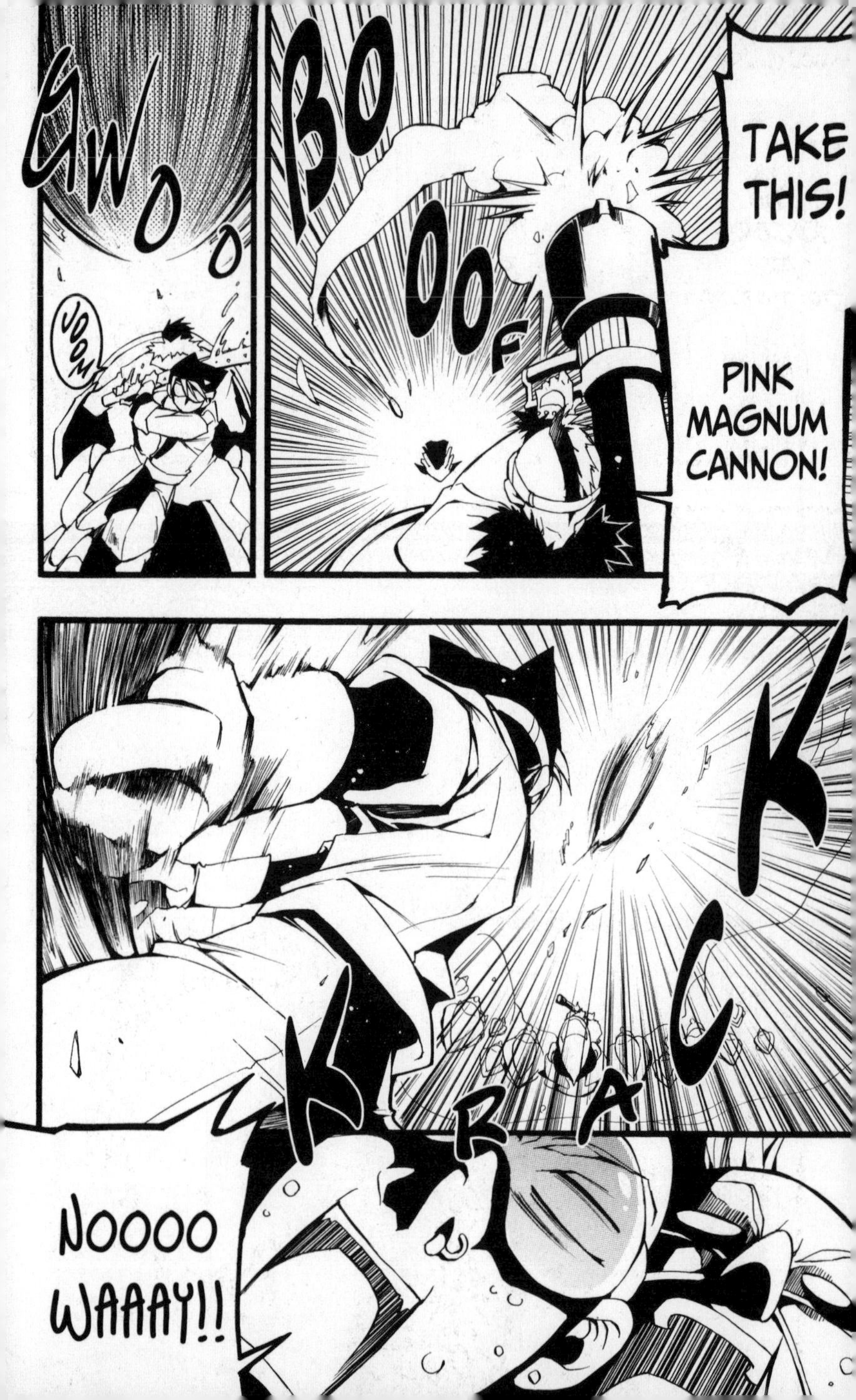
TAKE THIS!
PINK MAGNUM CANNON!
BOOOOF
GWOOO
VOOM
KRACK
NOOOO WAAAY!!

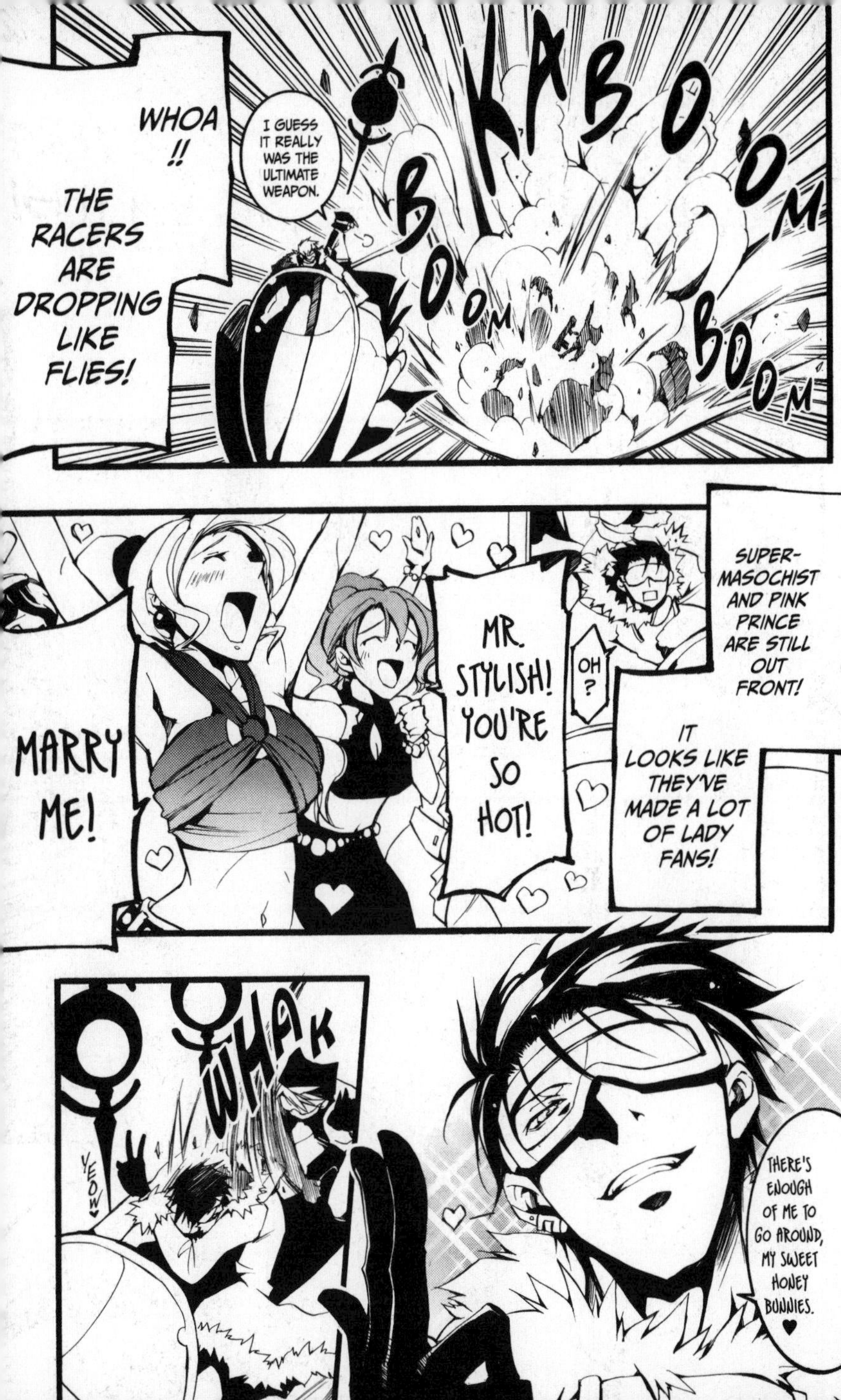
KABOOM
BOOM
BOOM
BOOM
I GUESS IT REALLY WAS THE ULTIMATE WEAPON.
WHOA!!
THE RACERS ARE DROPPING LIKE FLIES!
SUPER-MASOCHIST AND PINK PRINCE ARE STILL OUT FRONT!
IT LOOKS LIKE THEY'VE MADE A LOT OF LADY FANS!
OH?
MR. STYLISH! YOU'RE SO HOT!
MARRY ME!
THERE'S ENOUGH OF ME TO GO AROUND, MY SWEET HONEY BUNNIES. ♥
WHAK
YEOW♥

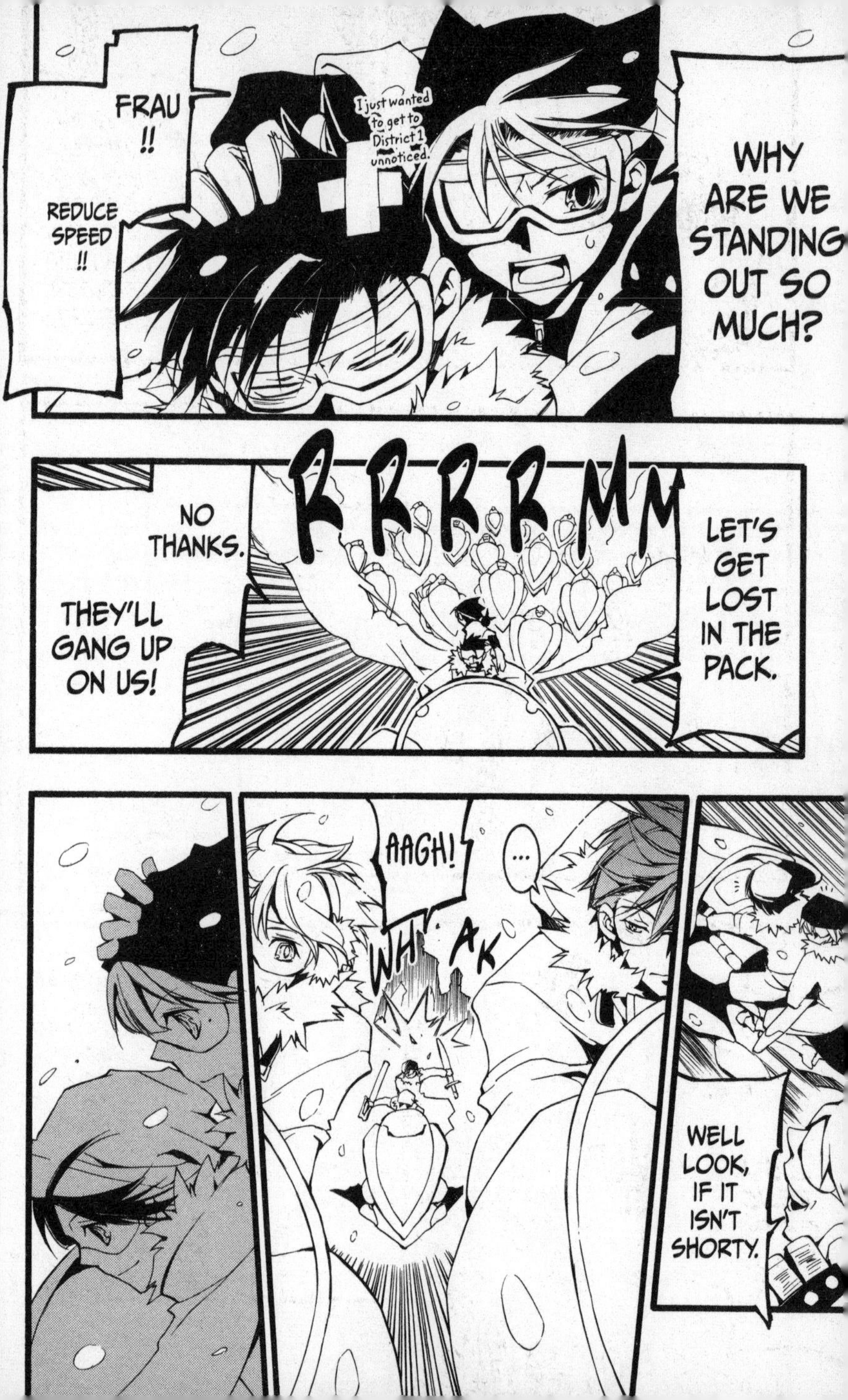
WHY ARE WE STANDING OUT SO MUCH?
I just wanted to get to District 1 unnoticed.
FRAU!!
REDUCE SPEED!!
RRRRRMM
LET'S GET LOST IN THE PACK.
NO THANKS.
THEY'LL GANG UP ON US!
WELL LOOK, IF IT ISN'T SHORTY.
...
AAGH!
WHAK

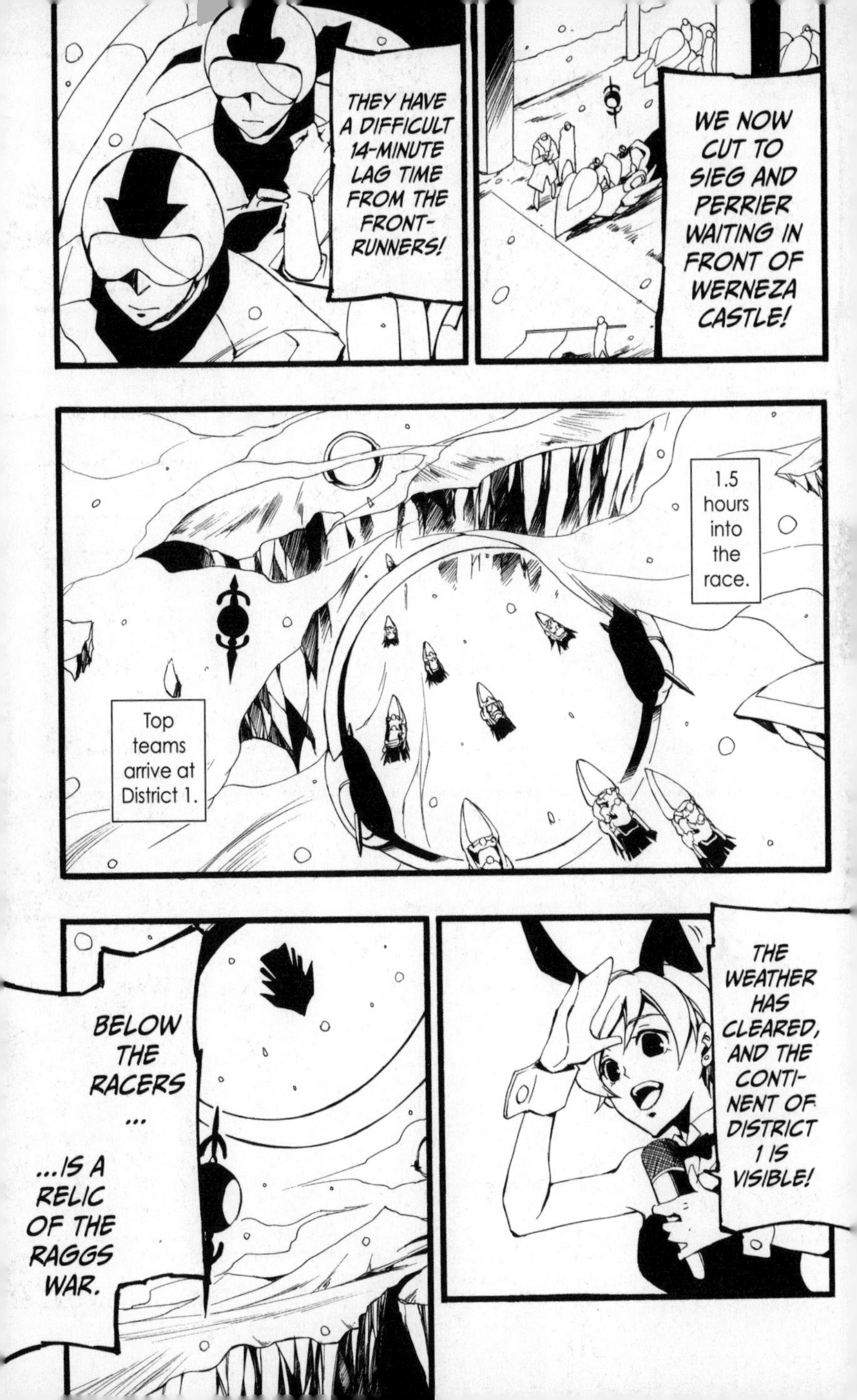
WE NOW CUT TO SIEG AND PERRIER WAITING IN FRONT OF WERNEZA CASTLE!
THEY HAVE A DIFFICULT 14-MINUTE LAG TIME FROM THE FRONT-RUNNERS!
1.5 hours into the race.
Top teams arrive at District 1.
THE WEATHER HAS CLEARED, AND THE CONTI-NENT OF DISTRICT 1 IS VISIBLE!
BELOW THE RACERS ...
...IS A RELIC OF THE RAGGS WAR.

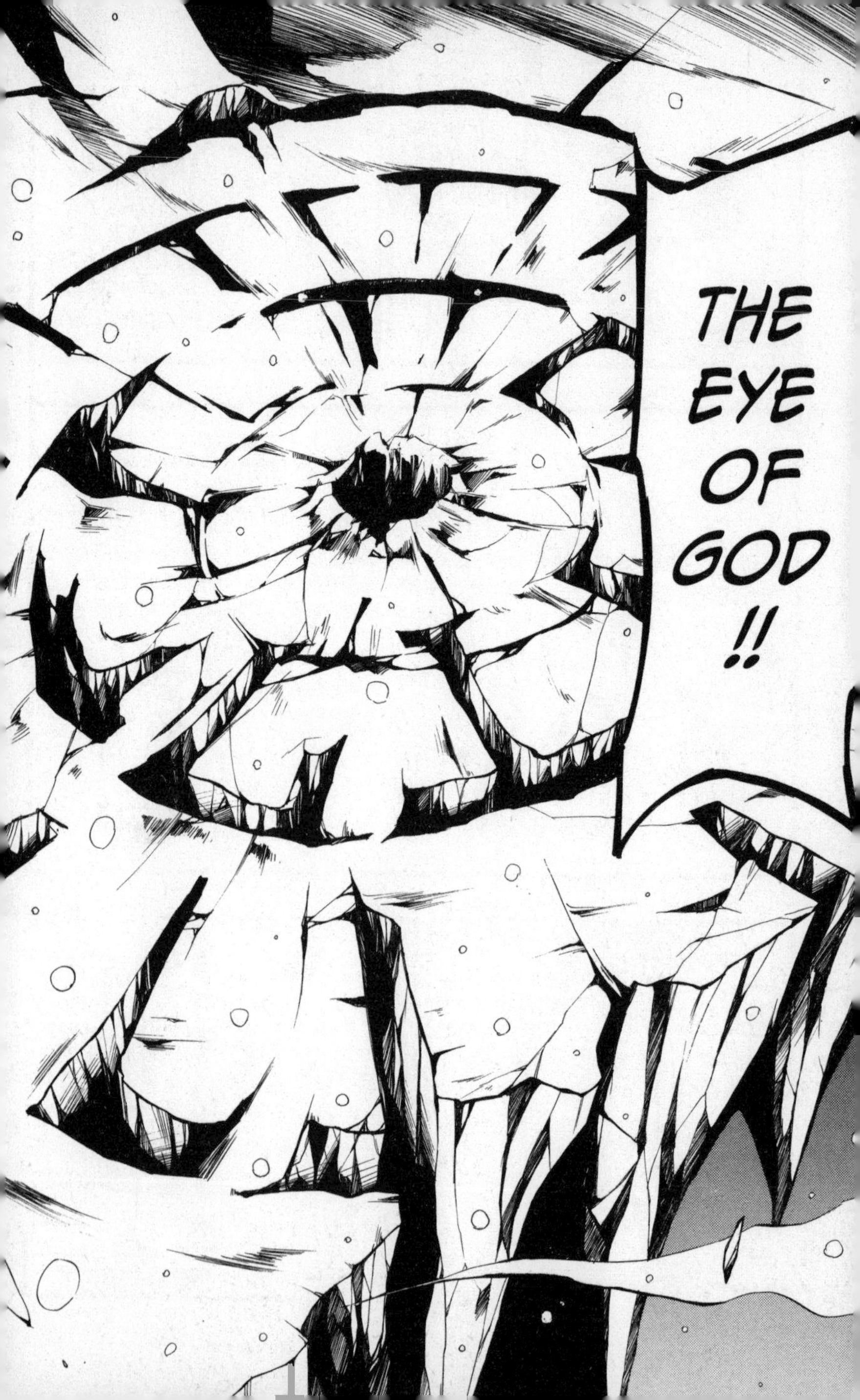
THE EYE OF GOD !!

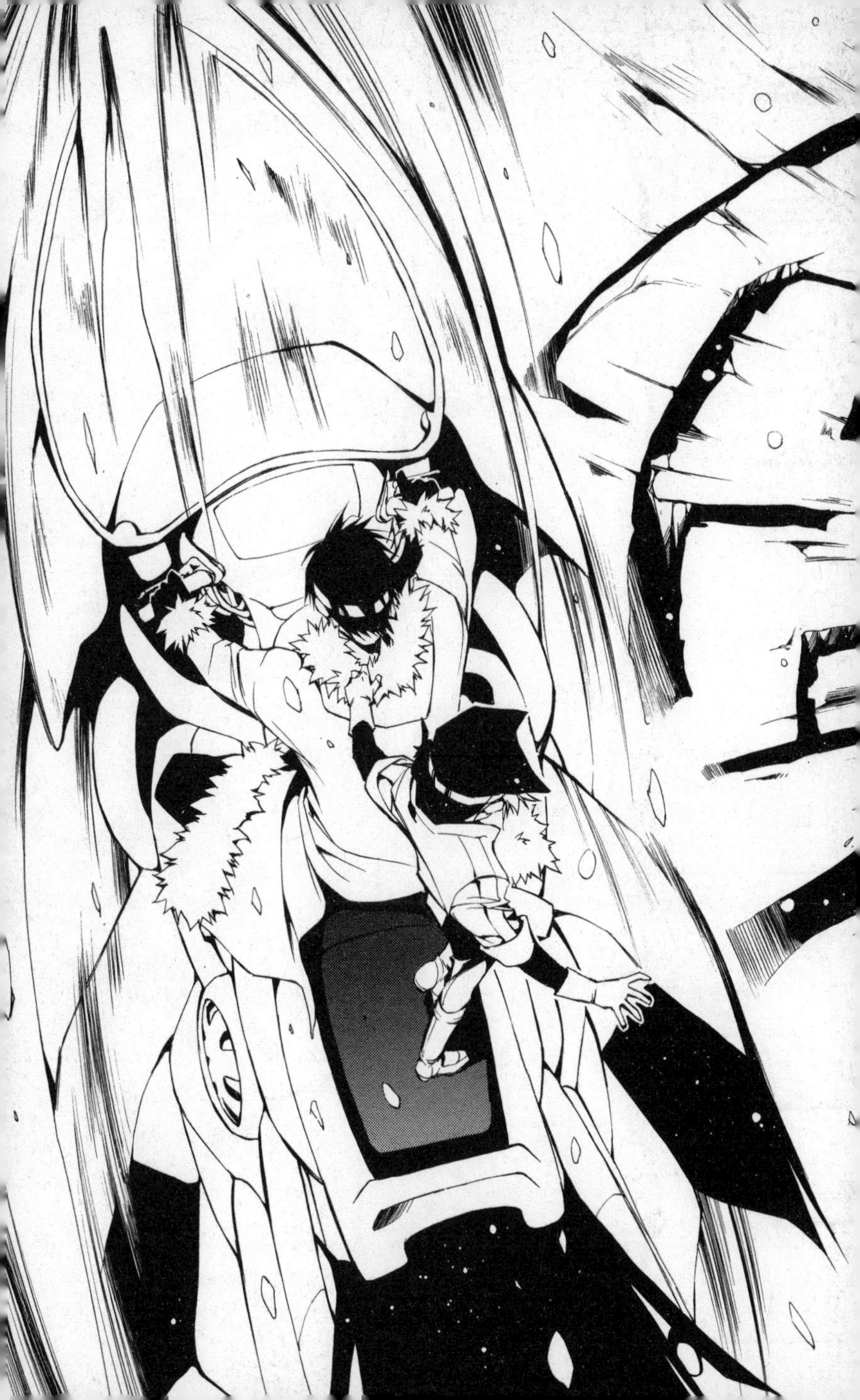

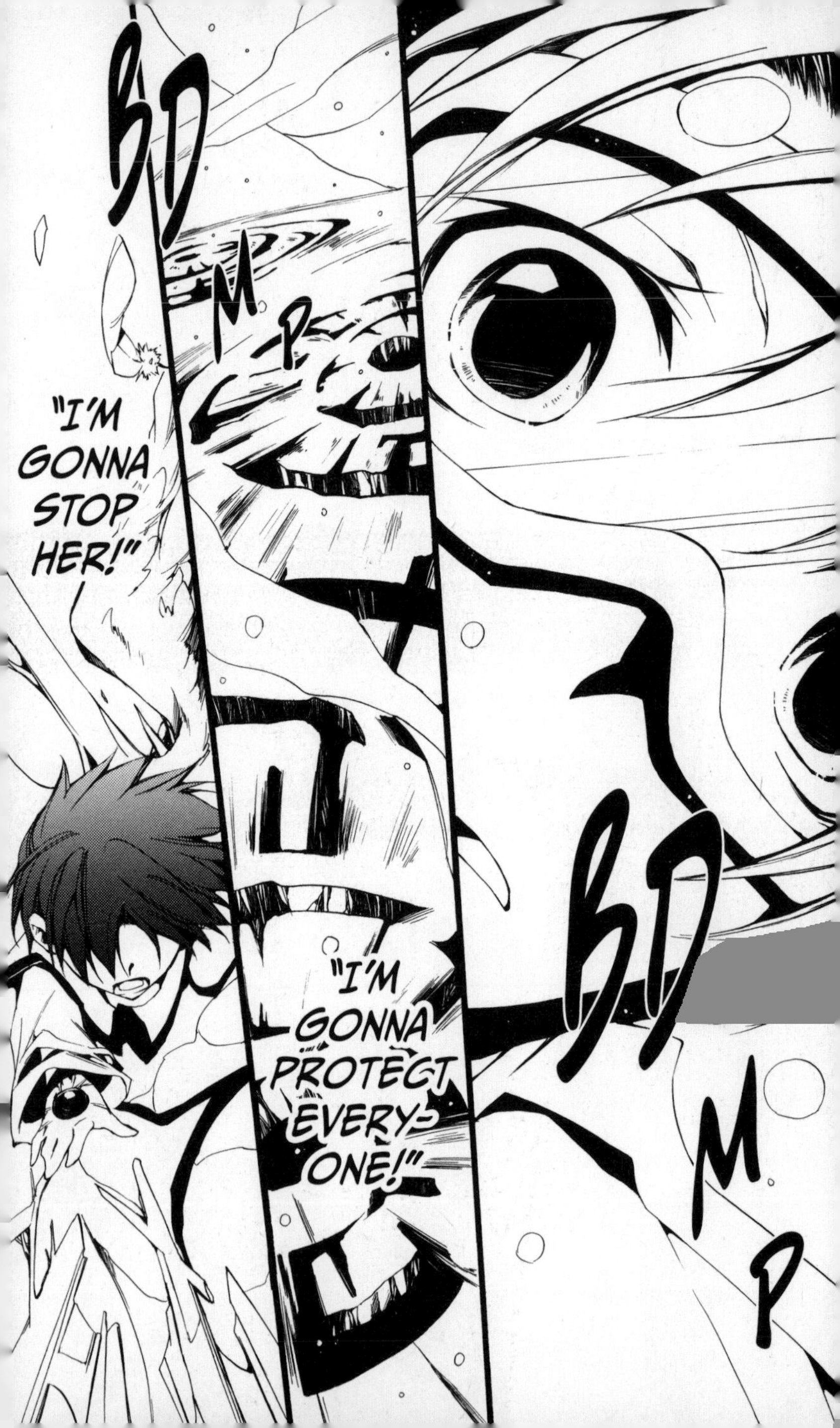
BDMP
"I'M GONNA PROTECT EVERY-ONE!"
BDMP
"I'M GONNA STOP HER!"

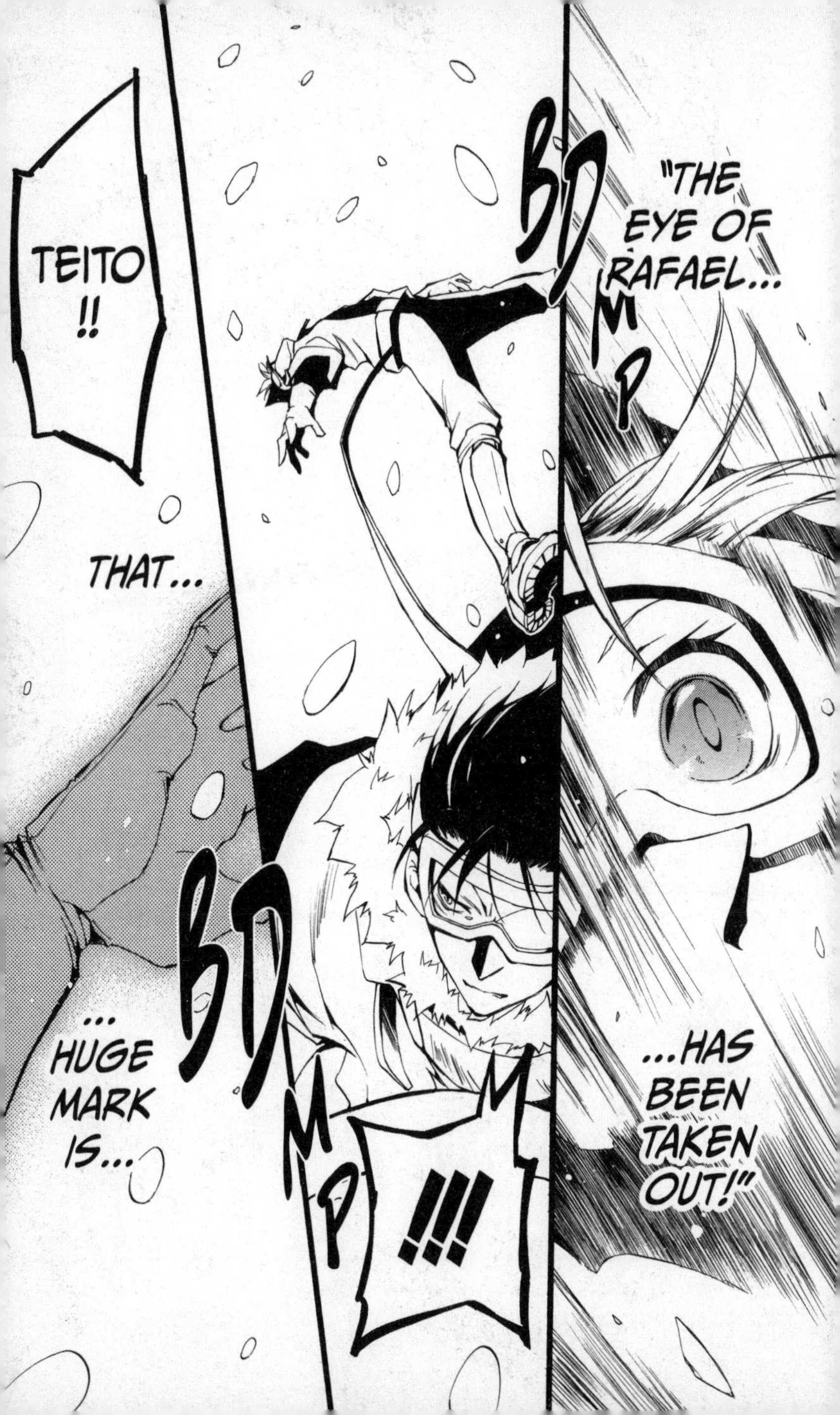
"THE EYE OF RAFAEL...
BDMP
...HAS BEEN TAKEN OUT!"
BDMP!!!
TEITO !!
THAT...
...HUGE MARK IS...

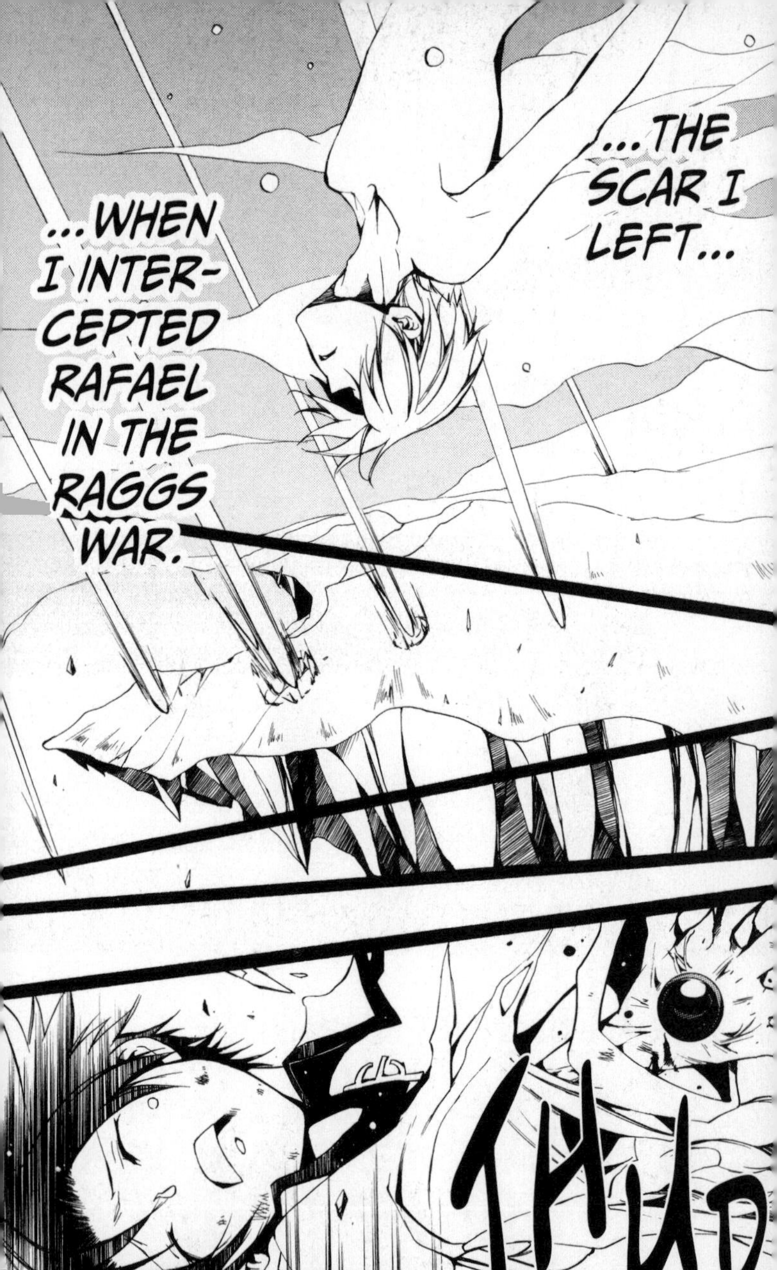
...THE SCAR I LEFT...
...WHEN I INTER-CEPTED RAFAEL IN THE RAGGS WAR.
THUD

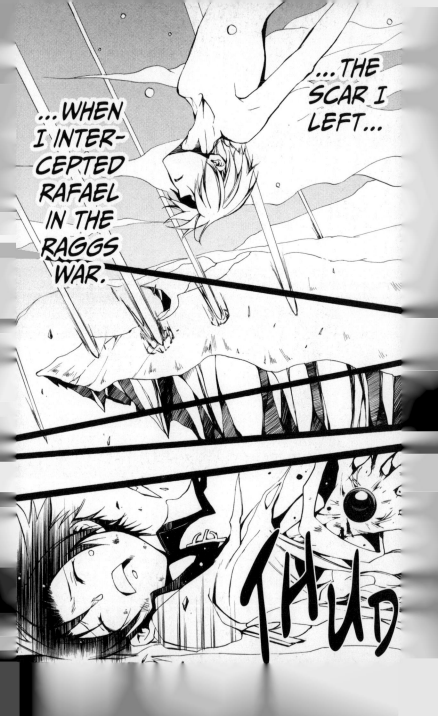

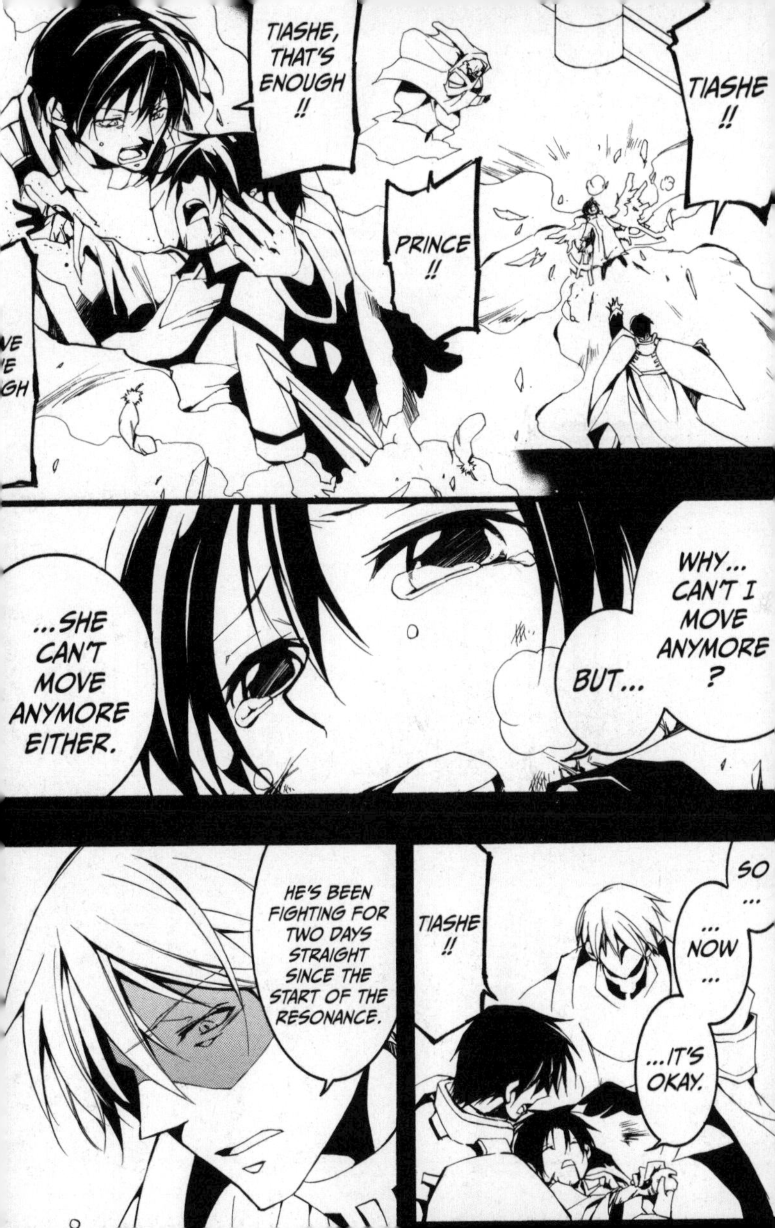
TIASHE !!
PRINCE !!
TIASHE, THAT'S ENOUGH !!
WHY... CAN'T I MOVE ANYMORE ?
BUT...
...SHE CAN'T MOVE ANYMORE EITHER.
SO ... ... NOW ...
...IT'S OKAY.
TIASHE !!
HE'S BEEN FIGHTING FOR TWO DAYS STRAIGHT SINCE THE START OF THE RESONANCE.

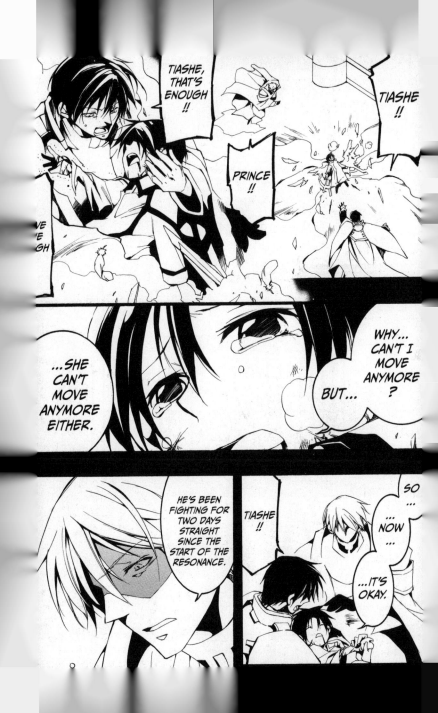

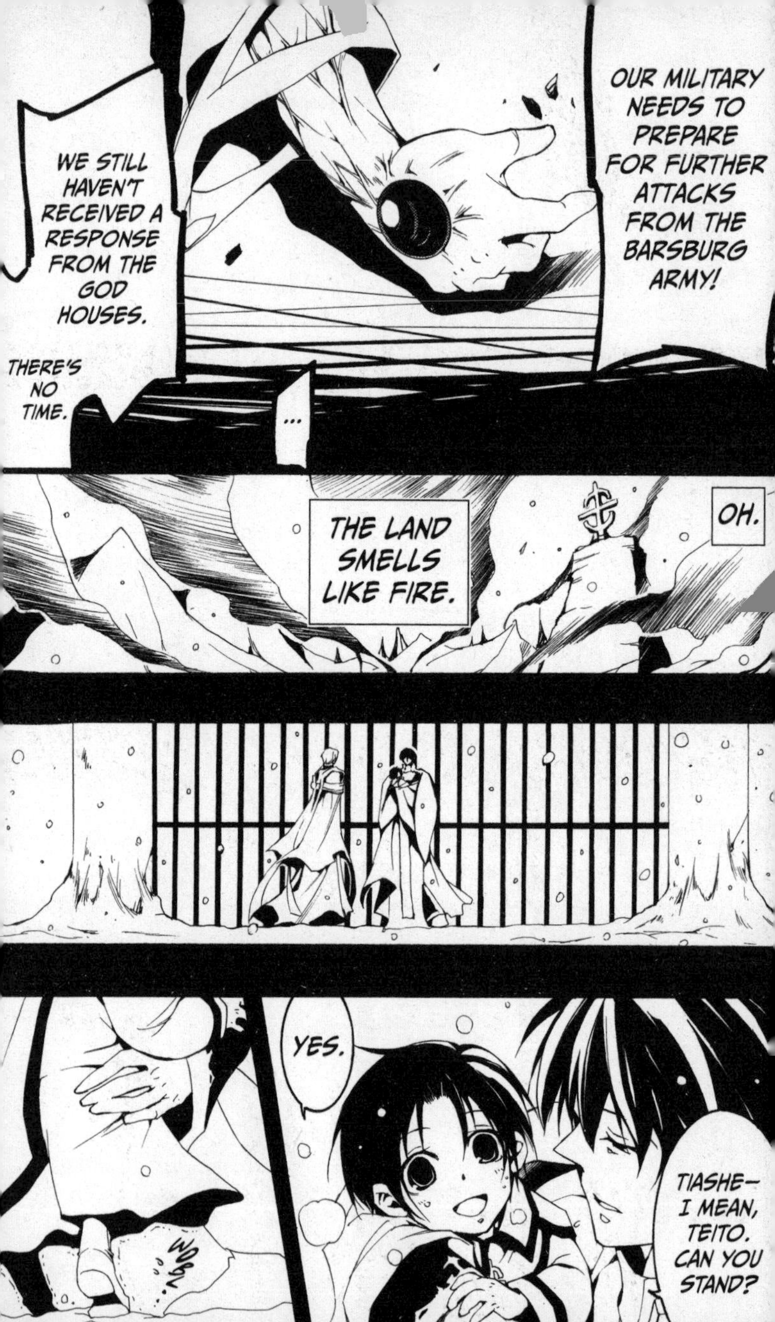
OUR MILITARY NEEDS TO PREPARE FOR FURTHER ATTACKS FROM THE BARSBURG ARMY!
WE STILL HAVEN'T RECEIVED A RESPONSE FROM THE GOD HOUSES.
THERE'S NO TIME.
...
OH.
THE LAND SMELLS LIKE FIRE.
TIASHE— I MEAN, TEITO. CAN YOU STAND?
YES.
WOBL...

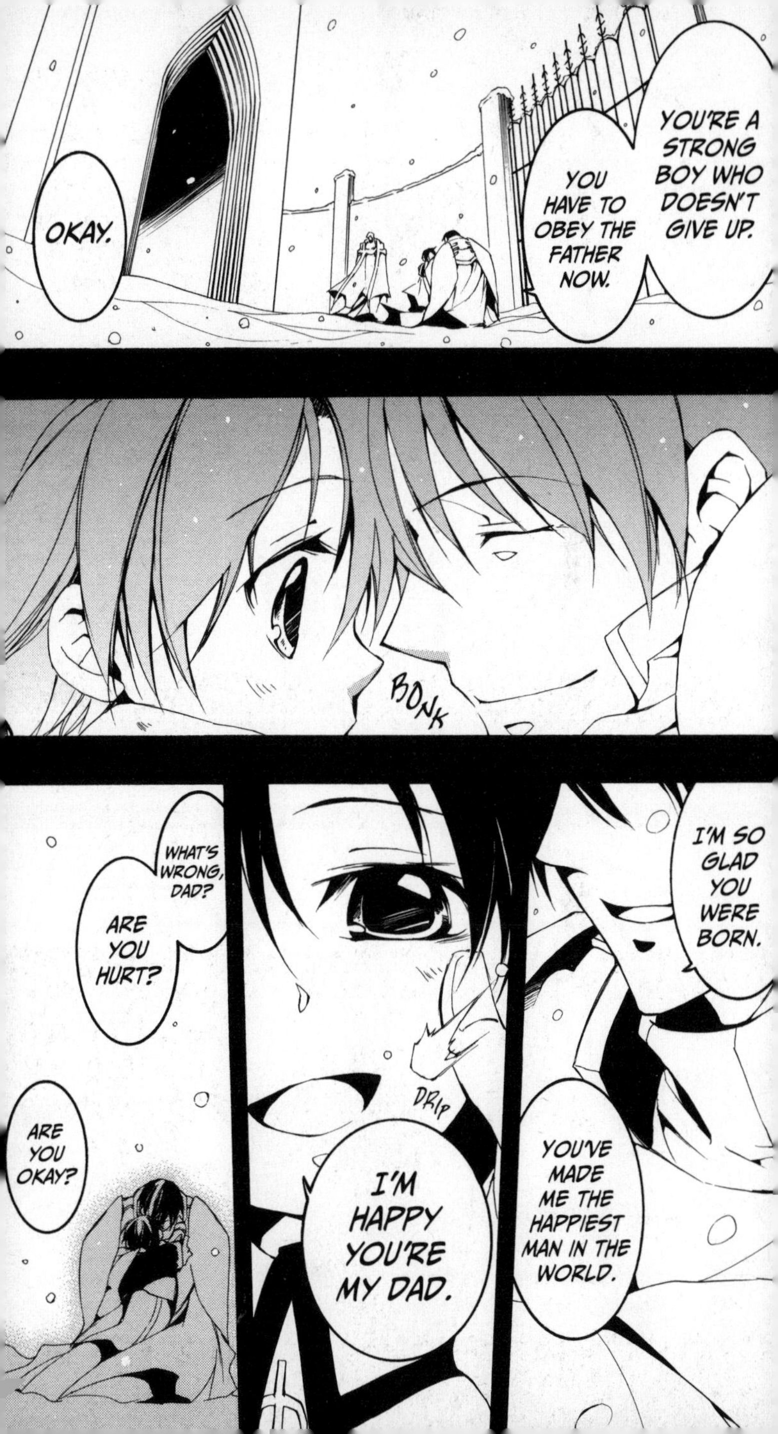
YOU'RE A STRONG BOY WHO DOESN'T GIVE UP.
YOU HAVE TO OBEY THE FATHER NOW.
OKAY.
BONK
I'M SO GLAD YOU WERE BORN.
YOU'VE MADE ME THE HAPPIEST MAN IN THE WORLD.
DRIP
I'M HAPPY YOU'RE MY DAD.
WHAT'S WRONG, DAD?
ARE YOU HURT?
ARE YOU OKAY?

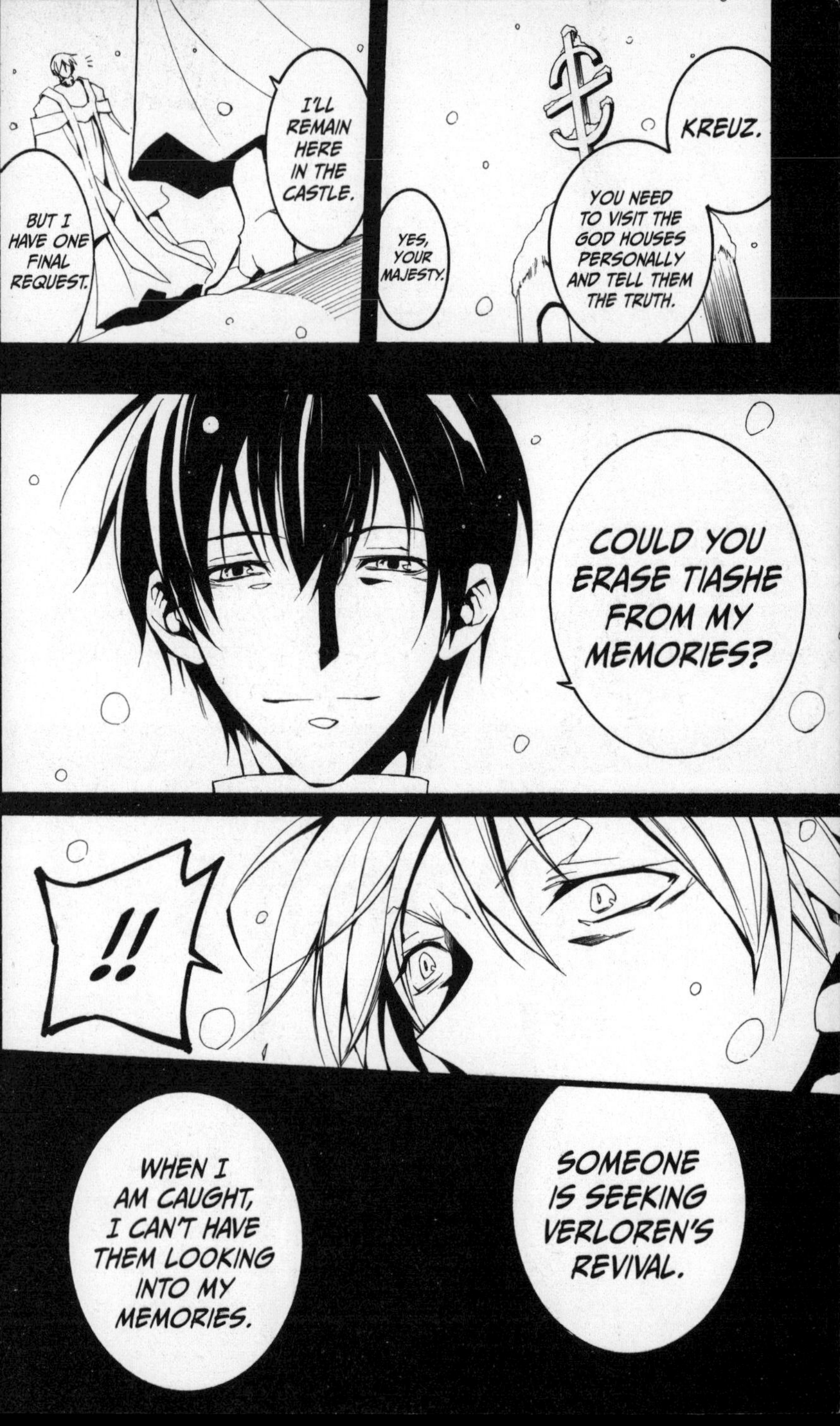
KREUZ.
YOU NEED TO VISIT THE GOD HOUSES PERSONALLY AND TELL THEM THE TRUTH.
YES, YOUR MAJESTY.
I'LL REMAIN HERE IN THE CASTLE.
BUT I HAVE ONE FINAL REQUEST.
COULD YOU ERASE TIASHE FROM MY MEMORIES?
!!
SOMEONE IS SEEKING VERLOREN'S REVIVAL.
WHEN I AM CAUGHT, I CAN'T HAVE THEM LOOKING INTO MY MEMORIES.

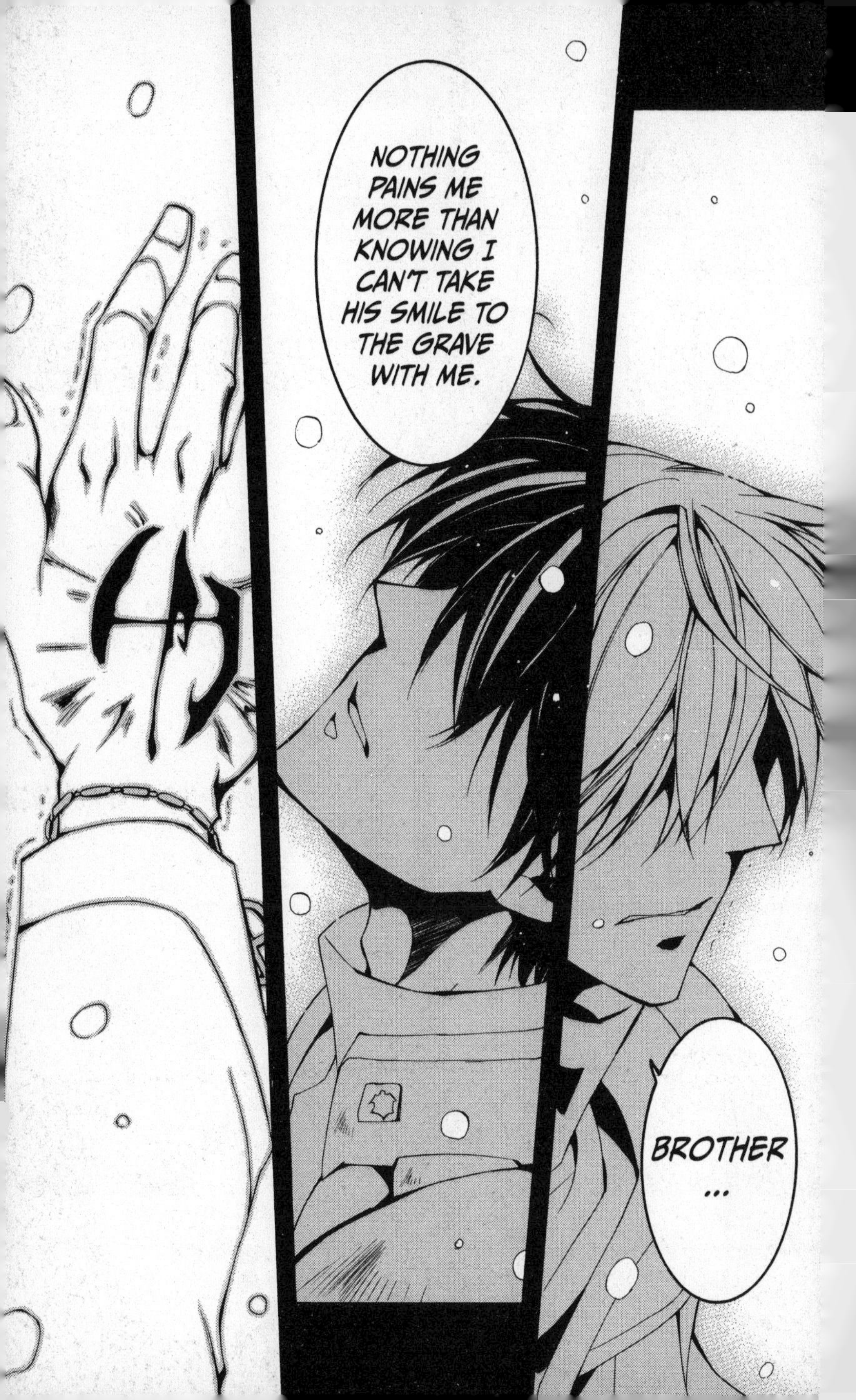
NOTHING PAINS ME MORE THAN KNOWING I CAN'T TAKE HIS SMILE TO THE GRAVE WITH ME.
BROTHER ...

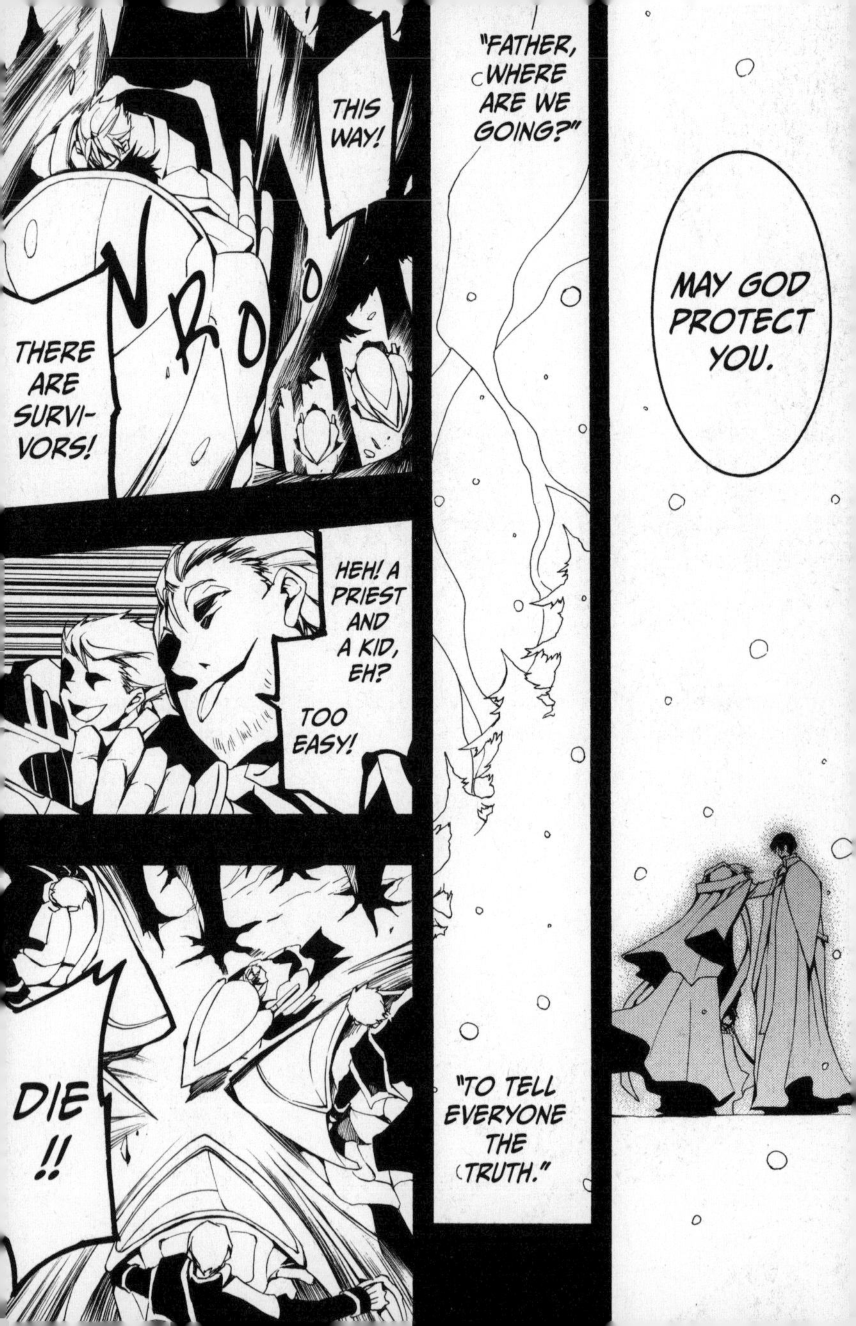
MAY GOD PROTECT YOU.
"FATHER, WHERE ARE WE GOING?"
"TO TELL EVERYONE THE TRUTH."
THIS WAY!
NROO
THERE ARE SURVIVORS!
HEH! A PRIEST AND A KID, EH?
TOO EASY!
DIE!!

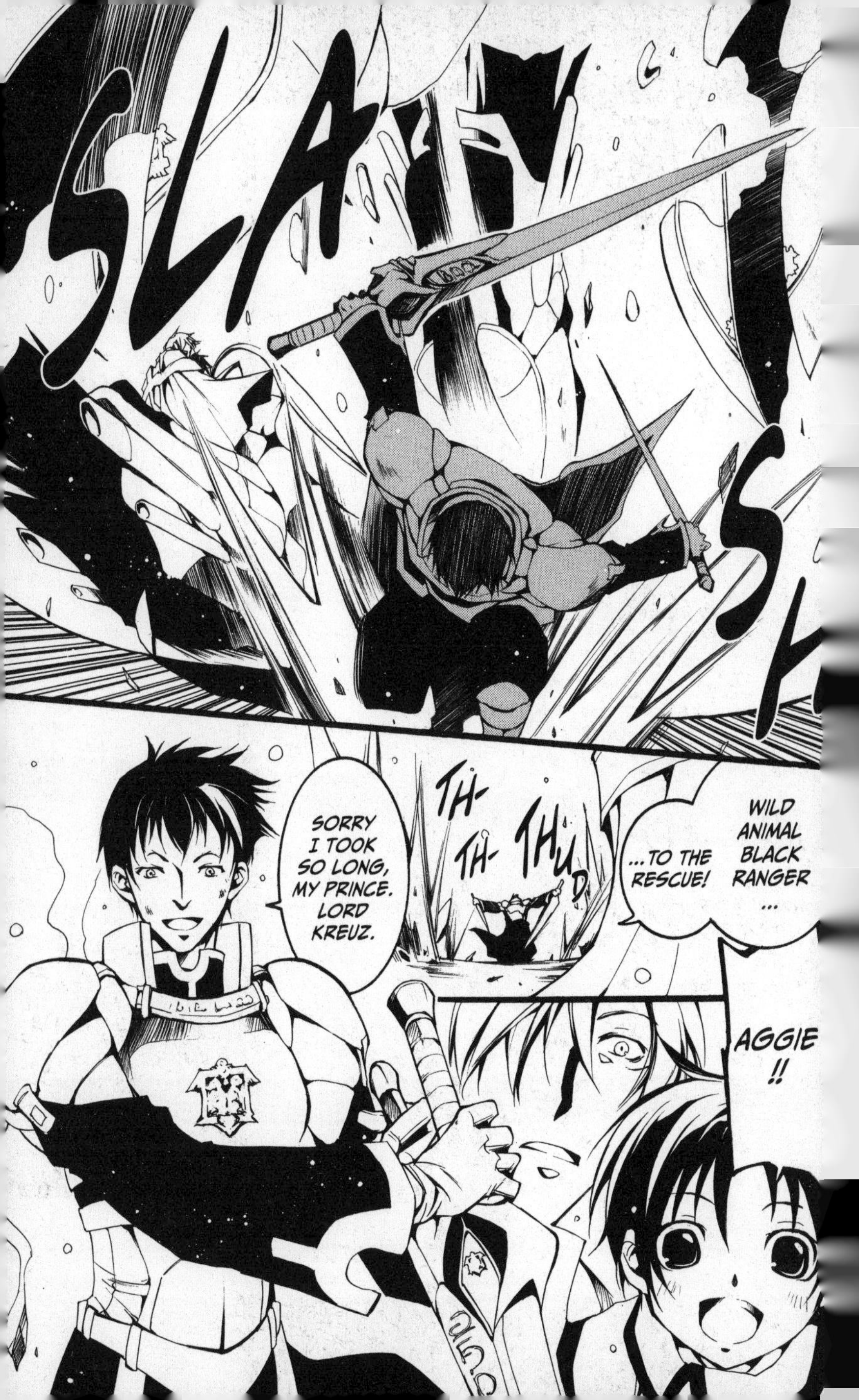
WILD ANIMAL BLACK RANGER ...
...TO THE RESCUE!
TH- TH- THUD
SORRY I TOOK SO LONG, MY PRINCE. LORD KREUZ.
AGGIE !!

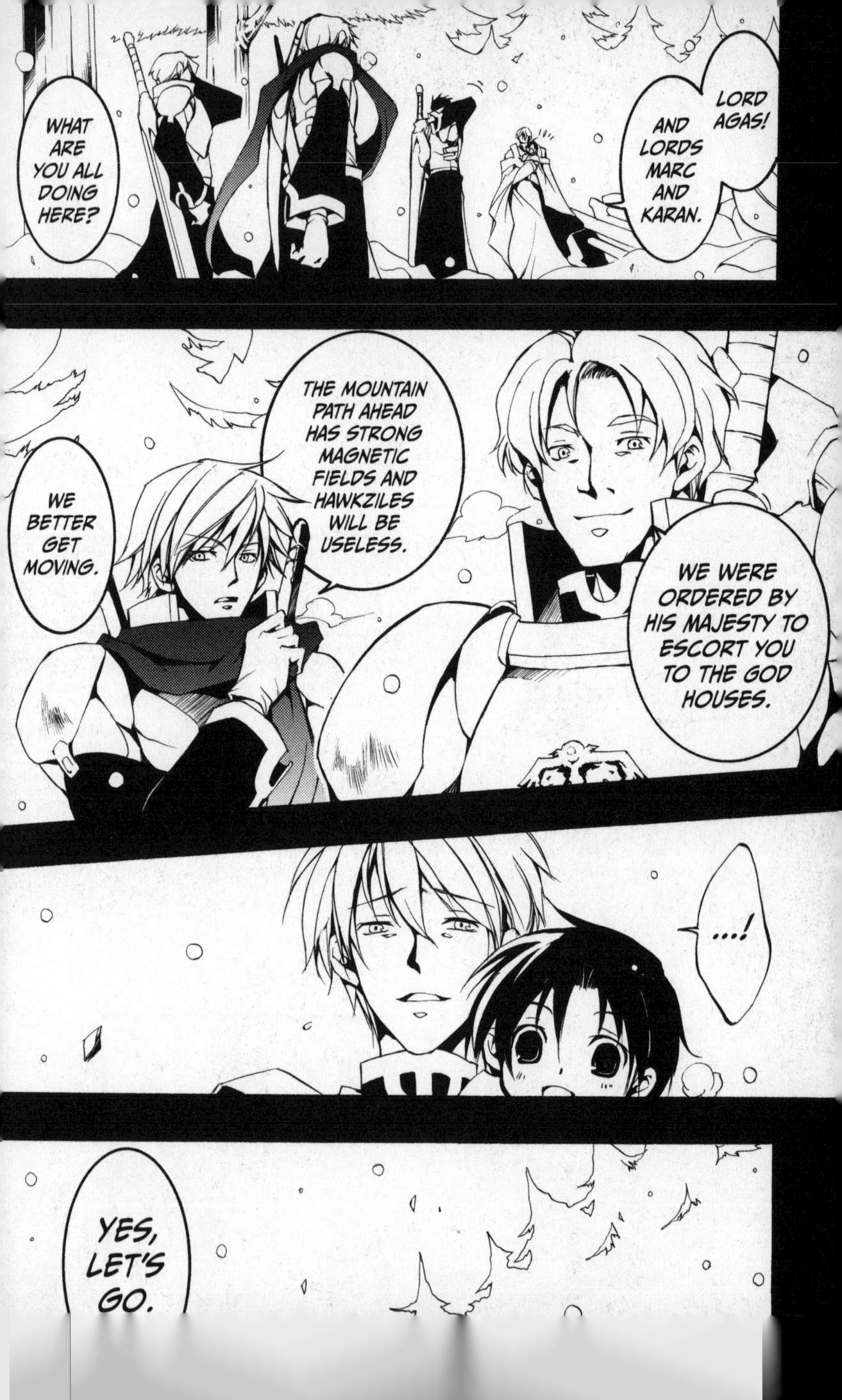
LORD AGAS!
AND LORDS MARC AND KARAN.
WHAT ARE YOU ALL DOING HERE?
WE WERE ORDERED BY HIS MAJESTY TO ESCORT YOU TO THE GOD HOUSES.
THE MOUNTAIN PATH AHEAD HAS STRONG MAGNETIC FIELDS AND HAWKZILES WILL BE USELESS.
WE BETTER GET MOVING.
...!
YES, LET'S GO.

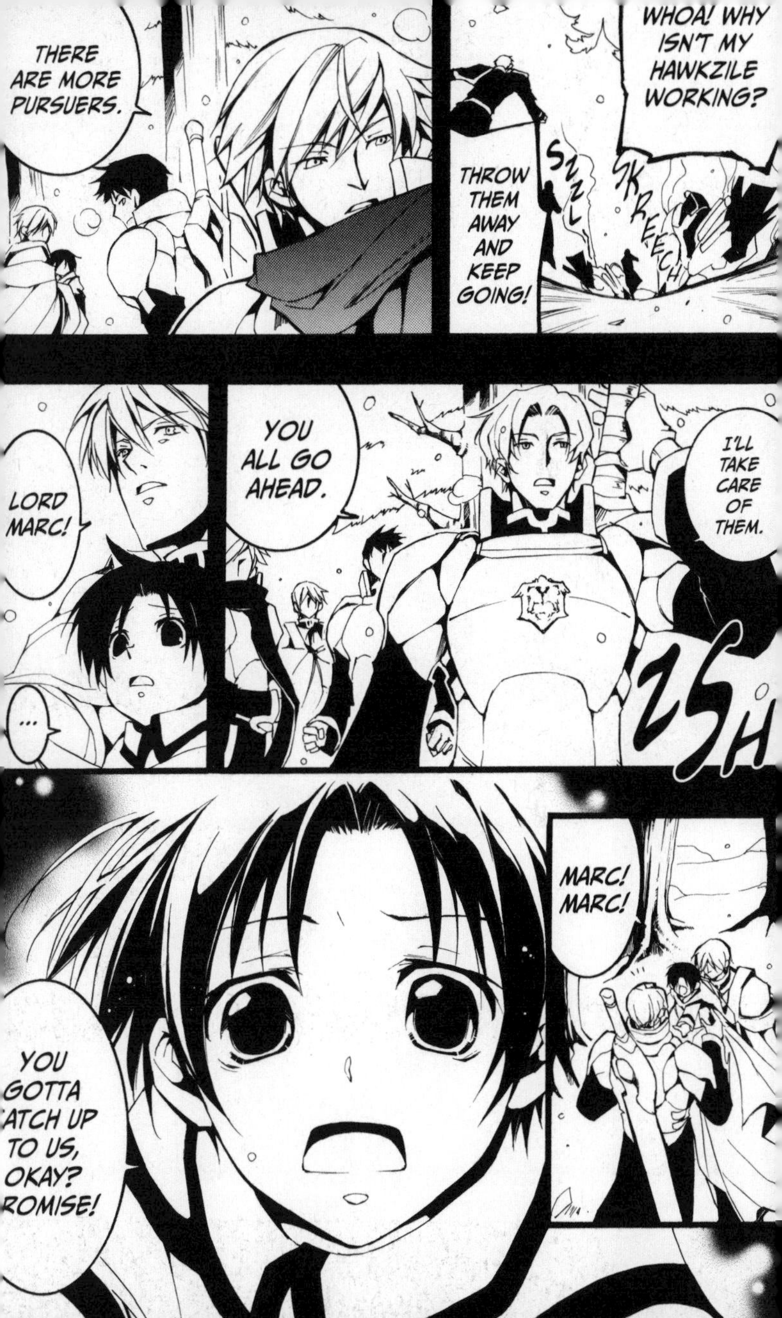
WHOA! WHY ISN'T MY HAWKZILE WORKING?
SIZZL
SKREECH
THROW THEM AWAY AND KEEP GOING!
THERE ARE MORE PURSUERS.
I'LL TAKE CARE OF THEM.
YOU ALL GO AHEAD.
ZSH
LORD MARC!
...
MARC! MARC!
YOU GOTTA ATCH UP TO US, OKAY? ROMISE!

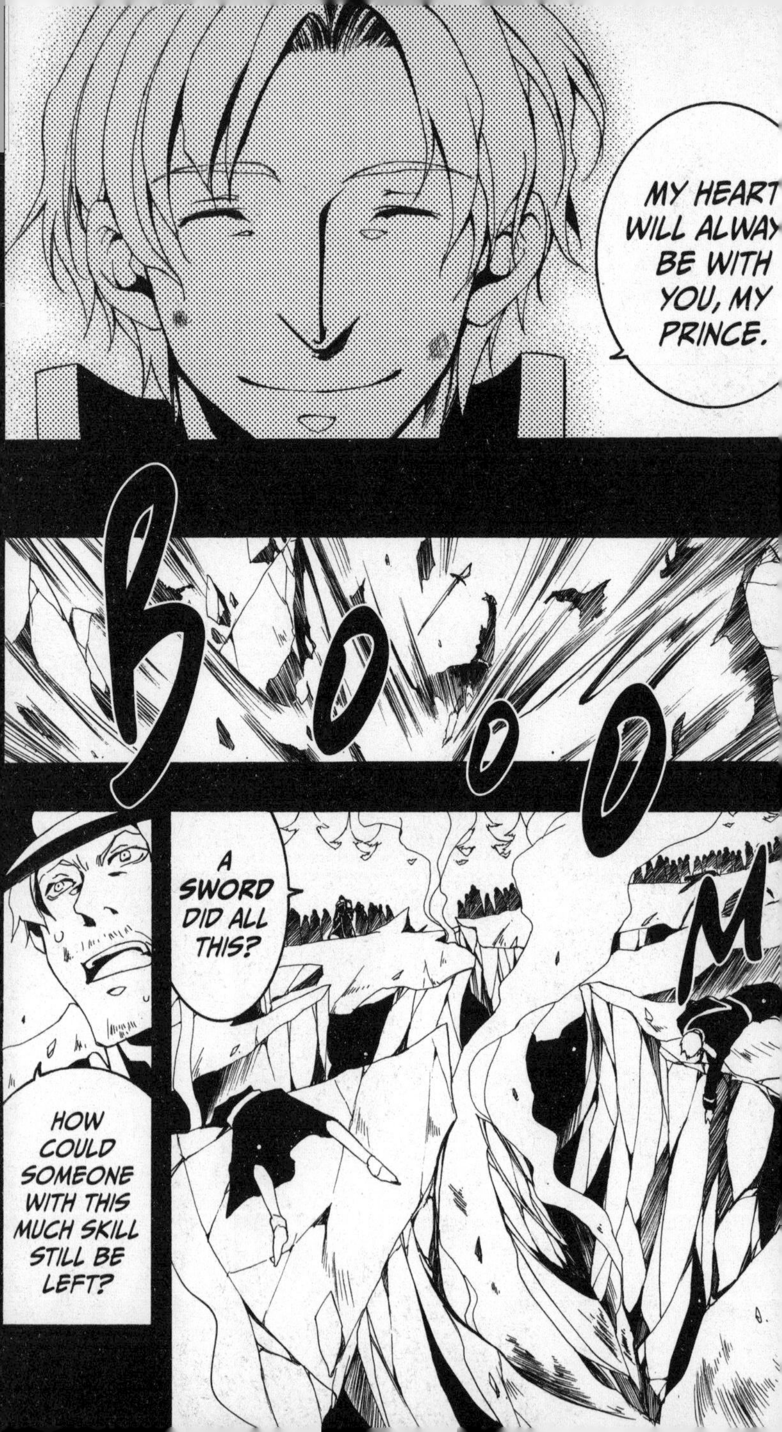
MY HEART WILL ALWAY BE WITH YOU, MY PRINCE.
BOOOM
A SWORD DID ALL THIS?
HOW COULD SOMEONE WITH THIS MUCH SKILL STILL BE LEFT?

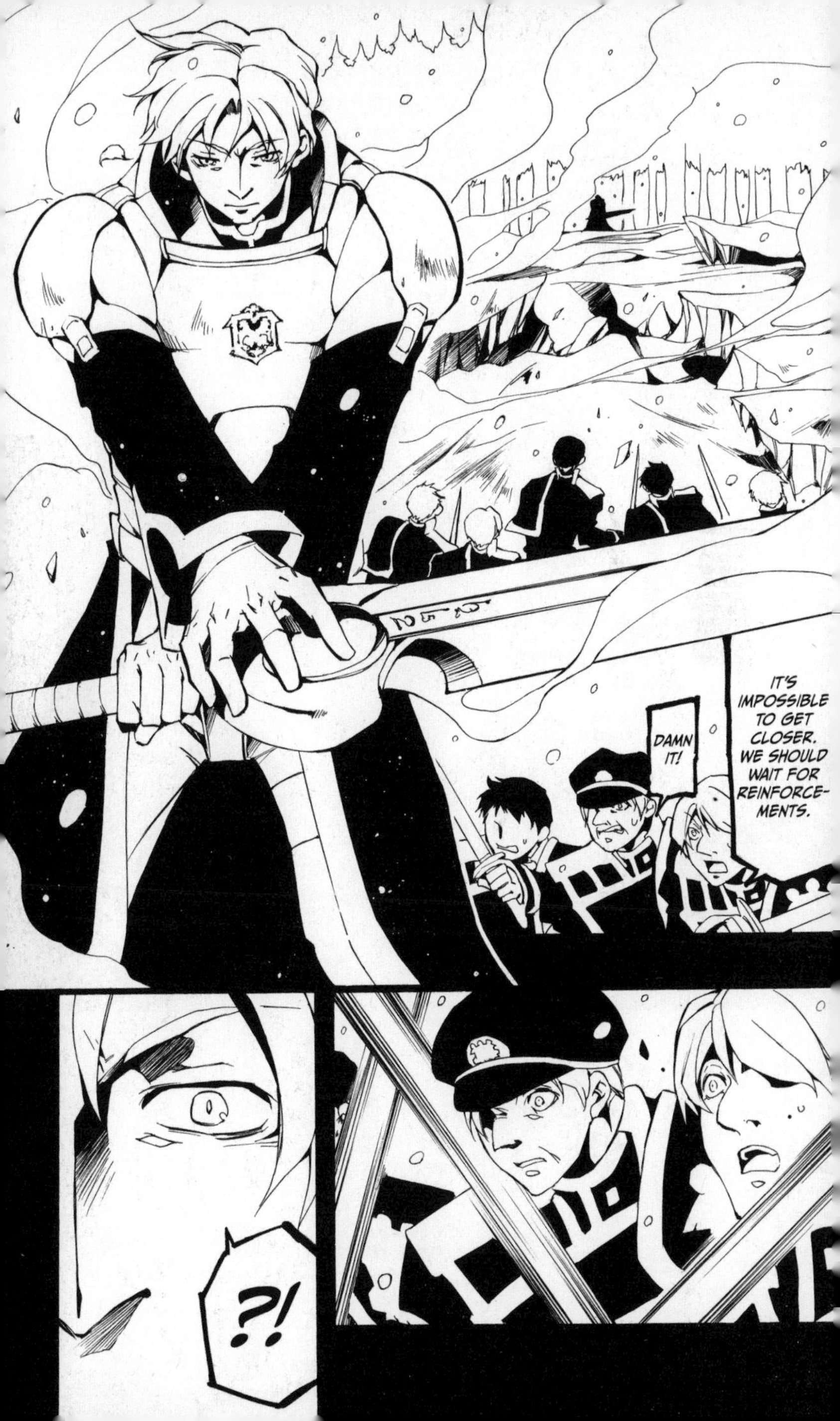
IT'S IMPOSSIBLE TO GET CLOSER. WE SHOULD WAIT FOR REINFORCE-MENTS.
DAMN IT!
?!

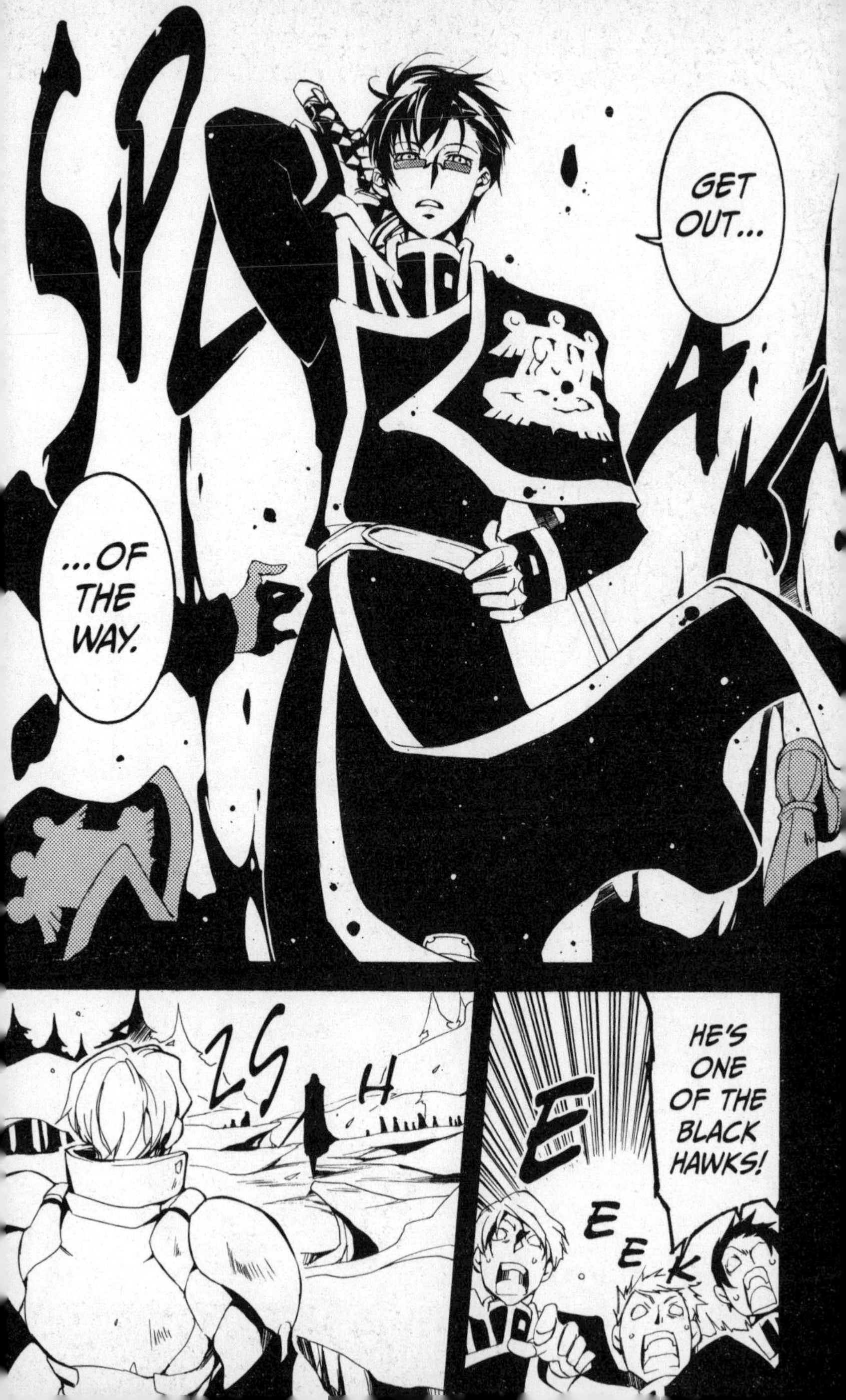
GET OUT...
...OF THE WAY.
HE'S ONE OF THE BLACK HAWKS!

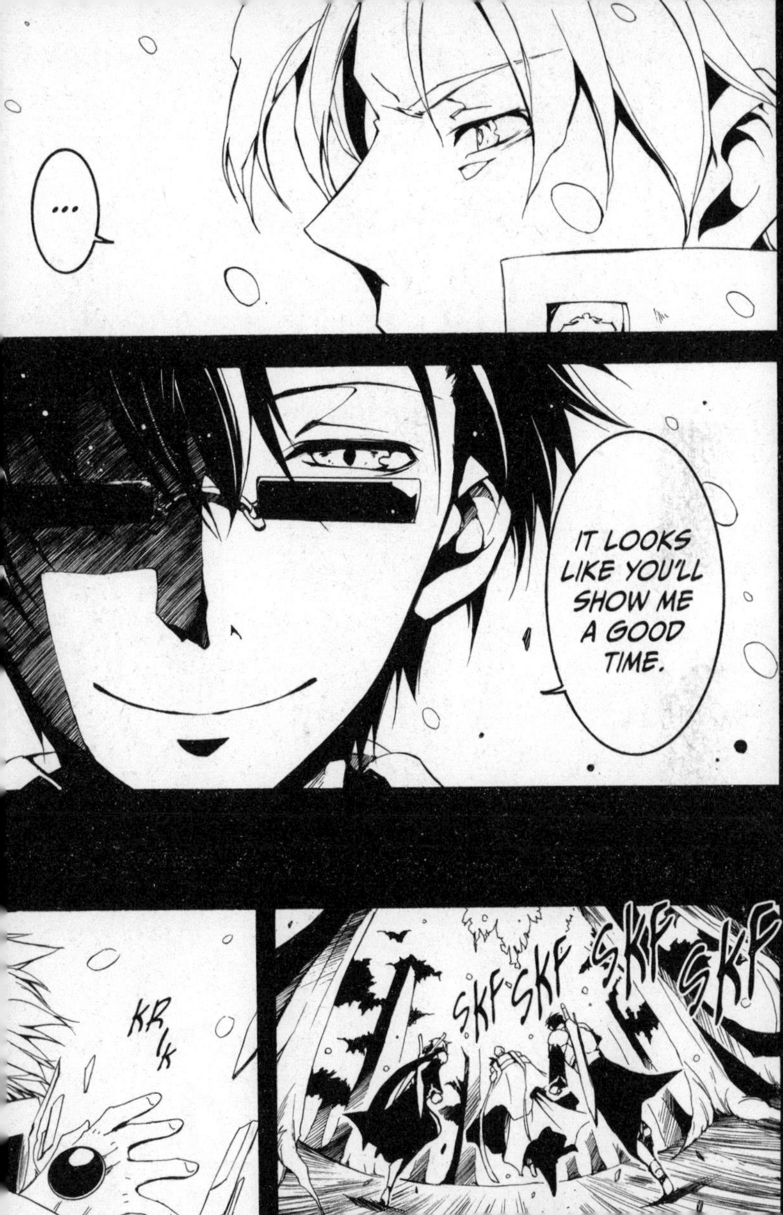
...
IT LOOKS LIKE YOU'LL SHOW ME A GOOD TIME.
SKF SKF SKF SKF
KRIK

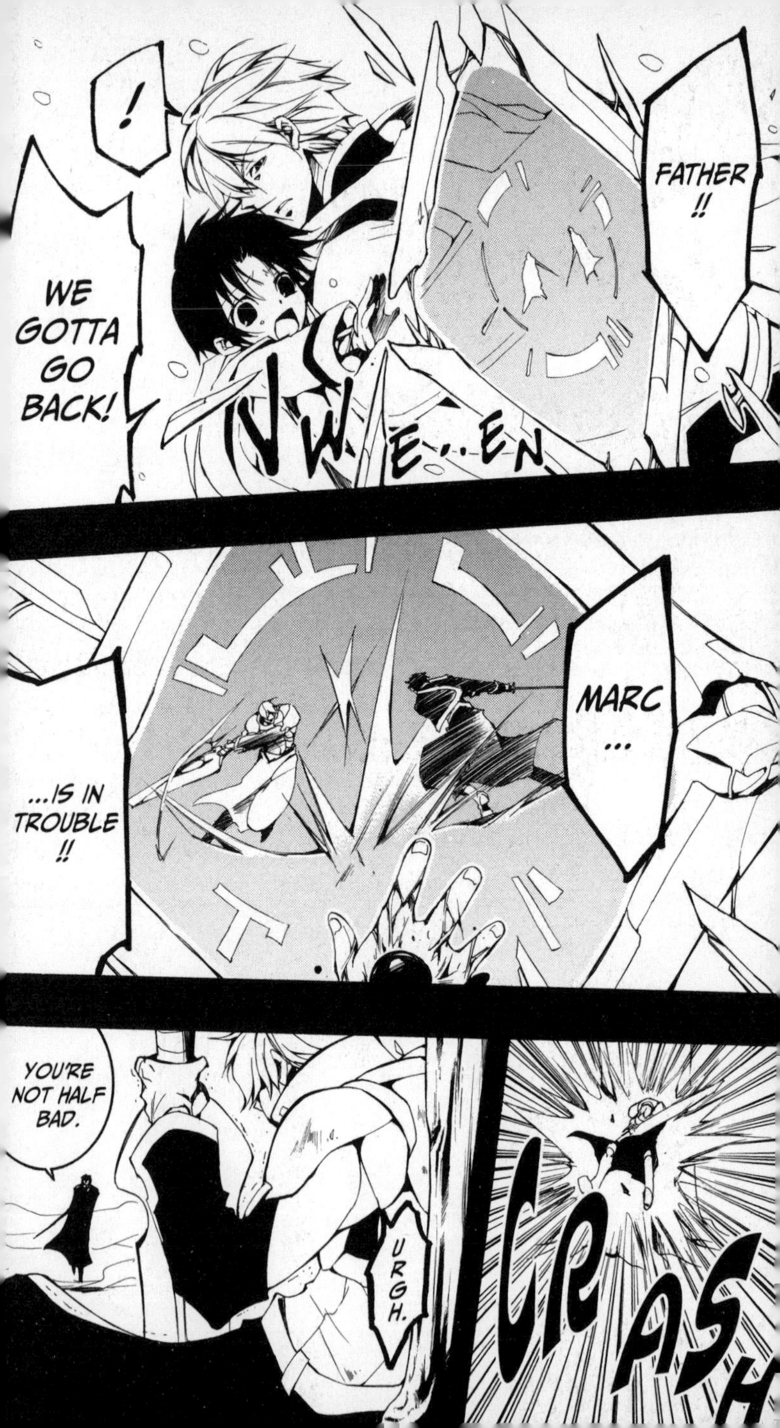
FATHER!!
!
WE GOTTA GO BACK!
VWE...EN
MARC...
...IS IN TROUBLE!!
CRASH
YOU'RE NOT HALF BAD.
URGH.

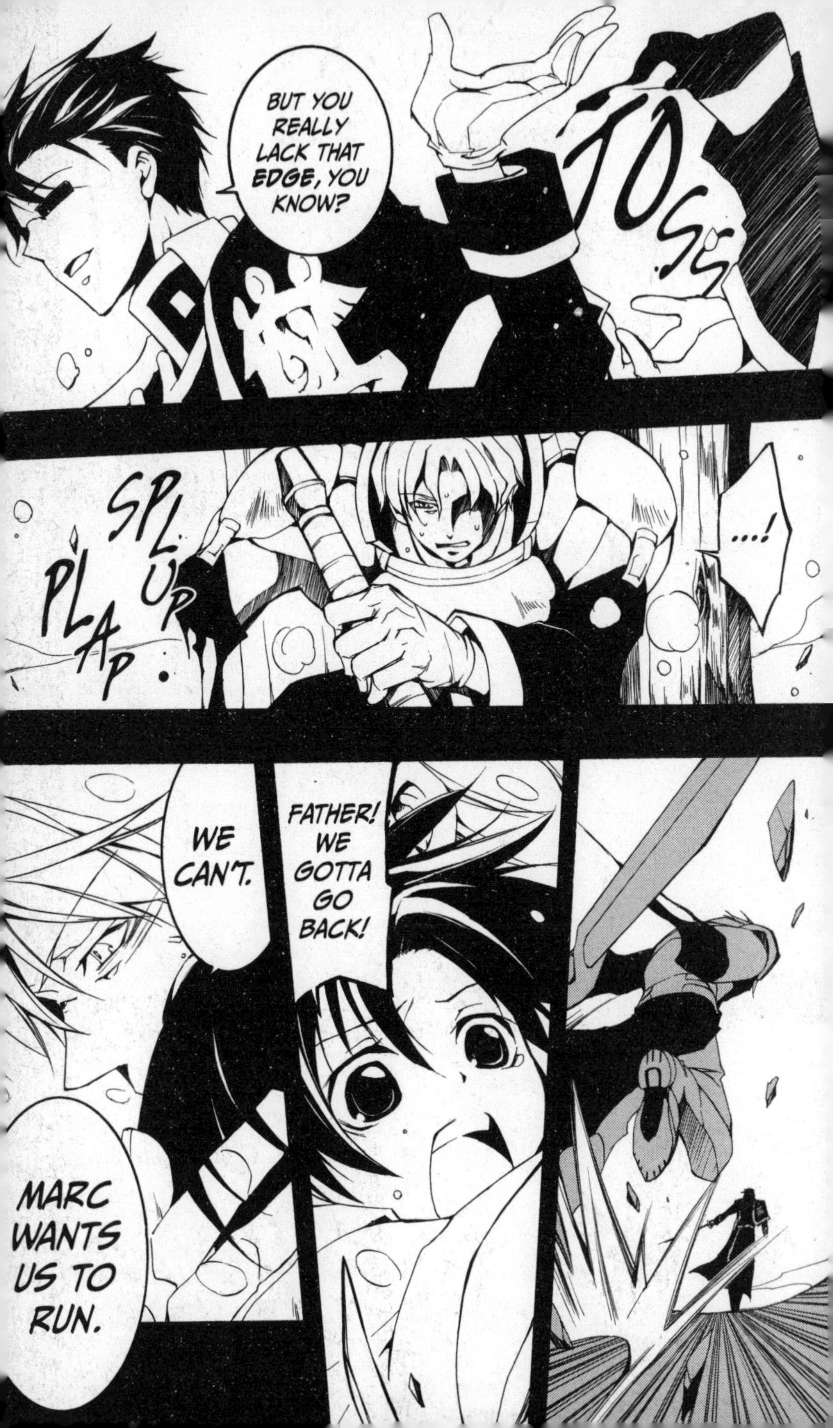
BUT YOU REALLY LACK THAT EDGE, YOU KNOW?
...!
SPLUP
PLAP
FATHER! WE GOTTA GO BACK!
WE CAN'T.
MARC WANTS US TO RUN.

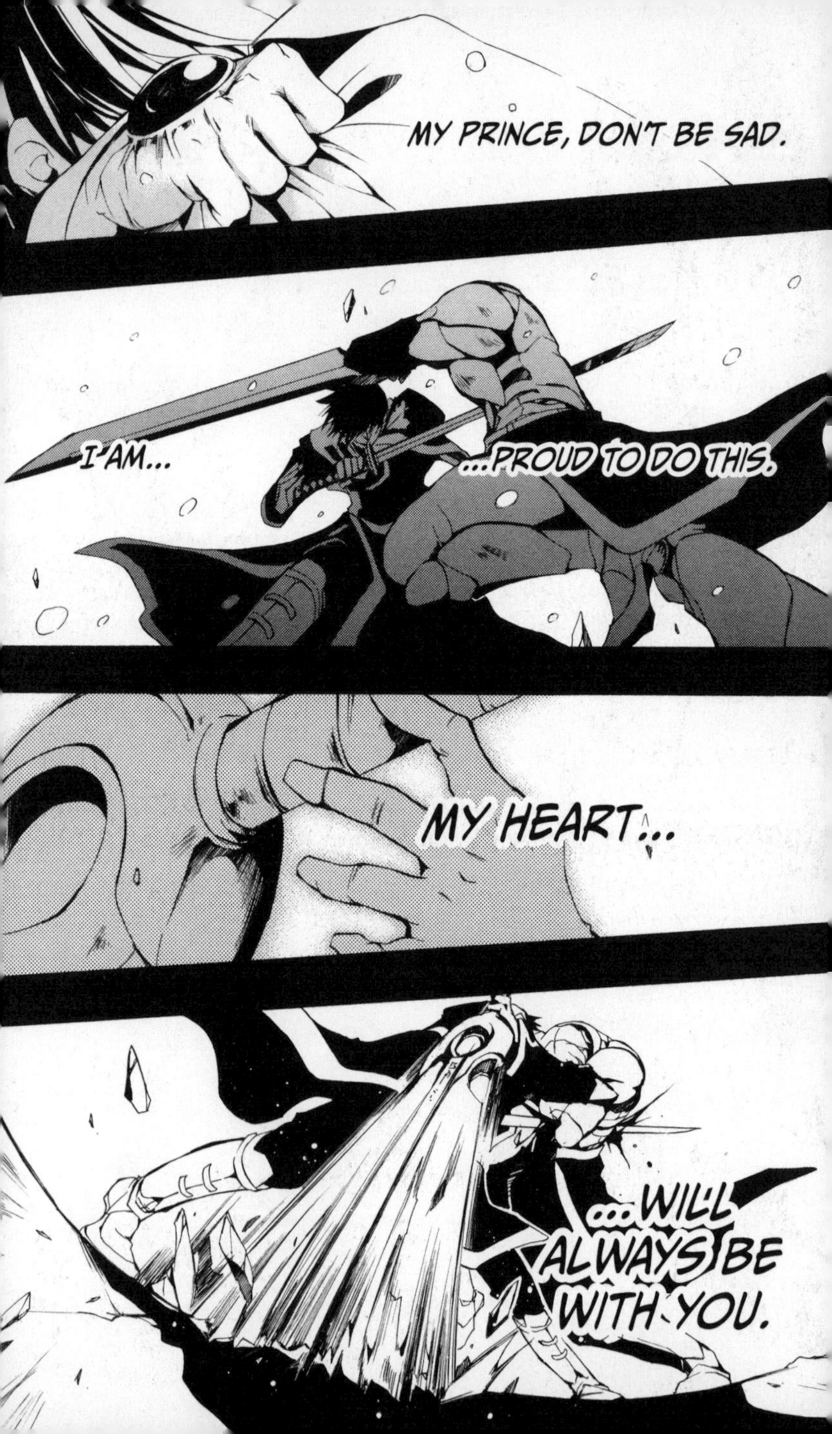
MY PRINCE, DON'T BE SAD.
I AM...
...PROUD TO DO THIS.
MY HEART...
...WILL ALWAYS BE WITH YOU.

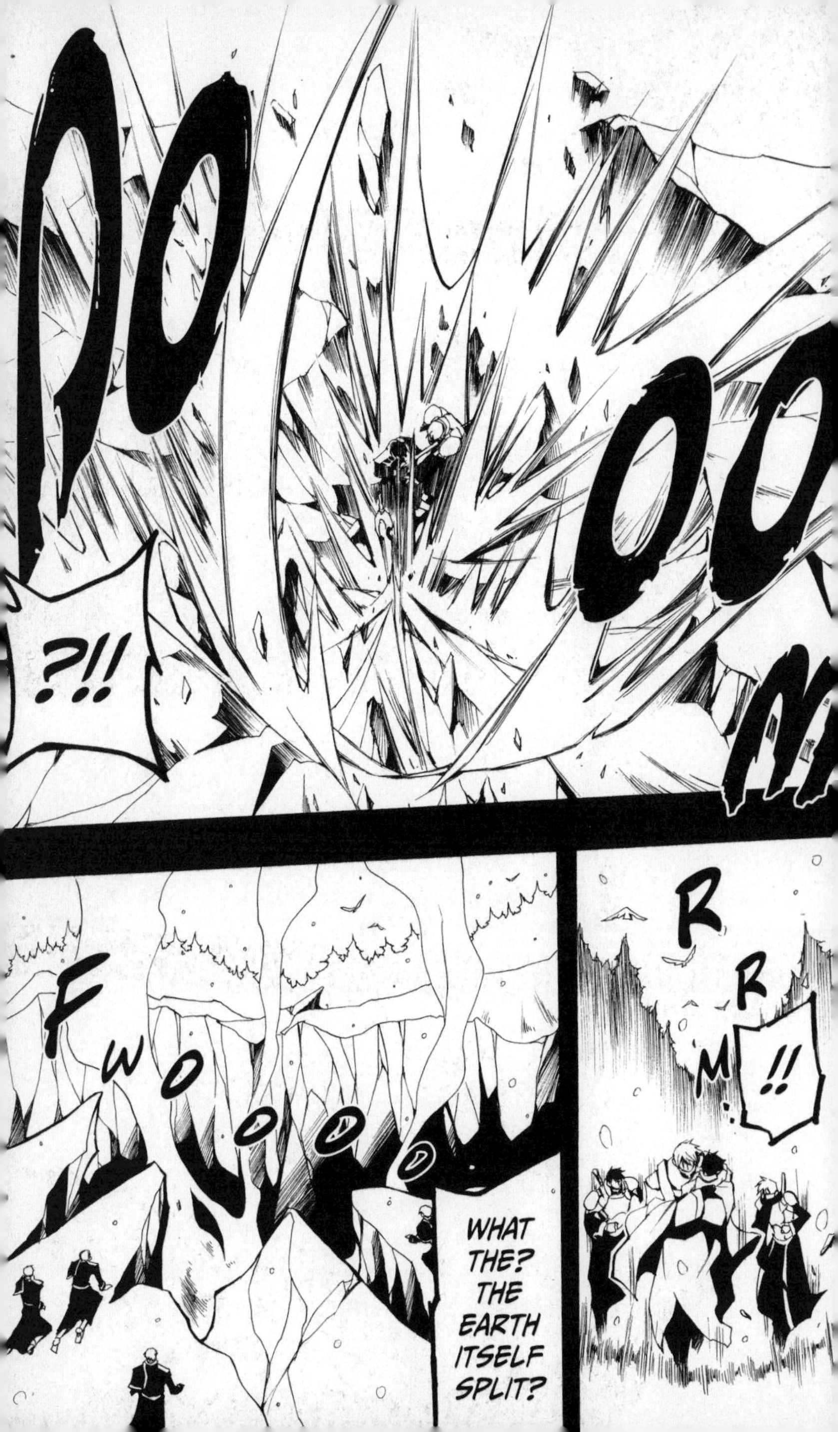

?!!
DOOOM
RRM
!!
FWOOOOOO
WHAT THE? THE EARTH ITSELF SPLIT?

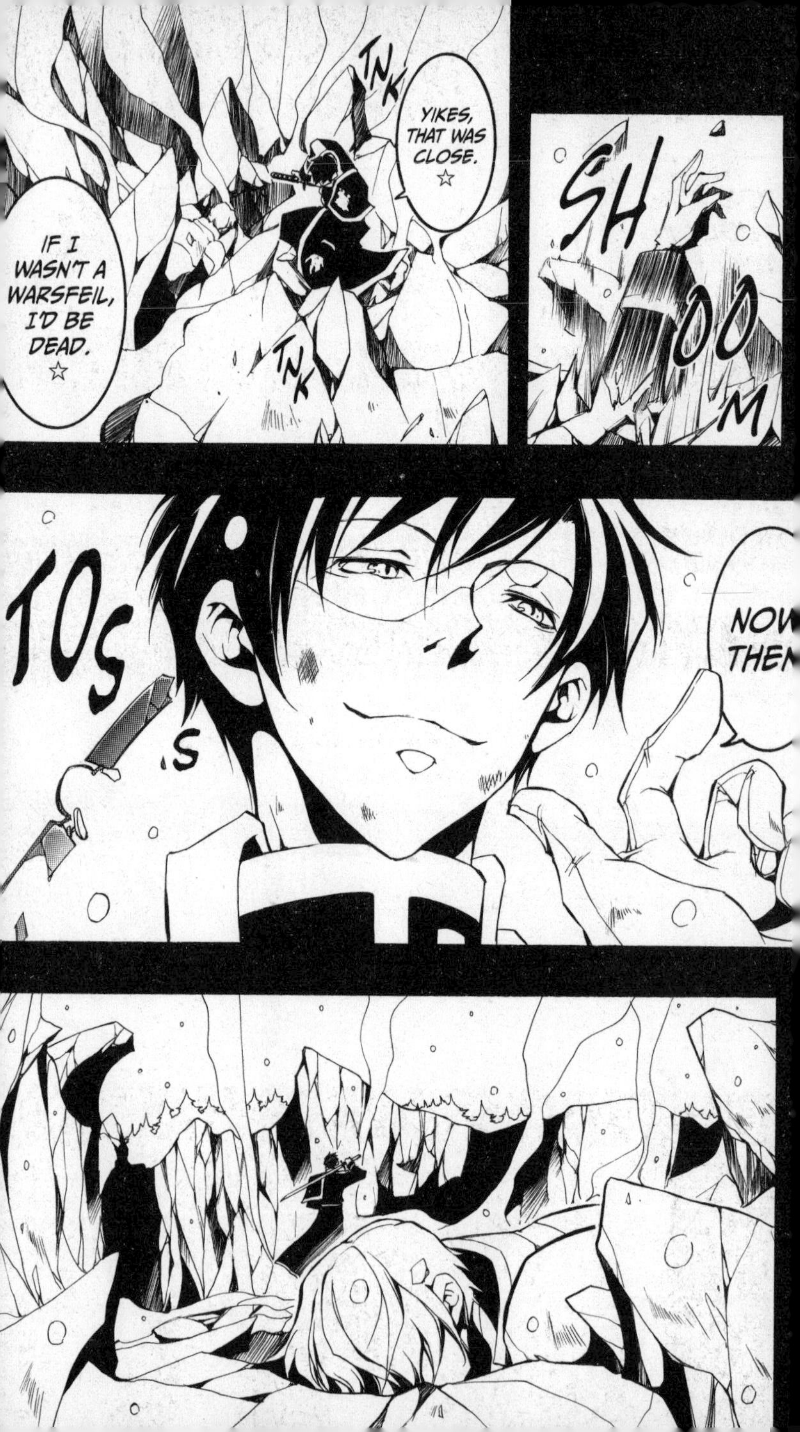
SHOOM
TNK
YIKES, THAT WAS CLOSE. ☆
IF I WASN'T A WARSFEIL, I'D BE DEAD. ☆
TNK
NOW THEN
TOSS

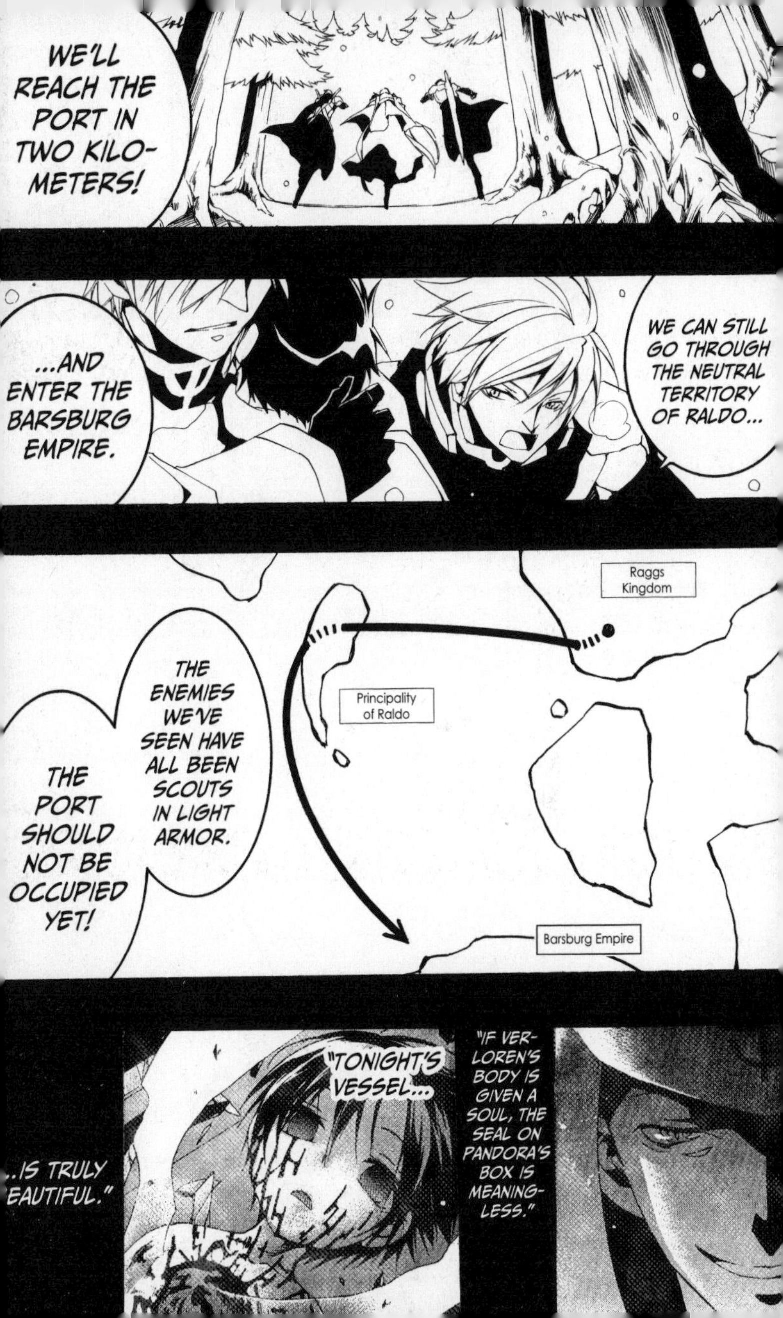
WE'LL REACH THE PORT IN TWO KILO-METERS!
WE CAN STILL GO THROUGH THE NEUTRAL TERRITORY OF RALDO...
...AND ENTER THE BARSBURG EMPIRE.
Raggs Kingdom
Principality of Raldo
Barsburg Empire
THE ENEMIES WE'VE SEEN HAVE ALL BEEN SCOUTS IN LIGHT ARMOR.
THE PORT SHOULD NOT BE OCCUPIED YET!
"IF VER-LOREN'S BODY IS GIVEN A SOUL, THE SEAL ON PANDORA'S BOX IS MEANING-LESS."
"TONIGHT'S VESSEL...
..IS TRULY EAUTIFUL."

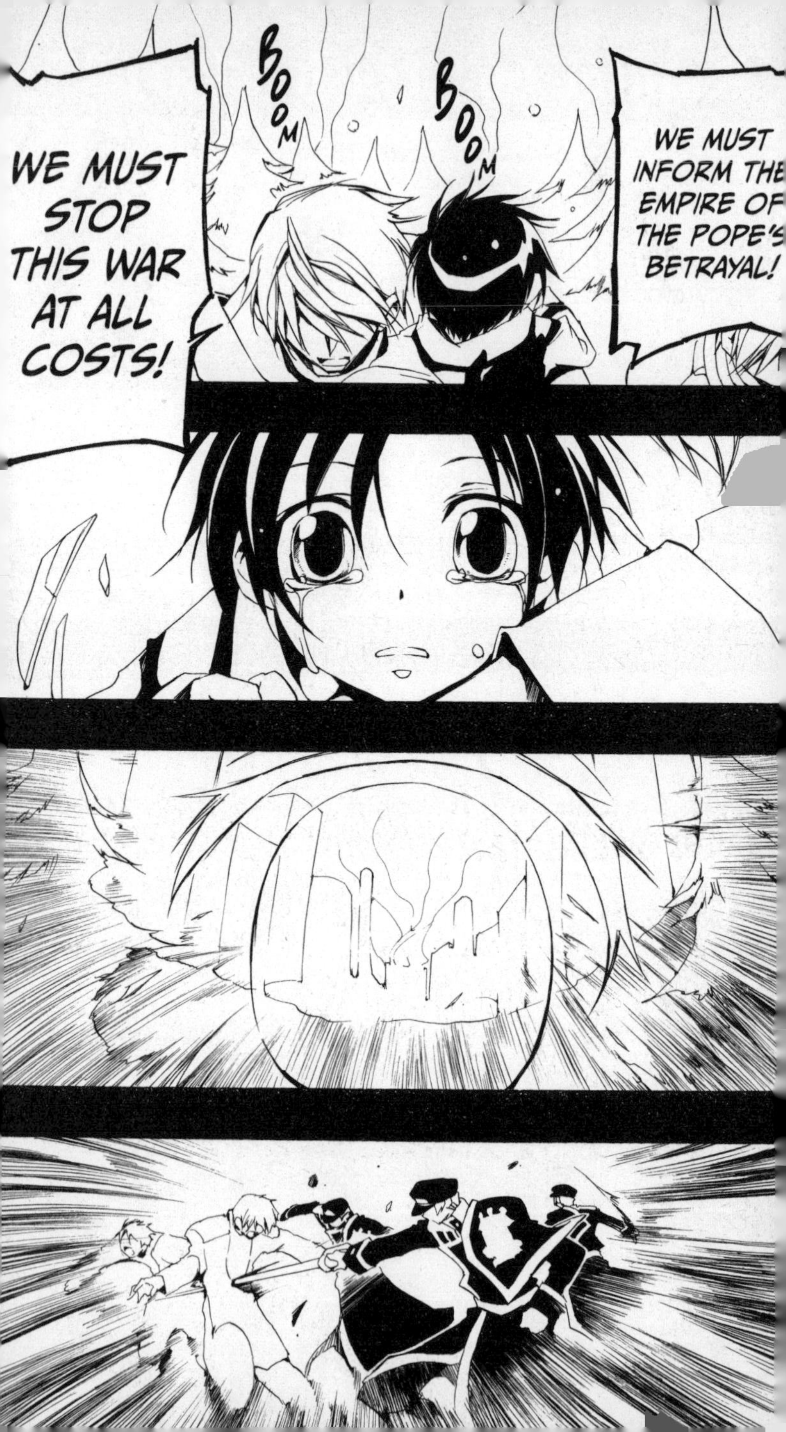
WE MUST INFORM THE EMPIRE OF THE POPE'S BETRAYAL!
BOOM
BOOM
WE MUST STOP THIS WAR AT ALL COSTS!

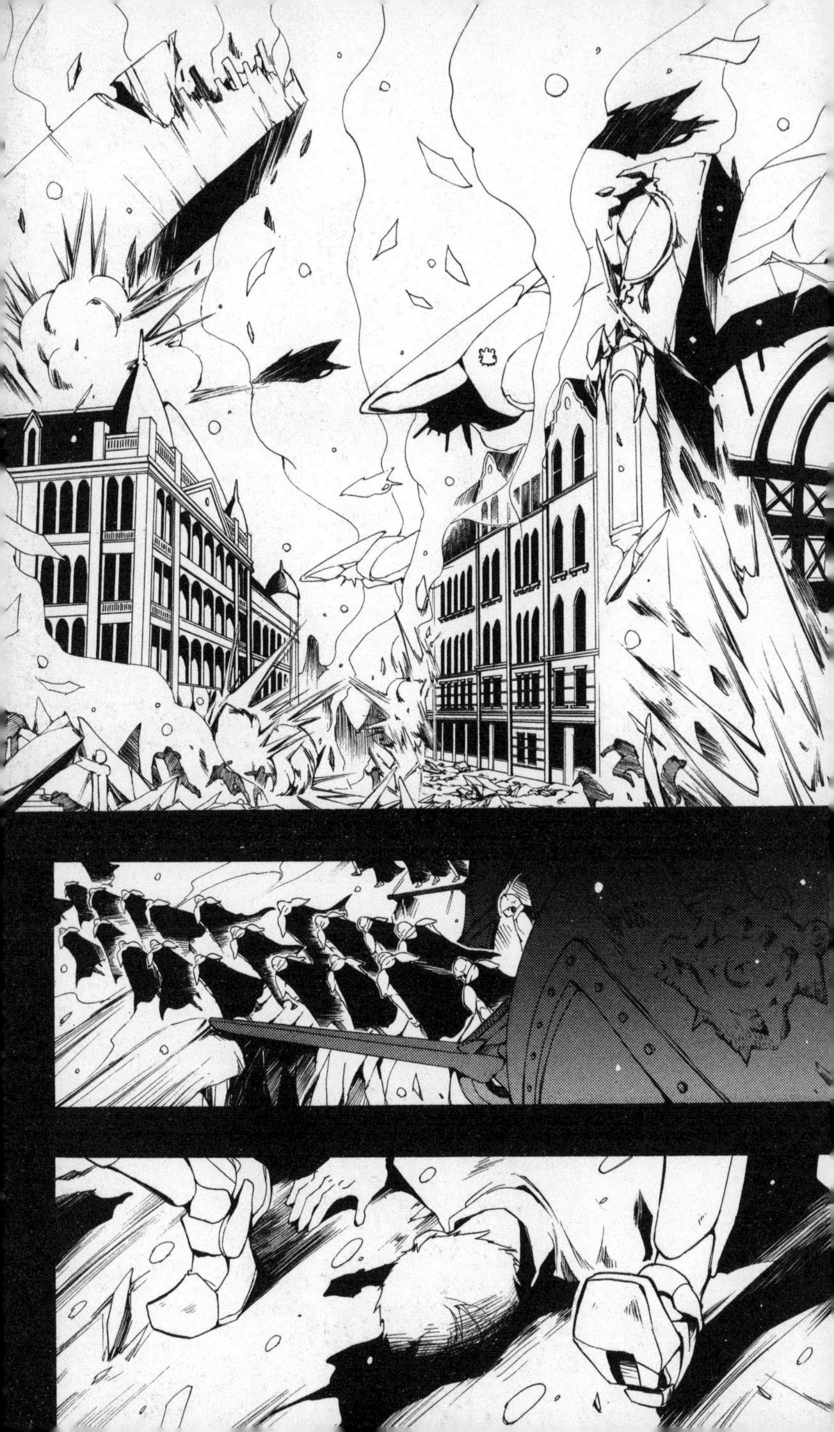

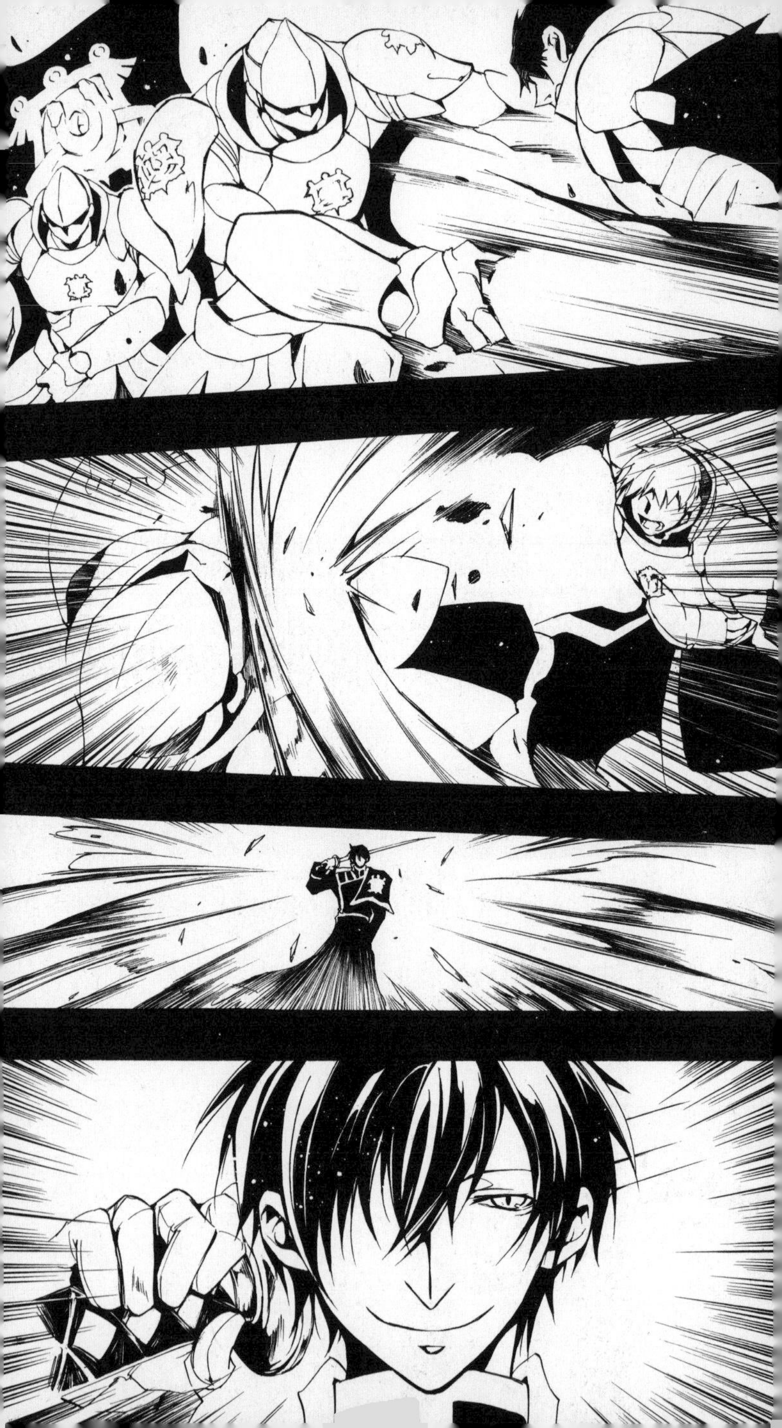

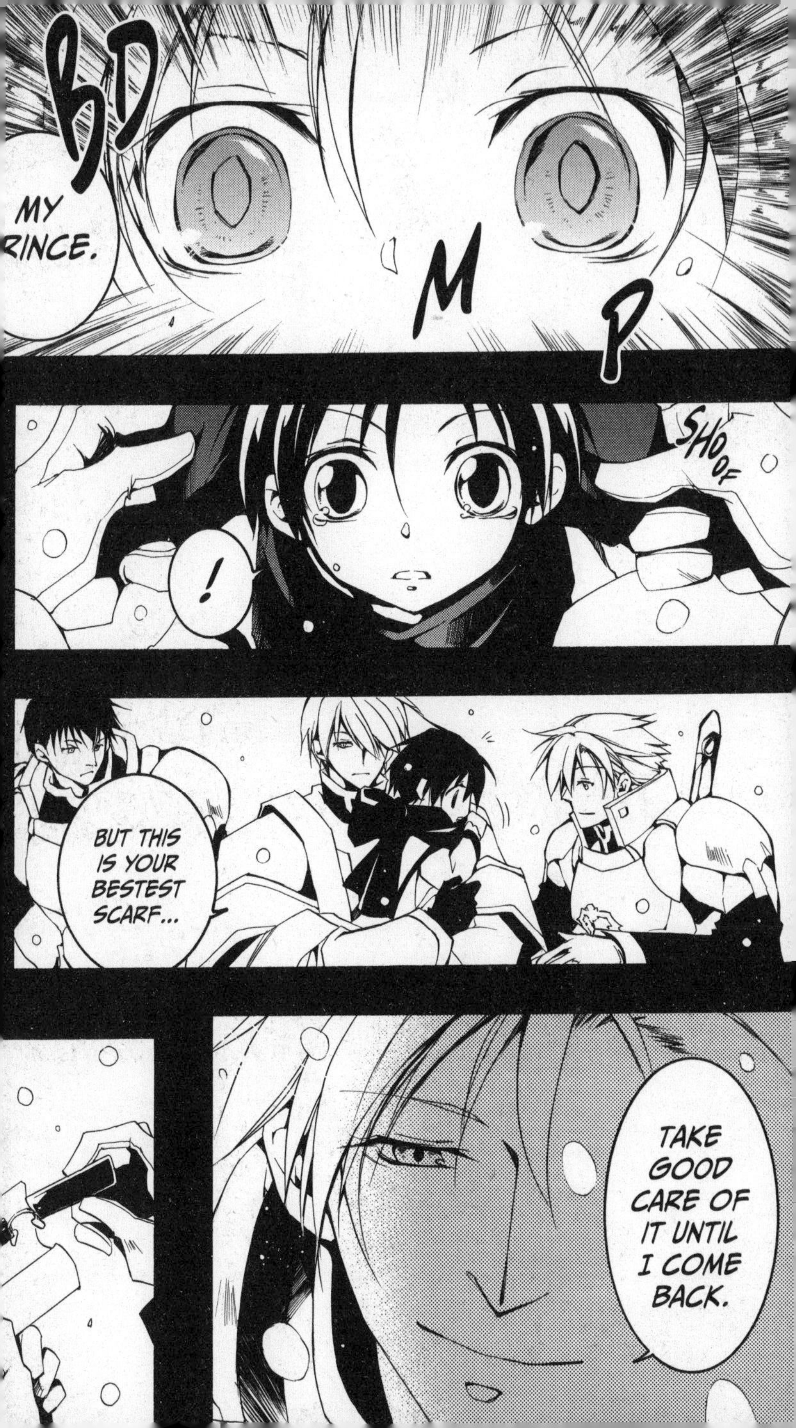
BDMP
MY RINCE.
SHOOF
!
BUT THIS IS YOUR BESTEST SCARF...
TAKE GOOD CARE OF IT UNTIL I COME BACK.

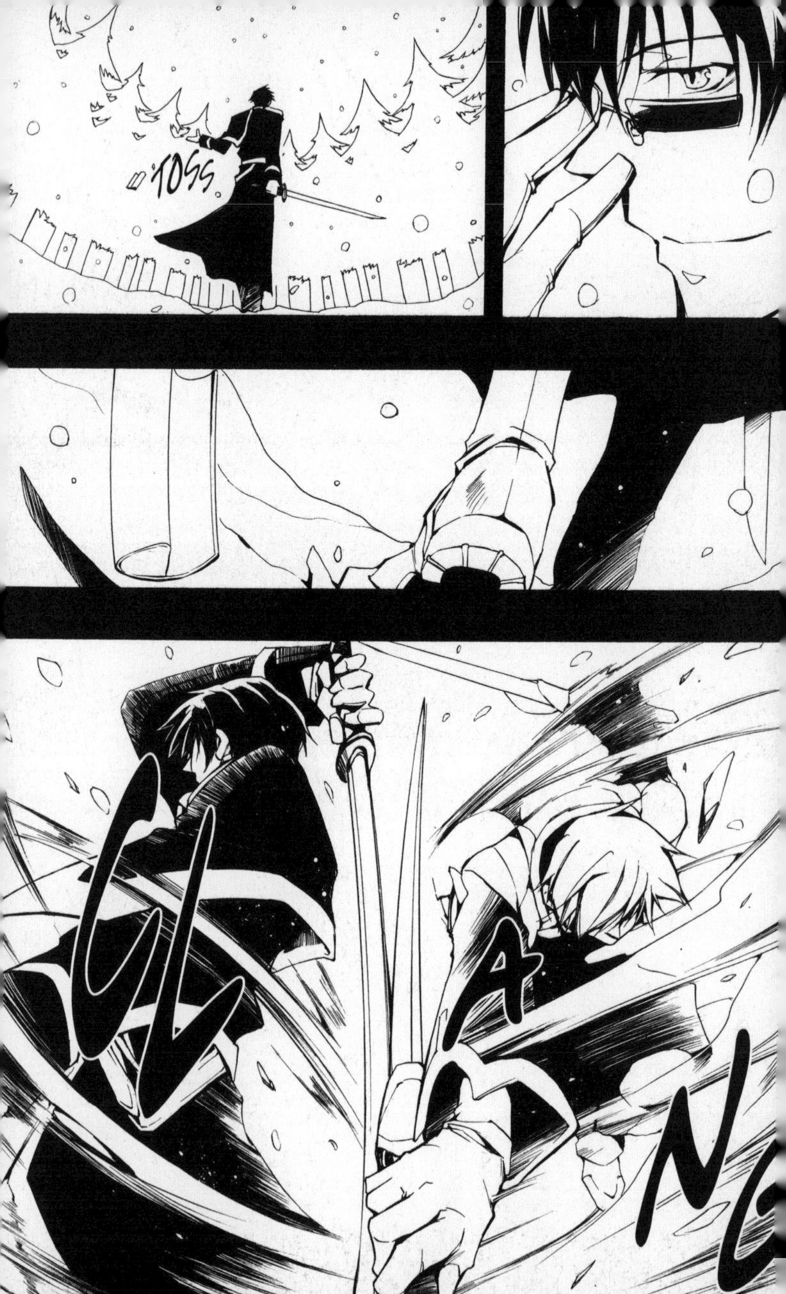
TOSS
CLANG

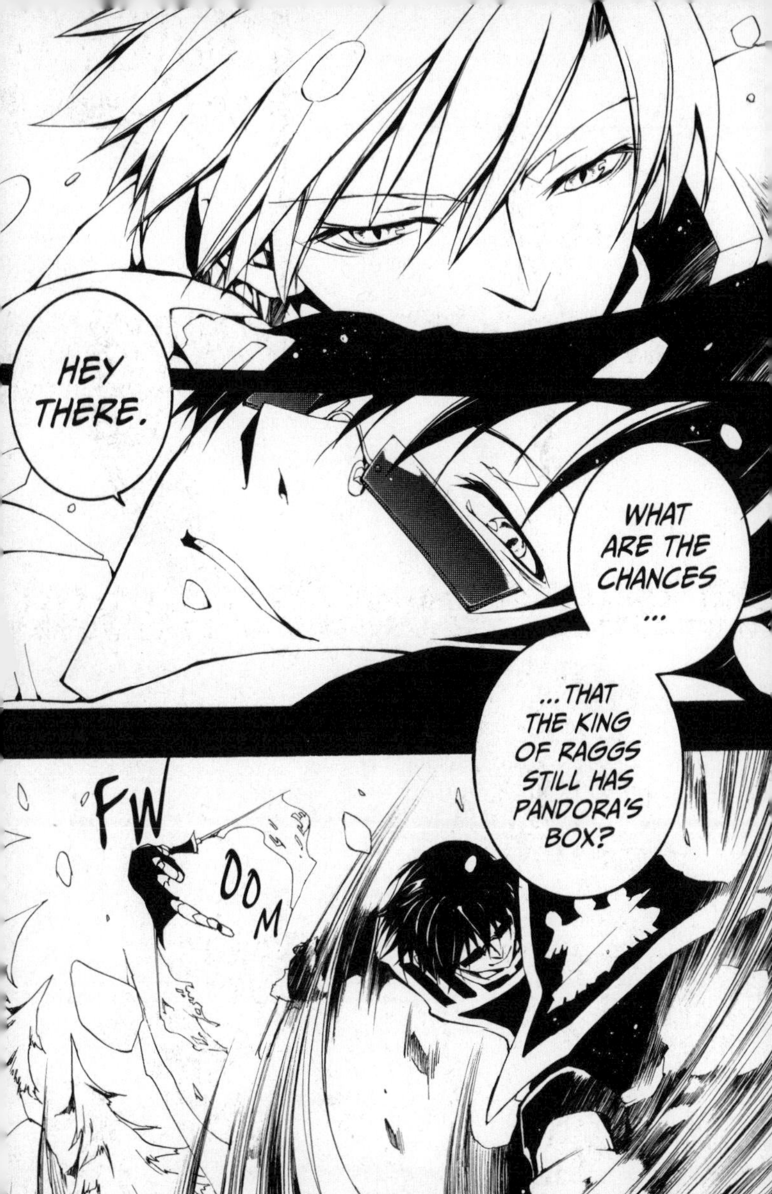
HEY THERE.
WHAT ARE THE CHANCES ...
...THAT THE KING OF RAGGS STILL HAS PANDORA'S BOX?
FWOOM

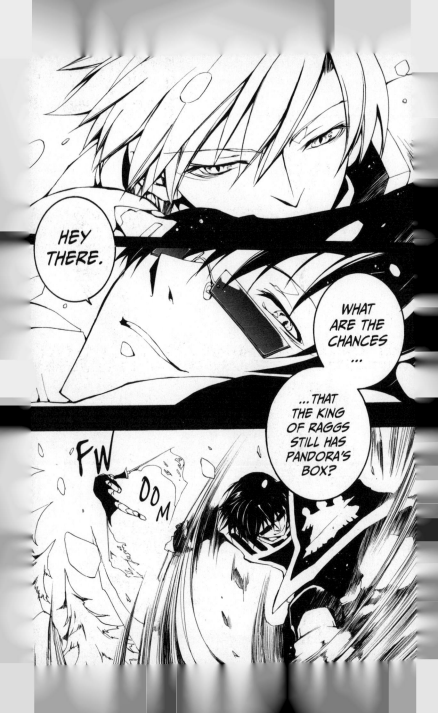

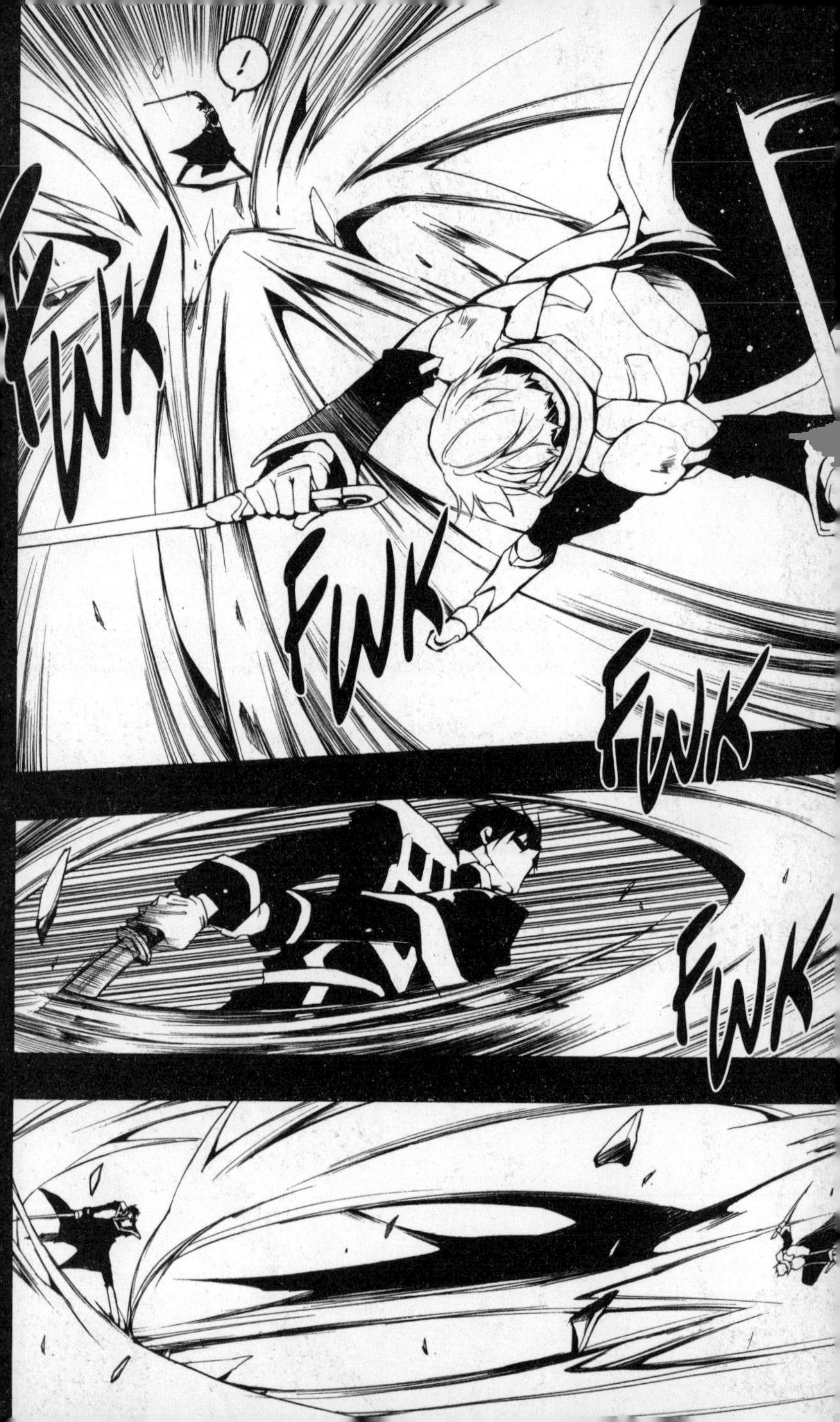

!
FWK
FWK
FWK
FWK

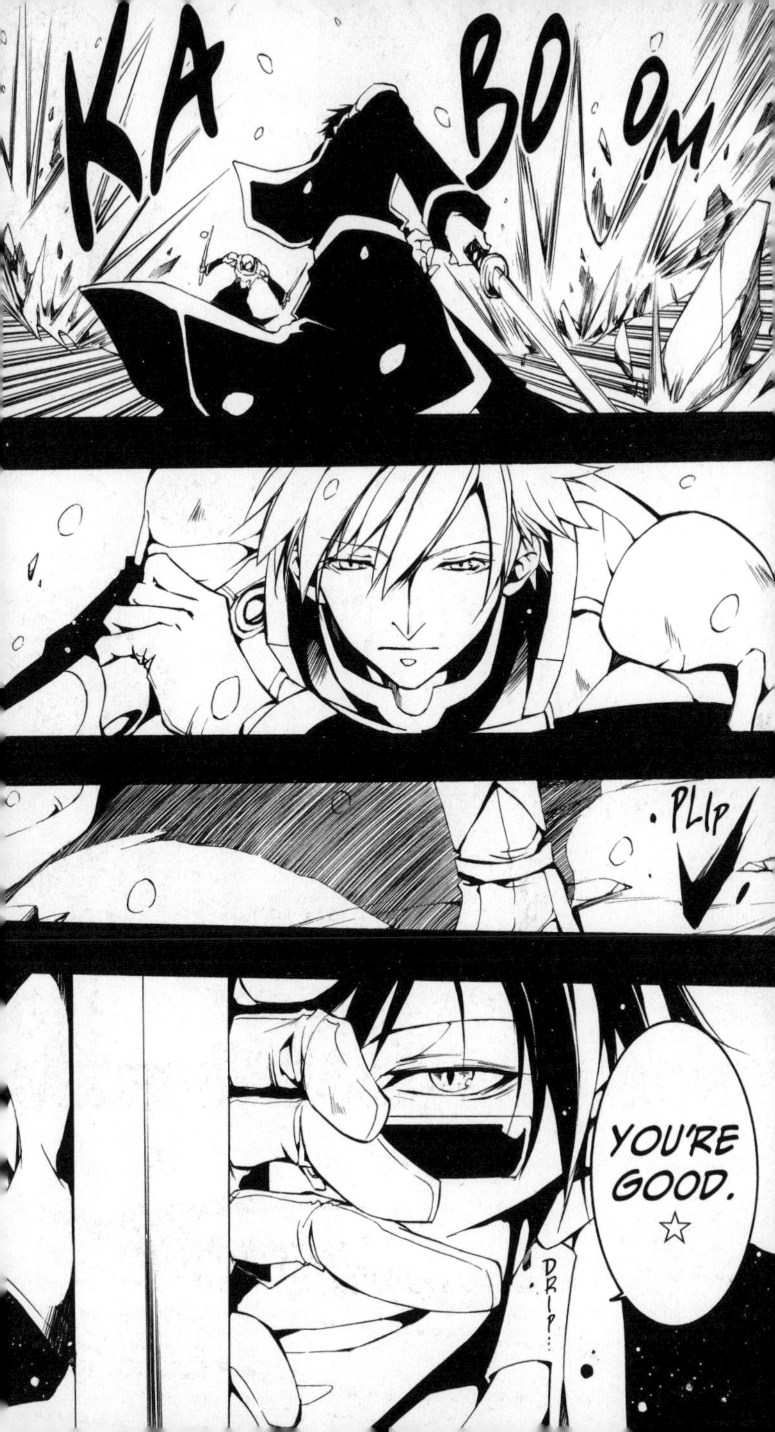
KA BOOM
PLIP
YOU'RE GOOD. ☆
DRIP...

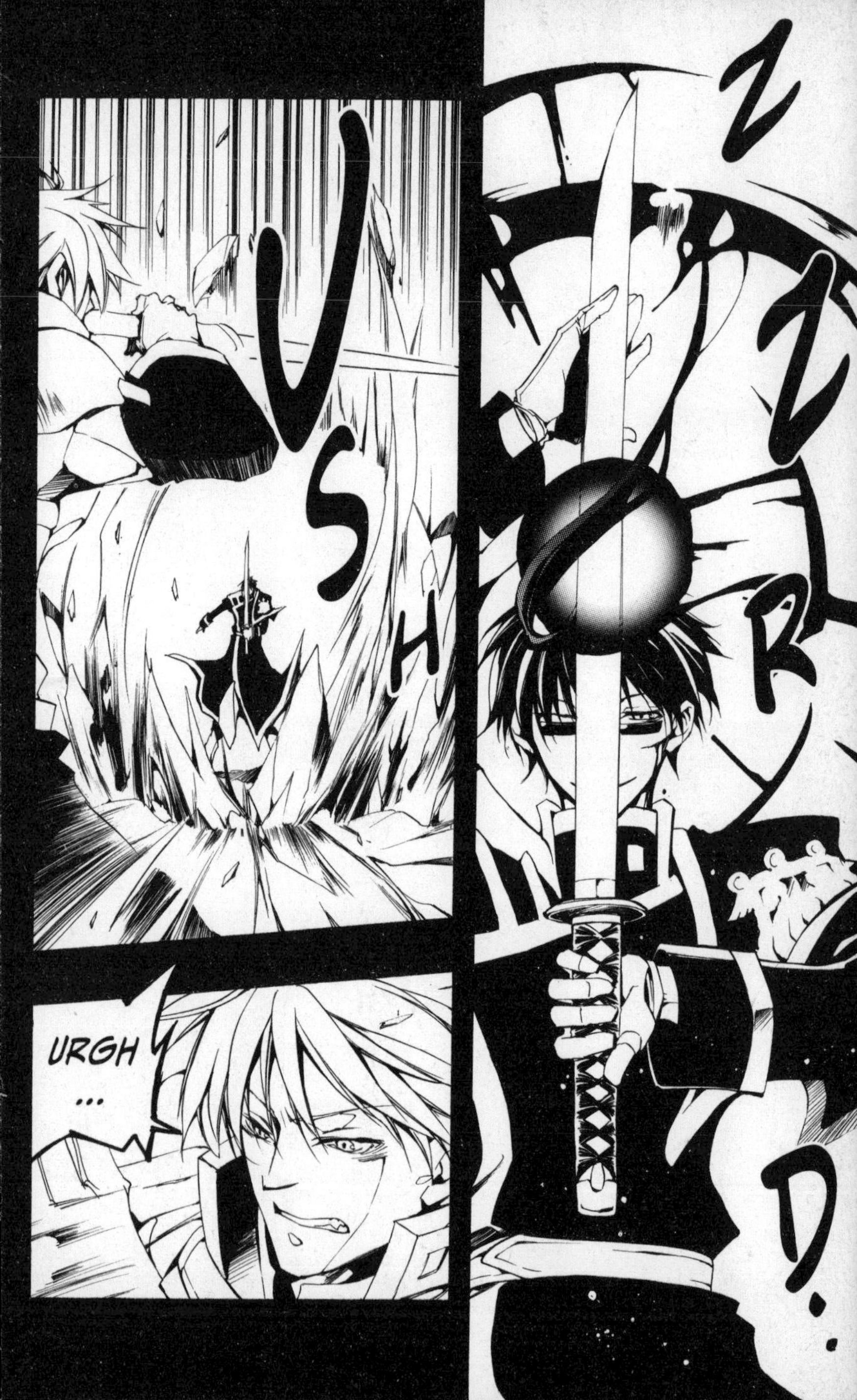
ZZRD...
VSH
URGH ...

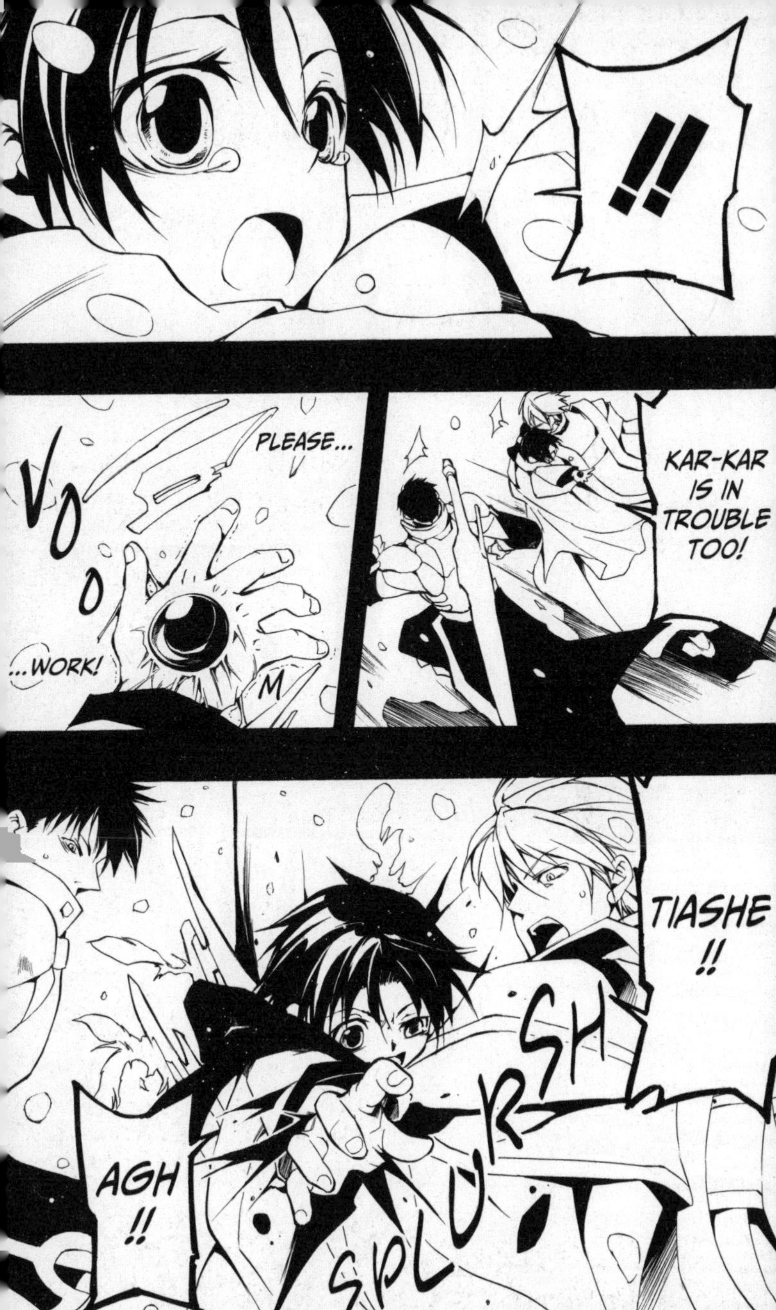
!!
KAR-KAR IS IN TROUBLE TOO!
PLEASE...
VOOM
...WORK!
TIASHE !!
SPLURSH
AGH !!

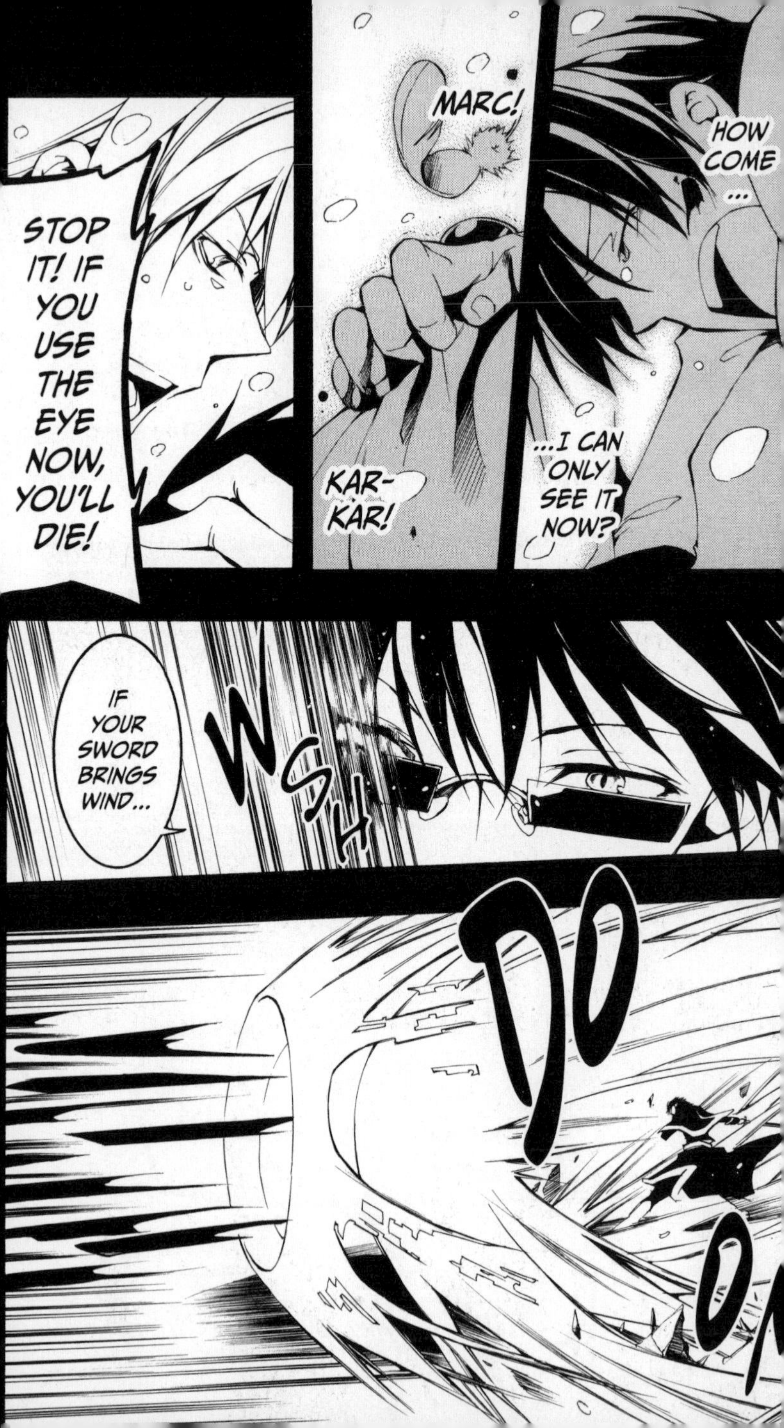
HOW COME ...
...I CAN ONLY SEE IT NOW?
MARC!
KAR-KAR!
STOP IT! IF YOU USE THE EYE NOW, YOU'LL DIE!
WSH
IF YOUR SWORD BRINGS WIND...
DOO

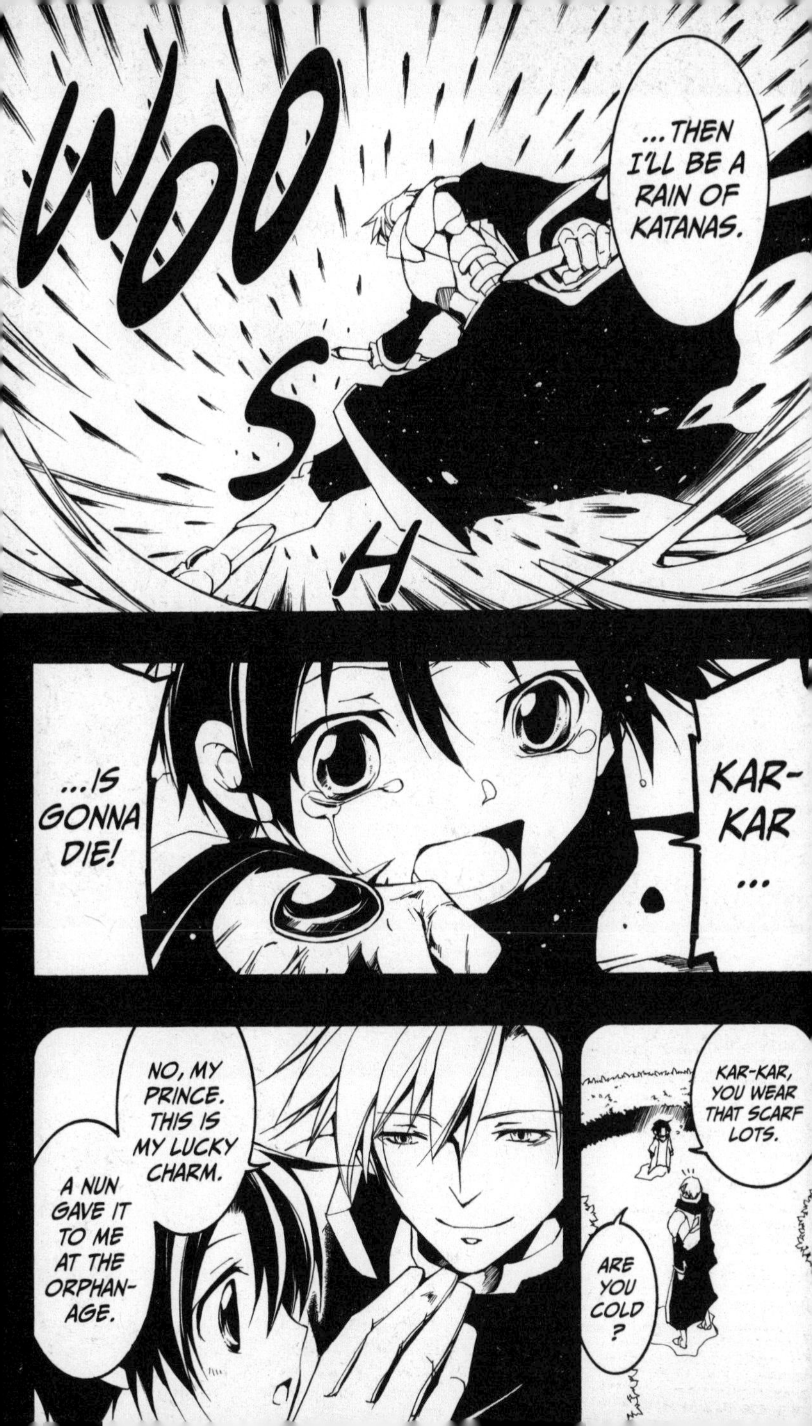
...THEN I'LL BE A RAIN OF KATANAS.
WOOSH
KAR-KAR...
...IS GONNA DIE!
KAR-KAR, YOU WEAR THAT SCARF LOTS.
ARE YOU COLD?
NO, MY PRINCE. THIS IS MY LUCKY CHARM.
A NUN GAVE IT TO ME AT THE ORPHAN-AGE.

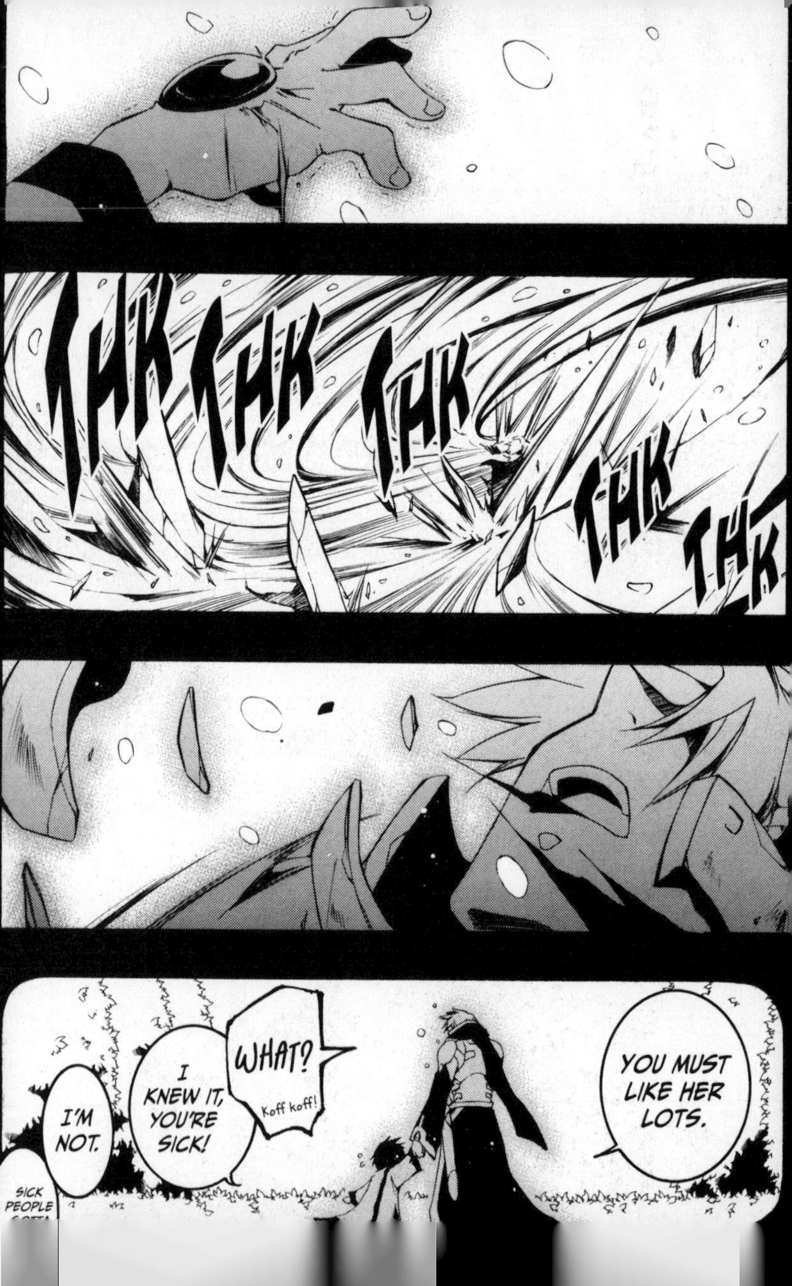
THK THK THK THK THK
YOU MUST LIKE HER LOTS.
WHAT?
Koff koff!
I KNEW IT, YOU'RE SICK!
I'M NOT.
SICK PEOPLE

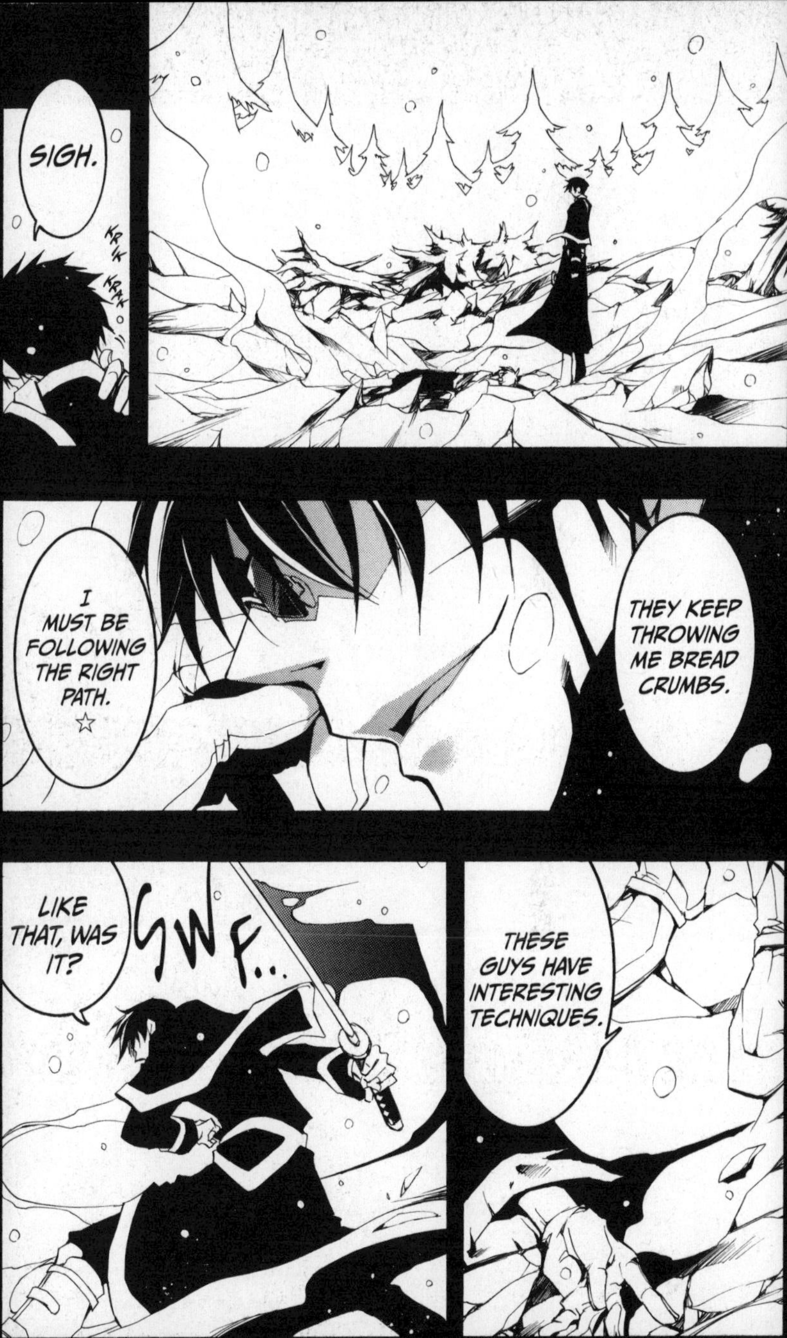
SIGH.
THEY KEEP THROWING ME BREAD CRUMBS.
I MUST BE FOLLOWING THE RIGHT PATH. ☆
THESE GUYS HAVE INTERESTING TECHNIQUES.
SWF...
LIKE THAT, WAS IT?

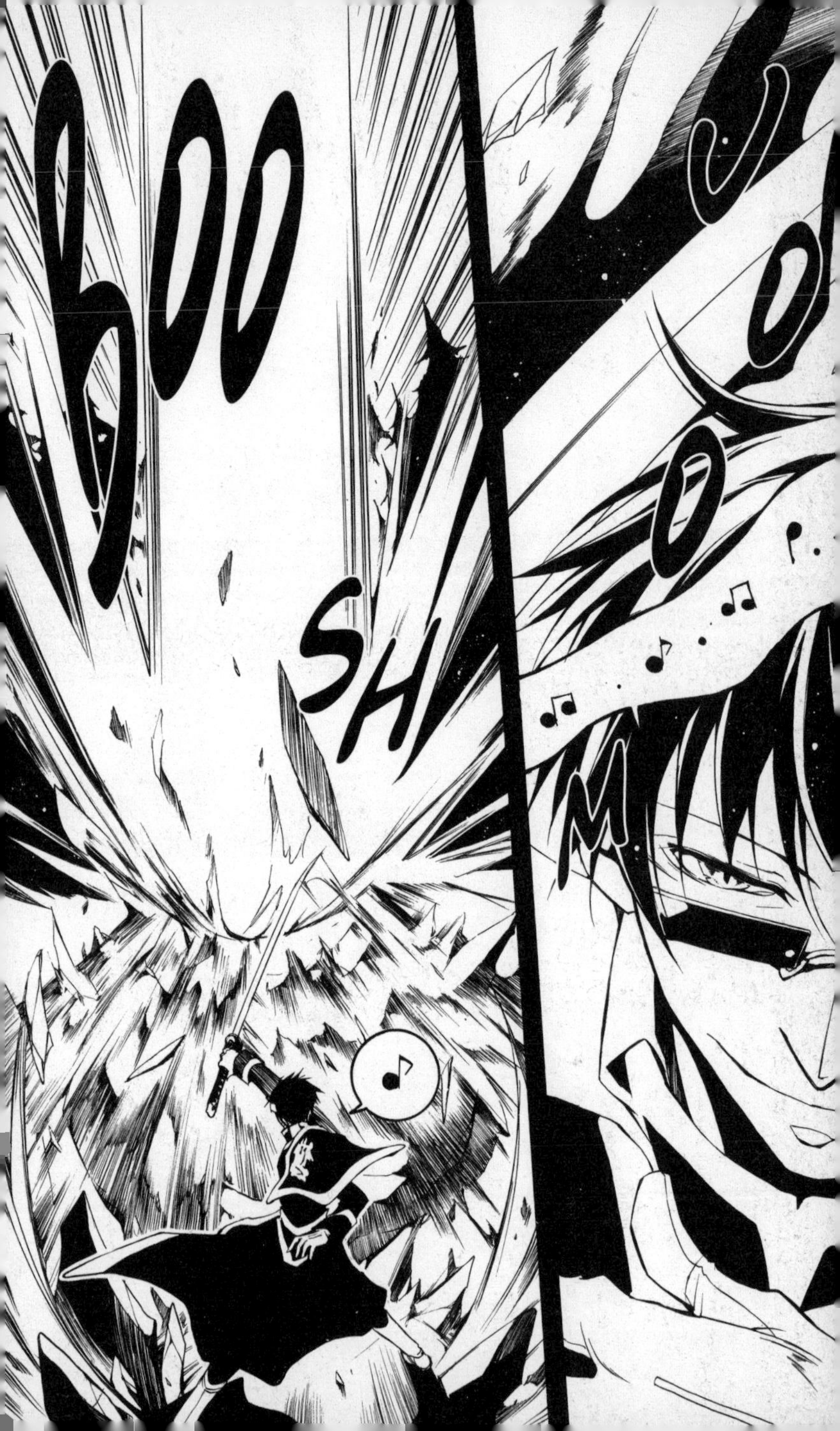
BOOO
SH

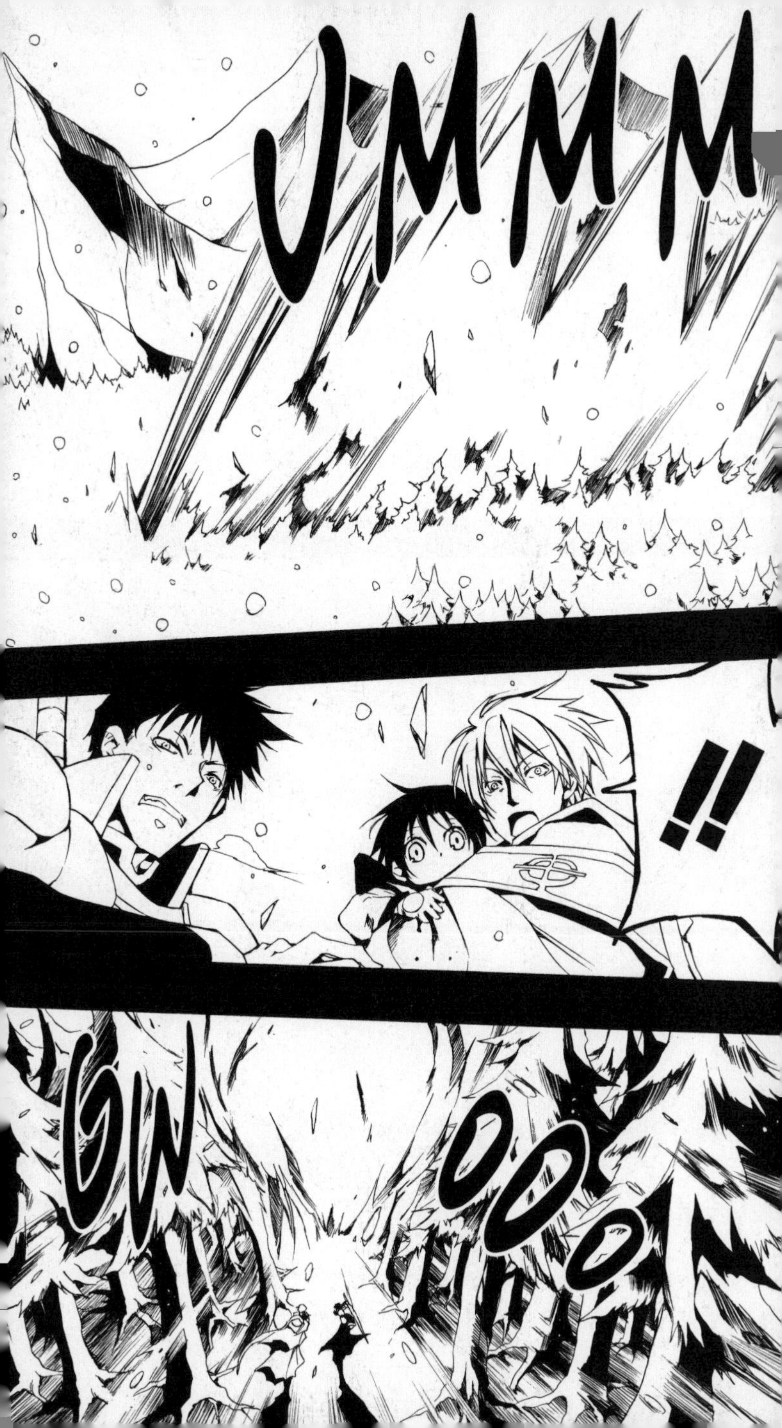
VMMM
!!
GWOOOO

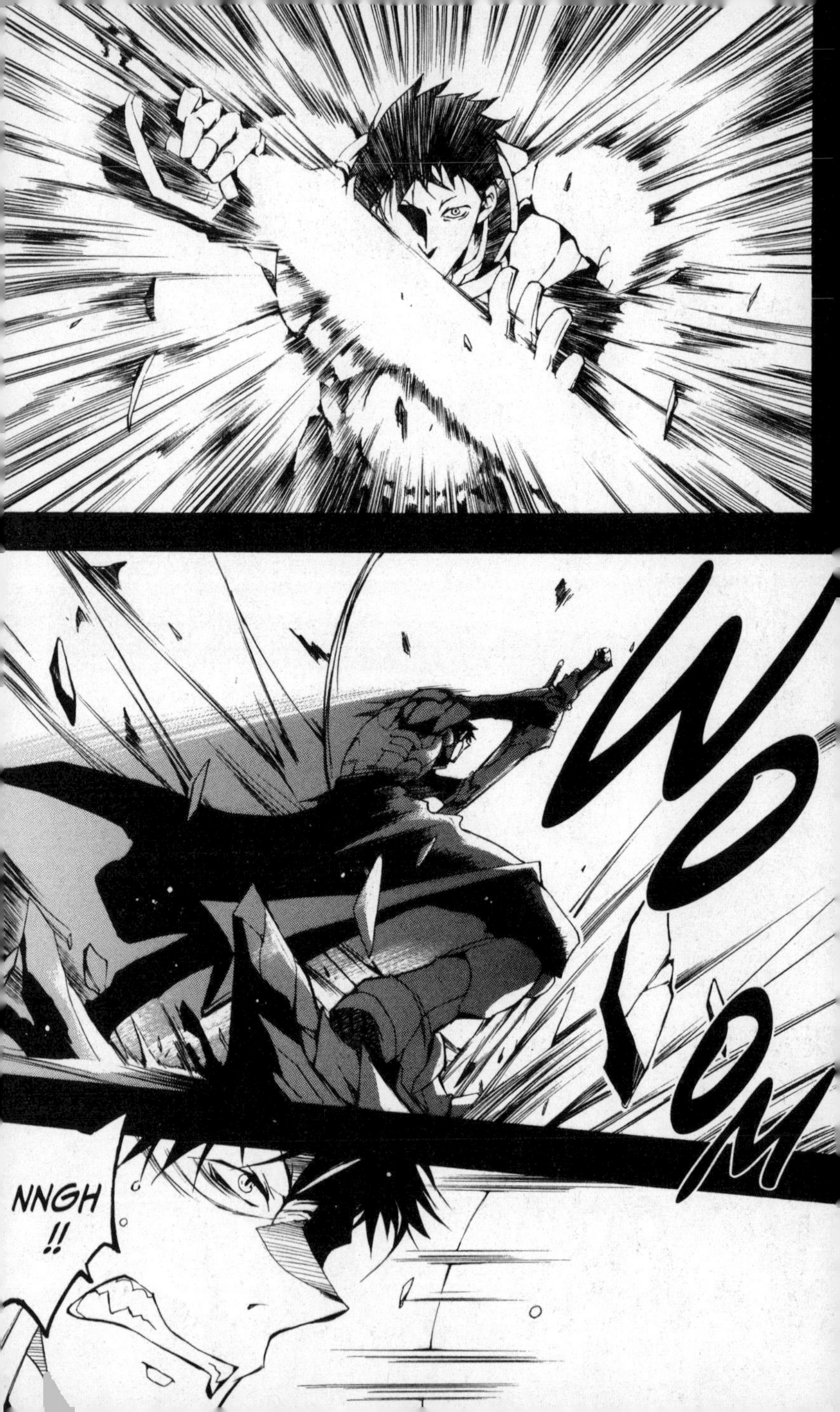
WOOM
NNGH !!

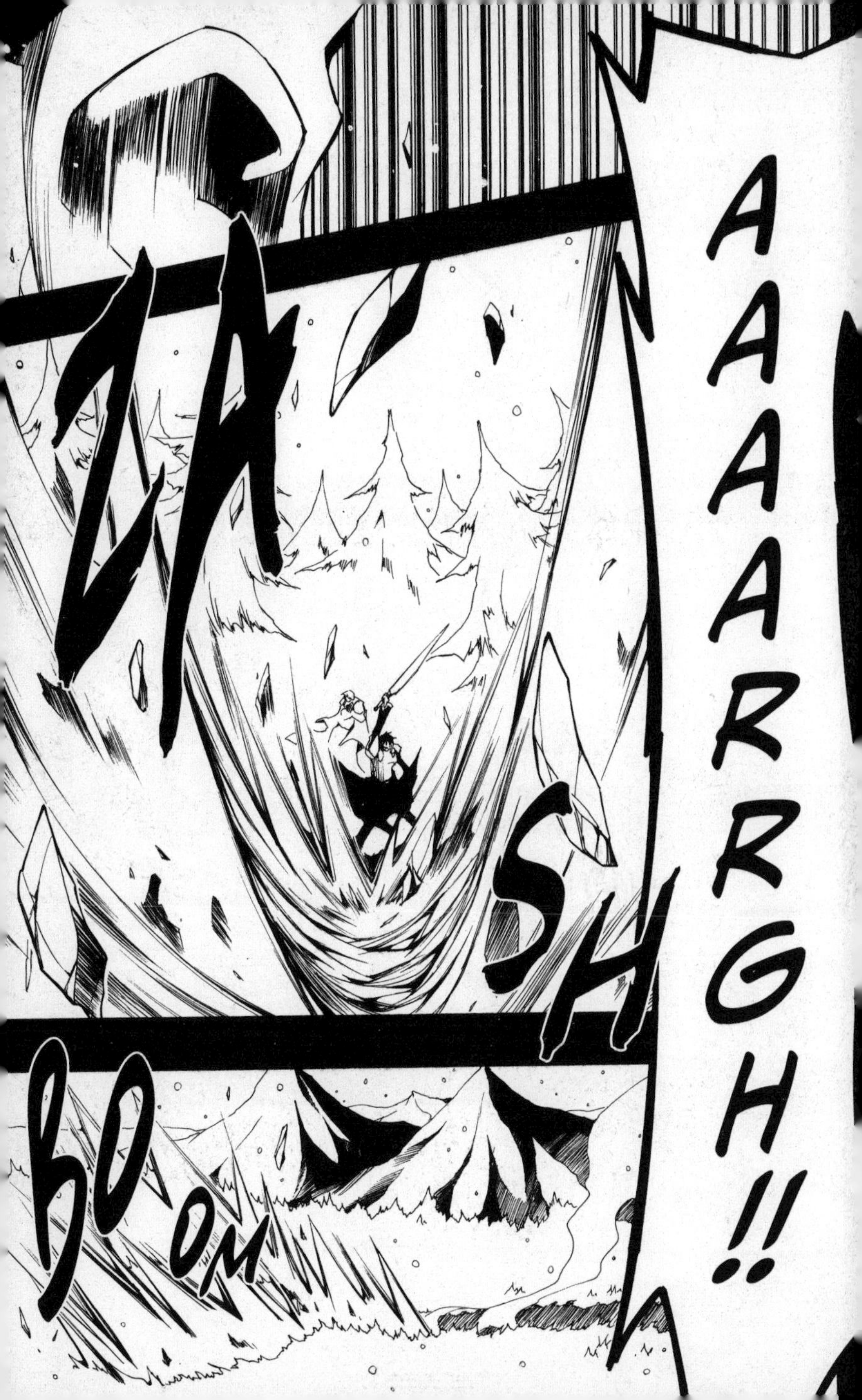
AAAARRGH!!
ZASH
BOOM

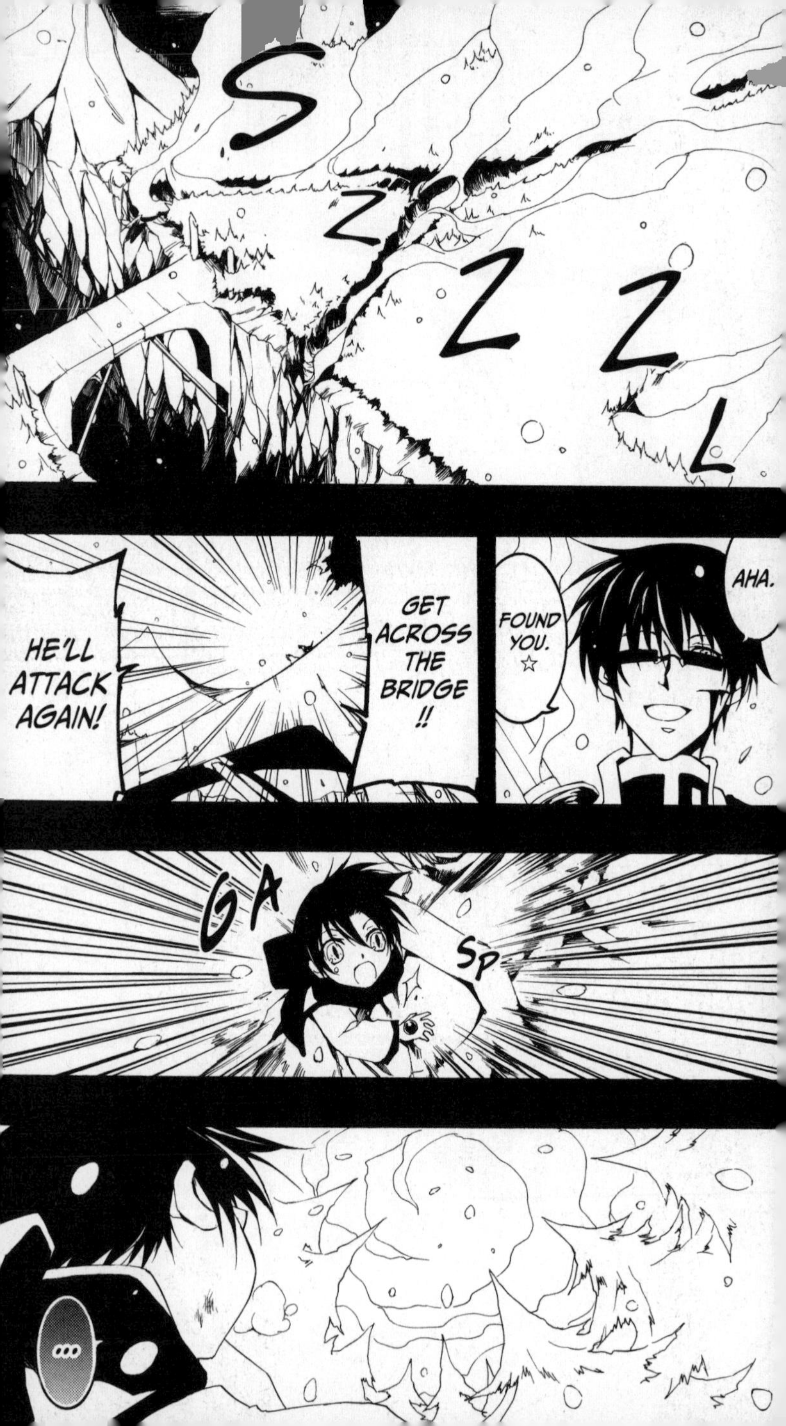
SZZZL
AHA.
FOUND YOU. ☆
GET ACROSS THE BRIDGE!!
HE'LL ATTACK AGAIN!
GA
SP
...

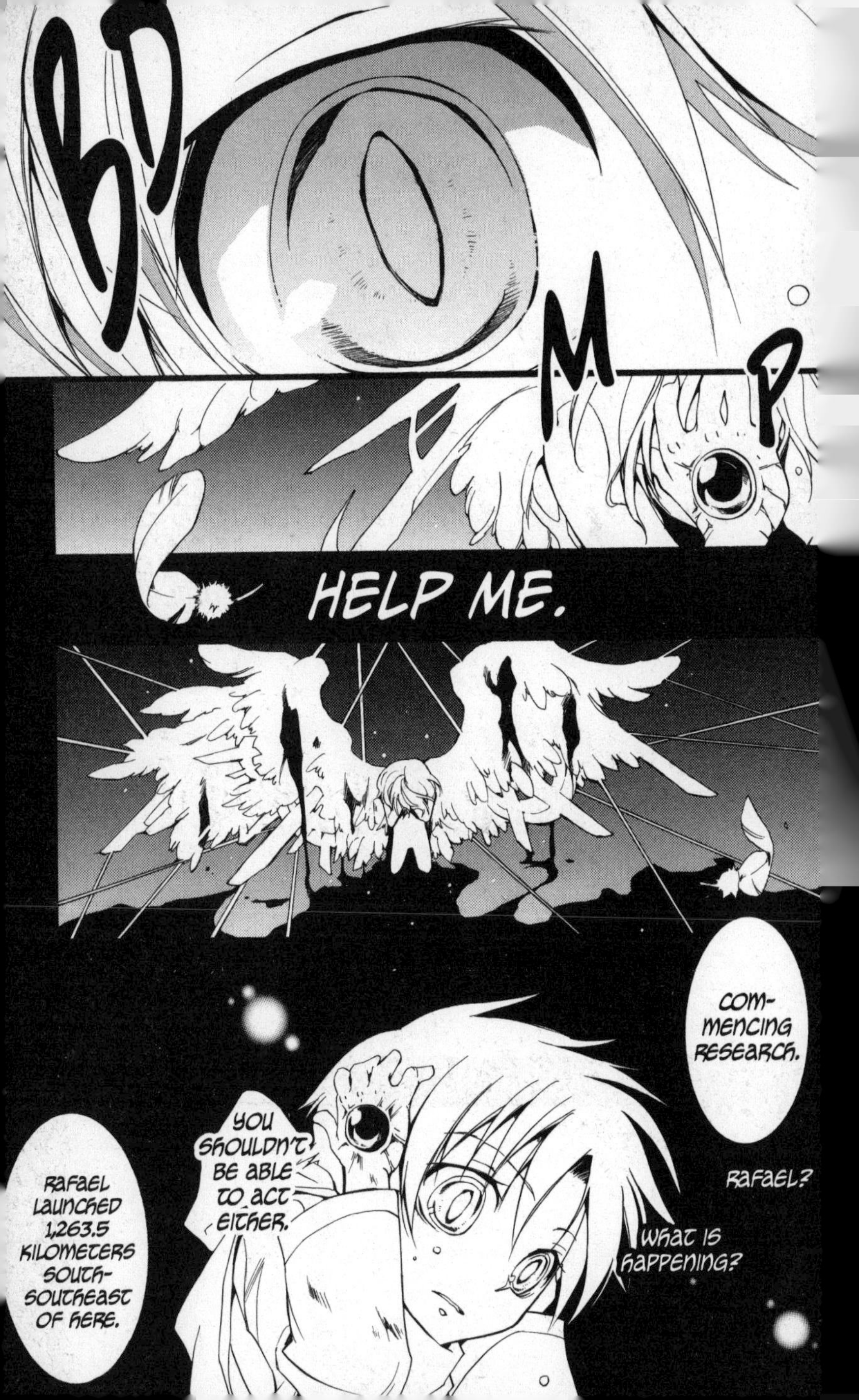
HELP ME.
COMMENCING RESEARCH.
RAFAEL?
WHAT IS HAPPENING?
YOU SHOULDN'T BE ABLE TO ACT EITHER.
RAFAEL LAUNCHED 1,263.5 KILOMETERS SOUTH-SOUTHEAST OF HERE.

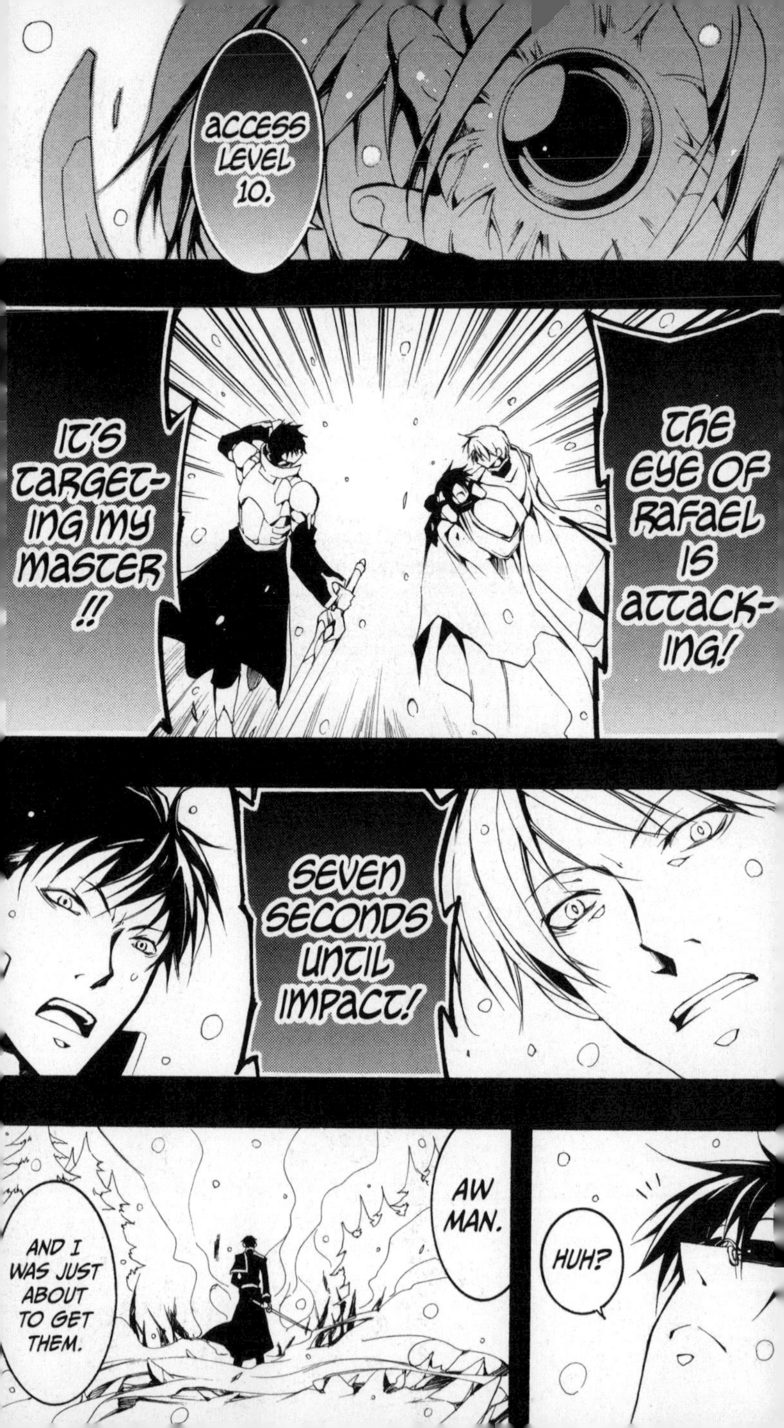
ACCESS LEVEL 10.
THE EYE OF RAFAEL IS ATTACKING!
IT'S TARGET-ING MY MASTER!!
SEVEN SECONDS UNTIL IMPACT!
HUH?
AW MAN.
AND I WAS JUST ABOUT TO GET THEM.

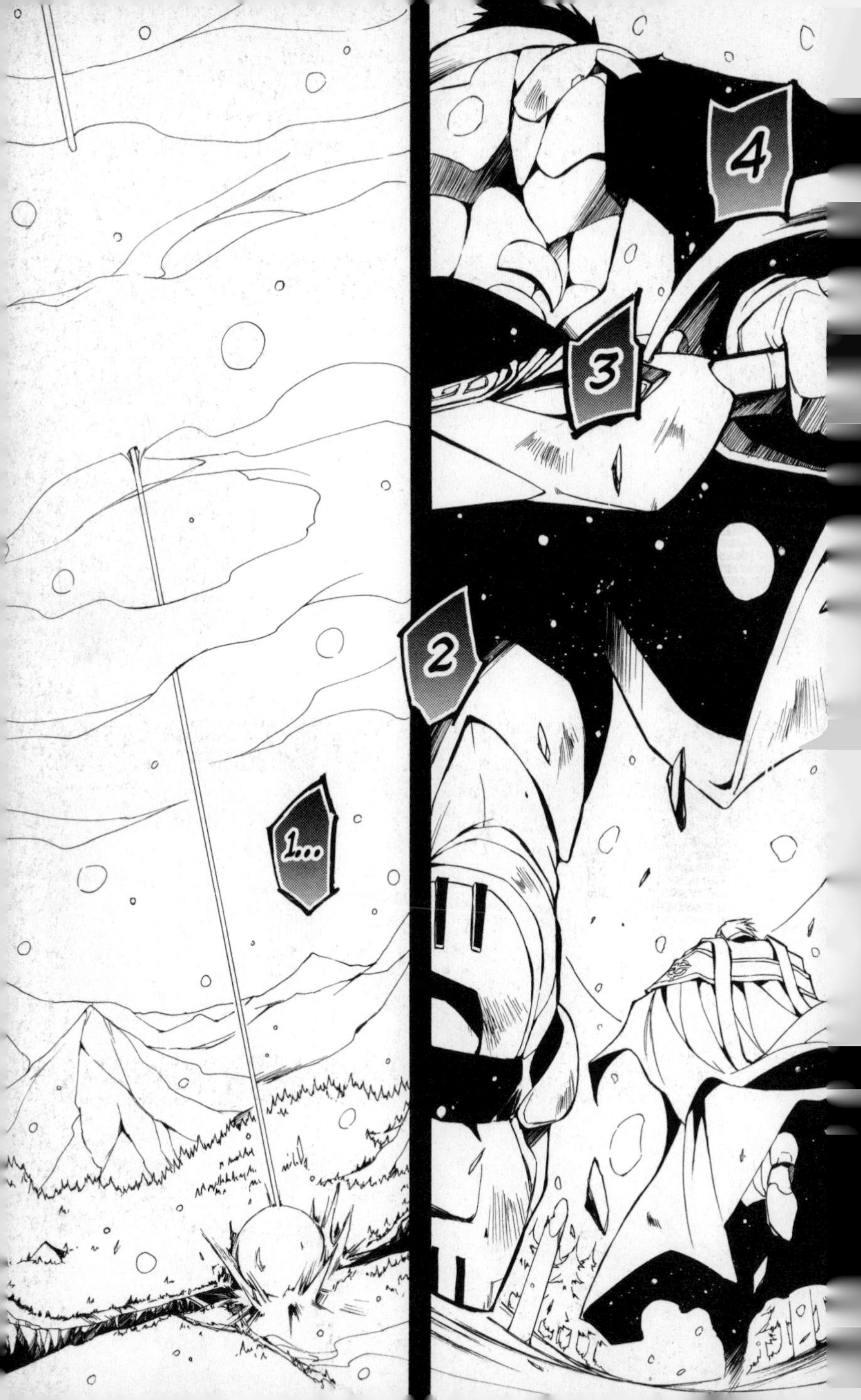
4
3
2
1...

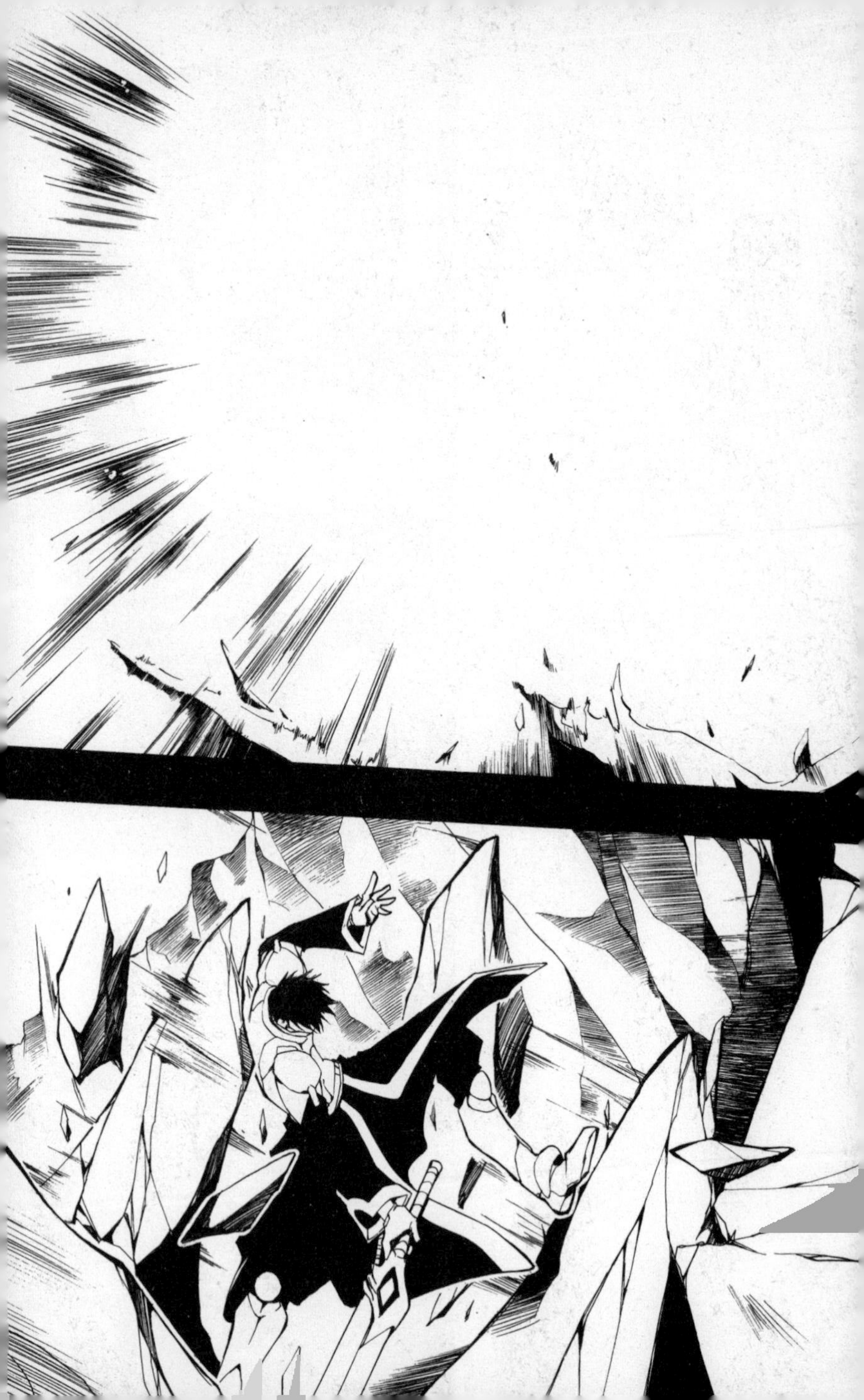

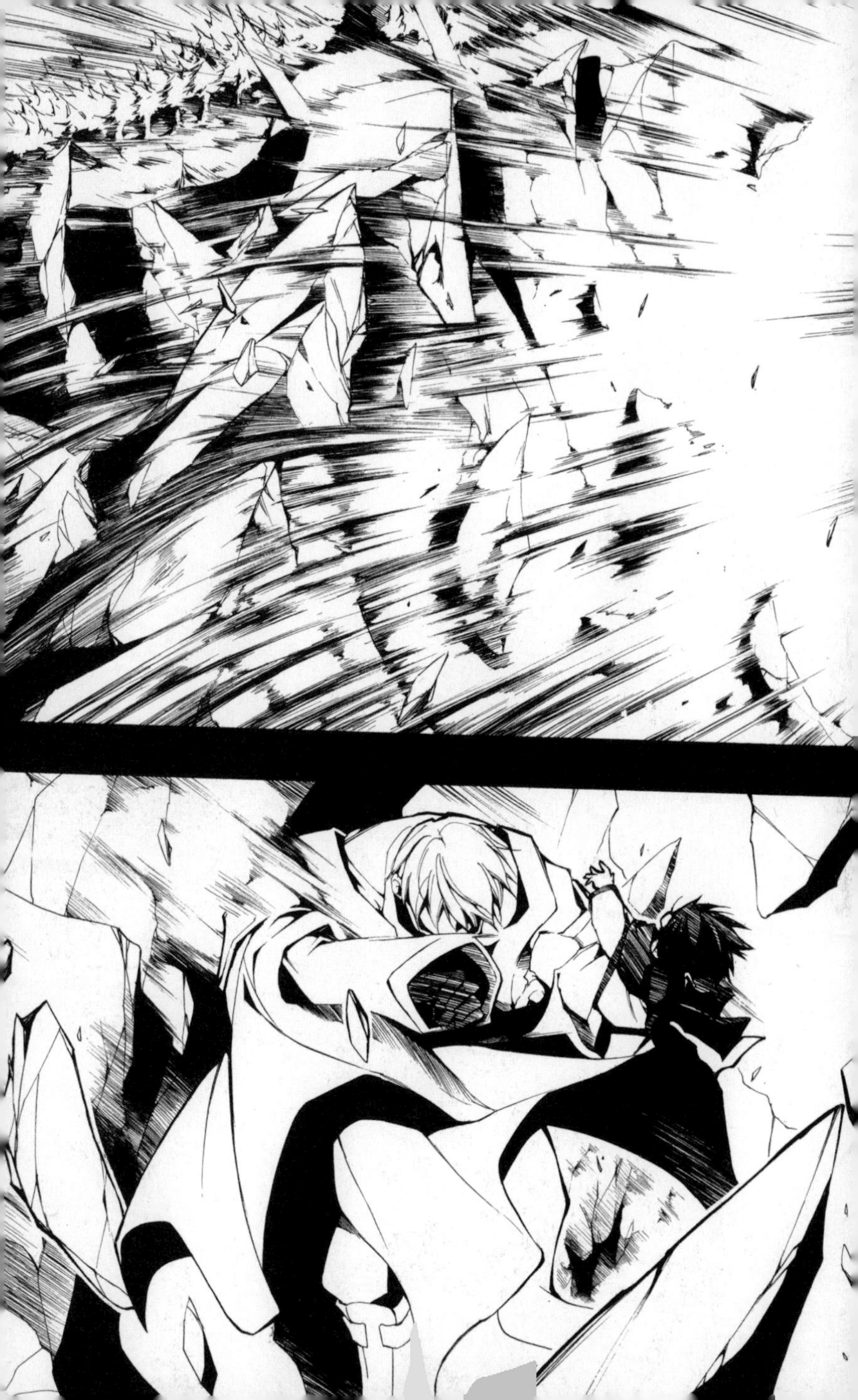

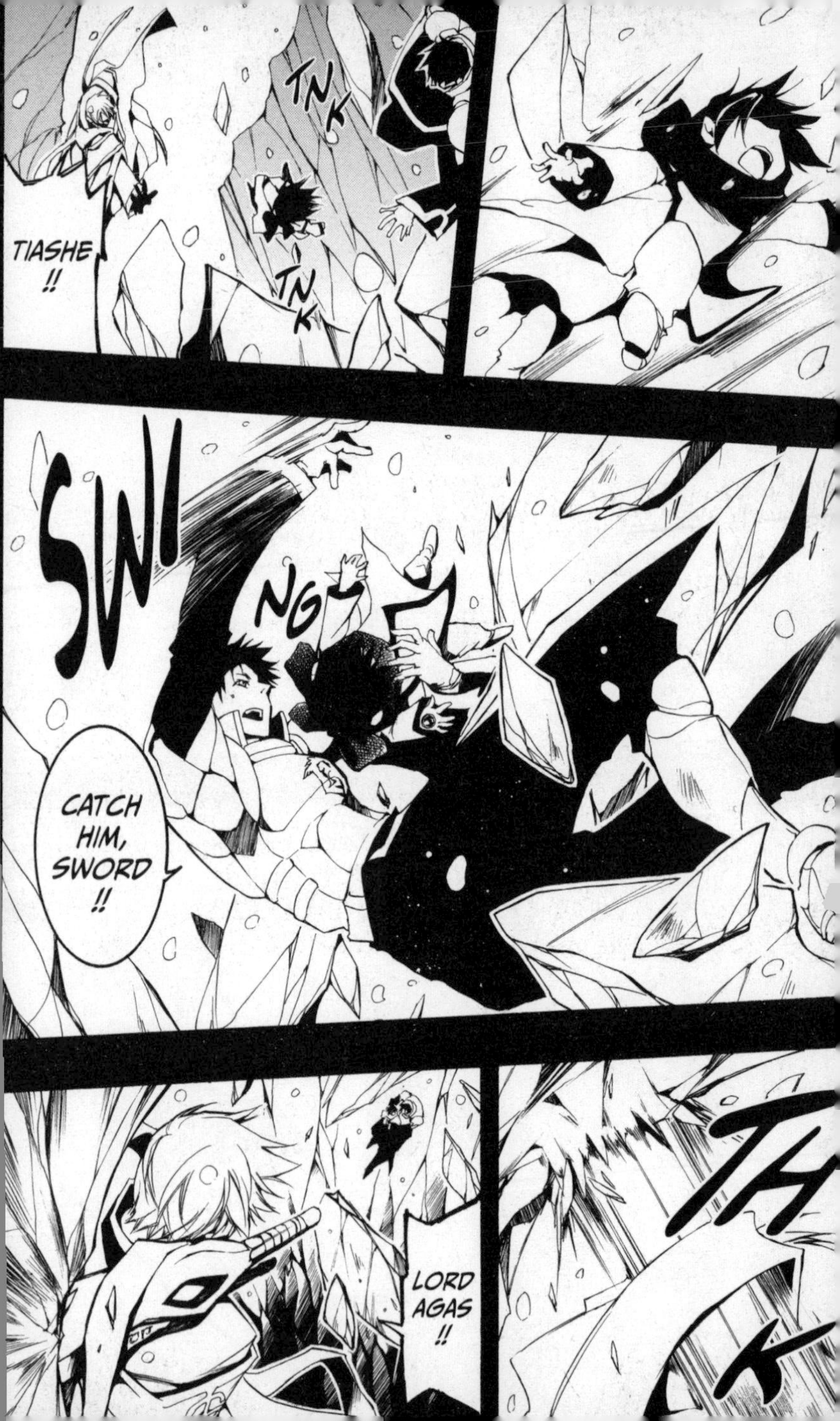
TNK
TIASHE!!
TNK
SWING
CATCH HIM, SWORD!!
THK
LORD AGAS!!

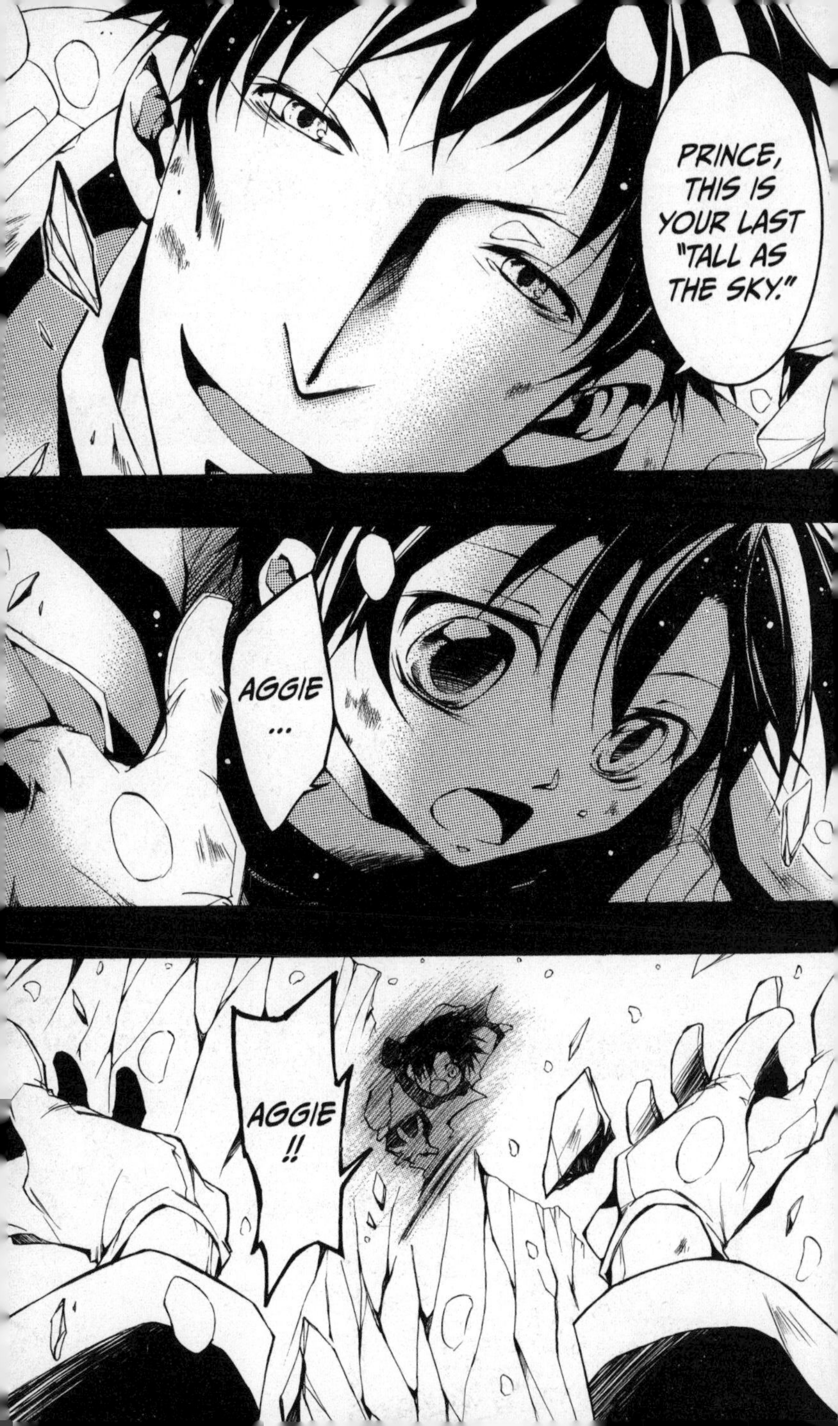
PRINCE, THIS IS YOUR LAST "TALL AS THE SKY."
AGGIE ...
AGGIE !!

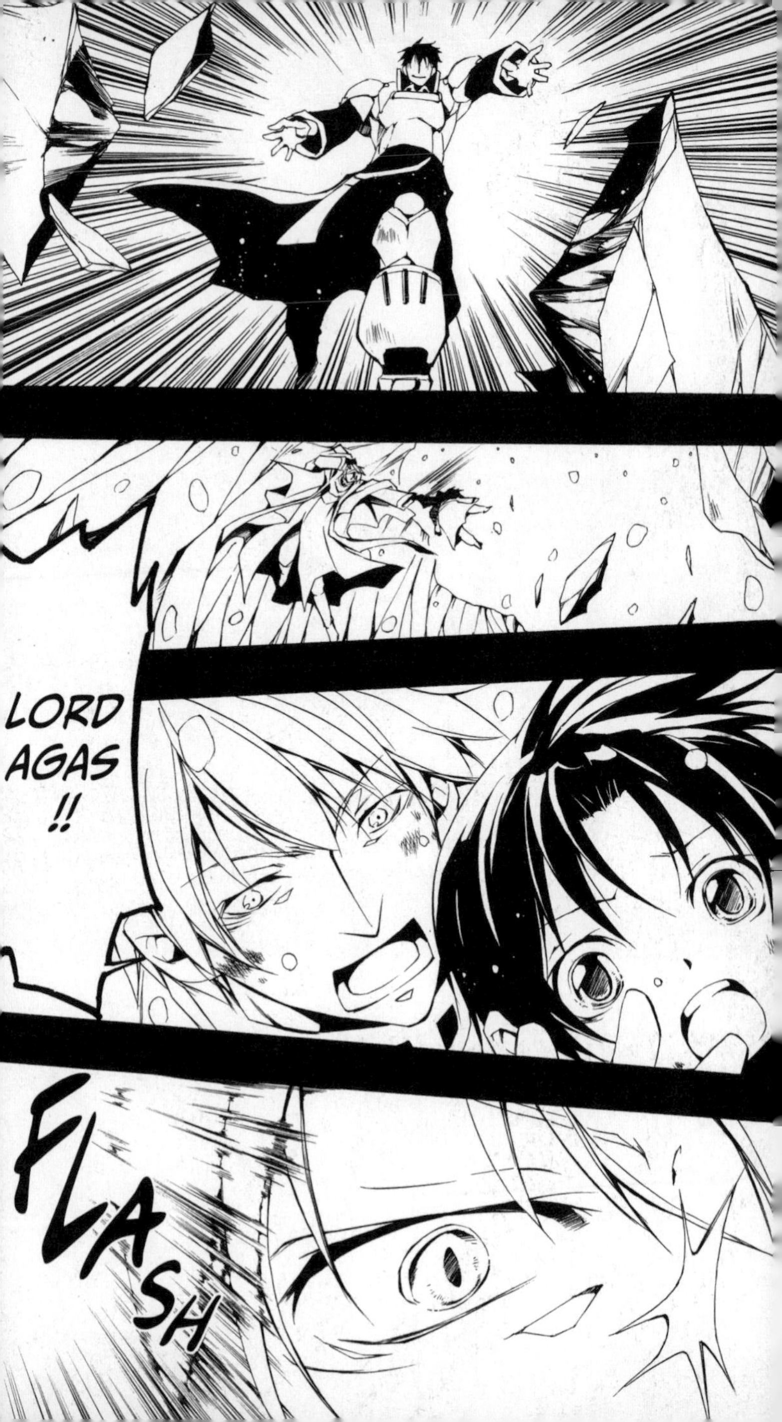
LORD AGAS!!
FLASH

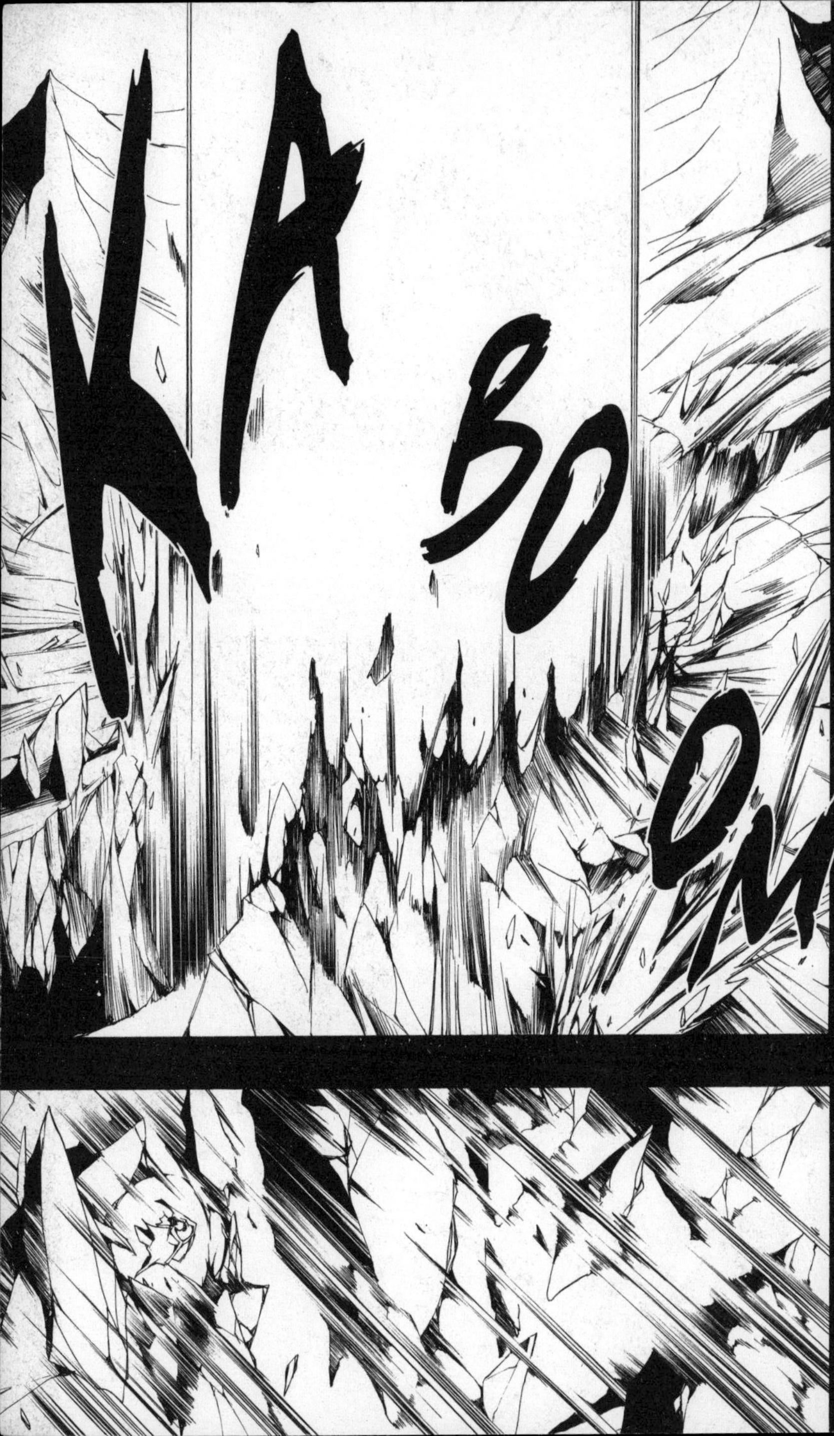
KABOOM

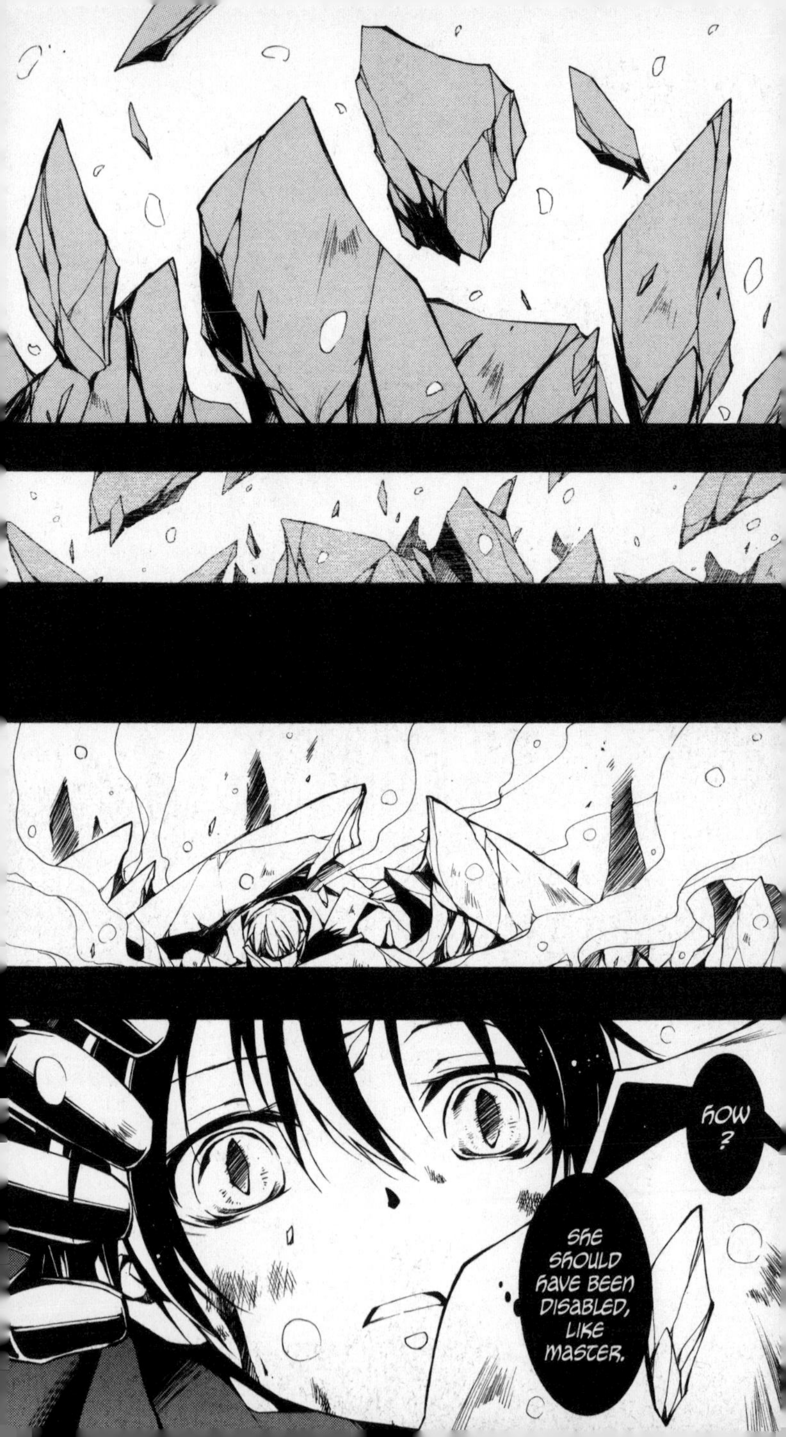
HOW?
SHE SHOULD HAVE BEEN DISABLED, LIKE MASTER.

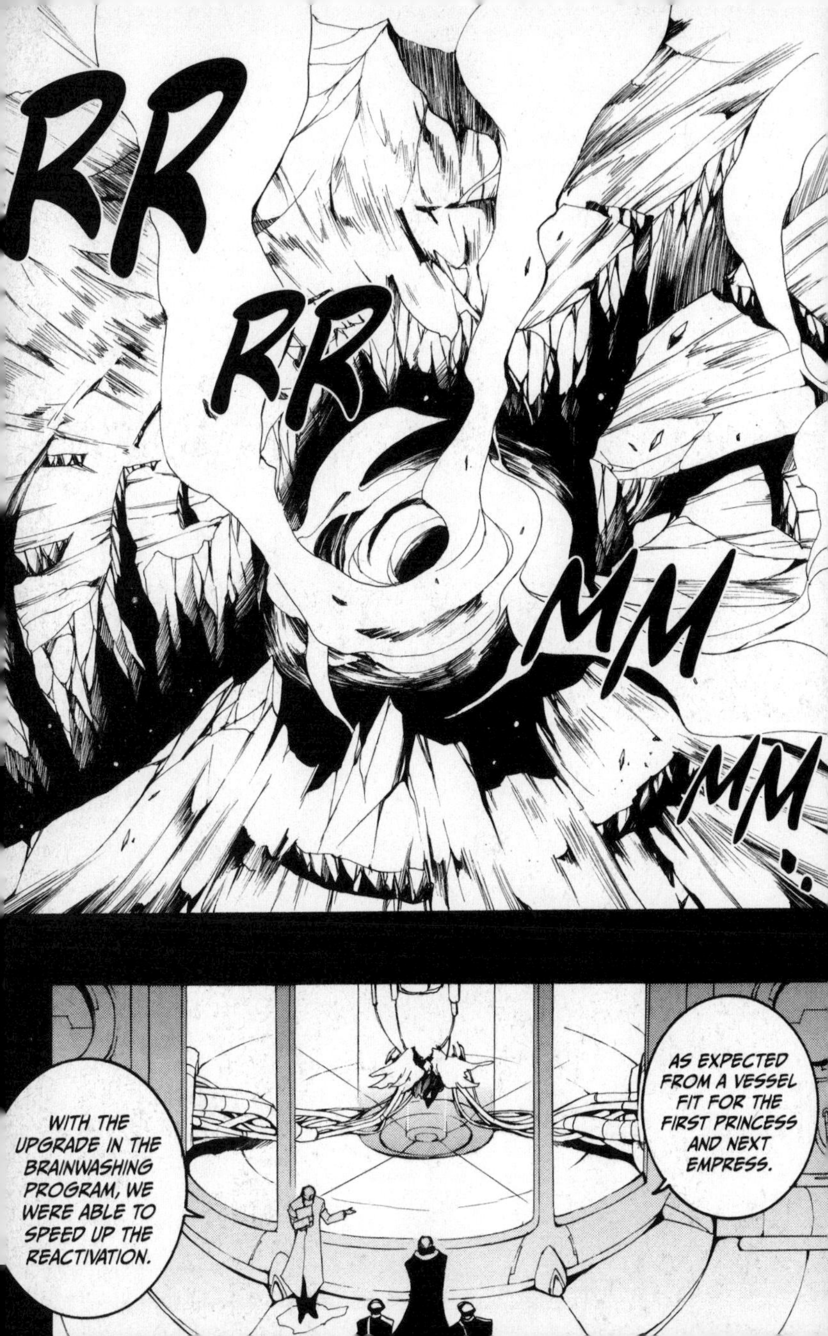
RRRRMMMMMM..
AS EXPECTED FROM A VESSEL FIT FOR THE FIRST PRINCESS AND NEXT EMPRESS.
WITH THE UPGRADE IN THE BRAINWASHING PROGRAM, WE WERE ABLE TO SPEED UP THE REACTIVATION.

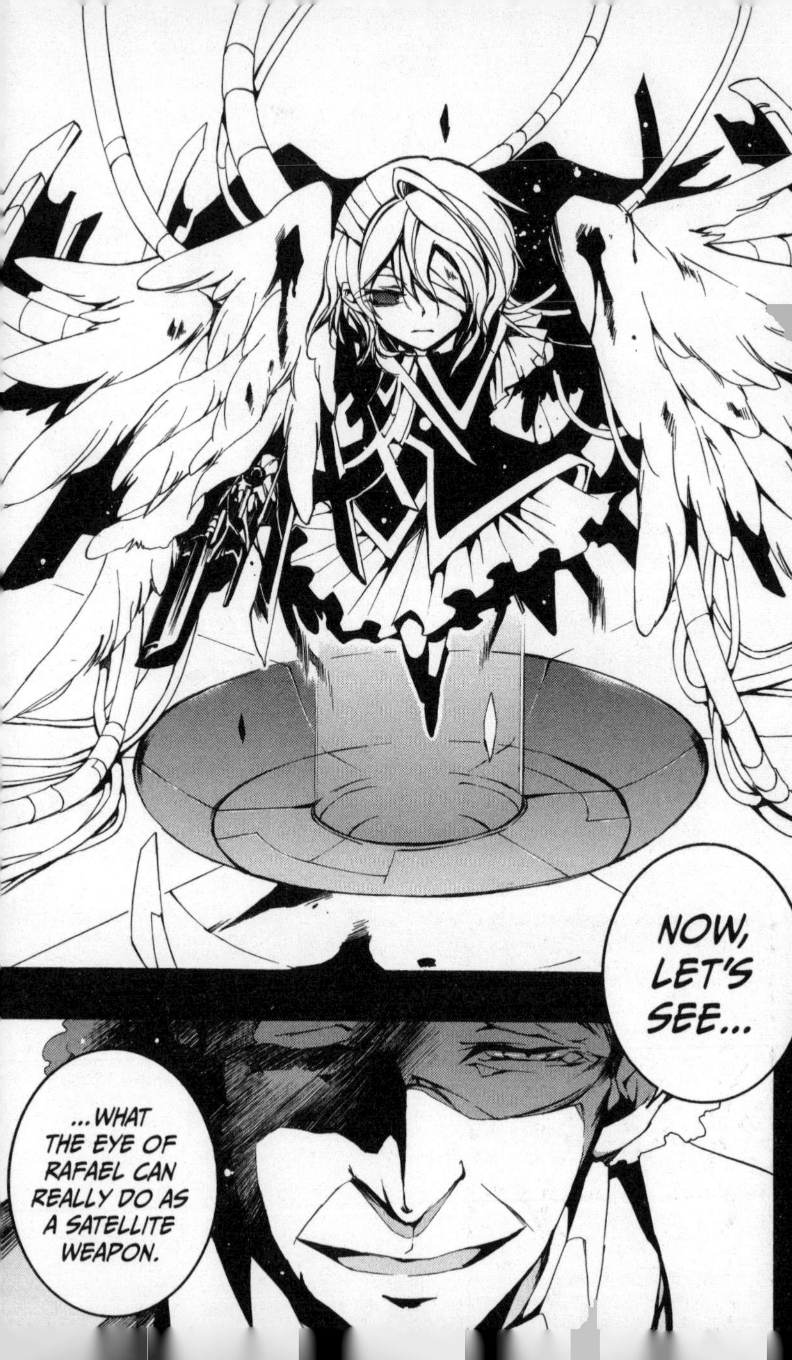
NOW, LET'S SEE...
...WHAT THE EYE OF RAFAEL CAN REALLY DO AS A SATELLITE WEAPON.

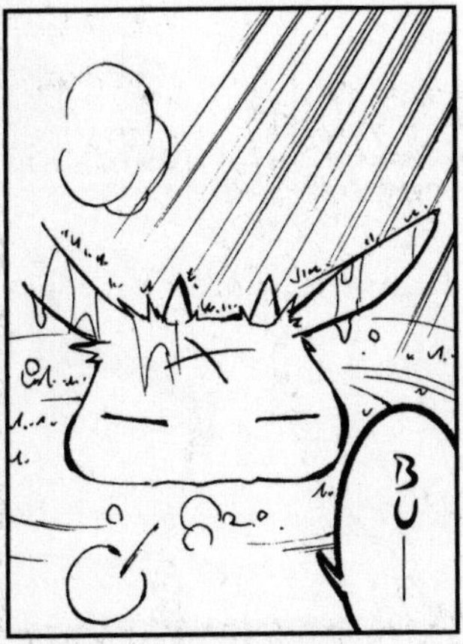
BU—

Bonus

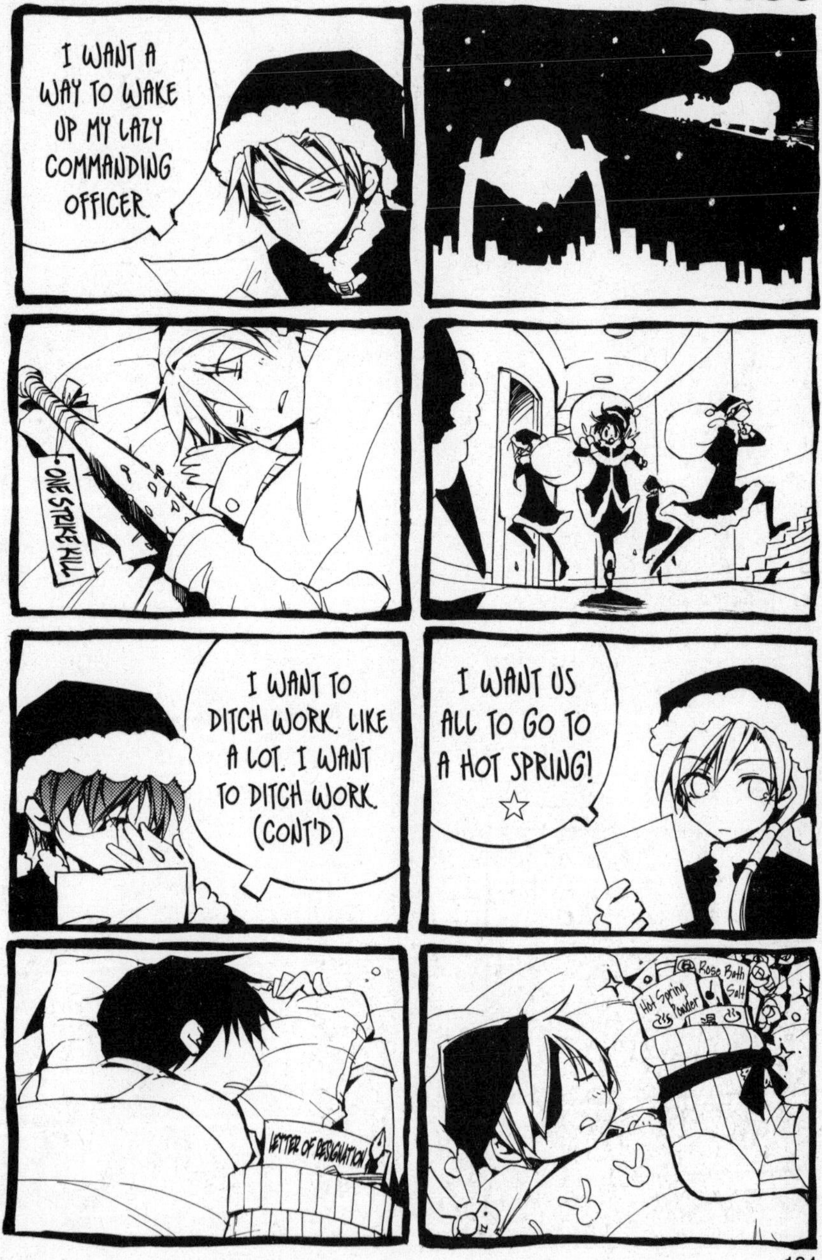
I WANT A WAY TO WAKE UP MY LAZY COMMANDING OFFICER.
ONE STRIKE KILL
I WANT US ALL TO GO TO A HOT SPRING! ☆
I WANT TO DITCH WORK. LIKE A LOT. I WANT TO DITCH WORK. (CONT'D)
Rose Bath Salt
Hot Spring Powder
LETTER OF RESIGNATION

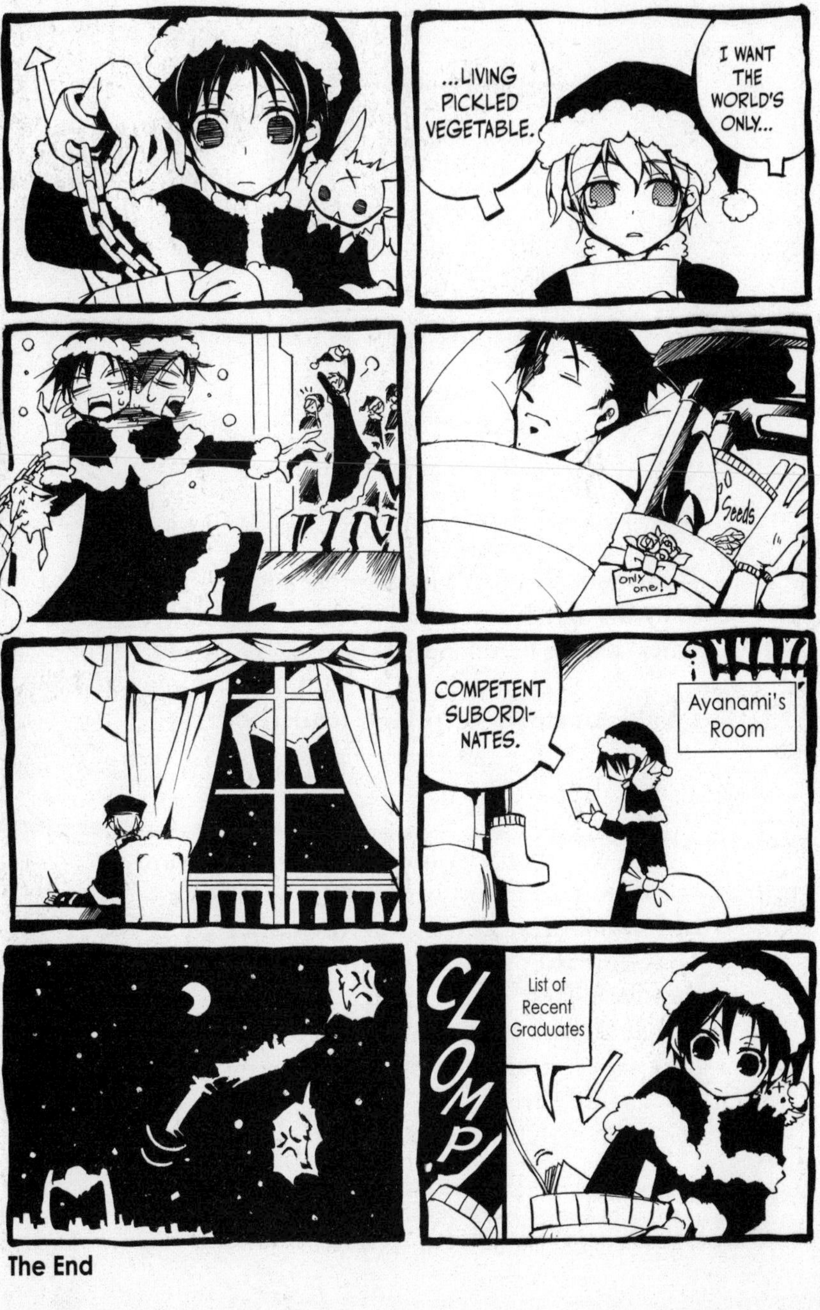
I WANT THE WORLD'S ONLY...
...LIVING PICKLED VEGETABLE.
Seeds
only one!
Ayanami's Room
COMPETENT SUBORDI-NATES.
List of Recent Graduates
CLOMP!

The End

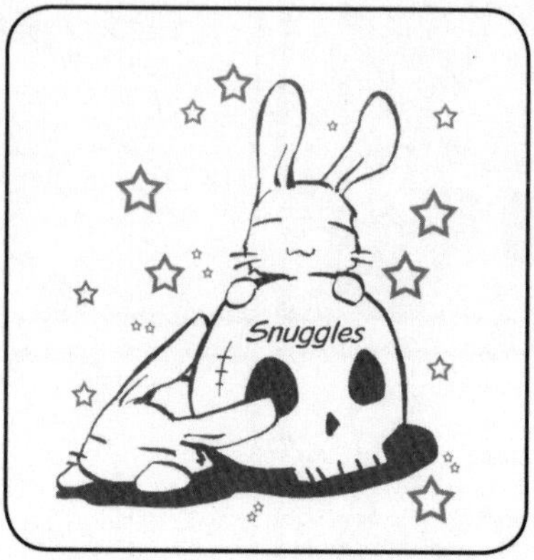
Snuggles

We've gone through a lot together since we met ten years ago. Now it's so natural to be around each other that we hardly notice the other one there.

—Yuki Amemiya & Yukino Ichihara, 2011

Yuki Amemiya was born in Miyagi, Japan, on March 25. Yukino Ichihara was born in Fukushima, Japan, on November 24. Together they write and illustrate *07-Ghost*, the duo's first series. Since its debut in 2005, *07-Ghost* has been translated into a dozen languages, and in 2009 it was adapted into a TV anime series.